Military Industry and Regional Defense Policy

Previous studies of military industrial policy in the developing world focused on political-economic effects. Using methodologies that focus on the production of complete weapons systems – a misleading gauge in a world of growing international defense cooperation – existing analytical models for military industrialization could not account for the rapid growth of Iraq's very significant military industry.

By examining in detail the military-industrial policies of India, Israel, and Iraq – three of the most powerful regional powers in the Cold War and post-Cold War eras – this book re-addresses the issue of military industrialization in the developing world. It focuses on the impact of security perceptions on policy-making in producer states, and makes use of recent literature re-examining the role of regional state sub-systems in international relations and recent historical studies of international technology and arms transfer.

By focusing on the political-military aspects of military industrial policies and examining how developing states have integrated military industries with national security policies, Timothy D. Hoyt creates a new framework for analyzing the rationale and effectiveness of these industries in the context of global and regional threats. This model explains the unusual development of Iraq's arms industry and the emergence of apparently similar industries elsewhere, while also providing new insights into the strengths and limitations of Indian and Israeli military industrial sectors.

This book will be of much interest to researchers and policy-makers of defense policy and military industry, international relations, and regional studies (Middle East and South Asia).

Timothy D. Hoyt is Professor of Strategy and Policy at the US Naval War College. He teaches and researches a range of issues including classic and contemporary warfare, strategic theory, conflict in the developing world, insurgency and terrorism, weapons of mass destruction, and security in the Middle East, Persian Gulf, and South Asia.

Cass military studies

Intelligence Activities in Ancient Rome
Trust in the gods, but verify
Rose Mary Sheldon

Clausewitz and African War
Politics and strategy in Liberia and Somalia
Isabelle Duyvesteyn

Strategy and Politics in the Middle East, 1954–60
Defending the northern tier
Michael Cohen

The Cuban Intervention in Angola, 1965–1991
From Che Guevara to Cuito Cuanavale
Edward George

Military Leadership in the British Civil Wars, 1642–1651
'The genius of this age'
Stanley Carpenter

Israel's Reprisal Policy, 1953–1956
The dynamics of military retaliation
Ze'ev Drory

Bosnia and Herzegovina in the Second World War
Enver Redzic

Leaders in War
West Point remembers the 1991 Gulf War
Edited by Frederick Kagan and Christian Kubik

Khedive Ismail's Army
John Dunn

Yugoslav Military Industry 1918–1991
Amadeo Watkins

Corporal Hitler and the Great War 1914–1918
The List Regiment
John Williams

Rostóv in the Russian Civil War, 1917–1920
The key to victory
Brian Murphy

The Tet Effect, Intelligence and the Public Perception of War
Jake Blood

The US Military Profession into the 21st Century
War, peace and politics
Edited by Sam C. Sarkesian and Robert E. Connor, Jr.

Civil-Military Relations in Europe
Learning from crisis and institutional change
Edited by Hans Born, Marina Caparini, Karl Haltiner and Jürgen Kuhlmann

Strategic Culture and Ways of War
Lawrence Sondhaus

Military Unionism in the Post Cold War Era
A future reality?
Edited by Richard Bartle and Lindy Heinecken

Warriors and Politicians
U.S. civil-military relations under stress
Charles A. Stevenson

Military Honour and the Conduct of War
From Ancient Greece to Iraq
Paul Robinson

Military Industry and Regional Defense Policy
India, Iraq, and Israel
Timothy D. Hoyt

Managing Defence in a Democracy
Edited by Laura R. Cleary and Teri McConville

Gender and the Military
Women in the Armed Forces of Western democracies
Helena Carreiras

Military Industry and Regional Defense Policy
India, Iraq, and Israel

Timothy D. Hoyt

LONDON AND NEW YORK

First published 2007
by Routledge
2 Park Square, Milton Park, Abingdon, Oxon, OX14 4RN

Simultaneously published in the USA and Canada
by Routledge
711 Third Avenue, New York, NY 10017

Routledge is an imprint of the Taylor & Francis Group, an informa business

First issued in paperback 2011

© 2007 Timothy D. Hoyt

Typeset in Sabon by Wearset Ltd, Boldon, Tyne and Wear

All rights reserved. No part of this book may be reprinted or reproduced or utilized in any form or by any electronic, mechanical, or other means, now known or hereafter invented, including photocopying and recording, or in any information storage or retrieval system, without permission in writing from the publishers.

The publisher makes no representation, express or implied, with regard to the accuracy of the information contained in this book and cannot accept any legal responsibility or liability for any errors or omissions that may be made.

British Library Cataloguing in Publication Data
A catalogue record for this book is available from the British Library

Library of Congress Cataloging in Publication Data
A catalog record for this book has been requested

ISBN10: 0–714–65714–X (hbk)
ISBN10: 0–714–68582–8 (pbk)
ISBN10: 0–203–96904–9 (ebk)

ISBN13: 978–0–714–65714–1 (hbk)
ISBN13: 978–0–714–68582–3 (pbk)
ISBN13: 978–0–203–96904–5 (ebk)

Dedicated to my wife Lisa, with all my love, and our children Liam, Ben, and Jon.
May their world be a better, more peaceful one than ours.

> *I study war and politics in order that my children may study science and mathematics, in order that their children may study art and music.*
> John Adams, *in a letter to his wife Abigail*

Contents

Acknowledgments xii
List of abbreviations and acronyms xiv

1 **Introduction** 1
   Military industry in the developing world 2
      The developing world: some structural considerations
      Regional powers
      LDC arms procurement
      LDCs and the international arms trade
   The study of LDC arms industries: analytical frameworks 7
      Structuralist/dependency approach
      Economic/development approach
      Dominance/world system approach
      Systemic/historical approach
      Existing frameworks: the missing variable
   Methods of analysis 17

2 **India** 22
   Background 22
      Indian security perception
      Military-industrial policy
      Structure of the Indian defense industry
   Nehru and the age of idealism: 1947–62 28
      Selected indigenous arms programs, 1948–62
   The age of realism: 1963–74 33
      Selected indigenous arms programs: 1962–74
   Hegemony unfulfilled: 1974–98 39
      Selected indigenous arms programs: 1974–98
   1998–2005: New threats and opportunities 56
   Conclusion 61

x Contents

3 **Israel** 67
   Background 67
      Israeli security perceptions
      The structure of the Israeli defense industry
   The pre-state period: 1920–48 74
   Development of military industrial infrastructure: 1948–67 75
      Selected indigenous arms programs: 1948–67
   The boom years: 1968–73 83
      Selected indigenous arms programs: 1967–73
   Overextension and decline: 1973–95 91
      Selected indigenous arms programs: 1973–95
   Managing security in an uncertain world: 1995–2005 105
   Israeli military-industrial requirements 106
      The future: niche production or military-industrial and strategic dysfunction?

4 **Iraq** 115
   Background 115
      Iraq's security perception
      Iraq's military-industrial base
   Embargo, diversification, and war: 1974–84 124
      Selected indigenous arms programs, 1974–84
   Pragmatism and victory: 1984–90 129
      Selected indigenous arms programs, 1984–90
   The 1990s: what might the industry have looked like? 138
   The enduring puzzle: Iraq's strategic weapons 143
      Ballistic missiles
      Chemical weapons
      Biological weapons
      Nuclear weapons
      Why we don't know – continuing gaps
   Conclusion 158

5 **Regional powers, security, and arms production: conclusions** 163
   Case studies: patterns and trends 164
      India
      Israel
      Iraq

Lessons learned: security and military industry 170
A security-based model of LDC arms production 171
    Category one: sustenance requirements
    Category two: quality maintenance
    Category three: ability to produce systems not available
        from other suppliers
    Category four: production of regional-specific weaponry
        and niche production
*Regional powers and military industry in the evolving
international system 179*

Notes	187
Select bibliography	268
Index	283

Acknowledgments

This book has been a work in progress for over 15 years, and as a result I cannot truly do justice to all the people who deserve thanks. I will mention a few, and apologize to those who must be excluded, either for reasons of space or at their own request. You all know who you are, and I am deeply grateful.

This book is based on my PhD dissertation, written at the Johns Hopkins School of Advanced International Studies – an experience made richer by my study with Michael Vlahos and George Liska. Robert Osgood and Roger Hansen served briefly as my graduate and dissertation advisors, respectively, before their untimely passing. Eliot Cohen was kind enough to take on the difficult task of inheriting a massive and unfocused dissertation project. I could not have completed my studies without his gentle and resolute prodding. It seems only right to express my deepest appreciation for the members of my dissertation committee – Eliot Cohen, Bruce Parrott, Robert Harkavy, Andrew Krepinevich, and Frederick Holborn. Their comments made this book a better one.

The initial impetus for this research came from a study of ballistic missile production I worked on at the Library of Congress' Congressional Research Service. Colleagues at Georgetown University's Security Studies Program – Bernard Finel, Audrey Kurth-Cronin, Jim Ludes, and Elizabeth Stanley – challenged my assumptions and pushed me in new directions. Faculty at the Naval War College provided crucial assistance and intellectual support, particularly Andrew Ross, Drew Winner, and George Thibault of the Distance Education Program – a fine colleague and a true gentleman. Special thanks are due to my many colleagues in the Strategy and Policy Department – the best of all possible academic homes.

Michael Eisenstadt, Ephraim Inbar, Gerald Steinberg, Ariel Levite, Avner Cohen, and Aharon Klieman all contributed to my understanding of Israeli defense industry and policy, whether they realize it or not. Tom Mahnken, Andrew Parasiliti, Ken Pollack, Tamara Wittes, Rich Lacquement, Ahmed Hashim, Bill Fuller, David Kaiser, Heidi Rutz, and George Baer challenged, and in some cases continue to challenge, my assumptions about Iraq. My work on India owes an enormous debt to Steve Cohen,

Devin Hagerty, Sumit Ganguly, Peter Lavoy, Tom Thornton, Rajesh Basrur, and Michael Krepon. Research assistants never receive the recognition they deserve, but I could not have finished this without the help of Chris Connell, Aaron Frank, Kate Dumouchel, and James Quinn. My parents – Bill and Kathy Hoyt – and my in-laws – Rob and Polly Wright – provided emotional, financial, and intellectual support. I love you all, and thank you so much for all your help in so many ways. Lisa and I are blessed to have you in our lives.

Finally, this book is dedicated to my own family. My wife Lisa has suffered with this project for over 15 years. Without her devotion and her strong editorial hand, this book would not have been completed. She is truly my better half, and this book is as much hers as mine. I love you, my dearest, and thank you for everything. I had hoped that my three sons – Liam, Benjamin, and Jonathan – would have the opportunity to live in a safer, more peaceful world, although events of the new century present new challenges. I can only hope this book contributes, in some small way, to a better understanding of how to resolve the threats and conflicts that are emerging in the developing world. I firmly believe that to achieve peace, we must understand war – and I hope this book contributes to both pursuits.

Wakefield, Rhode Island

Abbreviations and acronyms

AAM	air-to-air missile
ACDA	Arms Control and Disarmament Agency
ADS	Air Defence Ship
AEW	airborne early warning
ALH	Advanced Light Helicopter
ASM	air-to-surface missile
ASW	anti-submarine warfare
ASWAC	airborne surveillance and warning aircraft
ATBM	anti-tactical ballistic missile
ATGM	anti-tank guided missile
ATV	Advanced Test Vehicle
AWACS	airborne warning and control system
C3I	Command, Control, Communications and Intelligence
COIN	counter-insurgency
DPSU	Defence Public Sector Undertaking
DRDO	Defence Research and Development Organisation
ELINT	electronic intelligence
ECM	electronic counter-measures
ESM	electronic support measures
EW	electronic warfare
FAC	Fast Attack Craft
FAE	fuel-air explosive
FMS	Foreign Military Sales
GDP	Gross Domestic Product
GNP	Gross National Product
IAF	Israeli airforce
IAI	Israeli Aircraft Industries
ICBM	intercontinental ballistic missile
IDF	Israeli Defense Forces
IDFN	Israeli Defense Forces Navy
IGMDP	indigenous guided missile development programme
InAF	Indian Air Force
INS	Indian Naval Service

INSAS	Indian Small Arms System
IQAF	Iraqi airforce
ISG	Iraqi Survey Group
ISL	Israeli Shipyards Limited
ISRO	Indian Space Research Organisation
IRBM	intermediate-range ballistic missile
LCA	Light Combat Aircraft
LDC	less-developed country
MBT	main battle tank
MRBM	medium-range ballistic missile
MWS	major weapons system
OF	ordnance factory
OIF	Operation Iraqi Freedom
OSP	Off-Shore Procurement Funds
PAF	Pakistani Airforce
R&D	research and development
RPV	Remotely Piloted Vehicle
SAM	surface-to-air missile
ShShM	ship-to-ship missile
SIGINT	signals intelligence
SIPRI	Stockholm International Peace Research Institute
SP	self-propelled
SRBM	short-range ballistic missile
SSM	surface-to-surface missile
SSN	submarine (nuclear-powered)
TEL	transporter-erector launcher
UAV	Unmanned Aerial Vehicle
UNMOVIC	United Nations Monitoring, Verification and Inspection Commission
UNSCOM	United Nations Special Commission
WMD	weapon(s) of mass destruction

1 Introduction

This book examines three of the most important regional powers of the late twentieth century, assessing the relationship between changing security calculations and military experiences on military-industrial policy. This study provides a *security-based* context for evaluating arms industries of Less-Developed Countries (LDCs).[1] This perspective is often lacking in existing literature on military industries in the developing world, which focus on issues of economic opportunity costs and dependency.

Examination of the arms industries of *regional powers*, in this case India, Israel, and Iraq, is particularly important in the changing international environment. Regional powers represent the most prolific and sophisticated producers and consumers of arms in the developing world. They are also the states most likely to pose threats to regional and international stability. The security focus of most of these states, however, remains rooted in existing regional military competitions, and military and national security perceptions center on the capabilities of neighbors and traditional rivals.

Focusing on the relationship between regional security calculations and military-industrial policies serves two important purposes. First, it facilitates more sophisticated and accurate assessments of the motivation, development, and accomplishments of LDC military industries. Existing methodology provides inadequate means for measuring the relationship between national-security requirements and military industrial policy, and for assessing the practical benefits of LDC arms production.

In addition, this demonstrates that the security policies of developing states provide important indicators for their acquisition, assimilation, and development of dual-use or military technologies in the future. If security perception significantly affects military-industrial policy, understanding regional security concerns provides a framework for analyzing and possibly predicting technology assimilation and potential arms production in future aspiring powers. This study concludes with a model of *security-based* military-industrialization, suggesting new methodologies for analyzing the evolution and effectiveness of LDC military industries in the emerging international system and some policy implications.

2   *Introduction*

Military industry in the developing world

The accumulation of military strength and technological mastery in the developing world since 1945 is significant and impressive. In 1950, only a few states outside Europe and North America possessed the capability to manufacture and, with some foreign assistance, design military weapons, equipment, and ammunition.[2] By 1985, 55 LDCs produced arms of some kind.[3] Eight of these states accounted for over 90 percent of LDC arms production, and about a dozen states were considered 'major' LDC producers.[4]

The members of this 'Dirty Dozen' figure prominently in lists of potential proliferators of ballistic missiles and chemical, biological, and/or nuclear weapons.[5] They represent the predominant military actors in regional state subsystems in the developing world which have been the site of regional or superpower conflict and competition. Their intentions and capabilities, therefore, pose a greater potential threat to regional and, perhaps, global stability and security than the large number of smaller, less capable LDCs.[6] The evolving international system looks increasingly to regionalism as a potential solution to problems of security, economic development, and even ecological problems.[7]

Arms production by prominent regional actors requires careful evaluation for three reasons. First, these states often seek or possess the means to engage in and prolong military conflict with neighbors or states in adjoining regions; second, they may seek the capability to deter external intervention with locally produced weapons; and third, local arms production reduces the impact of supply constraints on their foreign and military policies. Accurately assessing the intentions and capabilities of these regional powers, therefore, represents an important priority and challenge for policymakers and analysts.

Existing surveys of LDC arms industries fail to adequately explain variations in LDC military-industrial policies both within and between regions. They also fail, in many cases, to identify or explain distinctions between the capabilities of the leading LDC arms manufacturers, which can be classified as 'regional powers,' and the larger number of LDC producers with modest or insignificant capacity. In particular, most existing analysis of LDC arms production fails to adequately assess national security perceptions and their impact on military preparedness, military industrialization and weapons acquisition.

The developing world: some structural considerations

The developing world consists of a number of interacting but still distinct regional state-systems which vary in size, influence, and importance to the international community.[8] Among the regional systems which have been identified since the early 1960s are South Asia, North Africa, and the

Middle East, and more recent studies examine the continuing development of various types of regional systems and balances of power.[9]

Academic interest in 'non-great' powers grew in the late 1960s, due both to the expansion of the number of states in the United Nations and the surprising survivability of presumably 'weak states.'[10] The international hierarchy of power is not adequately defined by only two tiers, however, whether they be defined as strong and weak, core and periphery, or developed and developing. At a minimum, there appears to be a narrowing of the economic and military gap between the most advanced countries in the developing world, including the so-called 'newly industrialized countries,' and the least advanced or smallest of the developed world. These states form a middle tier in the international hierarchy, and have been referred to as 'semi-peripheral' states.[11] They also tend to be the most powerful states in their regions.

Recent analysis explores the importance of regional security dynamics, which lie somewhere between analyses of systemic pressures and state-level decision-making on perceptions of military threats and opportunities.[12] Distinct regional 'security complexes' are formed in areas of cultural similarity, and are identifiable because the *primary* security relationships of states in the system are concerned with other states in the system. Relative indifference, as between Pakistan and Iran, signifies the effective boundary of a regional system. These complexes may overlap one another, and powerful states may have interests in more than one security complex.[13]

Analysis of regional systems illuminates the primary security relationships in the developing world. Although LDCs may share certain broad goals,[14] aggregation of the so-called Third World into a unitary actor or bloc is overly simplistic.[15] The developing world is part of a hierarchy of global power based on resource endowments, economic achievements, political influence, and military capabilities.[16] LDC military industrialization is most advanced in states which are deeply involved in regional political-military rivalries, or which boast significant military and economic advantages over most of their neighbors.[17] Nevertheless, these larger powers still face many of the security problems and dilemmas common to most developing states.

Assessing the nature of the security threat to an LDC is often problematic.[18] The internal fragility of the developing states is a powerful factor in their definitions of 'national security'. Not all LDCs actually face imminent invasion: most suffer more from internal threats to regime maintenance than from external threats of territorial absorption.[19] States whose primary concerns are threats to internal security, however, have little need to create sophisticated military industries. Many developing states also face potential external threats, from regional neighbors or outside forces. It is these threats which are most likely to create a demand for advanced military capabilities and an expanded military-industrial base.

Regional powers

Regional powers do not easily fit the traditional descriptions of 'great' or 'weak,' but exist as significant powers in a more limited sphere. Martin Wight identifies the regional power as a separate type of state, which exists not only as a dominant power within a regional subsystem, but also as a middle power in the extended international arena.[20] Regional powers occupy a hierarchically distinct position among LDCs, and have greater requirements for externally-focused military forces. Most analyses of regional powers focus on issues of scale, examining the potential for larger LDCs to work their way into the ranks of the so-called great powers, and concentrate primarily on states with relatively larger territorial, population, and economic resources.[21]

Regional powers, however, also compete with neighbors in fierce regional rivalries, and these competitions are often unevenly matched. These competitions tend *not* to result in outright conquest – a strategy of limited territorial occupation has become increasingly common in regional warfare.[22] Even the acquisition of limited amounts of territory, however, can significantly destabilize regional power balances. Iraq's aims in 1980 were limited to freeing the Arab population of Iran – which simultaneously would have secured Iraq's control of significant Iranian oil assets. Indian analyses of the Kargil War of 1999 believe Pakistan engaged in 'salami slicing' – whittling off small portions of Indian territory, which over time could significantly tilt the balance of power in the region by destabilizing India internally.[23]

Regional conflict therefore can force local states to solicit military assistance and alliance from external powers as a method of balancing power, or as a means of cementing or challenging regional hegemony. International support has not always proven reliable. Pakistan, for example, was subject to abrupt imposition of sanctions by its US ally in 1965 and again in 1990. The impact of arms supply constraints on India, Israel, and Iraq will all be discussed in later chapters. Regional powers may also find themselves the targets of multinational arms embargoes or arms transfer limits (Israel under the Tripartite Pact), of broad international sanctions (Iraq, 1990–2003), or of targeted supplier controls (India after the 1974 nuclear tests).

Ultimately, the primary security concern of regional states is the *immediate* threat, which is usually regional rather than international. In the words of Michael Handel: "The power of a state is thus best measured not against all other countries, but in relation to its neighbors, and by the degree to which the strength at its disposal matches its national goals and ambitions."[24] 'Balance of threat' theory, a derivative of the traditional balance of power calculation, argues that states assess threat in terms of aggregate power, geographic proximity, offensive capability, and aggressive intentions.[25] In a later article, Walt posits that small states are primarily concerned with *proximate* threats, even in the face of potential great power conflict on the horizon.[26]

Regional powers therefore allocate military expenditures primarily in response to local threats. However, the role of local military industrial policy in addressing these threats – a crucial element of LDC arms procurement policies – is rarely addressed.[27] Equally rare are studies in which regional conflicts are viewed as the primary motivation for LDC arms production and military expenditures.[28]

LDC arms procurement

Faced with threats to security or unfulfilled ambitions, LDCs must acquire military tools appropriate to national requirements. These tools range from basic items, such as uniforms, small arms, ammunition and tents, to extremely sophisticated and complex weapons and combinations of weapons, such as aircraft, tanks, ships, or missile batteries. The latter items often require foreign assistance for training, maintenance, production, and integration into national military structures.

Developing states have two security-based rationales for importing or producing high-technology weaponry.[29] Sophisticated equipment is often required to match arms available to potential adversaries. In most cases, this requirement is determined by the *regional* military balance and the force structures of neighboring states. For example, "[t]he essential objective of India's weapons acquisition policy is to ensure that the armed forces are always equipped with weapons that are qualitatively equal to those available to its adversaries."[30]

Sophisticated weaponry is also used to overcome quantitative deficiencies relative to major rivals.[31] Technology acts as a force multiplier: it can, properly used, increase the combat effectiveness of a military organization in a manner equivalent to or greater than an increase in its size.[32] Technology alone is not sufficient to ensure deterrence or defeat of the enemy. Military forces must be trained and organized appropriately to maximize the advantages of sophisticated equipment and take advantage of enemy weaknesses.[33] States which are inferior in either technology or military technique may attempt to compensate by attaining quantitative superiority, or may pursue asymmetric strategies or strategies of exhaustion.[34] The Vietnam War and the Soviet defeat in Afghanistan are cases of technologically inferior forces overcoming superior adversaries.

LDC arms procurement, therefore, must consider the same issues which affect military decisions in the developed world. If war is believed likely, states must prepare either for decisive and rapid defeat of their opponents or a long, drawn-out battle of exhaustion.[35] LDCs possess the same ability to overestimate their own capabilities or underestimate their opponents that developed states have demonstrated in five centuries of European warfare.[36] Whether the LDC seeks quantitative or qualitative advantage,

6 *Introduction*

or prepares for defense or aggression, it must still decide what weapons are necessary and whether to procure them at home or abroad.

LDCs and the international arms trade

The study of arms production in the developing world is intimately linked with analysis of the international arms trade. European mastery and application of various technologies and development of military organizations and operations which exploited those capabilities led to the creation of the colonial empires and, in a very real sense, to the modern international system.[37] The dominant industrialized powers of the early twentieth century remained the primary sources of arms technology during the Cold War and afterwards.

Interest in the expanding military capabilities of developing nations began in the late 1960s, when the transfer of weapons and production technology from the developed world shifted from surplus World War II equipment to advanced supersonic aircraft and missiles. These early trends were noted in two large studies by the Stockholm International Peace Research Institute (SIPRI) and the Massachusetts Institute of Technology.[38]

The study of arms trade relationships in the 1950–70 period emphasized characteristics of the international system that were historically unique.[39] The international arms market was dominated, temporarily, by two superpowers, as other producer states attempted to catch up with significant changes in conventional weapons technology, particularly in the aerospace sector, and simultaneously recover from World War II. The superpowers dominated both production of existing types of weapons and also development of new and increasingly sophisticated systems. Both superpowers unabashedly used arms supplies for geopolitical gain and ideological leverage. The potential for dependence and loss of political autonomy encouraged some LDCs to pursue strategies of import substitution, multiple sourcing for arms, or local or cooperative industrial efforts.

Interest in LDC military and military-industrial capabilities increased during the 1970s and 1980s. Developed states began selling extremely sophisticated arms to the periphery: these arms demonstrated significant effectiveness in regional conflicts.[40] Growing military capabilities, combined with policies of military-industrial autarky, self-sufficiency, and/or self-reliance,[41] raised the possibility of competition between developed and developing world arms industries in the near future.[42]

The combination of new producers, improved competition, and independence-maximizing policies contributed to significant changes in the international arms trade during the 1970–85 period. Superpower share of arms transfers fell from over 80 percent in the 1960s to 51.4 percent in 1985, while other developed suppliers increased their share to over 30 percent, creating opportunities for LDCs to avoid dependent relationships with superpower suppliers.[43] LDCs increased their share of arms exports from 5.9 percent of the global market to 16.6 percent in the 1974–84 period.[44]

This period marked the high point of both LDC arms industries and the international arms market. International arms exports boomed, due to increased oil wealth and new high-intensity regional conflicts, most conspicuously the Iran–Iraq War. Global arms imports grew from $22.9 billion in 1975 to $40.3 billion in 1984. LDC purchases increased from 72.7 percent of global imports to 80.1 percent; and imports to the Middle East and Persian Gulf grew from 30 percent of the global total to 43.3 percent.[45]

The international arms market collapsed after 1988. The value of the international arms trade declined 70 percent, from $74 billion in 1987 to about $22 billion in 1993.[46] The end of the Iran–Iraq War and the contraction of the international market nearly bankrupted the Brazilian defense industry.[47] Other LDC and developed arms industries suffered severely from reduced domestic and international demand. Studies of the international arms industry since that time focus on the impact of globalization and the effects of substantial contraction due to the end of the Cold War and falling defense budgets (particularly in Europe).[48] A few book-length studies have considered LDC producers in the post-Cold War period.[49] In general, however, interest in the topic has waned, and studies have focused on the impact of contraction on larger producers, and the changing nature of the arms market itself.[50]

The study of LDC arms industries: analytical frameworks

As mentioned above, study of LDC arms industries evolved from the study of the Cold War international arms trade. Moralist traditions found in these studies profoundly affect analysis of LDC arms production.[51] The moralist position criticizes both national arms industries and the global arms trade. Arms producers are viewed as pursuing profits at the expense of human lives, and weapons are blamed for international destabilization and as a primary, if not the sole, cause of military conflict. This position was widely accepted during the 1919–39 period, when critics blamed private armaments firms for fomenting wars around the globe and held these same firms responsible for World War I.[52] Many of the studies written in the 1970s took a similar tone.[53] LDC arms acquisitions and production receive special vilification. The purchase or production of arms purportedly strengthens militarist and anti-democratic forces in developing societies, which leads to increased repression and violation of human rights.[54]

The importance of the moralist position lies in its broad support among analysts of the arms trade and of LDC arms production. Moralist arguments are paramount in the field of peace studies, which is dominated by structural, rather than state-level, approaches. These place primary importance on theories of imperialism, dependence, structural violence, and dominance.[55] Prominent scholars and institutes in the peace studies field constitute some of the most influential and devoted analysts of LDC arms production.

Existing studies of LDC arms industries can be divided into three different groups. First are studies of individual states, either in article-length format or in individual volumes.[56] These analyses are often excellent and extremely comprehensive, but lack a comparative perspective. The second group is volumes which use multiple case studies. The case studies may include developed states for comparison, or may focus strictly on the developing world.[57] The third group is broad surveys, which analyze LDC production as a bloc.[58]

Four basic theoretical approaches are identifiable in the comparative works, used singly or in combination. These approaches are *structural/dependency*, *economic/development*, *dominance/world system*, and *historical/systemic*. Each approach focuses on different aspects of the motivation for LDC arms production, and proposes different methods for assessing its impact.

Each approach also has proponents and pessimists, who view developments as potentially beneficial or fundamentally detrimental to national political-economic health and stability. Proponents do not necessarily *advocate* given military-industrial policies – in most cases, they are agnostic. Proponents do, however, recognize that the trade-offs made by a given state in pursuing military-industrial policies may not be inherently harmful to the economy of the producing state, and that local production can in some circumstances represent a logical and cost-effective response to economic and security problems. Each of these approaches, and the arguments of its proponents and pessimists, will be examined briefly below.

Structuralist/dependency approach

The *structuralist/dependency* approach focuses on the hierarchical nature of politico-military power in the Cold War period.[59] The industrialized nations form the upper tiers of the international hierarchies of both military and military-industrial capability, while former colonies and developing states constitute the lower tiers. Throughout the Cold War period, LDCs relied on the transfer of technology, equipment, training, and knowledge from more industrially and militarily sophisticated powers. This dependence on outside supply made LDCs vulnerable to embargo or the threat of embargo, which could be used to influence their foreign and, in some cases, domestic policies.

Many LDCs have based their military-industrial programs, at least in part, on the need to overcome or mitigate potential dependence on outside suppliers. The issue of dependence has become an important, and in some cases the *only*, security-related variable in determining the effectiveness of

LDC military industries.[60] One analytically compelling method of assessing LDC arms industries consists of comparing the products and programs of LDC industries with programs and products developed in a similar time period in the developed producer countries in order to assess the effectiveness of import-substitution.[61] Other studies focus on the opportunity costs and structural inequalities between developed major arms manufacturers and the LDCs, measured in economic and financial terms as well as in terms of available industrial, scientific, educational, and economic resources.[62]

Proponents using this approach, typified by Andrew Ross, emphasize the importance of LDCs increasing their levels of self-sufficiency, and gradually improving import-substitution programs in various major weapons systems and in overall arms procurement.[63] Other studies favorably assess the growth of arms exports and technology acquisition by LDCs.[64] This position is exemplified by a model, entitled 'the ladder of production.'[65]

These proponents emphasize technology as a process. 'Technology is perhaps best understood as an abstract version of knowledge, an attitude towards life and a method for solving its problems.'[66] The ladder of production is viewed as a logical model of LDC military-industrial development, through which LDCs gradually absorb technological processes and concepts and convert them into military and industrial capabilities.

Pessimists focus on technology as a product, and on the inability of developing states to compete with established producers in the industrialized world. These studies focus on production of major defense items such as tanks, supersonic aircraft, and naval vessels, emphasizing the less-sophisticated nature of LDC defense products, their poor export performance, and the continuing LDC dependency on imports of advanced weaponry.[67] One of the most important aspects of this new dependency, according to pessimists, is the gradual shift among the major LDC

Table 1.1 The ladder of production

The ladder of production describes a 'rational' progression of technology absorption and production capabilities.

1. In the initial underindustrialized state, the LDC purchases foreign weapons systems, and relies heavily on foreign trainers, technicians, and advisors.
2. As the industrial and technical base matures. The LDC assumes greater responsibility for upkeep, maintenance, and repair of weapons, decreasing reliance on advisors and trainers.
3. After extensive familiarization with the new technologies, states move to local assembly of foreign weapons from imported components.
4. Assembly, in time, leads to licensed production with increasing proportions of local content and decreasing reliance on imported components and parts.
5. Technological assimilation through use and production, in theory, leads to eventual use of acquired infrastructure for local research and development (R&D), weapons design, and completely indigenous production.

producers from imports of finished products to imports of manufacturing technology, known as technological dependency.

The pessimists have a different model of LDC industrialization, called the import-substitution industries (ISI) model. This model assumes that the theoretical objective of all arms producers is to reach a state of autarky, competing at the international state-of-the-art in all major weapons systems. Using this objective as the ideal, the ISI model then compares unit costs of production, dates of introduction of systems of comparable performance ('technological age'), and occasionally R&D spending as an indicator of present and future competitiveness.[68]

The most influential pessimist critique is embodied in the various works of Stephanie Neuman. Neuman analyzes the potential for competitive LDC production and the continuing performance of major LDC producers against the superpowers in both export markets and in indigenous development and design of major weapons systems.[69] Neuman attributes the failures of LDC industries primarily to issues of scale. Most LDCs lack the scientific and technical expertise necessary to maintain a first-rate military-industrial base or a top-of-the-line research and development establishment. Failure to keep up with high-technology R&D condemns the LDCs to second-line products, forcing them to copy or acquire technology developed elsewhere and reinforcing the cycle of dependency. In addition, most LDCs lack the internal market necessary for the mass economies of scale necessary to keep unit costs low. This inhibits both production of new systems (imported systems of similar or greater quality are less expensive) and long-term export potential of LDC-produced weapons.

Economic/development approach

The *economic/development* approach focuses on the economic opportunity costs of LDC military-industrial policies. Proponent analysts note that, in many cases, military expenditure leads to positive effects on national economic growth.[70] LDCs seeking to maximize economic development, increase security, and achieve acceptance as symbolic equals of the industrialized world sometimes see military-industrial policies as a means of 'jump-starting' both economic and defense objectives.[71] Some studies indicate that LDC military expenditures and arms production can have positive impacts on the economy similar to those found in industrialized states.[72] Weapons manufacture becomes another means of manipulating economic growth and employment, and provides important options for national leaders seeking to maximize security within the constraints of limited budgets and resources.[73]

Most analysts using the economic/development approach are pessimists, and strongly oppose the concept of LDC military-industrialization.[74] From a strictly economic viewpoint, investments in civilian sectors often offer better returns than military-industrial programs. Many LDC military industries operate inefficiently. Once start-up costs, imported materials and technologies, and other foreign exchange expenditures are factored in, LDC unit costs generally exceed those of systems available on the international market. Additionally, the goods produced often prove inferior to those available from abroad at lower prices.[75]

Economic/development analysts propose an alternate set of models for LDC military industrialization. Some industries, including Brazil, Singapore, and Israel, are described as 'export-oriented' defense industries because of their interest and involvement in international arms exports. These industries, in many cases, will have to focus on sophisticated, high-technology products in order to compete with other international suppliers. Other states, such as India, seek primarily to provide satisfactory levels of long-term political independence, and are titled 'import substitution' defense industries.[76]

In producing these models, analysts implicitly assume that LDC military-industrial policies result primarily from consideration of economic factors, particularly the possibility of lucrative arms exports.[77] While economic factors certainly play a role in these decisions, some analysts conclude that states use the purported economic benefits of military industries primarily as a justification rather than a motivation.[78] Little evidence exists which would indicate that exports provide the primary incentive for *development* of an arms industry.[79]

Dominance/world system approach

The *dominance/world system* approach represents an off-shoot of North–South relations theories of the late 1970s.[80] This approach takes the developed/developing stratification of industrial, economic, and military capabilities noted in the *structuralist* approach and extends it. The dominance approach assumes that continuing subordination of the developing world constitutes a major priority of these higher-level states, and that the hierarchical structure is deliberately inflexible in order to maintain this subordination.[81]

This approach stresses the pernicious impact of technology on developing countries. Many of these writings, in fact, exhibit a strong anti-technology bias. Some analyses refer to a condition of 'technologism', peculiar to the West and inappropriate for LDC economic, military, or developmental requirements.[82] Others question the rationality of increasingly costly high-technology weapons which perform only marginally better on a unit-level than their less-expensive predecessors.[83] The trend towards increasing cost and complexity and diminishing improvements in unit capability is viewed as particularly harmful to LDCs.

This approach's analytical focus on high-technology and its relevance for LDCs is applied to both LDC military industries and LDC military requirements and tactics. Some analysts argue that LDCs have no

12 *Introduction*

requirements for high-technology arms, or else should restructure their armed forces to use low-technology means to counteract technological advantages available to the developed countries.[84] These analyses imply or state explicitly that the production of high-technology military goods by LDCs is unnecessary, wasteful, and provocative.[85]

The dominance approach also places particular emphasis on technological dependency and the recent surge in co-production and offsets as part of international arms deals.[86] According to this approach, the fact that LDCs now rely on established industrialized producers for manufacturing technology instead of finished products only indicates the extent to which dependency has been accelerated by LDC import-substitution policies.[87] Dominance theorists argue that reliance on manufacturing technology, available at enormous cost and rarely operable without significant foreign training and assistance, places labor-intensive developing economies more deeply into the cycle of dependency and continued economic and social vulnerability.[88]

Systemic/historical approach

The last of the major approaches to LDC arms production is *systemic/historical*. This approach accepts many facets of the other approaches, but attempts to put them in a historical framework by studying the production and trade in arms in other periods. Only a few book-length studies use this approach, but they are among the most important in the arms trade literature.[89]

The importance of the systemic approach lies in its comparative nature. Variations and continuities within the international arms market and the hierarchy of producers become easier to discern through examination of several different periods. This approach identifies a series of different 'tiers of production,' based on the diffusion of dominant military-related technologies and the skills, techniques, and infrastructure necessary for their production. This approach therefore represents a significant expansion on the 'developed/developing' stratification prominent in other approaches.

The analysis of the diffusion of military technology and arms production bears considerable similarity to Raymond Vernon's *product cycle*, originally identified in the context of the spread of civilian technologies,[90] which predicts the diffusion of manufacturing capability in the following manner:

1   A product is invented in one state, and sold first domestically and then later on the international market.
2   As new products are developed, declining economic returns on investment prompt the sale of production technology overseas and the establishment of foreign subsidiaries to take advantage of lower cost factors.

3 Absorption of manufacturing technology and know-how combined with lower production costs eventually allow the new manufacturer to export the product back to the original producer.

There are, naturally, significant differences between the production of military equipment, intended for defense of national territory, sovereignty, and interests, and the production of transistor radios, basketball shoes, and other civilian goods. States often attempt to maintain control over production and dissemination of critical defense technologies – the Soviets produced special low-technology versions of their weapons for export, and the US insists on end-user restrictions. Nevertheless, defense technology diffuses, through licensed production, espionage, reverse-engineering, or adaptation of dual-use goods based on related civilian technologies.

The most extensive systemic study identifies five different tiers in the arms production hierarchy, based on time of entry into the ranks of producers, infrastructure, and production capability.[91] This hierarchy is briefly described in Table 1.2.[92]

This expanded hierarchical structure, superimposed on several arms of transfer systems, illuminates the flexibility within and between tiers across various periods.[93] China and the Ottoman Empire, two of the earliest users of gunpowder, fell from the ranks of the leading producers by the eighteenth century. France, Germany, and the UK, which formed the first tier in the late nineteenth century, now constitute dominant members of the second tier. In each system, smaller developed producers and states in the periphery made up the lower rungs of the second tier and the third tier.

Even during the rise of industrialization and the dynamic growth of European military power, regional powers existed, and created military industries and capabilities subject to some of the same constraints that are evident today. The Ottoman Empire, Japan, and China, for example, all failed to compete industrially or militarily with European great powers,

Table 1.2 The hierarchy of production

Tier One:	States which *innovate* at the technological frontier, and therefore temporarily become the sole or dominant producers of a given arms technology.
Tier Two:	States which produce at or near the technological frontier, and are capable of *adapting* existing technology to market and security requirements.
Tier Three:	States which copy and reproduce (*apply*) existing technologies, but which do not capture the underlying process of innovation or adaptation.
Tier Four:	States which *acquire* and use existing technologies, but are incapable of production.
Tier Five:	States which either acquire technologies and cannot use them or which do no obtain them at all.

but used imported and locally-produced military technology to great effect in the sixteenth to eighteenth centuries.[94] Various Indian principalities in the seventeenth and eighteenth centuries built significant military forces based on locally-produced or imported arms.[95] In the early nineteenth century Egypt built a significant military industry based on French expertise.[96] In the late nineteenth century, both China and Japan developed local defense industries based primarily around regional military requirements.[97] In the case of Japan, military-industrialization contributed to both economic growth and, after the Russo-Japanese War, great power status. Arms procurement and production in less-developed states and regional powers, therefore, is a phenomenon demonstrated across a wide range of historical experience.

Disaggregating the hierarchy of production by considering it in different eras provides valuable insights into trends in the arms industry. Systemic analysts challenge the bias against licensed manufacture evident in other approaches. Licensed production, from this perspective, represents a natural and historically validated method for states to create or maintain competitive industries in times of significant technological change or increasing R&D or unit costs. When unit costs are low, and generations of equipment turn over rapidly, states replace their arsenals frequently and this in turn permits economies of scale that allow multiple major producers. As unit costs increase, the number of major producers falls, and more states are forced to rely on licenses and other transfers.[98]

Licensed manufacture played a critical role in World War II. The Japanese airforce was based on an amalgamation of US, British, French, and German technologies, Russia's T-34 tank was based on US designs, and the P-51 Mustang fighter only became effective after the US airframe was merged with a British Rolls-Royce Merlin engine.[99] Licensed production also played an important role in the re-establishment of Europe's arms industries after World War II. The US supplied billions of dollars in Off-Shore Procurement Funds, including joint NATO projects and licensed production efforts.[100]

Systemic studies use analysis of products, in the form of weapons produced, manufacture under license, share of export markets, and overall military and R&D expenditure, in an effort to understand the diffusion of technological *processes*. This contrasts significantly with other approaches to LDC arms production, which view the products as symptomatic of an apparently irrevocable position of dependency on the part of the developing world. By distinguishing multiple tiers of production and focusing on the historical process of technological change and diffusion, systemic analysis more accurately describes the position of both LDC and lesser industrialized producers in the global system.

Introduction   15

Existing frameworks: the missing variable

Each of these approaches complements one or more of the others, and illuminates certain facets of the global economy, the international arms market, and the international system as they affect LDC military-industrial decision-making. The focus on economic and system-wide factors, however important, ultimately fails to explain critical variables in the motivation for and capability of LDC arms industries. Existing studies of LDC arms industries frequently attempt to assess *effect* without adequately considering *cause*.

States acquire arms to defend themselves from aggression or to expand their own power over neighbors. The bulk of the current literature on LDC arms production virtually ignores the military requirements which drive arms purchases and production, and the military implications of production on local and regional security relationships. Over two millenia ago, Thucydides identified three motives which determine the actions of states: honor, self-interest, and fear.[101] Contemporary analyses of LDC arms production virtually ignore the issues of honor, which might also be defined as prestige, and fear (security), focusing primarily on self-interest defined in economic terms.[102] Political and security motives for arms production are reduced in these studies to fear of dependency and loss of autonomy.[103] Dependency constitutes an important factor, and experience of embargo inarguably remains a significant variable in LDC military-industrial policy.[104] This concept of dependence as the *dominant* security motive for LDC arms producers, however, demonstrates the existing focus on political-economic, rather than political-military, concerns.

Assessing the political-military considerations which drive LDC military industrial policy and arms procurement requires a different analytical focus. Objectionable though it may be to some analysts of LDC arms industries, the realist notion that the international system consists of individual states competing for survival, power, and hegemony in an anarchic environment remains a critical tool for analyzing many aspects of LDC military-industrial decision-making.[105]

The procurement of weapons reflects a state's perceptions of and response to security threats and political ambitions. Possession of arms or a reputation for successful use of arms provides the dual benefit of deterring potential aggressors from attempting to carry out their objectives by force, and the option of compelling other states to comply with national objectives through threats or force.[106] Weapons also provide the means, if diplomacy fails, to defend against enemy capabilities and/or attack enemy assets, including military forces, territory, or economic resources.[107] Consideration of military-industrial policy in the absence of these political-military realities risks 'missing the forest for the trees.'

Krause assesses the motivations for arms production as *pursuit of*

16 *Introduction*

power, *wealth*, and *victory in war*.[108] According to his analysis, only first-tier producers exhibit all three motivations. Their quasi-monopoly on state-of-the-art technology, developed first in response to *victory in war* (security/military) objectives and ambitions, allows them to exploit the technology not only for *wealth* (profit) but also in the *pursuit of power* – the transfer of new technologies in return for alliances, bases, and other political gains.[109]

Second-tier producers, initiating production after the innovators, are particularly active on the international market (*wealth*).[110] These producers have difficulty keeping up with the technological state-of-the-art, and often must export abundantly in order to reach the economies of scale necessary to lower unit costs. This includes the sale of production technology, if necessary, in order to maintain their defense industrial base. The third-tier of producers consists of late or inefficient industrializers: their rationale is primarily *victory in war*, defined as security, regional hegemony, or global status and prestige.[111]

Most weapons producers, both industrialized and developing, can be classified as 'partially dependent' on imported arms, manufacturing technology, or weapons designs – a circumstance that is only increasing in the emerging globalized arms industry. This reality of partial dependence, also referred to as self-reliance, is fundamental to understanding security policy in both developing and industrialized states. It reflects the changing nature of technology, the uneven distribution of technologies, skills, and capabilities, and the increasing complexity of warfare.

Most arms producers are neither superpowers nor first-tier producers. Weaker states must, in theory, pursue rational arms procurement and production policies, because of their fundamental lack of resources.[112] Many states attempt to acquire and maintain some domestic arms manufacturing capability and exploit existing comparative advantages.[113] Smaller industrialized second-tier arms producers maintain rational military-industrial policies designed to maximize political independence while maintaining adequate military capability vis-à-vis existing military threats and national ambitions.[114]

Estimating the effectiveness of LDC arms production, therefore, requires analysis of the security requirements and political ambitions of the producer states. Major LDC producers include North and South Korea, Egypt, Israel, Chile, Brazil Argentina, South Africa, Taiwan, China, India, Pakistan, Indonesia, Singapore, Iran, and Iraq.[115] These are states which exist in distinct regional state sub-systems, are involved in rivalries with neighbors, and suffered embargoes or threats to alliances which contributed to concerns over security. Balanced analysis of the costs, benefits, and effectiveness of their respective industries, therefore, must reflect the security environments in which they interact, national goals and ambitions, and experiences and expectations regarding the intentions of external powers in their regions.

Methods of analysis

The accelerating pace of technological change and the development of military techniques to convert new technology into decisive military capabilities forms a pattern which has dominated warfare, and by extension the international system, for centuries. This pattern manifests itself at any given time as a global military culture – a rough hierarchy of military capability.[116] The most advanced states in this culture have mastered the technologies and/or techniques that constitute the contemporary international 'state of the art.'

In effect, states *innovate, adapt, apply,* and *acquire* military skills in a manner similar to their acquisition of technology. States which function at levels closer to the global 'state of the art' have significant potential military advantages over states operating further from the global standard. One method of improving relative position in global military culture is through exposure to modern warfare and sophisticated military technique. Another method is to increase a society's exposure to and mastery of the technological skills and processes that are associated with the state of the art. A third is to increase familiarity and expertise with the major military technologies available on the global market.

The study of LDC military industries must encompass the efforts of middle powers to improve their position in the global military culture. Evaluation of industrial efforts also needs to reflect the applicability of production to regional security requirements. States rarely make rapid dramatic positive shifts in either global military culture or in the global hierarchy of production – but even some positive change signifies a substantial increase in military potential.

This study will examine three of the most influential and important LDC arms producers of the late twentieth century. Israel and India represent the two most persistent and sophisticated LDC producers in the Cold War period. Each state created large military industries producing a wide range of conventional and unconventional arms, and military-industrial policy in each state has been an important issue in both national security and economic debates since the late 1940s. Iraq, by contrast, provides an example of a recent industrializer.

These three states also represent different models of domestic political and economic development. India, the world's largest democracy, has one of the world's most powerful and autonomous civil services – and a tradition of virtual non-involvement by Parliament in security affairs.[117] Israel's highly participatory democracy demonstrates considerable sophistication and concern over military expenditures, foreign affairs, and national security – with the prominent exception of nuclear weapons development.[118] Iraq represents a classic totalitarian state, where wealth, authority, and decision-making are concentrated in the hands of only a few individuals and public participation in national security decisions is, at best, minimal.

18 *Introduction*

These distinctions are important in determining the relative importance of regime type and of bureaucratic and domestic political influences on LDC military-industrial policy.

As mentioned above, various authors have defined LDC production in terms of 'export-oriented' and 'import-substitution' models, while others have stressed the importance of domestic economies of scale. The relationship between these two separate variables is unclear. In order to compete effectively in the global arms market, a state must be competitive in at least some high-technology areas. This level of technological absorption only comes at substantial social and economic cost. Logically, only states with significant resource endowments would be able to afford these expenditures.

In fact, however, there is not a clear relationship between size and technological competitiveness, at least at first glance. Major LDC exporters have at various times included Brazil, China, Israel, South Korea, and Singapore – but never India, despite its vast resources and formidable scientific and technical establishment. Economic factors do not adequately explain international competitiveness in the arms sector.

When the security variable is included, however, structural factors may provide greater insight. As mentioned above, technology can act as a force multiplier in warfare, creating synergies and capabilities that allow smaller combatants to overcome quantitative disadvantages. It is possible that smaller size and resource endowments may act as a *positive* stimulant to more rapid technological absorption and innovation. This absorption will be reflected in the capabilities demanded by the military, and therefore (over time) those weapons produced by the country as part of a policy of self-reliance. Accordingly, smaller countries may have greater incentive to strive for globally competitive arms production than larger, relatively more secure countries.[119]

Each of these states, therefore, responds to different types of security threats with relatively different resource endowments and different political and economic systems. One critical issue for each is dependency – what level of extra-regional influence is acceptable in order to maintain national security? Another is technology and the importance of quality versus quantity. A third is the acquisition of unconventional weapons. This approach will identify common factors and create an additional, *security-based* model of LDC military industrialization.

In each case, the introduction will include a general discussion of the security dilemma and objectives for each state and an analysis of the potential of the arms industry at the end of the Cold War. Analysis of the state's military-industrial development will be broken into several periods, each bounded by significant international, regional, or domestic events or crises. Comparison of policy priorities and changes between these periods, as the level of threat fluctuated, permits assessment of the impact of these crises and threats on national military and military-

Introduction 19

industrial policy. This methodology also helps take the inevitable time lags associated with policy shifts and complex projects into account.

Specific military-industrial programs will be examined in each era, and when long-standing programs exist, such as aircraft production in India, they will be assessed in several different periods. Both conventional and unconventional weapon production will be examined. Projects will be analyzed based on the initial objectives of the program and the eventual impact of the program on military encounters, regional military capability, and deterrence. The context in which decisions were made will be a matter of particular emphasis. Weapons are often produced long after program initiation, when political and security conditions have fundamentally changed.

Technology will be analyzed as both a *product*, in terms of specific pieces of equipment, and also in terms of assimilation – the acquisition of knowledge, technical skills, and infrastructure. The definition of 'local production,' as a result, will take a lowest common denominator approach based on US policy concerning co-production, which includes any program that:

> enables an eligible foreign government, international organization, or designated commercial producer to acquire the 'know-how' to manufacture or assemble, repair, maintain and operate, in whole or in part, a specific weapon, communication or support system, or an individual military item.[120]

Prevailing methodology for the study of LDC arms industries relies primarily on analysis of Major Weapons Systems (MWS), defined as ships, aircraft, armored vehicles, and missiles.[121] The advantage of MWS as a unit of measure comes from relative ease of detection: they are easily quantified. 'Bean-counting' of major weapons systems, however, provides a demonstrably inadequate means of assessing military capability. Iraq's masses of armor and relatively large and sophisticated airforce proved nearly worthless in combat against Coalition forces. Focus on MWS *production* provides a similarly inadequate measure of industrial capability and national military-industrial priorities. Production of artillery ammunition, for example, may represent a far more important contribution to LDC military capability than the production of self-propelled artillery pieces, but only the latter are measured by current methodology. Existing methodology also fails to examine the development and impact of industrial facilities which specialize in repair and maintenance of existing military equipment.

This study therefore shall examine five categories of military-industrial production. These are, respectively:

1   *Endurance*: the basic building blocks of military strength, including small arms; light crew-served weapons such as machine guns and

20   *Introduction*

   mortars; 'dumb munitions' such as artillery shells, aerial bombs, and mines; auxiliary equipment such as tents, trucks, jeeps, uniforms, and tires; other miscellaneous but unsophisticated items, and capabilities for repair and maintenance of existing equipment.
2 *Non-platform weapons*: these include artillery pieces; battlefield rockets; various missiles; guided weapons; electronics systems; torpedoes; and other naval ordnance.
3 *Modification programs*: locally-designed modifications of imported equipment of all types.
4 *Major weapons platforms*[122]: armored vehicles; aircraft; large naval combat vessels (over 300 tons).
5 *Strategic systems*: chemical and biological weapons capabilities; nuclear weapons developments; long-range (over 100 km) missiles; cruise missiles; satellites and other space reconnaissance capability; and space launch vehicles.

The difficulty of obtaining accurate data on arms issues is well-documented.[123] Analysis based on the convenient and quantifiable factors of military spending and transfers of major weapons systems provides an inadequate picture of national military capabilities, priorities, and military-industrial capability. SIPRI estimates consistently understated the capabilities of major LDC producers such as Israel and Iraq.[124] They utterly failed to reflect endurance or modification capabilities which provide enormous benefits in actual armed conflict.

The majority of data publicly available focuses on weapons platforms (aircraft, ships, and armored vehicles), and places little importance on the trade in or production of electronics systems, light and medium arms, and munitions. Evidence must therefore be drawn from biographical, anecdotal, and secondary sources, as well as defense and military journals. Estimates of the effectiveness of logistics and maintenance systems will be primarily based on past combat performance and on evidence of the ability to produce significant portions of equipment locally. Consideration of technology as a *process* suggests that local maintenance can provide knowledge and skills which can lead to both enhanced military performance and military-industrial capability, and that local production can provide some of the skills and equipment necessary for improving local maintenance and support functions and, therefore, enhancing the effectiveness of existing equipment in combat.[125] Modification and modernization programs, using locally-produced or imported subsystems to upgrade weapons effectiveness and extend service life of existing equipment, will receive particular attention, as these provide evidence of the transfer of process skills and assimilation of technology.

Where appropriate and available, standard data has been provided as a general means of demonstrating changes in military priorities and procurement policy. This data is far from comprehensive, and often inconsistent.

Expressions of military expenditures as a percentage of Gross National Product (GNP) or Gross Domestic Product (GDP) give a rough estimate of the impact of military spending on a national economy, and changes in these figures may indicate increased or decreased concern with national security. Data provided by the Arms Control and Disarmament Agency is used in most of these tables for the sake of consistency. Estimates of military spending and exports, particularly in the Israeli case, differ widely, and some inconsistencies are, regrettably, unavoidable. Errors in application and interpretation of this data are the sole responsibility of the author.

The conclusion will discuss the ramifications for the study of LDC arms industries and the evolving international system, and present a *security-based* model of LDC industrialization that will, hopefully, spur further study. If *regional* security calculations dominate the military-industrial policies of significant LDC producers, this will both provide alternatives to existing analyses of military production and also a means, perhaps, for anticipating changes in the policies of future producers and aspiring powers. Focus on security issues as a policy determinant will encourage the development of new tools for assessing the rationality and cost-effectiveness of LDC military-industrial policies and the potential direction of these policies in the future.

2 India

Background

On August 15, 1947, after almost two centuries of European domination, India achieved its independence. The new Indian state's foreign policy eschewed violence as a means of settling disputes.[1] As a leader of the Non-Aligned Movement, India was theoretically committed to the concept of peaceful coexistence and resistance to participation in superpower blocs.[2] India refused to join either superpower alliance network:

> It was through 'subordinate alliances' for the purposes of defending their territories that the rulers of India lost their independence. By calling in a stronger power to help you in defending your independence, you subordinate your policies to the advice of the protecting power. Thus an alliance between states, which are not mutually dependent, but one of which is very much stronger while the other seeks protection, leads to the subordination of the weaker partner.[3]

India's quest for self-sufficiency in arms production reflects this elite preference for independence. In practice, however, India's behavior has been more traditional. The essentially realist doctrine of *mandala* remains a part of Indian political and strategic culture.[4] Non-alignment has been used in combination with more traditional means to further Indian regional and international objectives.

India seeks the prestige and authority of a major power, as well as recognition of its role as the dominant power in South Asia.[5] India's economic and cultural predominance within the region is indisputable.[6] Indian claims to great power status rest on a number of factors, including the size of its population, the talent and creativity of its scientific and technical sectors,[7] its status as the largest democracy in the world, and its leadership in the Non-Aligned Movement and role as the articulator of a moral alternative to Machiavellian international politics.[8]

The Indian military exerts only marginal influence in domestic and international policy. The Army represented one of the primary symbols of

Imperial authority, and repressed nationalist demonstrations in the pre-independence period.[9] The Congress Party did not trust the military after independence, and deliberately undermined its authority, stature, and prestige. Since 1962, the role and status of the military in Indian society has grown as a result of regional conflicts and international peacekeeping activities.[10]

The Indian armed forces have engaged in international conflicts or interventions on at least ten occasions since independence.[11] Partition between secular India and Muslim Pakistan was marked by vicious rioting, mass emigration, and war.[12] From 1960–72, India successfully annexed the former Portuguese colony of Goa, suffered an ignominious defeat to China in the Himalayan mountains, and engaged in three separate conflicts with Pakistan. The last of these, in 1971, resulted in the secession of Bangladesh and the achievement of regional hegemony under Prime Minister Indira Gandhi. In 1974 India demonstrated its nuclear capability – a capability that remained mostly theoretical until a second series of tests in 1998.[13]

In the 1980s and 1990s however, Pakistan's development of nuclear capabilities neutralized India's larger conventional forces.[14] India's armed forces engaged in border conflicts with Pakistan; helped suppress secessionist and insurgent movements in Punjab, Kashmir, and the northeast; intervened in Sri Lanka and the Maldives; and expanded in force structure and potential range of operations, including a series of aggressive military exercises on the Pakistani and Chinese borders. The utility of a large military as a prestige instrument was apparently attractive to political leaders, but India's foreign and national security policy suffered from what has been described as an 'absence of strategic thinking.'[15]

India's national security policies shifted substantially after the nuclear tests by both India and Pakistan in 1998.[16] India's test was prompted by both international and regional considerations, including the threat of broad international sanctions against states which did not fall under the Nuclear Nonproliferation Treaty.[17] Flawed assumptions regarding the utility of nuclear weapons in regional politics – particularly the belief that nuclearization would force Pakistan to accept Indian regional ascendance – were exposed in the Kargil conflict.[18] These events contributed to a new Indian security posture, including a public nuclear doctrine, the development of nuclear command and control structures, and increased emphasis on the role of the military in contributing to national security policy.

India's defense industry has been used as the primary example of an 'import-substitution' or import-oriented model of LDC military industries.[19] The arms industry reflects the desire of the Indian government for international prestige as well as military self-sufficiency, and has emphasized high-visibility development and production of the most modern types of major weapons systems. The contribution of these efforts to Indian military capability have been substantial – at least within the South Asian region. The weapons which have been produced, often at great expense, have maintained and expanded India's quantitative and qualitative military advantage over Pakistan.[20]

Indian security perception

Under the Empire, Indian security revolved around the concept of 'the barrack,' a series of concentric rings of states or geographic regions which provided a buffer for the Indian heartland. Imperial policy focused on physically subduing the inner ring of the barrack, including the northwest frontier, the Indian Ocean, and the Bay of Bengal, while neutralizing the outer ring through diplomacy, threat, and bribery.[21] The partition of India removed the former northwest buffer, and placed a hostile Pakistan with unrealized territorial ambitions next to the Indian heartland at the same time that a resurgent China loomed ominously in the northeast.[22] In addition, World War II demonstrated the vulnerability of the Indian Ocean to foreign interference.

Since independence, India has required military force to respond to security problems at four different levels: internal strife, regional conflict, extra-regional intervention from China, and superpower interference in the regional system.[23] Internal security threats arise from the multi-ethnic nature of the Indian state, and fall into two broad categories: communal or economic disturbances and separatist movements.[24] Most potential separatist movements are located in peripheral regions. Chief among these are the restless tribal areas of the northeast and Assam, where Mizo and Naga rebels have been armed by China and Pakistan.[25] Numerous other ethnic and communal insurgencies exist in India as well.[26]

In the West, Kashmir was largely absorbed into India in 1947, despite its Muslim majority population, and remains a regional flashpoint today.[27] Punjab is the home of most of India's Sikh population, and a nationalist movement seeking an independent Sikh homeland ('Khalistan') began a violent insurgency in the early 1980s.[28] Pakistan funded and supported insurrections in both regions. Kashmir continues to represent the most likely spark for a future Indo-Pakistani conflict, as demonstrated in both the 1999 Kargil War and the 2001–02 'Compound Crisis.'

Pakistan represents the only threat to Indian regional dominance.[29] The assumption that Muslims and Hindus required separate states inspired the creation of Pakistan, but India's successful incorporation of a large Muslim minority into an avowedly secular national framework implicitly threatens this 'two-state' concept. The Pakistani military plays an unhealthy role in domestic politics – experiments with democracy have been unsuccessful, and the army believes that its status as the defender of Pakistan and the primary symbol of national unity permits it to freely intervene in both domestic and foreign policy.[30] Pakistan and India engaged in three major wars and one serious border skirmish in the 1947–71 period. India seized the Siachen Glacier in 1984, sparking an ongoing border skirmish. Military exercises, unrest in Kashmir and Punjab, and border tensions nearly led to war in 1986–87 and 1990. A Pakistani military incursion across the Line of Control in Kashmir led to a limited war in the Kargil region in 1999, and terrorist attacks on the Indian parliament in New Delhi sparked a crisis that nearly led to war in both January and June of 2002. Pakistan has provided support for regional and international terrorist groups, but more recently has become an important US ally in the global war on terrorism.[31]

Indian policy towards both China and the superpowers has been fundamentally defensive, focusing on isolation of the region and deterrence of outside intervention. The Chinese threat also influenced India's development of nuclear weapons and long-range ballistic missiles.[32] Superpower threats were managed diplomatically, including India's Treaty of Peace, Friendship and Cooperation with the Soviet Union in 1971.

Military-industrial policy

India's defense industries are intended to provide those armaments and supplies necessary for national defense, and to ensure that India does not have to rely excessively on external supplies or foreign support. In the 1970s, there was a gradual shift from a policy of *self-sufficiency*, or the pursuit of autarky, to one of *self-reliance*, which allowed a higher level of defense imports from politically trustworthy and reliable partners – Western Europe and the Soviet Union.[33] Because military-industrial efforts reflect India's self-image and global status, the procurement process is subject to input from three groups: the military, political leaders and civil service bureaucrats, and economists. Each of these groups has different key interests, which vie for predominance subject to the availability of foreign exchange and financial reserves and changes in the security threat.[34]

The military desires to match the technological quality of weapons available to traditional foes, primarily Pakistan, and to respond rapidly to changes in the balance of forces. Importing proven weapons already under production in the major industrialized military powers provides the most satisfactory solution. Pakistan possesses very limited military-industrial capability, and must therefore purchase most major weapons systems abroad. India can then purchase a counter-balancing weapons system and be assured of reasonably quick delivery.

Political leaders and civil service bureaucrats attempt to promote India's political and military independence and to assert India's claim to great power status. These priorities require the establishment of a domestic military-industrial base which can design, develop and produce the equipment required by the military. The civil service plays a critical role in this process: India's military industries are specifically earmarked as the exclusive responsibility of the state sector in the Industrial Resolution Policy of 1948.[35] Bureaucrats and politicians prefer ambitious local R&D and production programs to foreign imports, arguing that only through extensive local industrial programs can India ever achieve independence.

Economists have a third perspective, strongly tempered by the limited availability of foreign exchange. Imports which fed the hungry or enhanced India's long-term economic development generally received priority for scarce resources.[36] Economists therefore supported a middle path – the import of manufacturing technology, which could be used to gradually increase India's military production infrastructure and capabilities. India must, according to this view, accept some dependence on supplies of spare parts and manufacturing technology in order to acquire technological skills and capabilities which can be transferred to the rest of the economy.

Analysis of Indian security policy is complicated by the virtual absence of any long-term planning. India never commissioned a white paper on defense in the twentieth century, and the role of the military in formulating national security remained minimal until after the Kargil War.[37] Security considerations, therefore, were generally defined in non-military terms, reinforcing perceptions that India lacks a coherent strategy.[38] Because India seeks recognition as a great power, military-industrial policy often appears to prioritize symbol over substance even though it has contributed significantly to national security.[39]

Structure of the Indian defense industry

In the 1990s, the Indian military-industrial complex consisted of 39 ordnance factories (with more under construction),[40] nine (later reduced to eight) defense public sector undertakings (DPSUs),[41] and a vast array of public and private research, development and small production facilities. A separate Defense Research and Development Organization (DRDO) oversees research and development (R&D) for local production, although some firms also do 'in-house' R&D as well. The DPSUs were either established by the government, or were taken over or merged with government firms in an effort to nationalize the defense industries.[42] Virtually all of India's defense production is in the hands of the public sector, with the exception of some dual-use items, components, and non-lethal equipment. Recent reforms are attempting to open up the defense sector for participation by private firms, including those with up to 26 percent foreign equity – but state controlled industries dominate the defense sector.[43] In 1995, the Indian government announced plans to increase self-reliance and local participation in defense procurement from 30 percent to 70 percent by 2005 – an effort that has not been successful.[44]

Defense Public Sector Undertakings (DPSUs)[45]

The DPSUs manufacture all of the locally-produced major weapons systems for the Indian armed services with the exception of tanks and artillery, which are produced at government Ordnance Factories. Several of the DPSUs, including Bharat Earth Movers Limited (BEML) and Praga Tools Limited (PTL), actually produce the bulk of their goods for the civilian or dual-use industrial sector, and are only marginally involved in the manufacture of defense equipment.[46]

Other DPSUs, particularly Hindustan Aeronautics Ltd (HAL), are involved primarily in the design, development, and construction of expensive and sophisticated weapons systems for the armed forces. HAL has developed 11 types of aircraft from in-house R&D and produced 13 types under license. It also supports the Indian Space Research Organization space vehicle program, along with Bharat Dynamics Ltd (BDL).[47] HAL suffers from low worker productivity levels, like most elements of the Indian defense sector. In 1999, HAL employed 50,000 workers, and produced $500 million in sales. In comparison, Israel Aircraft Industries employed 14,000 workers and produced $2 billion in sales.[48]

Bharat Electronics Ltd (BEL), Bharat Dynamics Ltd (BDL), and Mishra Dhatu Nigham (MIDHANI) are involved in the high-technology arenas, including electronics, missile production, sophisticated composite materials and super alloys. These sectors will be crucial if India wishes to compete in the international defense industrial sector in the twenty-first century.

Mazagon Dockyard Ltd (MDL) is India's major military shipyard. Goa Shipyard Ltd (GSL) and Garden Reach Shipbuilders & Engineers (GRSE) in Calcutta are venerable, smaller shipyards which manufacture corvette-sized combat vessels among other projects. All three shipyards produce primarily for the civilian economy.[49]

The DPSUs produce a wide range of military and civilian goods, ranging from blankets to supersonic fighters. They are responsible for producing a significant portion of India's defense requirements, and contribute to Indian research and development efforts in the armaments sector.[50]

Defense Research and Development Organization (DRDO)

Shortly after independence, the Indian government established the Science Research and Development Organization, to carry out and coordinate high-technology research and development with military applications. The Defence Science Service was established in 1952 to encourage young scientists in defence-related research. The technical development establishments of the three armed services and the Defence Science Organization were combined into the Defence Research and Development Organization in January 1958. The Defence Minister's Research and Development Committee was constituted in 1959–60 to consider all DRDO-related matters.[51]

DRDO received a major boost in the early 1980s under V.S. Arunachalam, expanding its research labs by over 33 percent. By 1991, DRDO included 49 laboratories and establishments, and over 1,700 'research establishments,' which Nehru once referred to as the 'temples of modern

India.'⁵² This number has now increased to 51 laboratories and establishments.⁵³ DRDO employs 5,000 scientists and approximately 25,000 technicians.⁵⁴ DRDO is responsible for almost all R&D for the ordnance factories, which have little or no 'in-house' capability.⁵⁵ DRDO labs cooperate with the R&D facilities at other PSDUs, including HAL, BEL, and BDL.⁵⁶

The Ordnance Factories

The Ordnance Factories (OF) function almost exclusively for military requirements, and produce most of the army's basic equipment. The Ordnance Factories are divided into five groups: the Clothing Group, the Ammunition and Explosives Group, the Weapons Group, the Armoured Vehicles Group, and the Vehicles Group, and are sited throughout the country.⁵⁷ The OF complex employed over 177,000 people in 1990, but this number declined to about 133,000 in 2002.⁵⁸

The OF complex produces a wide range of products including small arms, artillery, mortars, ammunition, vehicles, tanks and other armored vehicles, rockets, optical and sighting devices, and anti-aircraft guns as well as basic supplies such as rope, tents, and clothing.⁵⁹ OF production was roughly 80 percent of the value of DPSU production in 2001–02, and the OF complex hoped to utilize more of its surplus capacity in the production of civilian goods.⁶⁰ In 2002–03, the Ordnance Factories produced Rs6105 crores (61.05 billion rupees) in total value, of which Rs756 crores (Rs7.56 billion) were non-defense sales.⁶¹ The Ordnance Factories export to over 30 countries, but the value of exports was only Rs35 crores (Rs350 million, or roughly $8 million) in 2001–02.⁶²

The Ordnance Factories are now able to produce most of the weapons and auxiliary equipment required for the Indian army. The fact that most of these items lie in the low-to-medium range of technological sophistication makes local production for the ground forces easier to achieve and sustain.⁶³ The most expensive and sophisticated systems produced for the Army by the Ordnance Factories are tanks and other armored vehicles. The Ordnance Factories often, however, operate at very low rates of production, which reduces efficiency and increases unit costs.

Nehru and the age of idealism: 1947–62

During India's first 15 years of independence, the state suffered little external menace. Relations with China, the 'other' Asian power, were cordial, but rarely warm,⁶⁴ and India scrupulously avoided entanglements in other alliances. India's primary security concern was regional. Pakistan refused to succumb to India's 'natural' position of leadership in South Asia, failing in its military effort to rearrange the border in 1947–48 and in enlisting UN support for its position on Kashmir.⁶⁵ Pakistan signed the Baghdad

Pact in 1954, and eventually joined the CENTO and SEATO collective security agreements. By enlisting in US efforts to contain the Soviets in the Northern Tier, Pakistan assured itself of both modern arms and training.[66]

India solicited advice from Western experts on its defense needs and policies, but opted for an aggressive high-technology procurement strategy that exceeded its immediate defensive requirements.[67] The army was distrusted by the new nationalist leadership, who viewed it as a sectarian force which had supported an alien ideology.[68] The new Indian government exerted considerable efforts to find ways to reduce the status of the armed services, and the army in particular, in the first decade of India's existence.[69]

The Indian republic inherited 16 ordnance factories and one clothing plant after partition.[70] Nehru preferred autarkic arms production to arms imports, but military industry did not receive a high priority in India's first decade of independence. [71]

From 1946–50, HAL expanded its facilities to permit the overhaul and conversion of war surplus C-47 transport aircraft.[72] The government authorized design of several trainer aircraft, and a prototype of the piston-engined HT-2 first flew in 1951. The design was put into production, with 169 being completed by the end of the production run in 1958.[73] Aircraft manufactured and assembled under license in the 1950s included the Percival Prentiss Mk 3 trainer aircraft and the Vampire turbojet aircraft,[74] which served first as a frontline fighter and then as a trainer and reserve combat aircraft for two decades. The Indian government also persued licensed production of the Gnat fighter and the indigenous development of the HF-24 Marut fighter.[75] (See case studies). Aerospace technology was a particular concern, due to British efforts to use supply of jet engines for Vampire fighters to influence India during 1951 tensions with Pakistan.[76]

The appointment of V. K. Krishna Menon as Minister of Defence in April 1957 initiated a major change in Indian defense procurement.[77] He recognized, however, the political utility of controlling a large, centralized industrial empire.[78] A Defence Production Board was created in 1955 to manage all ordnance factories and to secure effective liaison and cooperation with civil industry.[79] The value of production at the Ordnance Factories doubled between 1958–59 and 1961–62.[80] Under Menon, India began negotiations for licensed production of a wide range of military equipment, and began an extremely ambitious series of aerospace projects.[81]

Indian arms procurement in this period reflected the relative status of the three armed services. The airforce received priority for imported arms, including the purchase of highly sophisticated Hunter fighters from the UK over the objection of both the armed services and the Finance Ministry.[82] India also began licensed production of the Soviet MiG-21.[83] From 1952–62, the InAF more than doubled in size and substantially increased its capabilities through the acquisition of advanced fighter and bomber aircraft.[84]

Navy funding totaled between 2 and 10 percent of the defense budget.[85] In the absence of a major regional naval adversary, navy funding represented the most expendable portion of the defense budget.[86]

The army presented a modest list of requirements to the Ministry of Defence in 1957–58. These focused primarily on improving army firepower, and replacing the motley assortment of vehicles and tanks in Indian inventory with more functional and uniform equipment.[87] These requests were used by the Ministry of Defence as part of the effort to expand the Ordnance Factories, but were not fulfilled until after the Himalayan War in 1962.

The Indian national security and military apparatus, in early 1962, exemplified the worst excesses of politically-motivated mismanagement. The Indian army possessed a rich tradition of professionalism and expertise, and acquitted itself capably in conflicts with Pakistan and Hyderabad.

Table 2.1 Indian defense spending, 1948–67

Year	Defense spending (millions of rupees) (a)	Defense spending (millions of constant $1960)(b)	Defense spending as per cent of Gross Domestic Product (c)	Military R&D spending (millions of rupees) (d)	R&D as percentage of defense expenditures (e)
1948	1,675	443			
1949	1,672	443			
1950	1,748	452			
1951	1,833	452			
1952	1,878	475	1.7		
1953	1,926	470	1.7		
1954	1,969	503	1.8		
1955	1,932	524	1.7		
1956	2,118	624	1.7		
1957	2,665	567	2.1		
1958	2,797	621	2.0	15.0	0.54
1959	2,699	577	1.9		
1960	2,774	582	1.9		
1961	3,046	625	1.9	31.2	1.0
1962	4,336	862	2.6	51.4	1.08
1963	7,306	1,409	3.8	71.4	0.87
1964	8,084	1,380	3.6	82.3	1.02
1965	8,651	1,346	3.6	97.2	1.1
1966	9,027	1,307	3.4	114.6	1.26
1967	9,535	1,185	3.1	116.0	1.20

Notes
a   Figures from *SIPRI Yearbook 1968/69*, p. 206, *SIPRI Yearbook 1978*, pp. 42–4.
b   Figures from *SIPRI Yearbook 1968/69*, p. 206.
c   Figures from *SIPRI Yearbook 1974*, pp. 214–15.
d   Figures from *SIPRI Yearbook 1972*, pp. 222–3.
e   Figures from *SIPRI Yearbook, 1972*, pp. 226–7.

The InAF had, on paper, acquired significant qualitative and quantitative superiority over its Pakistani counterpart, and was considered the most sophisticated airforce in Asia. The navy was larger and more powerful than any in the region, maintaining a large fleet of surface ships supported by an aircraft carrier.

Appearances were deceiving, however, and all three services suffered from serious logistics shortcomings. The InAF was unable to maintain its aircraft, and would have been in serious trouble had it attempted to fight against China in 1962.[88] The Navy's most modern vessels were inoperable due to poor maintenance and lack of spares.[89] The occupation of Goa in December 1961 openly exhibited weaknesses in logistics, planning, equipment, and interservice coordination.[90]

India's lack of preparedness was vividly displayed in the Himalayan War of 1962. In the autumn/winter of 1962, an aggressive Indian policy of extending control over disputed borders in the Himalayas backfired. The Chinese army attacked on two fronts with multi-division forces, and the Indian army was routed.[91] Chinese forces overran Indian positions, made their interpretation of the borders very clear, and then withdrew to those borders. This disaster forced a fundamental shift in Indian defense and military-industrial policies discussed in the next section.

Selected indigenous arms programs, 1948–62

Case study: fighter aircraft—Gnat (license) versus Marut (indigenous)

GNAT LIGHT FIGHTER AIRCRAFT

In the mid-1950s, India sought to acquire aircraft in response to expanding InAF requirements and rapidly changing aerospace technology. The InAF significantly outclassed the Pakistan Air Force (PAF) in the early 1950s and aggressively sought to maintain both qualitative and quantitative superiority.[92] The Vampire, assembled locally under license, lacked the capability of emerging designs, and competitive aircraft were sought from both the UK and France. The UK offered licensed production of the Gnat fighter aircraft, designed by Folland Corporation and recently rejected as too limited for RAF requirements.[93]

A purchase agreement was signed in 1956, with Folland agreeing to supply 25 intact aircraft initially, as well as 25 more in disassembled form. After that, HAL would begin licensed production of the Gnat at the Bangalore facility, including the Orpheus 701 engine.[94] By 1962, HAL announced that the entire engine was manufactured indigenously.[95] India acquired most of the technology when Folland folded in the late 1960s, and as a result HAL eventually produced over 85 percent of the airframe and 60 percent of the engine.[96]

The Gnat performed very capably in InAF service for over 30 years. The aircraft's simple, robust construction made it easy to use and maintain. In the 1965 conflict with Pakistan, InAF Gnats were praised for their effectiveness against PAF Sabres, and production rates were increased at HAL-Bangalore shortly after the conflict.[97] Modified versions of the Gnat stayed in service until the 1990s.

THE HF-24 MARUT

India's first attempt at indigenous design and production of a modern fighter aircraft was a disaster. India's success in assembly of the Vampire, and the rapidly advancing technology of jet aircraft engines in the 1950s, led to an Air Staff requirement for a Mach 2 combat aircraft in the mid-1950s. An indigenous program for design, development, and production of a supersonic fighter was established. At the time the Marut program was begun, India only barely possessed the capability to design and develop elementary piston-engined trainers like the HT-2, much less state-of-the-art supersonic fighters. As a result, expertise was imported from abroad in the form of Dr. Kurt Tank – a German engineer who also aided Argentine and Egyptian aerospace efforts in the early Cold War.[98]

The Marut was designed around the British Orpheus 12 engine produced by Bristol, and the original agreement covered the licensed manufacture of the Orpheus engine and all subsequent improvements.[99] Unfortunately for India, the Orpheus 12 project, linked with a European cooperative aerospace effort, was cancelled. Bristol offered to continue development if the Indian government would pay all costs, estimated at $9–10 million, but the Indian government refused and sought alternatives elsewhere.[100] As a result, when the first Marut was test-flown, it used Orpheus 703 engines and was substantially underpowered.[101]

India then sought engines from other sources.[102] An agreement was signed with the Soviet Union to redesign the RD-9 engines used on the MiG-19 to fit the existing Marut airframes. The Indians anticipated that an RD-9 powered Marut would only be capable of Mach 1.4, and still sought alternatives to upgrade the Marut Mk. 2 to true Mach 2 capability.[103] The cost of this experiment was $3 million, but the engines performed 30 percent below design specifications.[104]

The first ten Marut Mk I aircraft were obsolete when they entered service in 1964, relied heavily on imported parts and cost more than a comparable or superior aircraft imported from abroad.[105] The Marut design itself, while physically attractive, had fundamental flaws. According to one report, the plane was incapable of firing all four 30 mm cannon simultaneously.[106] Only 75 percent of the aircraft originally ordered were built.[107] Production of the Marut ceased in 1975, almost 20 years after the decision to begin development.[108] Despite the failure of the aircraft to fill its intended role as a Mach 2 interceptor, the Marut continued to serve with the InAF as a trainer and ground attack aircraft into the early 1990s.

'Endurance' requirements

India produced approximately 700,000 rifles in World War II.[109] The Lee-Enfield .303 bolt-action rifle remained standard issue in Indian service until the Himalayan catastrophe, despite efforts by the army to procure more modern weapons.[110] The semi-automatic Ishapore rifle, an inferior local variant of the FN-FAL rifle, was rushed into production, although it did not completely replace the Lee-Enfield as Indian army standard issue until 1974.[111]

Other major weapons platform projects

During this period, HAL produced a series of indigenous trainers, including the HT-2, the Marut Advanced Trainer (a version of the HF-24), and the HJT-16 Kiran trainer/COIN aircraft.[112] HAL also produced the British HS-748 transport aircraft under license, after an agreement was signed in 1959. Again, this program was far too sophisticated to HAL at this time, and the program suffered delays and problems with quality control.[113]

The age of realism: 1963–74

The Himalayan disaster wiped out India's moralistic policies of not accepting military assistance from superpowers.[114] Several Western states, including the US, provided both equipment and industrial infrastructure for India's rearmament.[115] Growing Indo-Soviet political ties offered some prospect of deterring China.[116] The navy acquired inexpensive Soviet *Petya* class frigates and *Foxtrot* class submarines, after the UK did not respond satisfactorily to Indian requests.[117]

India supported its procurement policy with a massive reorganization and recruitment drive in the military. Economies of scale for military industrialization, particularly small arms, munitions, and artillery, were readily available, as the number of military personnel increased by almost 50 percent from 1962–75.[118] Allocation for the army increased from a proposal of Rs2.4 billion in March 1962 ($US400 million) to Rs5.71 billion ($US800 million) in the 1963/64 budget.[119] The new Indian defense scheme aimed at fighting a two-front war, if necessary, by containing China in the Himalayas while simultaneously engaging and defeating Pakistan in Kashmir and Punjab.[120]

Production in the ordnance factories increased fourfold in the year after the Himalayan crisis.[121] Production of civilian goods at ordnance factories, which had reached a high of 28 percent of total production in 1956–57, declined to only 3.6 percent by 1979–80. The numbers of ordnance

Table 2.2 Indian military expenditures and arms imports, 1963–73

Year	Defense expenditures (millions of current $US)	Defense expenditures (millions of constant $1972)	Defense expenditures as percentage of Gross National Product	Arms imports (millions of current $US)	Arms imports (millions of constant $1972)
1963	1,238.31	1,676.84	3.74	189	257.7
1964	1,269.07	1,700.06	3.53	127	170.5
1965	1,876.23	1,715.97	3.70	136	179.3
1966	1,440.46	1,551.41	3.32	278	356.5
1967	1,290.67	1,523.33	3.02	101	125.5
1968	1,377.33	1,632.25	3.13	168	200.7
1969	1,468.00	1,663.49	3.02	142	161.8
1970	1,598.67	1,748.29	3.05	100	108.0
1971	2,038.50	2,144.71	3.69	235	242.9
1972	2,070.39	2,070.39	3.60	205	205.0
1973	2,287.62	1,890.65	3.12	180	170.4

Source: ACDA, *World Military Expenditures and Arms Transfers, 1963–1973*

factories increased from 22 in 1962–63 to 33 in 1980–81, and the number of employees increased from 25,000 in 1956–57 to 113,000 by 1973–74.[122]

The military industry prioritized specific military requirements, particularly lower-technology items, basic weaponry and munitions, which could be produced relatively easily by local infrastructure, and programs for the ground forces.[123] Ten specifically configured mountain units designed for Himalayan duty were equipped primarily from OF production. Six additional regular infantry divisions were raised during this period to face Pakistan.[124]

Pakistan attempted to infiltrate large forces of irregulars into Kashmir in August 1965, but this effort to provoke a rebellion failed.[125] When India crossed the ceasefire line in an effort to deny the infiltrators critical routes of entry into the province, Pakistan launched a major conventional invasion on September 1. Initial Pakistani tactical successes prompted India to expand the conflict, counterattacking in the Lahore region. Fighting quickly stalemated across the front, and a ceasefire took effect on September 25.[126]

The conflict provoked international intervention by both the West and China. On September 7–8, the US, UK, and Australia declared an arms embargo on both sides. This placed both sides under considerable logistic stress, although it appears that Pakistan was more seriously affected because of its dependence on US equipment.[127] The Chinese government threatened to intervene on behalf of Pakistan, and the withdrawal of US support forced Pakistan into a closer politico-military relationship with China.

A new Indo-Pakistani war took place in November and December, 1971, the result of civil strife in East Pakistan. The Indian government supplied arms, training, and eventually artillery and conventional military support to Bangladeshi rebels. Unlike previous Indo-Pakistani encounters, the 1971 war was sharp and decisive. Pakistani attacks on Kashmir were stopped within ten miles of the border, while East Pakistan was overrun in two weeks. The US intervened both diplomatically and militarily, sending the aircraft carrier *Enterprise* and escort vessels into the Bay of Bengal while seeking assurances that India did not intend to dismember West Pakistan.[128] After the collapse of Pakistani forces in the East, a ceasefire was negotiated.[129]

India relied increasingly on supplies of Soviet weaponry through the 1960s. It still maintained an effort to assure diversified arms supplies, primarily through licensed production efforts with Western European producers. The effort to reduce dependency was both expensive and time-consuming, and relatively few locally-produced major weapons systems saw combat in 1971. The majority of license-produced major weapons systems entered the Indian order of battle after 1971, evidence of the long time-lag between military-industrial decisions – taken after 1962 – and actual delivery.

Selected indigenous arms programs: 1962–74

Case studies: the utility of licensed production

THE VIJAYANTA TANK

The Vijayanta is a licensed version of the Mk. 3 MBT, a private venture designed by Vickers. The Vijayanta uses the same 650 horsepower diesel engine as the British Chieftain tank, which may explain the confusion of some writers who refer to it as an Indian version of the Chieftain.[130] The result was a lighter, more maneuverable and less-well armored tank than those fielded in most European armies, appropriate for India's limited transportation infrastructure. Gen. J. N. Chaudhuri, later Chief of Army Staff of the Indian army, was intimately involved in the establishment of specifications for the tank.[131]

An agreement was signed in August 1961 for the establishment of a heavy vehicle plant and the manufacture of 1,000 tanks.[132] The Avadi Tank Works were completed in 1965 at a cost of Rs160 million ($25 million), and a production schedule of 100 tanks per year was announced the next year.[133] Several hundred Vijayantas served during the 1971 war. According to one report just before the conflict, the tank was considered to be 'a breakthrough,' and was much more maneuverable than the Centurions still in service with the Indian army.[134] The 105mm gun provided an important potential advantage, outgunning any tank in the Pakistani Army.[135]

Reports of the Vijayanta's combat performance in 1971, however, are less positive. According to Brig. Gen. A.C. Cariappa, the Vijayanta's performance was so unsatisfactory that the Army 'was not confident enough to equip its armoured divisions with an indigenous tank', and the Vijayanta 'was relegated to the infantry divisions as anti-tank protection weapons which any gun or missile should accomplish with much less cost.'[136] India imported large numbers of T-55 tanks when Vijayanta production failed to reach anticipated numbers in the late 1960s, and these played a much more important role than the Vijayanta in the 1971 war.

MIG-21 FIGHTER AIRCRAFT

India sought supersonic aircraft to offset the two squadrons of F-104 Starfighters promised to Pakistan by the US in 1961, and as a result of delays in the Marut project. India established sites for the MiG-21 production effort at Nasik (airframe construction) and Koraput (engine assembly and manufacture).[137] The first six MiG-21s delivered to India were unimpressive, lacking modern fire control systems and demonstrating an extremely short combat radius.[138] Later deliveries provided an improved variant, and local participation and production was given a higher priority after the 1965 war with Pakistan.[139]

HAL produced the MiG-21FL, MiG-21M, and MiG-21bis, and modified the designs of the latter two aircraft to fit Indian needs and industrial capabilities. The MiG-21M was an Indian version of the MiG-21MF, with a powerplant which produced less thrust, but also required less titanium and fewer sophisticated construction techniques.[140] HAL MiG-21bis versions used modified MiG-21M wings, which were cheaper and easier to produce.[141] These modifications did not significantly degrade the aircraft's performance, but did ease dependence on expensive foreign components.

MiG-21 production has always required procurement of some parts from the Soviet Union.[142] In reality there has never been a 'completely' indigenous MiG-21 produced by India.[143] The Soviets supplied production technology in a five-step process, and eventually only some of the most complicated materials were imported.[144] While the MiG-21 initially cost more to produce in India than to import, a production run of close to 20 years and over 500 aircraft eventually saved considerable foreign exchange, as production continued into the late 1980s.[145]

The MiG-21 continues in service with the InAF today, and makes up a substantial portion of Indian combat strength.[146] Deliveries of spare parts remained a sensitive issue between India and the USSR, as did Indian efforts to sell parts or whole aircraft to other LDCs.[147] The industrial processes used in producing the MiG-21 were also applicable to licensed production of later generations of Soviet aircraft.[148] India is presently committed to a major upgrade of many of its MiG-21s (see below).

India 37

'Endurance' requirements

During this period India increased production of the new Ishapore rifle at the Ordnance Factories. Other production included the French Hotchkiss-Brandt mortar, originally requested by the army in the 1950s.[149] The percentage of Indian requirements met locally increased from 39 percent to approximately 50 percent in the 1963–66 period.[150] Licensed production efforts attempted to emphasize production of vital spares, but in 1970 the Indian Parliament (*Lok Sabha*) was notified that only ten days of spares were on hand for Soviet-model MiG-21 fighters and Mi-4 helicopters.[151] Nevertheless, India's endurance capabilities were certainly better in 1965 and 1971 than during the 1962 Himalayan conflict, when the InAF's Hunter and Vampire fighters were virtually unavailable for service due to lack of parts.[152]

Non-platform weapons

The Ordnance Factories produced the 75 mm Pack Gun/Howitzer Mk. 1, which equipped the mountain divisions of the Indian army and remained in service into the 1990s.[153] In 1972, India began deployment of the 105 mm Indian Field Gun, which was used to replace the obsolescent World War II-era 25-pounders still in service. This weapon is remarkably similar to the gun on the Abbot SP 105 mm supplied by the UK.[154] India also produced the L-70 Bofors 40 mm AA gun and a 106 mm recoilless rifle.[155] The SS-11 anti-tank guided missile was produced under license at BDL.[156] India also began production of the Soviet AA-2 Atoll air-to-air missile (AAM) under license.[157]

Major weapons platforms

HAL produced two French helicopters under license, the Aerospatiale SA 315B Lama (known as the Cheetah in Indian service) and the SA 316B Alouette III (known as the Chetak). The Chetak is one of the few complete systems manufactured at HAL to be exported to a 'developed country.' Unfortunately, it was exported to the Soviet Union, which raised some concerns about the safety of Western technology in Indian hands.[158] Negotiations for the Chetak began in early 1962, and by 1966 the French were buying spares from HAL to take advantage of low labor costs in India.[159] While the quality of the components was up to international standards, pilot training was apparently a problem – one analyst notes that in 1985, the Indian accident rate for the Chetak/Alouette III was *ten* times the world average.[160]

Strategic systems

The Indian missile program has been closely identified with the Indian Space Research Organization (ISRO).[161] In 1963, India launched a series of US sounding rockets from Indian soil. In 1965, the Indian government requested the design of the Scout sounding rocket from the US, which was unclassified at the time. This was provided, although US assistance to the space program ceased not long afterwards.[162] As the ISRO developed sounding rockets and later the SLV-3 satellite launch vehicle, India's defense industries pursued their own missile and rocket R&D program. DRDO's first Chief Comptroller, Maj. Gen. B. D. Kapur, instituted a foreign training program for Indian scientists, as well as a curriculum in basic rocketry at the Institute of Armament Studies. Kapur visited Switzerland in 1962, and agreed to a joint SAM development program known as 'Project Indigo' with the Swiss firm Contraves.[163] India's interest in advanced missile systems, while unrealizable in the 1960s, continued as an important part of DRDO's research program until the 1980s.

The Indian nuclear program began even before independence, when Dr. Homi Bhabha convinced his friend Jawaharlal Nehru that research in nuclear energy would be crucial to India's future. As early as 1946, Nehru stated that India would develop nuclear power for peaceful purposes, but that it might have to use the latest technological developments for security as well unless the international system changed.[164] Indian signed agreements with Canada and the US for the CIRUS reactor and supplies of heavy water in the 1950s. China's 1964 nuclear tests sparked a rare Parliamentary debate on the nuclear issue.[165] In late 1964, Prime Minister Shastri officially sanctioned a weapons program, focusing on reducing the time needed to build nuclear arms to six months.[166] Homi Bhabha, India's first atomic energy chief, argued for the start of an underground testing project, a program approved by Prime Minister Shastri but put on hold from 1966 until 1970 or 1971.[167] The Trombay plutonium-reprocessing plant was commissioned, producing sufficient plutonium for approximately two nuclear weapons per year.[168]

The pursuit of nuclear capabilities, therefore, occurred under the direct control of the Prime Minister and a few close associates. The nuclear weapons program utilized some of India's finest scientists, but had almost no military input. By the mid-1960s, after the deaths of both Nehru and Bhabha, the US was in the process of creating a nonproliferation regime to control the spread of nuclear weapons, and encouraged India to sign the Nuclear Nonproliferation Treaty (NPT). India rejected the Treaty, preferring to maintain a nuclear option, and continued its nuclear weapons program, culminating in a nuclear test in May 1974.[169]

Hegemony unfulfilled: 1974–98

India's security policy focused increasingly on threats from adjacent regions and relations with the superpowers during the 1970s. The 1968 decision by the United Kingdom to pull forces back from east of the Suez Canal left a power vacuum in the Indian Ocean, which was increasingly filled by US and Soviet naval squadrons. The new US facility at Diego Garcia was viewed with particular concern, as were improvements in Sino-US relations.

Until 1971, the primary concern was the land balance in the west and north. With relatively modest defense expenditures, and relying heavily on local production, India secured itself on both fronts. As India asserted itself regionally, and sought great power status, the navy received increased priority in budget allocation.[170] The navy's share of the *capital* portion of the defense budget grew from 7 percent in 1963 to 49 percent in 1975, indicating the importance of power projection and naval capability in Indian security priorities.[171]

The navy's new resources came at the expense of the ground forces.[172] Both the army and InAF began modest modernization programs, but the navy received priority. The navy began expanding and re-equipping in the mid-1970s, while the other services had only just begun modernization in 1979.

The Soviet invasion of Afghanistan in 1979 had an immediate impact on South Asia. The Reagan Administration extended a $4 billion aid

Table 2.3 Indian defense expenditures and arms imports, 1972–82

Year	Defense expenditures (millions of current $US)	Defense expenditures (millions of constant $1981)	Defense expenditures as percentage of Gross National Product	Arms imports (millions of current $US)	Arms imports (millions of constant $1981)
1972	2,047	3,982	3.5	210	408
1973	1,852	3,413	2.9	190	349
1974	2,149	3,639	3.0	190	321
1975	2,832	4,398	3.3	170	263
1976	2,907	4,271	3.2	490	719
1977	3,050	4,232	2.9	725	1,005
1978	3,502	4,525	2.9	290	374
1979	3,842	4,577	3.1	490	583
1980	4,303	4,704	3.0	700	765
1981	5,151	5,151	3.1	875	875
1982	6,223	5,870	3.5	1,200	1,131

Source: ACDA, *World Military Expenditures and Arms Transfers, 1972–1982*

package to Pakistan, including sophisticated F-16 fighter aircraft, M-48A5 tanks, and TOW antitank missiles. These new acquisitions, and the US training that accompanied them, significantly improved Pakistani conventional military capabilities. The US also permitted transfer of military and dual-use technology to China, raising the possibility that the PRC could enhance its military capability.

Indian security policy became less opaque and more explicitly military-oriented in the 1980s. The 'Indira Doctrine' asserted India's right to intervene in neighboring states if domestic disorder there threatened to spread to India.[173] The denial of external influence in South Asia became the unspoken focus of the 'Rajiv Doctrine,' providing the rationale for Indian intervention in Sri Lanka (July 1987–March 1990) and the Maldives (November 1988).[174]

Pakistan aggressively pursued nuclear weapons capabilities, and by the middle of the 1980s it was widely assumed that Pakistan had sufficient weapons-grade nuclear material to create at least one nuclear device.[175] This uncertain nuclear threat acted as a deterrent to Indian military action. It may also have encouraged Pakistan to take greater risks supporting separatist movements inside Indian territory.[176]

The Indian army attempted to reorganize in the 1980s to better prepare for modern mechanized warfare, including the creation of new mechanized infantry divisions and air assault formations.[177] Plans called for a capability to decisively defeat Pakistan in a short campaign marked by rapid armored advances.[178] A rapid victory was desirable for economic reasons – the 1971 war cost approximately Rs2 billion ($US250 million at the time) per week. Future wars were estimated to cost closer to Rs40 billion a week ($US2.5 billion, in 1990 dollars), by Indian calculations, and a decisive war might take 6–8 weeks.[179]

The military's role and authority in internal security expanded dramatically, assisting the large forces of local, state, and national police and paramilitary forces whose primary concern is to provide for internal security.[180] Conflicts in Punjab and Kashmir became so severe that by the early 1990s, approximately 40 percent of the Indian army was deployed on internal security duties.[181] Insurgents in both regions received Pakistani support.[182] From 1990–2003, India created 36 battalions of the Rashtriya Rifles, tasked specifically for counter-insurgency duties.[183]

Table 2.4 Rupee–US$ conversion rates, 1972–92

1972	1981	1983	1985	1987	1988	1989	1990	1991	1992
7.706	7.893	10.312	12.237	12.698	14.477	16.663	17.949	24.519	28.950

Source: The World Bank, *World Tables, 1994* (Baltimore, MD: The Johns Hopkins University Press, 1994), pp. 346–7.

India and Pakistan staged major military exercises which nearly escalated to war on two occasions during this period. The Brasstacks exercise (1986–87) was a major test of the Indian Army's capability to carry out the new doctrine of 'persuasive deterrence.'[184] Brasstacks was a year-long, four part series of exercises in which the mechanized forces of the Indian army carried out combined arms operations on an unprecedented scale close to the Pakistani border.[185] Pakistan responded by moving an armored division and other units to the border, which raised tensions and nearly sparked off a war. The objective of these maneuvers remains unclear. It is possible that the Indian leadership actually intended to provoke a war. *Operation Trident* – the reconquest of the northern areas and Pakistan-held Kashmir, ordered at the height of the crisis – was called off less than two hours before it was scheduled to begin.[186]

As the result of Indian misgovernance, an indigenous insurgency opened in Kashmir in the winter of 1989. Both political and military leaders in Pakistan saw this as an opportunity to re-open the partition issue.[187] The Kashmiri insurgency coincided with Indian and Pakistani winter military maneuvers, adding the threat of conventional escalation to an already volatile situation. Both India and Pakistan maintained alerted forces in the region, although reportedly neither moved heavy armored formations – avoiding a repetition of Brasstacks.

The 1990 crisis reportedly included the actual deployment of Pakistani nuclear weapons to air bases, although this has been disputed by many of the key players in India, Pakistan, and the US.[188] Robert Gates, the Deputy National Security Advisor, made an emergency visit to the region to defuse the crisis. President Bush and President Gorbachev of the Soviet Union issued a joint statement warning of the possible consequences of war in the region.[189] The Kashmir issue, in the eyes of the superpowers and the international community, had finally become irrevocably linked with nuclear weapons.

Both India and China took steps to improve their defensive positions and logistics capability in this period. In 1986–87, the Indian army and airforce held joint exercises in the Himalayas to demonstrate India's enhanced military capability and to act as political leverage in the continuing dispute with China.[190] According to anecdotal reports, a 1986–87 crisis with China at Somdurong Chu in the Himalayas led Indian military leaders to ask what nuclear options India had available to respond to a Chinese tactical nuclear attack.[191]

Throughout this period, India's conventional military capabilities dominated all other potential regional adversaries combined. Ambitious force modernization programs for all three services sought to upgrade Indian conventional military capability. These modernization programs did not appear to correspond to any existing threat, and were viewed with concern by neighbors in South Asia and adjacent regions.[192] In 1986–87, for the first time, India's defense budget exceeded 4 percent of GNP, and Indian R&D funding for advanced weapons increased by 800 percent in the 1980s.[193]

The collapse of the Soviet Union undermined Indian military readiness, decreasing the availability of spare parts and jeopardizing delivery of equipment on order.[194] Despite plans for the introduction of a number of new weapons systems and major increases in force structure, the period 1987–92 was marked by a decline in overall Indian military expenditure and arms imports.[195] This decline seriously affected both modernization efforts and readiness.[196] It also savaged ongoing programs at Indian defense industries.[197]

The decline of the superpower competition quelled many of India's fears of the US.[198] Improved relations with the US were slowed by policy disagreements, particularly regarding the transfer of dual-use technologies to strategic sectors of the Indian economy.[199] US nonproliferation concerns frequently prevented technology transfer, causing great resentment in India.

India faced further hardship from a financial crisis, which required the government to begin a major economic liberalization effort in the 1989–92 period.[200] This crisis inflated India's external debt and ran down foreign exchange reserves.[201] Indian economic reform worked, and worked fairly quickly.[202] As the economic situation improved, India increased the defense budget.[203] The low cost of Soviet-model equipment after the collapse of the Warsaw Pact invited exploitation, and at times it appeared that Indian military procurement policy consisted primarily of periodic spending binges in the former Eastern bloc.[204]

In the early 1990s, India reverted to military-industrial and security policies reminiscent of the Nehru period. Improved relations with external powers, including China, encouraged Indian governments to follow a policy focused on regional military concerns and global symbols of power. The portion of the defense budget dedicated to research and development increased steadily, from 1 percent of the military budget in the 1960s to approximately 2 percent in 1977, and over 3 by 1982.[205] From 1989–93, R&D spending increased from 4.2–4.9 percent of the defense budget.[206] This increase was initially associated with increased numbers of major weapons platforms in development. By the 1990s, however, it appeared geared more towards technology acquisition.[207]

Local projects in the development stage included the Arjun tank, the Light Combat Aircraft, the Advanced Light Helicopter, the Delhi-class missile destroyer, projects for the design of aircraft carriers and nuclear submarines, a series of missile projects, and a new line of small arms. These projects all suffered from inconsistent political support and sporadic funding, with the important exception of the Indigenous Guided Missile Development Program (IGMDP) (see case study). The low level of funding

Table 2.5 Indian defense expenditures and arms imports, 1981–91

Year	Defense expenditures (millions of constant $US)	Defense expenditures (millions of constant $1991)	Defense expenditures as percentage of Gross National Product	Arms imports (millions of constant $US)	Arms imports (millions of constant $1991)
1981	3,542	5,288	3.3	1,100	1,642
1982	4,175	5,868	3.5	2,800	3,936
1983	4,667	6,304	3.5	1,300	1,756
1984	5,188	6,708	3.6	1,300	1,681
1985	5,527	6,895	3.5	2,600	3,244
1986	6,064	7,367	3.6	3,200	3,888
1987	6,870	8,090	3.8	3,000	3,533
1988	6,944	7,874	3.4	3,700	4,195
1989	6,742	7,314	3.0	3,900	4,231
1990	7,487	7,787	3.0	1,700	1,768
1991	7,189	7,189	2.7	800	800

Source: ACDA, *World Military Expenditures and Arms Transfers, 1991–1992*

alloted to these projects suggests that bureaucratic interests and symbolic factors, rather than any pressing military commitment or pursuit of genuine self-sufficiency, drove their continued existence.

Selected indigenous arms programs: 1974–98

Case studies: licensed versus indigenous production
Aircraft: MiG-29 versus LCA

THE MIG-29 'FULCRUM'

The Indians were offered the option of purchasing the MiG-29 during the visit of Defense Minister Ustinov, in early 1984. India's plans to license-manufacture the Mirage 2000 probably encouraged the Soviets to take steps to maintain a valued customer.[208] The Fulcrum had not even entered Soviet service at this point, so the InAF was being offered a truly 'top-of-the-line' fighter. Shortly after Ustinov's visit, India declined the option of licensed production of the Mirage 2000.[209]

Although a MiG-29 deal was triumphantly announced in mid-1984,[210] India backed out of the deal when they realized they would get the export version of the MiG-29.[211] A new deal was signed two years later, when the Soviets finally agreed to provide the 'real' version to India.[212] The aircraft, originally intended for delivery in April or May of 1987, began arriving in January, due to increased Soviet production.[213] Reports of negotiations for licensed production followed quickly.[214]

44 *India*

The MiG-29 never entered production in India. Competition with the indigenous Light Combat Aircraft (LCA), funding restrictions, and problems obtaining necessary components from the former USSR all contributed to delays in the program.[215] An official government report, while not citing the MiG-29 aircraft by name, chronicled numerous problems with the operation of a Soviet aircraft acquired in the late 1980s. Included among these problems were premature failures of over two-thirds of the available engines, non-availability of critical radar components and maintenance/repair facilities for avionics, and a failure on the part of responsible authorities to fund and construct engine overhaul facilities.[216]

The inability of the Indian government to produce either the MiG-29 or the LCA (see below) jeopardized both the aerospace industrial base and InAF modernization. India urged Malaysia, for example, to purchase the MiG-29 under the assumption that HAL could provide maintenance, spares, and upgrades.[217] India recently signed a deal to buy navalized versions of the Fulcrum to equip its naval air arm – but the aircraft will be built in Russia.[218]

THE LIGHT COMBAT AIRCRAFT (LCA)

HAL began research and development on a Light Combat Aircraft early in 1980, and the aircraft has undergone a series of radical changes in design and specification since that time.[219] Initially, the aircraft was viewed as a replacement for the MiG-21 interceptor in the InAF inventory with a secondary ground-attack role. HAL was already working on an engine designed specifically to provide extra power in tropical conditions.[220]

In 1985, the government announced that it had accepted the HAL design, and ambitiously planned for the flight of a prototype aircraft in 1989.[221] The design changed late the next year, however, after a visit by then-US Secretary of Defense Caspar Weinberger, who permitted the transfer of the General Electric F-404 engine (used in the F/A-18 Hornet) to India. The LCA program was not proceeding on schedule, so the import of the 11 GE F-404 engines might allow prototypes to fly at an earlier date *and* secure US technological assistance on the GTX Kevari engine.[222]

The LCA design has clearly undergone considerable modification since the original conception – the LCA's performance is comparable to a late-model F-16 or Mirage 2000.[223] These technological enhancements have contributed to the substantial delays. The InAF hopes to have six in service by 2008–09, aiming eventually for 80 percent indigenous content.[224] India's aircraft industry is much less efficient economically than the aerospace industries of Israel, Germany, and even Japan, each of which faced crises in aircraft production during the 1990s.[225] This raises questions about the unit costs and eventual number of aircraft purchased by the InAF, which grew frustrated with delays in the LCA program over a decade ago and sought other alternatives. While the InAF 'muddled through' the 1990s without substantial modernization, LCA delays and costs imposed great hardships. Lack of a replacement for the aging MiG force contributed significantly to the InAF's high accident rate in the 1990–2003 period.[226]

T-72 (license production) vs. Arjun (indigenous development)

T-72 TANK

India signed an agreement to purchase the T-72 in 1980.[227] A decision to produce the system under license was reached at the end of 1983.[228] The first T-72s produced in India entered service in 1988.[229] Production of the T-72 continued into the mid-1990s, but both Western and Indian sources report that the Avadi plant was utilized at a rate far below potential capacity.[230]

According to some observers, the T-72 program represents one of the most effective licensed-production endeavors by the Indian defense industries.[231] It has been reported, for instance, that the license-produced T-72 has a higher level of indigenous content than the locally designed Arjun.[232] Iraqi T-72s, however, performed poorly in the Gulf War, and demonstrated unexpected vulnerabilities.[233] In spite of these flaws, though, the T-72 represented a substantial improvement over the older Vijayantas and T-55s in Indian inventory, and was the most modern tank available in the South Asian region in the 1980s and 1990s.

Ambitious plans to modernize the T-72 force – 'Operation Rhino' – have begun. Around 150–200 tanks will receive a full upgrade, including a new fire control system and power pack, reactive armor, and navigational systems. The rest of the force will receive a partial modernization.[234] India has purchased the related T-90S, which will be produced at Avadi in the future, indicating a continued reliance on Russian designs.[235]

ARJUN TANK

The original requirement for an Indian tank design was issued in 1970, with deployment intended for 1985. In 1982, it was reported that all of the major subsystems, including engine, transmission, armor, fire control, and armament, were proceeding well, and that 'major breakthroughs' had occurred.[236] The tank's requirements were completely rewritten shortly thereafter, leading to substantial delays in development and production.[237]

Ambitious requirements intended to anticipate changes in 'state of the art' technology led to unfulfillable demands on Indian designers and industries. Substantial effort was put into developing a 1,200–1,500 hp engine, but engine tests proved the design unacceptable.[238] Other problems identified at the first technical trials in July 1988 included lack of an auxiliary power unit, poor transmission, exceedingly low average track life, failures in the hydro-pneumatic suspension system, poor maintenance, and failures in the main gun and fire control system.[239] Senior army officers say the tank is too heavy, and will cause problems with both tactical and strategic mobility.[240]

The Arjun is modeled after Western tank designs, with a high 'castle' turret and substantial emphasis on fire suppression systems and overall survivability. The tank utilizes many locally-produced subsystems, including the fire suppression system, night vision equipment, and nuclear-biological-chemical warfare protection systems.[241] The locally-designed 120 mm rifled gun is controversial.[242] The Arjun is also too heavy for most of the bridges in the region.[243]

At present, 124 tanks have been ordered to equip two tank regiments. India is also pursuing a 155 mm SP artillery version using the Arjun chassis.[244] An Arjun 2 variant is reportedly already in development, and India is also experimenting with a 'Tank EX' version using a T-72 chassis and an Arjun turret.[245] Overall, the Arjun has suffered unusual delays even for an Indian program and the program can only be judged as a failure – like the HF-24 Marut it will be produced in limited quantities for primarily symbolic reasons.

New directions for Indian Military Industry

THE INDIGENOUS GUIDED MISSILE DEVELOPMENT PROGRAM (IGMDP)

The IGMDP was initiated by the government, with the intention of cutting the design-production-deployment cycle from 10–15 years down to 8–10 years.[246] In order to carry out this extremely ambitious effort, an innovative policy of integration was instituted. Every effort was made to ensure maximum commonality of subsystems and technologies and minimize duplication of effort and wasted time. The IGMDP effort included 19 defense research laboratories, seven universities, and seven other institutions (including the ISRO). Production takes place at 19 public sector units, eleven ordnance factories, nine private sector corporations, and two other organizations.[247]

The IGMDP encompasses research, design, development, and production of five separate missiles – Agni (MRBM), Prithvi (SRBM), Akash and Trishul (SAM), and Nag (ATGM). The Trishul was first tested in the mid-1980s, and is designed to have a faster reaction time and to be more resistant to electronic countermeasures (ECM) than Soviet-model SAMs. The system lacks thrust vector control facilities, which makes the minimum range larger than comparable imported systems in service. The Trishul was intended to serve both the army and the navy.[248]

Trishul's initial rapid development, however, did not translate into rapid deployment. The Trishul was supposed to be deployed with the Indian Navy in 1992, but still had not reached deployment status in

2003.[249] India opted to buy Russian and Israeli short-range SAMs instead. After over 70 flight tests, the Trishul remains ineffective.[250] The failure of the Trishul, and the inadequate performance of Russian replacements, delayed the deployment of both local and foreign-produced surface ships for the Indian Navy.[251]

The Prithvi is a single-stage tactical missile that carries conventional and unconventional warheads and reportedly has an accuracy of 50–250 meters at maximum range.[252] With a 1,000 kg warhead, the range is only 150 km: the maximum range of 250 km is attainable only with a 500 kg payload. The Prithvi was first tested on February 25, 1988.[253] Prithvi has been deployed in the 222nd and 333rd Artillery Groups, and two additional groups (444th and 555th) are currently being raised. Prithvi will form an important component of a new artillery division authorized in 2003.[254] A naval version called the *Dhanush* is under development, to be launched from surface ships.[255]

The Nag is reportedly a third-generation 'fire-and-forget' ATGM using imaging infrared homing technology with top-down attack capability which will be mounted on vehicles or attack helicopters.[256] Despite the apparent sophistication and reported success of the Nag, India also arranged licensed production of vast numbers of MILAN-II ATGMs.[257] As of early 2004, the Nag still had not entered serial production.

The Akash program suffered serious delays due to lack of the software necessary for operation of the phased array radar, which is integral to the missile system.[258] The Akash will have a 25 km range, and a 'ramrocket' engine. There are reports that the Akash has been proposed as a possible ATBM, but its lack of range and limited launch speed probably make this impractical without significant modification. The Akash was designed in both ground and ship-based versions.[259] In late 2003, analysts reported that the Akash would not be deployed, but would remain a technology demonstrator at DRDO.[260]

The most important program is the Agni series of ballistic missiles. The initial variant, also called the Agni Test Demonstrator (TD), was a two stage rocket developed from the first stage of the SLV-3 space launch vehicle, and using the Prithvi twin-engined liquid fuelled motor as a second stage.[261] The range of the Agni system is about 2,500 km (1,500 miles).[262] After the first Agni test launch, on May 22, 1989, then-Prime Minister Rajiv Gandhi proudly told Parliament that the Agni was not a 'weapon system', but a demonstration of technology.[263] The Agni was tested again on May 29, 1992 with a reported range of 1,550 miles, and a payload of 500–1,000 kg (sufficient for a nuclear warhead). A successful third test launch of an extended range version of the Agni was carried out in early 1994.[264] Agni TD, a platform-launched liquid-fueled missile, was not an efficient weapon, prompting the development of a more survivable version.

Agni 2, a substantially more sophisticated missile, was first tested in 1999, tested again in 2001, and has now entered production and is

48 *India*

preparing for deployment. Agni 2 is a mobile, two-stage, solid-fueled missile with a range of approximately 2,000–3,000 kilometers.[265] The first stage of the Agni 2 has also been deployed as a shorter-range variant called the Agni 1 with a 700 kilometer range.[266] Agni 1 is the first nuclear delivery system specifically configured for covering Pakistani targets.[267] Agni 1 will be deployed in the Indian army's 334th Artillery Group, and Agni 2 will be deployed in the 335th Artillery Group.[268] An Agni 3 version and an ICBM called the Surya, are reportedly in development.

The IGMDP focused on close interaction between research and production, and certainly produced some results in a much shorter time than most indigenous R&D efforts. The production and deployment records of the five missiles, however, suggest that the program was far from a complete success. It remains one of India's most remarkable military-industrial achievements, and set the stage for potentially more successful missile projects.

There are a number of reasons for IGMDP's comparatively strong showing. First, limited access to technology transfer forced a higher priority for indigenous research and development than in other defense-related projects. Second, private and educational institutions were deliberately integrated into the R&D and development process on a major scale for the first time. Third, there is considerable technological overlap between the space program and the IGMDP, particularly in the Agni TD project. Fourth, missile design and development is relatively simple, especially when compared with other aerospace technologies (particularly aircraft). Finally, there was unusually close coordination between military users and designers.[269]

IGMDP also capitalized on existing research. An important research effort, predating the IGMDP, was 'Project Devil,' which attempted to reverse-engineer the Soviet SA-2 SAM used by the Indian military. The ultimate objective of this program remains unclear: one view is that it was intended to convert SA-2 technology for SSM use.[270] Other reports state that it was an effort to reverse-engineer and produce the SA-2 indigenously.[271] The end results of the program were the construction of two liquid-fuel motors, later used as the basis of the Prithvi program and several failed prototype systems.[272]

'Endurance' requirements

India produces a range of small arms, including the Ishapore SLR rifle, a Belgian 9 mm pistol and the Sterling Mk. 4 submachine gun, as well as 9 mm, 7.62 mm, 0.303 inch, and 12.7 mm ammunition.[273] In the early 1980s, DRDO made a commitment to develop a new series of 5.56 mm small arms for the Indian armed forces called the Indian Small Arms System (INSAS). Both Heckler & Koch of Germany and Steyr of Austria offered to provide for India's immediate needs and transfer technology worth $4.5 million for free. These offers were declined and DRDO spent the next decade, and approximately Rs2 billion (about $US100 million in 1990), reinventing a family of small arms based heavily on Steyr and H&K technology. In the meantime, India imported AK-47 rifles from former Warsaw Pact nations to fill requirements.[274] The INSAS finally entered service in the late 1990s.[275]

India also produced 51 mm, 81 mm, 120 mm, and 160 mm mortars and ammunition. A full line of munitions was also in production in this period, including 105 mm, 120 mm, and 125 mm tank ammunition, as well as anti-tank and anti-personnel mines, aerial bombs, and naval ammunition.[276] The Ordnance Factories continued to produce the bulk of India's non-weaponry equipment needs, although severe shortages of trucks and other logistics systems were reported in the 1990s.[277] Shortages in spares and stockpiles plagued all three services – evidence that endurance capabilities did not receive a high priority.[278] Items produced in India – from blankets to night vision goggles – were imported from abroad, and munitions supplies reached dangerously low levels for key equipment like the Bofors 155 mm heavy artillery piece.[279] Local production of the 125 mm tank shell for the T-72 tank suffered from poor quality control – Israeli-manufactured shells had to be imported during the Kargil war, and recent reports suggest defective rounds still plague the army.[280]

The Ordnance Factories were not the only organizations working on endurance requirements in this period. DRDO maintained three naval systems laboratories at Cochin, Bombay, and Vishakhapatnam, which pursued torpedo, sonar, and sonobuoy research.[281] Some efforts were made to support maintenance of Soviet systems no longer in production in Russia, including a $210 million overhaul facility for the Soviet SA-6 missile at Meerut.[282] Indigenization of spare parts for Russian equipment remains a priority today.[283]

Non-platform weapons

The 105 mm Light Field Gun entered service with the Indian army during this period. This weapon is easily deployed by helicopter – an important advantage for Indian army mountain divisions.[284] The purchase of the Bofors FH-77B 155 mm gun/howitzer included options for licensed production and the establishment of a new ordnance factory for ammunition production.[285] Both the counter-trade offsets and the establishment of the local munitions production line were marked by serious delays and difficulties.[286] Ammunition manufacture suffered long delays, but by 2000 India was producing 155 mm ammunition for the Bofors guns.[287] Spare parts remained a problem, and had to be imported from Sweden on an emergency basis during the Kargil War.[288] The Bofors played a critical role in Indian military operations during that conflict.

The SS-11 anti-tank guided missile was produced under license at BDL

50 *India*

through the 1980s, and India produced the Milan and Milan II under license.[289] India also produces a version of the Soviet *Grad* 122 mm rocket, and the BM-21 rocket launcher.[290] This rocket may be capable of carrying cluster munitions produced at the Ordnance Factories. India is producing the 'Pinacha' rocket and Multiple Barrel Rocket Launcher, a 214 mm weapon capable of firing cluster or high-explosive payloads up to 40 km.[291]

ELECTRONIC EQUIPMENT

Growth in the military electronics industry expanded significantly, particularly in the aftermath of the 1971 War. In 1973, production of military electronics had a value of Rs330 million: this nearly quadrupled to Rs1,260 million by 1983.[292] India's military electronics industry – dominated by BEL, with some contribution from HAL – is far from comprehensive or self-sufficient: many critical systems are imported, and some others have been in development for decades.

BEL produced sonar systems for the Indian navy, particularly the Advanced Panoramic Sonar, Hull Mounted (APSOH) sonar system.[293] BEL also produces naval communications systems and a variety of fire control and gun control equipment, radars, and antennae.[294] BEL began delivery of the Indra-1 and Indra-2 low altitude surveillance radars to the Indian armed forces in 1989.[295] BEL also produced night vision equipment, communications equipment, console systems, and tank fire control systems for the ground forces.[296]

Modification projects

TANK PROGRAMS

The mechanical failings of the Vijayanta were corrected after 1971, and production continued until the 1980s. Over 1,600 Vijayantas were produced,[297] and by the end of the production run the Vijayanta had reached 95 percent indigenous content by value.[298] Vijayanta modifications in development or production include: a special SP artillery version known as the Catapult; an armoured recovery vehicle; a bulldozer version; and a modification for bridge-laying.[299] At least 1,100 Vijayantas remained in service in the 1990s, comprising almost half of the Indian army's 58 tank regiments.[300]

GNAT/AJEET FIGHTER/TRAINER

In the aftermath of the 1971 war, a decision was made to produce an upgraded version of the Gnat, to be called the Ajeet. HAL agreed, in 1972, that such a project was feasible and within the capabilities of the company.

The primary purpose for the program was to increase the Gnat's limited range and payload in order to provide greater ground attack capability.[301] The project experienced enormous delays, considering the relatively simple nature of the modifications required.[302]

The Ajeet represents one of the few instances of extensive modification and upgrading of an existing design by the Indian aerospace industry.[303] Approximately 80 Ajeet strike fighters were fielded by the InAF in the 1980s, eventually retiring from service in 1991. Ajeets also served, unsuccessfully, as trainers for new InAF pilots.[304] The Gnat/Ajeet project, which provided effective combat aircraft to the InAF for 30 years, represents one of India's most successful military industrial programs.

Other major weapons platforms

OTHER ARMORED VEHICLES

India produces the Soviet BMP-2 armored infantry fighting vehicle, known in Indian service as the Surath. Production facilities were established in 1985, and production began in 1987.[305] The BMP chassis was intended as the basis for a series of armored vehicles. India also completed an agreement with Slovakia for purchase and eventual licensed production of armored recovery vehicles based on the T-72 chassis.[306]

OTHER AIRCRAFT PROJECTS

The InAF required a replacement for the aging Canberra bomber to perform deep strike and interdiction duties, but it was only in the late 1970s that sufficient hard currency could be found to fill this need.[307] The ruling Janata Party encouraged the armed forces to look at non-Soviet options. The Jaguar was finally selected on the basis of cost and delivery schedule.[424] Licensed production of the aircraft was arranged at the HAL-Bangalore facility.[308]

Pakistan's acquisition of modern F-16A fighter-bombers in the mid-1980s prompted India to buy new fighters.[309] Negotiations for the MiG-23/27 began in the summer of 1980, and a deal including licensed production options was signed in the summer of 1983.[310] Production facilities at Nasik were established in mid-1984, and HAL has produced at least 100 MiG-27s with gradually increasing local content.[311] It has also begun modification projects to extend service life and improve performance.[312]

France agreed to provide the Mirage 2000, with an option for licensed production in India.[313] An initial batch of 40 aircraft was purchased, with a later batch of nine being ordered in the 1980s. More recently, ten more aircraft have been purchased, with mid-air refueling capability.[314] The licensed production option was eventually rejected to pursue other projects, particularly the MiG-29 program discussed above. It may be renewed at a later date, depending on resources or the performance of the LCA, as part of an additional purchase of up to 130 new aircraft.[315]

A critical shortcoming is the lack of an advanced trainer. The InAF's accident rate is one of the world's highest, and can be attributed to decreased flying time and lack of an advanced transition trainer.[316] Despite the failure of the Ajeet trainer version, India put off purchase or production of an advanced trainer for over two decades. This problem was only resolved with the recent agreement to purchase British HAWK trainer aircraft.[317]

The early 1980s also saw the initiation of a series of other licensed and indigenous programs at HAL, which were intended to provide for Indian needs in the 1990s. A replacement for the domestically-produced Alouette IIIs led to the Advanced Light Helicopter (ALH) program. (See case study). HAL-Kanpur produces the Dornier-228 utility aircraft, which entered service with the InAF and Indian navy as a transport, liaison, and maritime surveillance aircraft in the mid-1980s.[318]

The HS-748 aircraft, a licensed version of the Avro 748, served as a transport aircraft and trainer with the InAF, as well as functioning as a civilian airliner. The airframe was intended to be used for the Aerospace Surveillance and Warning Control aircraft (ASWAC), a concept in development since the early 1980s.[319] The ASWAC system suffered from severe delays, the result of both teething troubles and bureaucratic struggles.[320] The ASWAC program was abruptly and tragically terminated after a spectacular crash killed most of the design team in 1999.[321] India has since abandoned the ASWAC project, instead pursuing purchase of Israel's PHALCON airborne radar system.[322]

ALH HELICOPTER

In 1971 India entered an agreement with Aerospatiale of France (producer of the Alouette III and the Lama) for design of a new single-engine helicopter. In 1977, the InAF requested that the program be modified to a two-engine design, a recommendation which was accepted by the government in 1979.[323] This effectively led to the cancellation of the single-engine project, despite the fact that HAL had nearly completed the design.[324]

In 1984, the Indian government entered into a seven-year contract with MBB of Germany for the design and development of the new twin-engined ALH.[325] The twin-engined design was intended to replace not only the Chetak and Cheetahs presently serving in the Army and Coast Guard, but also to serve in a naval version for ASW work. The ALH is designed so that the rear fuselage, engine, and tail assembly can be married to a tandem front fuselage (presently in the early design stage) for a battlefield support/anti-tank role.[326] It has also been specifically configured for the operating conditions of the Himalayan region. Western analysts praised the project as successful and smooth-running: an unusual compliment for an Indian design.[327]

It now appears that the ALH program was delayed just short of production in the early 1990s.[328] HAL attempted to market civilian versions of the helicopter in India and abroad, advertising that operating costs are 50 percent lower than for other helicopters in its class due to the fuel-efficient French engine.[329] More recently, as additional funding became available, the ALH – now known as the 'Dhruv,' has entered production for the Indian armed forces and for export.[330]

SHIPBUILDING

The expansion of the Indian navy was accompanied by an increase in the use of local shipyards for production of naval vessels. The major projects are briefly outlined below. After a spurt of significant local production effort in the 1980s, however, India's shipyards lay idle for almost a decade, creating a problem of block obsolescence in the surface fleet by the late 1990s.

SHISHUMAR ATTACK SUBMARINES

In the late 1970s, India began searching for a European partner to collaborate in the construction of diesel attack submarines at the Mazagon Dockyard in Bombay. A deal was signed in 1981 with Howaldtswerke-Deutsche-Werft AGN (HDW) of Germany, calling for the construction of two Type 1500 submarines to be built in Germany, and for two more to be constructed in Bombay at the Mazagon Dockyards from German parts. Some 350 Indian technicians were trained in Germany, and German advisors were made available to advise on licensed production of the submarines in India.[331]

The German-constructed boats were commissioned in 1986, and delivered to the Indian Navy in February 1987.[332] In early 1984, Mazagon Dockyards began the assembly of two Type 1500 submarines from parts. Prime Minister Indira Gandhi dedicated the opening of the new construction facilities, and stated that the two boats assembled in India would enter service in 1987 and early 1988, respectively.[333] The Indian government also announced its intention to take up the option to construct two further boats under license at Mazagon, planning for a total of at least six Type 1500 boats in Indian service by the mid-1990s.[334]

The *Shalki*, first of the Type 1500 boats to be assembled in India, finally was launched in September 1989, and was commissioned into the navy in March 1991.[335] Construction suffered from serious delays and abysmal quality control – none of the pressure welds on the first Indian-built boat passed inspection in 1986, an indication of extremely poor work at Mazagon.[336] The second submarine, known as the *Shankal*, was finally

54 *India*

commissioned in May 1994.[337] The option to produce the fifth and sixth submarines under license was cancelled in 1987–88, due to a combination of financial constraints and technical difficulties. Overall, the project proved too complex for Indian industry.

NUCLEAR SUBMARINES

There have been persistent reports that India is attempting to produce an indigenous nuclear attack submarine called the Advanced Technology Vehicle (ATV). Licensed production of attack subs, in theory, could provide the expertise and technical skills to design and build an indigenous SSN. One report alleges that a commission was set up in 1977 to study the project.[338] Other reports refer to a standing SSN program since 1970.[339]

The Indians became the first developing country to receive a nuclear submarine from a superpower. A 'Charlie-I' class SSGN (named *Chakra* in Indian service) was leased from the Soviets in January, 1988 for a period of three years.[340] Official announcements stated that the vessel was purchased for training purposes only, and it is reported that the submarine was extremely unreliable and unsafe, which necessitated its return.[341] Research on the ATV continued throughout this period, but never approached the production stage.[342] Current projections anticipate ATV production in 2007 at the earliest, and reports hint at more leases from Russia.[343]

AIRCRAFT CARRIERS

In the opinion of Indian navy leaders, the Indian navy requires three to five aircraft carriers.[344] In 1988, it was reported that the cost of an indigenous conventional aircraft carrier would be Rs7–8 billion (approximately $500 million in $US 1988).[345] Despite the cost, however, a plan was announced in 1989 to build two conventional aircraft carriers at Cochin, India with French assistance. Due to limited construction dock capacity, the design was restricted in size to about 28,000 tons with the capacity of 30–40 aircraft and helicopters.[346] Serious design finally began in 1999, and facilities for building the vessel – called the Air Defence Ship (ADS) – were opened in early 2003.[347] More recent reports state that the ship will be 37,500 tons, with a speed of 28 knots, and will be ready by roughly 2011.[348] This will be the largest military vessel ever constructed by India.

LEANDER CLASS FRIGATE

Six *Leander* class frigates were produced under license at Mazagon Dockyards in the 1970s.[349] The last two ships produced, the *Taragiri* and *Vindhyagiri*, received extensive modification, including the removal of ASW mortars to increase hangar space for the helicopters and the addition of

SS-N-2 Styx SSM launchers and two triple ASW torpedo tubes. The Indian Navy planned that the earlier ships would also be modernized and brought up to the standards of these last two vessels.[350]

GODAVARI CLASS FRIGATE

The *Godavari* class frigate is an indigenous Indian design, based on a 'stretched' version of the *Leander* class. The *Godavari* has a displacement of 3600 tons, and a top speed of 27 knots, and is armed with Soviet missiles, Western electronics and two helicopters for ASW work. There are reports that due to the variety of Soviet, Western, and indigenous systems on the ship, there were problems with equipment compatibility.[351]

The Type 16-A, or *Brahmaputra* class frigate, is a modification of the *Godavari*. The lead ship took 13 years to produce, finally entering service in 2000. The other two sister ships entered service by the end of 2004. Although the class has a formidable missile armament, the lack of appropriate SAM systems – due to failures in both the *Trishul* project and in Russian alternatives – contributed to the delay in actual deployment. A follow-on system – the Type 17 – is currently in production, based on Indian and Russian technology. Three vessels have been laid down, but the IN plans a total of 12 vessels. The Type 17 is reportedly a 'stealth' ship, with a small radar profile.[352]

DELHI-CLASS (TYPE 15) DESTROYER

The largest locally-produced warship to date is the Type 15 Destroyer Program. The lead ship – the *Delhi* – was launched in early 1991, with two others on order.[353] The *Delhi* was intended to field a combination of Soviet and Indian electronics and weapons systems, including ESM/ECM, EW equipment and sonar by Bharat Electronics Ltd. and Indian-built SAM (possibly the indigenous Trishul) and ShShM missiles.[354] Failures in the Trishul program have forced India to purchase Israel's Barak SAM system.[355] All three Delhi-class ships are now in service.

VIBHUTI CLASS CORVETTE

This license manufactured version of the Soviet *Tarantul I* class corvette contributes significantly to the surface ship strength of the Indian Navy, although this ship is too small for a major oceanic role. The 450 ton *Vibhutis*, which are literally packed with missile launchers (four SS-N-2C and one SA-N-5), differ from the original *Veer* design in having different machinery, a 57 mm gun instead of the Soviet 76 mm, and an improved and upgraded set of countermeasures equipment.[356]

KHUKRI CLASS CORVETTES (TYPE 25)

The *Khukri* is the first major warship to be entirely designed and built by India. The new corvette boasts a heavy armament of SSMs and SAMs, in addition to a 76 mm gun and a Chetak helicopter for ASW duties (eventually to be replaced by the ALH). The *Khukri* uses a number of locally-designed combat electronics systems, including the navigation unit, combat data system (except in the lead ship), ESM system, and air search radar (all built by BEL).[357] Later versions of the *Khukri* use the SS-N-25 ShShM, a significant improvement over the older SS-N-2.

Strategic systems

The 160 kg Aryabhatta satellite was launched in 1975, followed by the Bhaskara I (June 1979) and Bhaskara II (November 1981). The Soviet Academy of Sciences also provided assistance in the establishment of a satellite tracking and ranging station (STARS) in Tamil Nadu, which entered operation in 1978.[358] On July 18, 1980, the indigenous Space Launch Vehicle-3 (SLV-3) launched a 35 kg Rohini satellite into orbit.[359] With this test, India became only the seventh nation to successfully put a satellite into space with an indigenous launch vehicle. The link between the Indian Space Research Organization and DRDO was made explicit with the establishment of the Indigenous Guided Missile Development Programme (IGMDP) in 1983.[360]

India developed a substantial chemical weapons production capability in the 1980s, which was declared under the Chemical Weapons Convention and is in the process of being scrapped. In 1988, India declared to the 3rd UN Disarmament Conference that it had no chemical weapon arsenal. In 1997, while signing the Chemical Weapons Convention, it acknowledged possession of an arsenal, but the details remain confidential.[361] India also reportedly has some biological weapons (BW) capability, and pursues BW programs for primarily defensive purposes.[362] India's nuclear developments will be discussed below.

1998–2005: new threats and opportunities

The South Asian security environment changed dramatically after the Indian and Pakistani nuclear tests of May 1998, and then again after the calamitous terrorist attacks of September 11, 2001. Both events foreshadowed new Indo-Pakistani crises, as each state sought to capitalize on the new security situation. Pakistan hoped to exploit the increased international concern over regional stability, provoking a crisis in the Kargil region in 1999 in an effort to put pressure on India for concessions in Kashmir. The terrorist attacks of September 11, 2001 rejuvenated the US–Pakistan defense relationship, but also strengthened Indo-US relations.

After a terrorist attack on the Indian Parliament building in December 2001, India authorized an unprecedented military mobilization and attempted to use coercive diplomacy to force Pakistani concessions and to undermine the US-Pakistan relationship. These efforts led to regional crisis, but were only modestly successful. Any crisis in the region now takes place under the threat of regional nuclear escalation and of rapid international diplomatic intervention.

Military input to India's nuclear program has been strictly limited by India's military leadership. One of the most outspoken advocates of Indian nuclear capability was the former Chief of Army Staff, General Krishnaswamy Sundarji, and Indian army officers have desired a voice in the program since the 1960s.[363] Despite these rare exceptions, India's strong tradition of civilian dominance of civil-military relations has largely isolated nuclear debates from professional military advice. It was not until 1988 that the then-Chief of Staff of the InAF and a small cadre of air force officers independently initiated notional planning for a nuclear force.[364]

In the late 1980s, regional crises – Brasstacks in 1986–87 and a border crisis in 1990 – took place in conditions of nuclear opacity. Both states were strongly suspected of possessing nuclear weapons, and of having some means (probably airborne) of delivering those weapons in combat.[365] The post-1998 crises were fundamentally different, because both sides possessed tested and verified nuclear weapons capability.[366]

On May 11, 1998, India simultaneously detonated three separate nuclear devices – one reportedly a thermonuclear device, one a roughly Hiroshima-sized fission device, and the third a miniaturized, subkiloton device.[367] Two days later, India staged two more tests of subkiloton devices. One of the subkiloton devices reportedly used a reactor-grade, rather than the purer weapons-grade, mix of plutonium.[368] On May 28, 1998, after over two weeks of intense diplomatic activity, Pakistan also tested nuclear devices. The number of tests is still contested – Pakistani authorities claimed five, but other analysts were unconvinced.[369] Two days later, on May 30, Pakistan tested another device, which it announced was 'miniaturized.'[370] The yields of both Indian and Pakistani tests remain disputed, but seismic evidence unquestionably confirms that both states detonated nuclear weapons.[371]

The new Vajpayee government believed the nuclear tests fundamentally changed India's policy options and security conditions, both within the region and internationally. L. K. Advani, India's hard-line Home Minister, insisted that India's tests would make Islamabad '.. realize the change in the geostrategic situation in the region' and 'roll back its anti-India policy, especially with regard to Kashmir.'[372] He suggested that India's demonstrated nuclear power would allow it to intervene forcefully across the Line of Control in response to future attacks in Kashmir.[373]

Although Indian elites recognize the threat posed by Pakistan to Indian territory and security, they often deny that Pakistan should play an important role in determining Indian *nuclear* policy.[374] The official explanations of the nuclear tests emphasized extra-regional or international factors, only mentioning Pakistan in the context of Chinese missile and nuclear proliferation to Islamabad.[375] The military implications of the nuclear tests did not receive much emphasis. Perhaps the most telling comment was an interview with Prime Minister Vajpayee:

> India has never considered military might as the ultimate measure of national strength. It is a necessary component of overall national strength. I would, therefore, say that the greatest meaning of the tests is that they have given India *shakti*, they have given India strength, they have given India self-confidence.[376]

All of this suggests that India's elites focused primarily on the symbolic, international ramifications of the tests, and not nearly as carefully on the potential regional security impact. This emphasis on symbols rather than hard security concerns is reflected historically in much of India's post-independence foreign and national security policy.[377]

In the eyes of many analysts, the 1998 nuclear tests, and more importantly Pakistan's prompt counter-tests, actually degraded Indian security in the near-term. Indian *military* leadership recognized this possibility but it appears to have been largely rejected by Indian political elites.[378] According to the Indian Kargil Review Committee Report, as early as 1991 the Joint Intelligence Committee anticipated that Pakistan would use its nuclear capability to limit Indian conventional retaliation in the event of low-intensity conflict.[379] Shortly before the Kargil operation was discovered, Pakistan's Chief of Army Staff General Pervaiz Musharraf announced that while nuclear weapons had made large-scale conventional wars obsolete in the subcontinent, proxy wars were very likely.[380]

The Kargil War of 1999 was the first war in a nuclearized South Asia, and arguably the first real war between two nuclear states. Pakistan attempted, for reasons that are still unclear, to use military coercion against India, infiltrating about 2,000 regular and irregular troops over the Line of Control near Kargil.[381] This operation would also provide substantial support for the insurgency in Kashmir, and draw off the attention of Indian security forces.

Both India and the international community interpreted this move as an invasion of Indian sovereign territory across an established border. Significantly, India did not escalate or expand the conflict by crossing the Line of Control or the border – a tactic India had first used in 1965.[382] Both India and Pakistan may have alerted and/or deployed nuclear weapons and delivery systems during the crisis.[383]

The Kargil experience contributed to significant changes in Indian nuclear and military doctrine. India's Draft Nuclear Doctrine (DND) was issued in August 1999.[384] The DND articulated a need for a survivable second-strike force, but also suggested that unlike the US-Soviet competition, retaliation did not need to be immediate – only assured. In early 2000, Minister of Defense George Fernandes announced a new 'limited war doctrine,' stating that there was a 'strategic space' in which conventional combat could take place without triggering nuclear deterrence.[385] Both doctrines aimed at denying the Pakistanis any advantage through the threat of nuclear escalation in the future.[386]

The December 13, 2001 terrorist attack on Indian Parliament caused an alarming crisis in the region. India initiated an unprecedented military buildup in response. Indian reports state that the Indian airforce and Indian commando forces were prepared to strike dozens of militant bases and several major military targets within two weeks after the December 13 attack.[387] The crisis was temporarily resolved in January 2002, after concessions by the Pakistani government.

In May of 2002, the crisis re-emerged in an even more dangerous manner. An attack by terrorist forces on the Kaluchak barracks resulted in the deaths of dozens of innocent women and children. India responded by combining India's Eastern and Western Fleets in the North Arabian Sea, placing paramilitary forces in Jammu and Kashmir under formal military command, and reportedly preparing another series of military strikes before the monsoon season began in mid-June 2002.[388] Again, efforts to coerce Pakistan into significant concessions did not achieve decisive results.

In early 2003, India's nuclear doctrine was formally approved, and a national command authority established as part of a formal command and control apparatus for the nuclear arsenal.[389] A new Strategic Force Command has been created and secure posts for the National Command Authority are now under construction.[390] The Indian navy is trying to carve out its place in the nuclear establishment, currently dominated by airforce bombers and army ballistic missiles.[391] India's nuclear structure remains, then, a work in progress.[392]

As India enters the twenty-first century, it appears to have embarked on a major military modernization effort. The 1999–2000 budget increased funding for space and nuclear-related activities by significant amounts. The 2000–01 budget, reflecting the Kargil Crisis of the summer of 1999, called for a 28 percent increase in defense spending.[393] By 2003, defense appropriations were Rs65,300 crores – roughly $15 billion. Despite the large annual increased throughout the 1998–2003 period, however, real growth in the defense budget was only modest due to inflation, and defense spending in 2003 still amounted to only 2.4 percent of GDP.[394]

The army remains the predominant service in terms of prestige and budget allocations – the army share of the 1999–2000 budget was 55.29 percent, compared to 14.8 percent for the navy, 22.49 percent for the airforce, 6.07 percent for research and development, and 1.35 percent for defense production.[395] Indian military leaders recently asserted that India's conventional edge has declined significantly in an Indo-Pakistani conflict – from 1.75:1 in 1971, to roughly 1.5:1 in 1990, to approximately 1.22:1 today.[396] One report states that the Indian military is now 'vast but hollow.'[397]

In terms of new equipment, the army is purchasing new equipment in response to the Kargil conflict – but while artillery fire control radars and mountain gear have moved to the top of the priority list, the 'big ticket' item remains the purchase of the T-90 tank.[398] Significant increases in expenditure for the Ordnance Factories suggests that maintenance, spares, and logistic capabilities are also receiving renewed emphasis – ordnance factory sales increased from Rs5,522 crores in 2000–01 to Rs6,105 crores in 2001–02.[399] However, reports stated that the ordnance factories still suffered from some quality control problems.[400] In addition, Indian Unmanned Aerial Vehicles programs – a priority for the army – appear to be inadequate, and are being replaced by Israeli imports.[401] Indian industry is also working on battlefield radars for the army, but these will compete with possible US imports.[402]

In 2004, the navy appears to be on the verge of halting a decade-long decline that included an institutional crisis with the dismissal of the Navy Chief in late 1998.[403] According to Naval Chief Admiral Madhavendra Singh, the navy ordered no ships from 1985–95 – and this shortfall is being made up by both domestic production and foreign orders.[404] As mentioned earlier, naval construction represents one of India's most successful local military industrial programs. According to Admiral JG Nadkarni (IN, retired), this is because the Indian Navy has been largely successful at defining its own requirements and keeping DRDO out of its programs – a significant condemnation of India's leading defense R&D organization.[405]

New production currently in the works includes the ADS, the Type 16A and Type 17 frigates mentioned earlier, and an impending arrangement for local production of French-designed *Scorpene*-class conventional attack submarines.[406] Other naval technologies in research or production include light and heavy torpedoes, a hull-mounted sonar array (HUMSA), a submarine sonar, a dunking sonar for helicopters, EW systems, and a naval variant of the LCA aircraft.[407] India has also tested the supersonic BrahMos anti-ship missile, jointly developed with Russian assistance, with a range of roughly 300 kilometers and a 300 kilogram warhead.[408]

The lack of an advanced trainer, aging equipment and rigorous flight schedules for InAF have led to a very high accident rate in the last decade. Efforts to procure an advanced jet trainer have only recently been successful.[409] HAL began research on a stealth aircraft – the Medium Combat Aircraft – in 1997, although it is unlikely to enter production in this decade.[410] India and Russia are reportedly cooperating on design of a fifth-generation supersonic fighter aircraft.[411]

Reported efforts to expand the InAFs squadron strength from the current 39 to 60 will require a massive increase in resources, particularly given the loss of 300 aircraft to accidents since 1990.[412] Current efforts to maintain InAF strength include upgrading older MiG-21bis aircraft with Russian assistance.[413] Deployment of the LCA is intended to begin this decade.[414] Acquisition and licensed production of the very sophisticated Russian Su-30MKI has begun, but the program suffered significant delays in setting up production.[415] In the meantime, the InAF will continue to rely heavily on older MiG-21 airframes, and will probably continue to lose aircraft to accidents at a rate of 20–5 per year.[416]

India clearly intends to field a range of nuclear forces.[417] The DND does not explicitly rule out tactical nuclear weapons, despite its adherence to a no-first-use policy, and some Indian analysts have discussed the tactical nuclear option.[418] India currently possesses sufficient weapons grade plutonium to create an arsenal of roughly 60 weapons. Using its more abundant stocks of reactor-grade plutonium, a less-efficient material for weapons design, this number could increase significantly, to the 750–1,000 range.[419] Some Indian analysts have been calling for further tests to include both thermonuclear devices and neutron bomb technology.[420]

India's space capabilities have also been substantially upgraded. The head of India's Space Research Organization has promised an unmanned mission to the moon by 2008.[421] India has launched eight remote sensing satellites, nine communications satellites, and one meteorological satellite. The Technology Experiment Satellite launched in 2001 reportedly has one meter resolution, and the Cartosat series preparing for launch in 2004–05 will have resolutions of 2.5 meters (Cartosat 1) and one meter (Cartosat 2), respectively. India's PSLV can now launch a 1,500 kilogram payload, and cooperation with Israel on space technology appears extremely promising.[422]

Conclusion

For nearly 50 years India pursued, and failed to achieve, the elusive goal of 'self-sufficiency' — independence in production of all major combat equipment. The shocking experience of the Himalayan War forced India to reconsider its security policies. The policies of Nehru's successors reflected a more self-interested approach, and the traditional utility of military capability received increased emphasis. India's arms industries spent the 1960s responding to immediate requirements caused by the wars with China and Pakistan.

The defeat of Pakistan in 1971 firmly established India as the predominant power in the subcontinent. Indian military capability expanded to attempt to fill new sets of security objectives, including an increased maritime role in the region and a self-perceived role as 'regional policeman.'

Ironically, India's military expansion did not yield enhanced security. As Indian military expenditures climb, the majority of spending is still committed to the ongoing antagonism with Pakistan.

How has the Indian arms industry fulfilled the primary objectives of the Indian government? Despite its failure to ascend to the higher tiers of the arms production hierarchy, India's military industry has significantly affected the military balance in the subcontinent. India has been successful in reducing dependence on foreign suppliers through local design, development, assembly, and/or production of military equipment.

A critical requirement for the Indian armed services has been to maintain significant quantitative advantages in primary weapons systems over Pakistan, as well as to maintain adequate stockpiles of munitions and equipment to permit the waging of high-intensity conflict. The Indian arms industry has provided these benefits for all three services, although not always consistently. In 1971, over half the InAF's aircraft, half of the helicopter force, and approximately 25 percent of the tank fleet were models which India assembled or produced locally, although some of this equipment had been imported as a finished product.[423] Indian production provided small arms, munitions, and light and medium weapons for the ground forces for 30 years, as well as providing unsophisticated munitions for the air force and navy. Although it receives little notice from Indian or other analysts, the bulk of India's defense production is substantially more sophisticated than that of China, due primarily to India's willingness to utilize licensed production. For example, India produced the MiG-21 before the PRC, and India's T-72, *Delhi*-class destroyer, and SU-30MKI are significantly superior to existing Chinese models.

In the words of one recent Indian Chief of Army Staff: "Modernization is a relative term. The question is: modernization for what? Basically, in India, we have to keep reasonably up with our neighbors. So, if neighbors forces get modernized, then we also have to get modernized to that extent."[424]

This explains part of the preference for licensed production. It adequately responds to most military needs, provides leverage against supply blackmail by external powers, and demonstrates Indian military and industrial capabilities. Only a few countries are capable of manufacturing supersonic aircraft, or large surface warships, or sophisticated diesel attack submarines. Indian industrial capability therefore reflects India's self-image as a growing power and a great nation.

India produced approximately 47 percent of the value of all major weapons systems acquired since 1965.[425] This large industrial effort should, in theory, provide the means to produce, maintain, and repair significant portions of the Indian military's major equipment, providing leverage against dependency on foreign supply and the means to assure sustained military operations in short-term and extended conflicts. In practice, this has not been the case.

Table 2.6 Local share of value in Indian major weapons systems procurement

	1965–70	1971–75	1976–80	1981–85	1986–90	Total
Primarily indigenous production as percentage of overall procurement	31.4	40.3	34.9	34.4	22.7	30.2
Licensed Production as percentage of overall procurement	17.7	21.0	15.1	12.7	18.3	16.8
Indigenous production as percentage of imports	61.8	104.5	68.2	65.1	38.4	56.9
Licensed production as percentage of imports	34.9	54.4	29.9	24.0	31.1	31.6
Combined local production as percentage of imports	96.7	158.9	98.2	89.2	69.4	88.5
Combined local production as percentage of total procurement of major weapons systems	49.2	61.3	49.5	47.1	41.0	47.0

Source: SIPRI data found in Ian Anthony, 'The "third tier" countries: production of major weapons', in Wulf, *Arms Industry Limited*, 370–3, 382–3. See pp. 368–9 for methodology. I have combined some of the data and created additional columns in order to further illustrate the range of indigenous efforts.

One of the most attractive theories in the study of LDC arms production is the concept of the 'ladder of production,' discussed briefly in Chapter 1.[426] India has consistently violated this theoretical ladder, skipping or ignoring steps in pursuit of symbolic goals. It has regularly rejected the possibility of incremental improvements to existing arms based on local R&D, preferring instead to purchase or develop entire new systems. The separation of the Indian defense sector from private industry minimizes the impact of imported defense production technology on the national economy.[427] In the aerospace sector, sophisticated manufacturing technology imported at enormous expense has had virtually no impact on the national economy.

Separation of the defense and private sectors was originally encouraged because quality standards in the civilian sector were often much lower than those in the defense industries. As India has integrated with the global economy, however, quality in many sectors now approaches or exceeds Western standards. Retiring Chief of Army Staff Sharma insisted that the government must make sure that Ordnance Factories and DPSUs 'become more competitive in the market economy, and we should also diversify much of our needs to the private sector so that the competition among our own businessmen is available and that in itself will reduce prices.'[428] Prime Minister Vajpayee recently noted the need to involve the military in defense research and development, and to ensure that the users of technology be firmly in the loop, as well as the desirability of having the private sector involved in R&D and production efforts.[429] The fact that these remarks are necessary more than 50 years after independence merely emphasizes the inadequacy of Indian military-industrial policy. Better utilization of India's enormous scientific establishment could substantially increase Indian military industrial competitiveness and alleviate technological shortfalls in the existing force structure.

Research and development, with the exception of the IGMDP, has been sloppy and poorly supervised.[430] The LCA project has now dragged on for almost 25 years, and the aircraft remains years from serial production. The GTX 'Kaveri' turbine, intended as its power source, has been under development for two decades. India's efforts to indigenize production often, in the words of one analyst, results 'in a constant endeavour to reinvent the wheel.'[431]

Government reports condemn long delays in major projects. The former director of DRDO, Dr. V. S. Arunachalam, admitted that 'in our eagerness to get major projects, we gave unrealistic timeframes and very low budgets.'[432] Dr. Abdul Kalam, director of DRDO, identified critical problems in the Indian R&D establishment, including poor interaction with end users, overemphasis on in-house R&D projects, and poor administration of available funds.[433]

Availability of funding for projects is a particular sticking point, whether in the R&D or production stages. The Indian budget process rarely facilitates extended funding commitments. The budgeting process is designed to maximize civilian oversight of defense procurement, and complicates the possibility of easily shifting funds or of maintaining consistent production rates over extended periods.[434] Lack of a prepared national security policy or strategy severely complicates long-term planning and coordination of industrial strategy.[435]

Some signs of positive progress are apparent. A recent announcement, creating a $5.5 billion fund for modernization, may alleviate this problem.[436] India has also committed nearly $1 billion (Rs50 billion) to advance payments for foreign equipment, hopefully avoiding continued delays in the AJT, *Gorshkov*, and PHALCON purchases.[437] The Indian government has allowed foreign firms to purchase up to 26 percent of the share capital of certain defense related industries. The government also announced its decision to set up a Defence Procurement Board and take a long-term perspective on procurement needs 15–20 years in the future.[438]

Serious weaknesses are evident in management of existing industrial programs. India has always been concerned about the availability of spare parts, and the possibility that the USSR or other suppliers would practice 'spare parts diplomacy.'[439] Despite this, insufficient priority has been given to manufacture of spare parts for Soviet equipment.[440] In 1993, the Indians needed to import small items, including hose pipes, rubber bungs, seals, and hydraulic oils for the MiG-21 aircraft and T-72 tank.[441] Only months later, India went on a foreign shopping spree which included land mines, 125 mm tank shells for the T-72, and artillery rounds for 130 mm cannon.[442]

The most notable weakness in Indian defense industry, however, is the virtual absence of a significant refit and modernization capability. The great strength of the incremental approach and the 'ladder of production' is the gradually increasing ability to modify existing equipment for the local combat environment or to extend service life.[443] India's defense industry focused almost exclusively on the production of major weapons systems and platforms, and relied on imported subsystems and armaments. The result is an industrial base which can design and produce airframes, but which has difficulty installing a different radar or an improved air-to-air missile to improve performance.[444] The Indian arms industry should be capable of far better, given the amount of resources expended.

India could now benefit substantially from a transfer of technology and expertise from the civilian sector, and a general opening of the defense sector to new ideas and competition. India boasts a surfeit of talented scientists, technicians, engineers, and computer programmers who could make substantial contributions to the Indian defense industry. Aircraft upgrades, for example, are becoming increasingly dependent on software modifications, and India boasts one of the most vibrant computer programming industries in the world. The fact that the Indian ASWAC airborne early warning system could be held up over inadequate computer software suggests how inefficiently Indian defense industries are coordinated with the private sector.

The IGMDP therefore offers a potential model for future Indian military industrial efficiency and success. Unlike previous Indian programs, the IGMDP had rigorous standards, efficient management, and strict deadlines for development and funding. The IGMDP is the first major Indian R&D program which has incorporated both public and private sector technology establishments with consistent military support and oversight in the testing and development stages. There is no indication as yet, however, that this level of integration is being replicated in other Indian projects.

If a local solution is not immediately available, however, India has been careful in maintaining and creating new access to foreign technology. The most important new venue is the 'Glide path' – the gradual opening of technological transfers from the United States as part of the warming of Indo-US relations.[445] India has agreed to participate in a missile defense program with the US, raising the possibility of both Indo-US technology cooperation and also transfers of the US-Israeli Arrow system to India.[446] The US recently offered to sell F-16 and F/A-18 aircraft to India, including technology transfer and licensed production rights. Differing perceptions of the role of technology in the relationship may still limit Indo-US cooperation, however.[447]

Indo-Russian cooperation continues to blossom. The BrahMos

represents a significant achievement, and may be deployed in 2004.[448] India and Russia are also discussing a new beyond-visual-range missile, merging an existing project at the Russian firm Novato with R&D work being done at DRDO.[449] India has agreed to help Russia develop its Glonass satellite navigation system – a deployment that could have significant military impact.[450]

Finally, the Indo-Israeli defense relationship continues to be extremely fruitful for both sides – one of the first examples of significant defense cooperation by mid-level producers in the new globalized defense industry. The PHALCON project, which the US denied to China, is a crucial demonstration of that relationship, and of US comfort with technology transfer to India.[451] India also seeks to work on missile projects with Israel, using Israeli expertise to flesh out DRDO's ideas – including the Dhanush ship-launched ballistic missile.[452] Space cooperation, noted earlier, remains a serious possibility as well.

Skillful use of existing industrial infrastructure and more sophisticated foreign partners creates a genuine opportunity for India's military industry to make significant strides in the near future. Given the history of poor management and bureaucratic interference, it would be imprudent to hope for a rapid success. But as India's military begins serious new plans for modern warfare, the role of Indian industry will be critical in determining the technological sophistication of India's forces, in maximizing the effectiveness of India's defense budget, and in determining India's overall military capability on both a regional and global stage.[453]

3 Israel

Background

Israel possesses the most technologically-sophisticated military industry of any developing country.[1] Israel's rapid military-industrial development is astonishing: in the period from 1940–90, the Israeli arms industry evolved from the manufacture of small arms and explosives in tiny basement factories to the production and modernization of supersonic fighter aircraft, sophisticated missiles, tanks, and electronics systems.[2]

Israel's defense industry developed in response to its abnormally threatening security condition. Limited economic resources and constrained access to the international arms market forced the new state to carefully integrate military-industrial development into its overall economic and national security planning. The close links between the Israeli Defense Forces (IDF) and their military-industrial base facilitated the research and development (R&D) of unique and sophisticated combat equipment tailored for the Middle East environment and the changing dimensions of the Arab threat. Careful deliberations by political and military leadership nurtured specific sectors of the industry which filled critical needs, occasionally over the objections of economic counsel.

For the most part, Israel's early military-industrial policy stressed short-term preparation over longer-term preparedness. Threats to Israeli survival were deemed imminent, and long-term investments in expensive infrastructure were seen as generally counterproductive. Investments in repair and maintenance, as well as the gradual acquisition of sophisticated modernization and modification capabilities, fulfilled most of Israel's military requirements at minimal expense.

This practical approach to industrial development, characterized by the 'ladder of production' model described in Chapter 1, began to unravel after the Six Day War of 1967. Diplomatic isolation, national pride, and increased economic resources contributed to a new belief that indigenous 'across-the-board' manufacturing capabilities were essential to Israel's security. The lure of 'blue-and-white' projects, designed and produced in Israel, nearly bankrupted the defense budget in the unhappy case of the

Lavi fighter aircraft. During the 1990s, economic limitations, the changing nature of the threat to Israel, and the unique characteristics of US military assistance re-shaped Israel's military-industrial infrastructure and policy.

Israel's military-industrial experience typifies both the most positive and negative aspects of less developed country (LDC) policies. Bolstered by a close relationship with political leaders and the military, local industry has reached internationally competitive levels in select technological niches and areas of comparative advantage, including electronics and missiles. Other manufacturing sectors in the economy have benefited from the defense programs and their high standards of manufacturing and technological competitiveness. But Israel also succumbed to the lure of 'self-sufficiency,' and squandered scarce economic resources on high-profile but ultimately unsuccessful projects like the Lavi. The Israeli case offers many lessons for prospective LDC producers.

Israeli security perceptions[3]

The state of Israel existed, until recently, in one of the most unrelentingly hostile national security environments imaginable. As the only non-Arab state in the Middle East, Israel became the focus of Arab animosity and pan-Arab ambition. The survivors of the Holocaust who fled to Israel after World War II found themselves faced with renewed threats of cultural and national annihilation. The ultimate objective of the Arab states has been defined as 'politicide' – the murder of the *politeia* or political entity of Israel.[4]

The absence of potential regional allies forced Israel to seek sufficient military strength to deter or defeat an Arab coalition assault alone. As a result, Israeli national security policy emphasized the military aspects of security.

> This security concept was intended to come to grips with a military dilemma: how to defend against an existential military threat in conditions of non-existent defensive space (lack of territorial depth), quantitative inferiority (in terms of force ratios) and weak military staying power relative to that of the adversary.[5]

Geographic constraints and limited economic and manpower resources determine Israeli military policy. To narrow the resource gap and incorporate new immigrants into the economy, rapid economic development and industrialization is a priority.[6] Israel's small size, vulnerable borders, and highly concentrated population require the IDF to take the war to enemy territory as quickly as possible, in order to limit civilian casualties and damage to infrastructure.[7] Israeli policy demands decisive victory in every conflict, assuming that each military encounter is merely a 'round' in an extended war with the Arab world.[8] The first significant Israeli military defeat might mean national annihilation.

IDF strategy is therefore driven by requirements to 1) limit casualties, 2) fight on enemy territory, 3) win quickly, and 4) win decisively.[9] These requirements demand an offensive approach to fundamentally defensive goals.[10] The IDF must depend on superior quality in order to offset Arab mass, demanding the highest levels of competence from an army which is primarily composed of part-time reservists. The highest possible standards of efficiency in operations, maintenance, and repair are critical in order to limit procurement expenditure but maximize available military capability. Israel must be able to fight, if necessary, in complete isolation from external suppliers, and be able to call upon all national resources in the event of crisis. These all-encompassing requirements profoundly affected the evolution of Israeli military industry.

The structure of the Israeli defense industry

The structure of the Israeli defense industry reflects both the socialist leanings of the early Labor governments and the gradual expansion of the private industrial sector. In the aftermath of the Six Day War, Israel made a distinct effort to incorporate private firms into the defense industry, a policy which was most successful in the electronics industries.[11] Economic constraints from the mid-1980s onward forced the Israeli defense industry to lay off thousands of workers – employment in the defense sector fell from 62,600 to 46,500 from 1985 to 1989 – and drove larger firms to export and diversify in order to survive.[12] Israel exported a very high percentage of its total military production – 70 percent in 1994 – and arms exports reportedly climbed from $2.2 billion to $3.3 billion from 1992–98.[13] By 2000, Israel was the fifth largest arms exporter in the world, behind Russia, France, the UK, and the US.[14]

Israel's arms industries and military-industrial policy have been forced to evolve in substantial new directions since the end of the Cold War.[15] Nevertheless, it was the unique geopolitical environment of that Cold War – the superpower competition, Soviet support for Arab nationalism, and the gradual development of a US-Israeli security relationship – that determined both the size and scope of Israel's military industrial infrastructure and its global role. What follows is a snapshot of the Israeli arms industry in the immediate post-Cold War period and a discussion of recent trends.

Government controlled industries

MASHA is the Hebrew acronym for the Renovation and Maintenance Centers of the IDF Logistics Branch. One of these centers has specialized since the 1950s in renovation and modification of armored combat vehicles, beginning with World War II surplus halftracks and Sherman tanks.[16]

In the 1970s, MASHA was assigned responsibility for manufacture of the Merkava tank, although manufacture of most of the parts was subcontracted. The IDF is thus unique among Western producers in that it not only designed its own main battle tank, but is also ultimately responsible for its production.[17] The IDF Communications and Intelligence Branches are also reportedly major designers and, in some cases, producers of appropriate equipment.[18]

RAFAEL is the organization tasked with research and development and production of some of Israel's most sophisticated defense systems. RAFAEL has been responsible for the development of over 100 different weapons systems for the IDF since 1967.[19] The original function of RAFAEL was research and development (R&D), with the responsibility for production of systems accepted by the IDF being passed on to other firms. This research and development included a substantial role in Israel's nuclear weapons program.[20] In the late 1960s, RAFAEL became a 'closed economic unit,' financed completely by means of development and production contracts. By 1986, RAFAEL had 6,500 workers, 70 percent of whom were engaged in R&D activity and 30 percent of whom were engaged in actual production.[21]

RAFAEL designs and develops the 'cutting-edge' equipment required by the IDF and unavailable elsewhere. The entire Israeli guided missile program was conceived and initiated at RAFAEL, which also designed the PYRAMID television-guided glide bomb and other precision-guided munitions.[22] RAFAEL designed the TAL 2 cluster bomb to meet IAF requirements at a time when the US refused to supply these weapons.[23]

RAFAEL has suffered from the changed international environment – employment fell from over 7,500 in 1986 to 4,100 in 1999.[24] The need to become self-financing also moved RAFAEL's priorities from pure research and development to actual production and competition with other producers in both Israel's industry and abroad.[25] RAFAEL's exports – presumably a major money maker – lagged well behind other Israeli firms as a percentage of total output.[26]

Israel Aircraft Industries (IAI) is structured into four divisions, with a total of 17 plants.[27] These divisions are Aircraft, Technologies, Electronics, and Bedek (the division responsible for maintenance, upgrading, and overhaul). In 1999, the workforce was just over 14,000, down from a high of over 22,500 in the mid-1980s.[28] IAI not only manufactures a variety of systems for all branches of the IDF, but also exports to approximately 80 different countries.[29] By the early 1990s, IAI was engaged in joint ventures and cooperative projects with 20–30 US companies, and had demonstrated some success selling to the US military.[30]

IAI specializes in refitting combat aircraft for both the IAF and a wide range of potential foreign customers. The firm produced and modernized aircraft for IAF needs, in addition to a range of tactical missiles. IAI provides for the other IDF services as well, including small armored vehicles, and patrol vessels for the navy. IAI's Elta division is a leader in the manufacture of electronics systems, producing a wide range of ground and air-based electronic warfare and electronic intelligence systems.[31] IAI has also become the leading producer of RPV/UAVs in the world.

IAI produces components for other major commercial aircraft producers, including Boeing and McDonnell Douglas.[32] IAI hopes to enter the international space technology market, particularly the manufacture of small satellites for commercial use.[33] IAI remains a powerful exporter. In 1994 79 percent of its total production was exported, and by 2000 IAI exports reached $1.7 billion – 8.2 percent of all Israeli non-diamond exports.[34]

TAAS (Israeli Military Industries) provides a wide variety of equipment for all three services and for the export market.[35] The company produces hundreds of different items, including light arms, ammunition, tank guns, air fuel tanks, artillery rockets, chaff/flare and other decoys and towed assault bridges.[36] Sales to the IDF accounted for about 40 percent of total sales in the early 1990s, with the rest being accounted for in the export market.[37] TAAS products include a number of now-famous weapons and munitions designed and developed specifically for Israeli needs, including the Uzi submachine gun, the Galil family of infantry weapons, and 'Hetz' 105 mm tank ammunition.

TAAS has been particularly hard hit by changes in the industrial environment. Employment at the firm fell from 14,500 in 1985 to 3,800 in 1999.[38] According to a recent report, TAAS received over $1.3 billion in government subsidies in the past decade.[39] TAAS has suffered from the increasing importance of US military assistance in the defense budget, and was forced to take a larger role in the export market in an effort to increase revenues. While exports reached 53 percent of total production in 1994, TAAS suffered a catastrophic 33 percent decline in sales the following year, emphasizing the vulnerability of export dependence.[40] Efforts to merge the major firms (IAI, TAAS, RAFAEL) or even to consolidate core business functions between them have been largely unsuccessful, and TAAS has apparently been the major loser from inter-industry competition.[41]

Israel Shipyards Limited (ISL) produces commercial vessels and warships for the Israeli navy, including the Reshef and Aliya class missile attack craft. ISL suffered severely in the late 1980s, when the Israeli government terminated contracts with the shipyard and purchased Sa'ar 5 corvettes from a US firm. Drastic cost-cutting measures stabilized the yard's financial situation, which also engaged in increased maintenance work for the US Navy's Sixth Fleet.[42]

Public-sector corporations[43]

Tadiran is Israel's leading electronics firm, established to ensure that the IDF had access to competitive electronics and communications equipment.

A full line of communications equipment is produced, ranging from personal radios and portable equipment for individual soldiers to long-range communications and C3I networks, including significant international business.[44] Military sales, which reached 60 percent of total sales in the mid-1980s, but declined to the 45 percent mark – a low level for any Israeli defense firm. This was achieved primarily through increased concentration on lucrative civilian technologies, such as portable radios and consumer electronics. The company suffered severely during the late 1980s, laying off 50 percent of its workforce.[45]

Elisra, a subsidiary of Tadiran, is the primary producer of electronic warfare equipment in Israel, specializing in airborne self-protection systems. Elisra is involved in projects for the IAF, Navy, Signal Corps, and Intelligence, and sales to the IDF account for about 43 percent of total sales. Half of these are airborne systems, including the SPS-2000 (a self-protection system designed for front-line aircraft, like the F-15 and F-16), the SPS-1000, designed specifically for the aircraft upgrade market, and the SPS-65, designed for helicopters and low-flying aircraft.[46] The company also produces a variety of ELINT systems, as well as ESM/ECM systems for installation on the new Sa'ar 5 corvette and other Israeli navy vessels.[47]

In 1999, elements of Tadiran and Elisra merged to create a powerful electronics conglomerate with significant export potential – over $300 million in sales in 1999 alone. The new Elisra Group consists of Elisra Electronic Systems, Tadiran Spectralink, Tadiran Electronic Systems, BVR Systems Ltd., and Stellar. Elisra Group exports roughly 60 percent of total sales, but only 7 percent to the United States, and has also apparently diversified substantially into the non-defense market.[48]

Private firms

El-Op Electro-Optics, half-owned by Tadiran, is an important producer of electro-optical systems, both for the IDF and for export markets.[49] The primary areas of El-Op expertise are laser designators, night-vision equipment, and Heads Up Displays for various aircraft. El-Op produces a number of systems used by the US military and the IDF, including electronic and electro-optic susbsystems used in the US Apache attack helicopter, and the Rangefinder Target Designator Laser used in IAI's Night Targeting System for Cobra helicopters. El-Op also produces the Multisensor Stabilized Integrated System, used on Israeli fast patrol boats for tracking and passive surveillance of both surface and air targets,[50] and is a contractor in the Matador tank fire control system.[51]

Elbit was established in 1966 with the objective of developing and producing advanced computer-driven equipment for Israeli military requirements.[52] Like Elisra, Elbit managed to increase sales during a time of major defense cutbacks, an indication of both IDF priorities and of the ability of

Israeli electronics firms to compete in the international arena. Military sales account for approximately half of Elbit sales ($300 million in 1991), and about two thirds of the company's net profits.[53] The company has thrived due to the increased importance of defense equipment upgrades, which Elbit performs on land, sea and air systems. The primary consumer of Elbit products is the US military (45–50 percent of sales), followed at a great distance by the IDF (20 percent).

Present projects at Elbit include the Phantom 2000 upgrade program for the IAF and the central mission computer for IAF F-16s. Elbit performs upgrade work for the aircraft of several foreign countries, including Northrop F-5s, MiG-21s, and the Czech L-39 trainer.[54] Elbit provides the fire control system for the Merkava tank, integrates similar systems into both Western and Soviet-bloc equipment, and produces a range of artillery fire control systems.[55] The company has also developed command and control, ESM, and ELINT equipment for naval vessels,[56] and is one of the few manufacturers in the world fully integrated ELINT/ESM systems for submarines.[57]

In 1999, Elbit and El-Op merged to create a firm with employment of roughly 4,000, revenues of $720 million, and a varied customer base divided roughly evenly between Israel (25 percent of sales), the US (25 percent), Europe (30 percent), and the rest of the world (20 percent).[58] According to *Defense News*, 94 percent of Elbit's revenues came from the defense sector, compared to only 60 percent for Elisra Group. This suggests that Elbit is more dependent on exports than Elisra, and at greater risk from the inherent fluctuations in the international arms trade.[59]

Israel has a large number of smaller firms that act as producers and sub-producers of military systems and components. *Rada* – an example of these small firms – produces superb equipment for the IAF and international clients. Rada specializes in computers, automatic test equipment, and airforce ground support equipment. Because of the high quality of its test and maintenance equipment, the firm is involved in large numbers of international aircraft upgrade programs.[60] Rada's two most important products have enormous force multiplier effects, but cannot easily be quantified because the systems themselves are inconspicuous and highly sensitive. The first is the Automatic Test Equipment (ATE). According to Israeli reports, this system can substitute for multiple highly trained technicians.[61] The second system is the computerized Data Transfer Equipment (DTE), originally designed for the F-16 and now used on F-5s and Mirage-type aircraft as well.[62] The DTE transfers mission data from electronic cartridges to avionics computers, and processes information much more rapidly than the original US system. This allows greater efficiency and increases the effectiveness of the aircraft in combat, while also simplifying post-mission analysis.[63] Small, efficient electronics firms like Rada are now capable of making a major impact on the quality of IDF equipment, particularly in the aerospace sector.

The pre-state period: 1920–48

The Israeli Defense Forces (IDF) evolved from small groups of Zionist settlers, who formed independent self-defense cells as early as the 1880s to defend Jewish settlements against attack.[64] In September 1907, ten men founded a secret organization called *Bar-Giora*, named after the leader of the Jewish revolt of AD 70.[65] In 1909, a larger group calling itself *Hashomer* (Watchmen) was formed, never numbering more than 100 members.[66]

Arab riots and attacks in 1920 prompted the establishment of the larger and better-organized Haganah, which eventually provided the basis for the IDF at independence in 1948.[67] It was under the auspices of the Haganah that semi-permanent cottage-type military industries were first established by Jewish settlers. Early local production efforts included hand grenades, home-made bombs, and other explosives. TAAS (Ta'asiya Zvai'it), the forerunner to Israeli Military Industries, was founded in 1933, and began budgeting for research and development of weapons in 1937.[68]

During World War II, a series of underground factories were established which produced small arms, including the versatile and easily produced Sten submachine gun, ammunition, and 2-inch and 3-inch mortars.[69] By 1948, TAAS was manufacturing grenades, rifles, 'Dror' light machine guns, British and 'Davidka' model mortars, Sten guns, and PIAT anti-tank weapons, as well as ammunition for all of these weapons.[70] Israeli military leadership recognized the value of these industries: 'The condition of the Haganah is far from satisfactory. In the matter of arms we have become noticeably better off, by acquisition and independent manufacturing.'[71]

The leaders of the Haganah felt that these light arms would be sufficient to suppress local Arab resistance. David Ben Gurion, chairman of the executive of the Jewish agency (Yishuv) and later the first Prime Minister of the state of Israel, was not convinced.

> We would not be up against the Arabs of Palestine, but the Arab states. The Haganah, operating as an underground movement, could neither produce heavy weapons nor train its members in their use. We must therefore buy heavy weapons in good time and lay the foundations for an industry capable of building them. Clearly with the end of the war the United States would dismantle a large part of its arms industry. An effort must be made to obtain our necessary machinery from this source.[72]

Shortly after the end of World War II, TAAS purchased large amounts of sophisticated arms production machinery from the US at the scrap metal rate of $75 per ton.[73] Research, development, and industrial infrastructure constituted a high priority. In 1946, the budget for the Haganah was

670,000 Palestinian pounds, of which 200,000 were devoted to the arms industry. In 1947, the budget was increased to 770,000 Palestinian pounds, of which 310,000 were earmarked for industrial programs.[74] The formation of the IDF in 1948 included the establishment of the Science Corps, which combined research and development organizations from all of the services and government establishments.[75]

Development of military industrial infrastructure: 1948–67

Israel lost over 6,000 dead in the War of Independence, which amounted to approximately 1 percent of the 1948 population.[76] Combat in the conflict was relatively unsophisticated – the few tanks available to the IDF, for example, saw little action.[77] Most of the fighting was done by units of brigade size or smaller, with light wheeled vehicles, small arms, mortars and some light artillery. As a result, while the IDF's local industrial base made a significant contribution to the War of Independence, it could not guarantee security in the future.

The new Israeli state under the leadership of David Ben Gurion established a two-track diplomatic and industrial policy to ensure supply and maintenance of adequate arms. On the one hand, Ben Gurion actively pursued a strategy of allying with a great power patron.[78] Israeli diplomatic efforts during much of this period focused on obtaining access to or membership in the Western defense community. At the same time, however, Ben Gurion also initiated efforts to establish a sophisticated domestic defense industry.

The period 1949–55 saw the establishment and expansion of the firms which eventually became the primary producers in the Israeli defense industry. TAAS, for example, expanded production over 50 percent by 1953.[79] Emet, renamed RAFAEL in 1959, combined the Science Corps of the various branches of the IDF, and began research and development of a series of rockets, guided weapons, and missiles.[80] MASHA began renovation and maintenance of the IDF's diverse equipment stockpiles.[81]

As early as 1950, Ben Gurion advocated establishing an aircraft industry. His initial proposal was the establishment of a maintenance plant which would produce spares for the 30 different types of aircraft then in IAF inventory. The plan was opposed by economists and military advisers, who argued that the Israeli market was too small to warrant a major investment in the aircraft industry, and that such an effort would either exceed Israel's technical capacities or drain skilled labor to an unreasonable extent.[82] Ben Gurion insisted, and in 1952 the Cabinet authorized the establishment of Bedek, which would overhaul and refurbish IAF aircraft, gradually assume responsibility for overhaul and maintenance of both civilian and military aircraft which Israel desired to purchase, and maintain El Al, Israel's national airline.[83]

Ben Gurion also supported the establishment of an electronics firm

(Tadiran) in response to the IDF's requirements for batteries, again over the strong objections of economic advisors. At least initially, Israeli batteries and transistors were not as good as imported competitors. In order to satisfy entrepreneurs who wished to create an Israeli electronics market, the new firm agreed to sub-contract heavily to the private sector, and to limit its production for the local civilian market to only 50 percent to encourage competition.[84] This effort at import-substitution was the first step in the creation of what later became a world-class defense electronics industry.

Ben Gurion reorganized the IDF and the Defense Ministry in 1950, reflecting concern over the IDF's reluctance to cooperate in military-industrial development. The Defense Ministry was given jurisdiction over finances and the acquisition, development, and production of new arms.[85] In 1953, Ben Gurion decided that the nation's service sectors would be tasked to provide support for the IDF, so that duplication of effort in medical, transport, and other sectors would not be necessary.[86] The new principle was coined as 'Let the army prepare solely for the battlefield, and let all the nation's services provide support in wartime.'[87]

Israel's rudimentary protectionist policies focused on defense-related areas: chemicals, metals, and machinery were considered particularly critical.[88] Grants from the United States, financial transfers from the Jewish diaspora, and the Reparations and Restitutions Agreement with the Federal Republic of Germany (signed in 1953) provided the capital necessary for development of industrial infrastructure.[89] Acceptance of the German reparations payments was extremely controversial.[90] German reparations helped provide funding and dual-use technology for Bedek and the Israeli metals industry, including establishment of the Urdan Works and major funding for Koor Industries.[91]

Despite Ben Gurion's ambitious plans, Israel's military industry evolved on something of an ad hoc basis in response to IDF requirements and needs. The Tripartite Agreement between the US, UK, and France attempted to balance and limit the quality and quantity of arms provided to Middle East states.[92] The lack of a reliable source of arms necessitated that Israel purchase whatever equipment was available from any supplier, regardless of the effects on standardization and maintenance, creating a logistics nightmare.

Financial constraints also limited the IDF's ability to procure new equipment. The IDF therefore emphasized 'self-help' policies – the most modern available equipment was procured, regardless of source, and modified to fit Israeli needs.[93] High rates of operability and high standards of maintenance for all equipment became major priorities.[94] Throughout this period, the budding Israeli arms industry was forced to provide spare parts for a variety of incompatible systems on a trial and error basis.[95] These 'endurance' sectors constituted the most crucial contributions of the Israeli defense industry in this early period.

As in most developing countries, the ground forces received priority – their capabilities were most integral to defending national territory. In addition, ground forces generally rely less on expensive technology and are therefore less expensive to equip. Lack of financial resources and assured suppliers forced the IAF to rely on used and frequently obsolescent equipment acquired from a variety of sources.[96] The navy had the lowest priority, and was virtually ignored, as was the potential strategic role of the airforce.[97]

On October 27, 1955, Egypt's President Nasser announced the finalization of an arms agreement with Czechoslovakia which would provide Egypt with hundreds of sophisticated Soviet-model tanks and aircraft. Israel quickly negotiated an agreement with France calling for supply of jet aircraft, tanks, and ammunition stocks. Israel agreed in return to participate in planning and carrying out joint military operations against Egypt. These operations eventually included the British, and became the Suez campaign of October 1956.[98]

Table 3.1 Israeli military expenditures, 1948–67

Year	Defense expenditure (millions of current Israeli pounds) (a)	Defense expenditures (millions of constant $1960) (b)	Defense expenditures as percentage of Gross Domestic Product (c)
1948	16	26.4	
1949	22	36.2	
1950	28	49.2	
1951	49	78.0	
1952	49	49.9	4.4
1953	49	39.7	3.6
1954	50	35.8	2.8
1955	57	38.6	2.5
1956	122	77.1	4.6
1957	183	109.2	5.9
1958	212	122.5	5.9
1959	243	138.8	5.9
1960	294	163.1	6.6
1961	313	163.1	5.9
1962	396	183.7	6.1
1963	511	228.1	6.7
1964	700	296.9	8.0
1965	825	325.3	7.9
1966	1,131	346.7	9.8
1967	1,772	557.4	14.7

Sources:
a *SIPRI Yearbook 1968/69*, p. 206; *SIPRI Yearbook 1974*, p. 214.
b *SIPRI Yearbook 1968/69*, p. 204.
c *SIPRI Yearbook 1973*, p. 241.

Despite the close relationship between France and Israel, some effort was made to diversify weapons supplies after the 1956 campaign. Israel acquired major weapons from several other NATO states as well. Centurion tanks were purchased from the UK, and the Federal Republic of Germany was used as a conduit for both German surplus weapons (such as M-48 tanks) and covert US arms supplies in the early 1960s.[99] The French connection, however, was most critical for Israeli defense planning.

From the Israeli perspective, industrial and technological cooperation was at least as important as French arms shipments. The Israelis looked at the growing French arms industry as a model of industrial development. Military industry therefore provided a means of acquiring and absorbing the latest industrial techniques and technologies.[100] France, in turn, sought a partner who could assist it in developing and maintaining the highest technological standards, and was particularly interested in the success of Bedek and Emet in the fields of aeronautics and missile development, respectively.[101]

The most obvious manifestation of Franco-Israeli cooperation was in the aerospace sector. Bedek, now known as IAI, expanded and began licensed production of a modified version of France's Fouga Magister trainer aircraft in 1960.[102] French assistance in establishing the Dimona nuclear facility was crucial to the development of Israel's nuclear weapons capability.[103]

During this period, Emet (now renamed RAFAEL) was involved in a series of sophisticated missile development projects, including the Gabriel ShShM, the Shafrir AAM, the Luz air-to-surface missile (ASM), and the Shavit/Jericho SSM.[104] Cooperation with the French on the manufacture of solid-fuel rocket motors was particularly important, but at this same time Israel independently developed inertial guidance systems later used on the Gabriel missile and other systems.[105]

The successes of the 1956 Sinai Campaign convinced the IDF that future operations should aim for a rapid victory, based on mobility, armored assault, and air superiority. This decision put a priority on the acquisition of tanks and aircraft. Production of either, with the exception of the Fouga Magister trainer, was temporarily beyond the capability of the arms industry, but local modifications and upgrades provided valuable infrastructure for later efforts, and substantially increased the capabilities of older weapons purchased from abroad at relatively little cost.

The money saved by modifying major land weapons was then available for the purchase of Mirage fighters and other systems which could not be acquired or duplicated through Israeli efforts.[106] The IDF was aware that military technology was advancing much more quickly than the capacity of Arab social structures to absorb it – a condition which fundamentally favored Israel and its emphasis on qualitative superiority.[107] IDF Chief of Staff Moshe Dayan emphasized continuing development of sophisticated equipment even though the 1956 Sinai Campaign demonstrated IDF shortages in critical areas including small arms and basic transport.[108] The military-industrial effort reached its peak in the creation of new weapons for the tiny Israeli navy. The combination of the locally developed Gabriel missile and the imported Sa'ar attack craft produced a naval capability uniquely suited to Israel's needs at minimal cost (see below).

From 1958–67, in real terms, defense expenditure increased by approximately 15 percent per year, while GNP expanded about 5 percent per year.[109] Industrial investment increased from 109.6 million Israeli pounds in 1956 to 527.7 million in 1964.[110] Growth in the defense industries was twice the rate of growth in other industrial sectors.[111] Local defense industries produced few major weapons systems during this period, but an extensive industrial infrastructure was established for both research and development and, if necessary, production of new weapons.[112] The arms industries were the only economic sector which avoided losing skilled personnel to emigration during the recession of 1965–67.[113]

At the end of this period, Israel experienced the economic and political pressures of maintaining an advanced military-industrial infrastructure. The Arava transport, designed for both commercial and military markets, became a 'make-work' project to maintain employment at IAI. The IDF was unwilling to purchase the aircraft, but the program continued as a means of ensuring continued employment at IAI during the recession of 1965–67.[114] The Arava decision could not be justified on economic terms, nor under the wide umbrella of national security.[115] The Eshkol government funded the program to protect against 'brain drain,' and to ensure that the infrastructure for a national aerospace manufacturing capability existed.[116]

By 1966, Israeli arms supply was diversified among several European states, and a sophisticated military-industrial infrastructure had been created. Strong political support, rational and focused economic investment, and dedicated R&D programs in this period provided Israel with a significant level of independence in production of small and light arms and ammunition, and the capability to carry out relatively sophisticated modification projects for existing weapons.[117]

Selected indigenous arms programs: 1948–67

Case study: technological innovation and the Israeli navy

The end of the Sinai conflict found the Israeli navy (IDFN) in disarray. The most neglected of Israel's three armed services, its three old destroyers could not protect Israel's pre-1967 coastline from Arab raids.[118] The loss of a single destroyer would be a national catastrophe: in addition to the loss of the ship, the 200 crew members included highly trained (and possibly irreplaceable) technicians. By early 1960, IDFN leaders were considering a number of unorthodox options in order to find a role that the navy could perform effectively given its current limitations.[119]

The IDFN reassessed its needs based on Israel's short war assumption. It required fast naval units, large cruising radii, smaller crews than contemporary destroyers, but at least their equivalent in firepower.[120] A design which could, if necessary, be manufactured in Israel at ISL was preferred. The Jaguar-class patrol boat being built in the Federal Republic of Germany (FRG) met all these requirements, once suitably modified.[121] Armed with ShShMs under development at RAFAEL the Sa'ar project created an entirely new and effective kind of surface combatant, allowing the IDFN to protect the coast and carry out an aggressive naval campaign against a distant Arab sea blockade.

At the time, this was the largest and most complex project ever undertaken by Israeli industry: based on unproven new technology, it would 'make or break' the navy.[122] The IDFN tripled the number of men passing through the officers training course in order to manage the project and learn the new technical skills required by the new state of the art equipment.[123] The IDFN closely linked the program to national industrial capabilities at ISL to ensure adequate repair, maintenance, and replacement of vessels. Development of the Gabriel missile took eight years, and cost approximately $11 million. The first dozen Sa'ar boats were built at a cost of approximately $5 million each. This estimate may not include the cost of weaponry and electronics, which were added after the ships reached Israel. Nevertheless, in 1967 Israel could buy eight Sa'ars for the cost of one surplus destroyer.[124] The Israeli navy not only found an appropriate solution to its dilemma – it found one which could be afforded with the resources available.

The new Reshef-class missile boat, designed and produced by ISL in response to Israel's expanded post-1967 coastline, had better armament and sea-keeping abilities, greater endurance and-range, and slightly slower speed than the original Sa'ar.[125] Israel's new fleet of attack craft proved itself in the October War of 1973. The IDFN sank 15 Arab ships, at least half of which were destroyed by Gabriels, and lost none.[126] The close links between military and industry, combined with a willingness to innovate in the face of apparently insoluble security problems, provided an inexpensive and effective solution which became a model for other LDC navies in the 1970s and 1980s.

'Endurance' requirements

As early as 1954, basic aircraft maintenance was underway at the Bedek plant. Within a year Bedek was overhauling engines for the IAF which had formerly been sent to France for these services.[127] By the 1960s, sales of locally produced spare parts and engine overhauls had become a profitable export business for IAI.[128] Israel was reported to be self-sufficient in the production of spares for the IAF, and local manufacture accounted for 90 percent of ordnance and ammunition requirements.[129]

Non-platform weapons

By the mid-1960s, Israel was self-sufficient in the manufacture of small arms.[130] Among these weapons was the famous Uzi submachine gun – over 1.2 million had been exported by early 1995.[131] The Soltam firm became a major producer of mortars, including large-caliber Finnish Tampella designs under license. Production of artillery received a low priority.[132]

Weapons: modifications programs

ARMORED VEHICLES

Israel's tank force has traditionally depended upon a relatively small number of modern, top-of-the-line tanks, when these are available, and a much larger number of older models which have been upgraded, modified, and sometimes almost completely reworked to Israeli specifications. Israel could not acquire modern tanks until after the Sinai Campaign, when the UK agreed to sell Centurions for the first time. Older Shermans, available from a variety of sources, constituted an important part of the IDF tank force.[133]

Overhauls of the Sherman and Centurion tanks provided substantial increases in performance. Shermans were upgraded with higher velocity 75 mm guns, and later with special medium velocity 105 mm weapons, extending their useful combat life by at least a decade.[134] The newer Centurion was mechanically unreliable compared to the older and simpler Shermans. These problems were eventually resolved by replacing the engines, and older models had their 20-pounder guns replaced by NATO-standard 105 mm weapons. The Israelis made over 2,000 modifications to the Centurion, which greatly improved its mechanical reliability.[135]

The IDF bought used halftrack infantry carriers for $5,000 each, and adapted them for local conditions. New models of the same equipment would have cost $40,000 each.[136] The IDF fielded home-made SP artillery using the Sherman tank chassis with French and locally produced Soltam 155 mm howitzers.[137]

AIRCRAFT

The IAF relied on France for modern aircraft through 1967, and the Mirage III served with great distinction in 1967 and 1973.[138] The Mirage III was modified by IAI to fit IAF requirements, including strengthened wings, increased ordnance capability, and installation of an Israeli electronics package instead of the original system.[139] Israeli engineers proposed a series of modifications for the Mirage III fighter which were later incorporated into the production model of the Mirage V.[140]

Strategic systems

BALLISTIC MISSILES

Israel began development of surface-to-surface rockets and missiles in the early 1950s. The SSM project at RAFAEL produced a number of prototypes which were generically named Luz, and tested in land, sea and air-based modes. The name Luz has appeared at least once in major Western defense journals to describe a system believed in production, and according to one Israeli report was actually fielded with the IDF in 1962.[141]

The Jericho missile, according to Western reports, was conceived of as a collaborative effort between France and Israel. Israel was extremely concerned about Egyptian missile development at this time, as German scientists actively assisted Egypt in designing and producing several types of rockets in the early 1960s.[142] The Shavit sounding rocket was developed with French assistance and first tested in July 1961.

Responsibility for the Shavit/Jericho project was transferred back to Dassault of France in the mid-1960s, when the new Eshkol government decided to slow down the Israeli nuclear program in 1963.[143] The first MD-620 (Jericho I) test failed on December 23, 1965. A second test in March 1966 was successful, and the missile and technology were later transferred to Israel.[144] Some reports state that two different missiles, the MD-620 and MD-660, were developed with the help of Dassault of France. Two of 50 MD-660 missiles, with a 450 km range, were reportedly delivered to Israel before the imposition of the French embargo in January 1969.[145]

NUCLEAR WEAPONS

Israel is widely believed to possess a considerable arsenal of nuclear weapons.[146] Franco-Israeli cooperation on nuclear power and weapons development began in the mid-1950s.[147] Negotiations were highly compartmentalized and secretive, and many aspects of the deal took the form of oral agreements rather than written documents – in fact, some of the documents contained false data.[148] The IDF was not involved in the initial negotiations or practical considerations – these were all handled by Shimon Peres.[149]

Throughout the late 1950s France assisted in the construction of the nuclear reactor at Dimona, and in the design of the Jericho missile. A number of Israeli scientists resigned from the Israeli Atomic Energy Commission in 1958. It has been argued that this was a protest over the secretive nature of nuclear weapons research.[150] More recent analysis, however, suggests that the resignation was entirely procedural, and was not a rejection of the nuclear program by the civilian scientific community.[151]

Ben Gurion and Peres took great pains to disguise the costs of the nuclear program. According to Avner Cohen's analysis, the cost of the nuclear program in 1957 was roughly 15 percent of the defense budget, and nuclear-related expenditures then doubled in 1958. Funding for the nuclear program, therefore, substantially exceeded national outlays for research and development, which averaged 11 percent from 1960–67. The nuclear budget came from private sources, including fund raising in the United States. The amount was kept secret, to avoid comparisons with the IDF budget (and possible competition for financial resources) or a more vigorous domestic debate on the nuclear issue. Israel informed the United States in 1961 that the entire nuclear agreement with France totaled $34 million, including all ancillary facilities. Shimon Peres, however, cites the cost at closer to $80 million.[152]

Under Levi Eshkol's leadership, the program was increasingly used as an insurance policy – a means of obtaining US political and later military support in return for non-weaponization and non-testing.[153] The first US–Israeli security dialogue took place in July 1962, and a later meeting between Eshkol and President Johnson from June 1–3, 1964 contributed to better US-Israeli relations – although Johnson remained concerned about the Israeli nuclear program, and insisted on regular visits by US scientists.[154]

RAFAEL played an important role in providing components for the nuclear program, and tests at the facility were crucial to weaponization.[155] By 1966 or 1967, Israel had produced sufficient plutonium for at least one nuclear weapon, and reportedly assembled nuclear devices at the height of the 1967 crisis.[156]

The boom years: 1968–73

Israel's stunning success in the Six Day War had immediate ramifications for Israeli defense and military-industrial policy.[157] Israel's European arms supply sources dried up after the conflict, and while the US began providing arms, it used them as a political tool for influence in the Arab–Israeli conflict.[158] The dramatic defeat of the Arab coalition led to a united commitment by the Arab states to destroy Israel, codified in the 'Three no's' declaration at the Khartoum Summit later in 1967.[159]

The Israeli arms industry expanded dramatically in this period, as defense expenditures skyrocketed.[160] Employees in the defense sector rose from less than 10 percent of the total labor force in 1966–67 to over 19 percent in 1973, including about 12,000 new employees at TAAS and IAI.[161] Defense industry employment jumped from 14,000 in 1966 to 34,000 in 1972.[162]

Military industrial growth from 1966–73 was four times the rate of other industrial growth.[163] The average rate of growth in the metals and electronics industries combined was 13 percent per year, and growth in electronics alone was approximately 30 percent per year. From 1968–74, investment in metals and electronics accounted for about one third of all Israeli investment, which increased the share of these two industries in all non-diamond industrial exports from 15 percent in 1967 to 38 percent in 1980.[164] Military industrial production increased fivefold over the 1966–73 period, reaching $500 million in 1973.[165] Israeli investment in defense research and development reportedly increased by over 300 percent between 1966 and 1972.[166] For the first time, the government encouraged private firms to bid for defense contracts and become more involved in the defense sector. Elbit and El-Op, prominent firms in the electronics sector, were founded during this period.[167]

The occupation of the Sinai, the Golan Heights, and the West Bank provided Israel with strategic depth and favorable defensive terrain for the first time in its history.[168] The combination of this new 'comfort zone' and the proven weaknesses in the Arab armies led to an underestimation of the level of Arab threat, and an assumption that war with the Arab states was unlikely in the immediate future.[169] The IDF became more influential in determining weapons acquisition policies, and redistributed resources towards longer-term projects in Israel at the temporary expense of more immediate requirements.[170] The IDF increased procurement of locally produced goods by 86 percent from 1967–72.[171] The growing costs and uncertain reliability of weapons suppliers made economic arguments for military-industrial expansion more attractive.[172]

After 1967 Israel found itself in a single-supplier defense relationship. While the Soviet Union quickly resupplied the Arab forces after their

Table 3.2 Israeli military expenditures and arms imports, 1963–73

Year (Israel)	Defense expenditures (millions of current $US)	Defense expenditures (millions of constant $1972)	Defense expenditures as percentage of Gross National Product	Arms imports (millions of current $US)	Arms imports (millions of constant $1972)
1963	215.67	285.59	8.58	20.0	27.3
1964	288.67	362.12	9.91	69.0	92.6
1965	312.33	357.30	8.96	46.0	60.6
1966	408.00	429.01	10.64	37.0	47.4
1967	635.86	672.12	16.32	23.0	28.6
1968	709.43	837.85	17.70	55.0	65.7
1969	964.00	1,135.94	21.35	163.0	185.8
1970	1,382.29	1,484.03	25.92	232.0	250.7
1971	1,463.85	1,491.25	23.75	257.0	265.7
1972	1,490.95	1,490.95	21.62	214.0	214.0
1973	3,953.10	3,255.72	45.41	1,717.0	1,625.9

Source: ACDA, *World Military Expenditures and Arms Trade, 1963–73*

defeat, Israel's European suppliers showed progressively less support, and eventually cut off sales altogether. Israel had ordered 50 Mirage V aircraft from France in 1966. The French government blocked delivery of the Mirages, which Israel had already paid $70 million for, but permitted the transfer of spares for existing Mirage III aircraft in IAF service until 1969, when a complete embargo was imposed.[173] The French embargo also affected delivery of the remaining Sa'ar missile boats, which had to be stolen by teams of Israelis from Cherbourg in December 1969.

In 1966, Israel arranged to purchase the new Chieftain main battle tank from the UK, with an option for licensed production in Israel. After field trials, the Israelis proposed over 70 modifications, which were promptly incorporated into the design. In November 1969, just days before the contract was to be signed, the British backed out and canceled the agreement.[174]

As a result, the Israelis found themselves abruptly reliant on the US for supply of their two most important combat systems: tanks and aircraft. The US was unwilling, however, to supply the most modern M-60 tanks to Israel, instead selling older M-48s which the IDF promptly modified to the equivalent of an M-60.[175] While the US was willing to deliver A-4s to the IAF, it refused to provide the significantly more sophisticated F-4E Phantom II multi-purpose fighter until October 1968. In a meeting with Assistant Secretary of Defense Paul Warnke on October 22, 1968, however, Foreign Minister Eban and Ambassador Yitzhak Rabin heard the *quid pro quo* for these aircraft:

> the United States wanted Israel to sign an unprecedented document. ... We were asked to consent to a US presence in and supervision of every Israeli arms manufacturing installation and every defense institution engaged in research, development, or manufacture – including civilian research institutions such as the Weizmann Institute of Science and Israel's universities.[176]

Under these circumstances, it is not difficult to understand Israel's concern over the reliability of the US arms pipeline. The arms industry began developing indigenous 'blue-and-white' weapons systems, including the Merkava tank, new versions of the Sa'ar fast attack craft, and the Kfir fighter, which could supplement or replace imported systems in the event of future pressure or embargo. Because of the long-lead times associated with development and production of major weapons systems, most of these items did not enter service until the mid-to-late 1970s.

The growth of the capability and the political influence of the arms industry inspired debate between factions of the IDF, led by Yitzhak Rabin, former IDF Chief of Staff, and the political leadership and Shimon Peres, former head of the Defense Ministry. Rabin emphasized Israel's long-term vulnerability in the absence of strong US support. Peres supported diversified supply through European sources including the UK, Germany, and France, and also encouraged the growth and support of the local defense industry.[177]

The two factions clashed on prioritization of local industrial efforts. Rabin favored procurement of major systems from foreign suppliers, which offered guaranteed delivery schedules, lower prices and combat-tested equipment. Rabin supported an Israeli industrial infrastructure for maintenance and modification of existing systems, and particularly opposed projects with high unit costs. Peres strongly supported domestic production of major systems as a means of hedging against foreign embargo. He also noted that the industrial capability already existed: it seemed only logical to use it, if only to maintain the capability.[178]

Rabin's views illustrate a critical concept in Israeli, and other LDC, arms procurement. Israel consistently needs to make choices between *konenut* (short-term preparedness, focusing on immediate order of battle) and *hitkonenut* (preparation, or augmenting future capabilities). This condition is not unique to Israel – all states must choose between short-term requirements and long-term investments and research when making defense allocations. Israel's existential vulnerability, however, makes these considerations more immediate and perilous than in most countries.

In the 1967–73 period, Israel placed greater priority than ever before on *hitkonenut*.[179] Despite the impressive achievements of both the IDF and the Israeli military industries during this period, the close fit between security policy, military doctrine, and military-industrial priorities began to unravel. The psychological impact of the recovery of almost all of historic Israel was almost overwhelming, and possession of the new territories led to debate over IDF military doctrine. Should Israel adopt a static strategy of defending the border, or exploit its new-found strategic depth and conduct a mobile defense somewhere inside the new boundaries?[180] The decisive victory of June 1967 turned into an extended conflict along the new borders, known as the War of Attrition, which increased in intensity as Egypt attempted to inflict unacceptable casualties on the IDF, and dragged on for several years to an unsatisfactory stalemate.

Important lessons of the War of Attrition were neither absorbed into doctrine nor passed onto the defense industry in terms of requirements for future systems.[181] The IDF failed to adjust to Arab advantages in firepower, and underestimated the importance of combined arms.[182] The IAF paid insufficient attention to the ever-thickening Arab air defense belts based on imported Soviet SAMs.[183] Many of the Israeli-produced countermeasures which resulted from the 1973 war could have entered service earlier, if the lessons of the War of Attrition had been properly assimilated.

On October 6, 1973, Israel was attacked on two fronts by a well-armed and highly motivated Arab coalition led by Egypt and Syria, with supporting contingents from numerous other Arab states. After serious initial setbacks – according to some reports, on October 9, 1973 Minister of

Defense Moshe Dayan was disturbed enough to order the arming of Israel's arsenal of nuclear weapons [184] — the IDF was able to stabilize the situation on both fronts. The Israelis were then able to successfully launch sweeping counterattacks in the Golan Heights and the Sinai leading to eventual termination of the war.[185]

Despite the overall success of the IDF, the war exposed grave deficiencies in Israel's military forces, overall preparedness, and doctrine. Israeli military intelligence was surprised by the Arab attack because of its incorrect assessment of Arab intentions and capabilities.[186] The IDF was surprised on an operational level by new Arab tactics derived from previous Arab-Israeli conflicts and based on new technologies, including anti-tank guided missiles (ATGMs) and surface-to-air missiles (SAMs). The Arabs for the first time had access to SCUD SSMs, which provided the Arabs with a weapon which could hit Israeli cities with impunity.[187]

Israel's mobilization and logistics capabilities were severely tested, and inadequate stockpiles of ammunition and spare parts led to critical shortages during the fighting. The IDF deliberately thinned out spares and stockpiles after the War of Attrition in order to focus resources elsewhere. A stockpile of 105 mm tank ammunition sufficient for 30 days of combat would have cost $250 million, a considerable portion of the Israeli defense budget at this time.[188]

Lack of tank transporters forced reserve armored units to move on their own tracks, which increased maintenance problems and breakdowns. Distribution of ammunition was poor, and artillery units received a low priority despite front-line units' desperate need for covering fire and support.[189] The IDF estimates that only 40 percent of its tank ammunition ever reached the front.[190] The overall cost of the conflict was frightening – perhaps as much as an entire year's Gross Domestic Product.[191]

Local military-industrial efforts demonstrated their effectiveness in key aspects of the conflict. Israel dominated naval operations during the war. Israeli missile boats destroyed at least 15 Arab naval craft with no losses to themselves.[192] The IDF was able to quickly repair damaged tanks and put them back into service, and the refitted Centurions and M-48s proved superior to any tanks in the Arab armies.[193]

Israeli-built and modified Mirages, Neshers, and Baraks were the preferred aircraft for air superiority missions, releasing the more versatile American-built F-4s for attack sorties. Although over a quarter of the IAF was lost during the war, the IAF dominated air-to-air encounters, destroying 277 Arab planes while losing only six.[194] Finally, during the actual fighting, RAFAEL was reportedly able to analyze SAM wreckage, and come up with 'the technological means to cope more successfully with the enemy's missile threat.'[195]

The near-disaster of 1973 prompted the commitment of even larger national resources, both financial and intellectual, to ensure Israeli security. Between 1961 and 1975, annual military expenditures increased by 12 times in constant dollars, and increased fourfold as a percentage of GNP. In comparison, in real terms, GNP only increased by three times.[196] While this growth was significant, particularly relative to Egypt, the income of the Arab states as a whole was increasing due to the rising price of oil.[197] Iraq's increasing economic strength and political intransigence was a serious concern. Iraq's GNP increased from approximately 50 percent of Israel's in 1972 to almost twice Israeli GNP in 1979 – all as a result of rising oil prices.[198]

The most important result of the war, however, was to shake Israel's confidence. Casualties were high, costs to the economy were severe, and Arab use of oil as a political tool threatened Israel with political isolation.[199] Oil wealth also permitted the Arab states to expand their armed forces quantitatively, and to purchase new weapons which qualitatively were almost a match for the best IDF systems.

Selected indigenous arms programs: 1967–73

Case study: major weapons platforms

THE MERKAVA TANK

The decision to design and produce the Merkava resulted directly from the British government's decision to cancel joint production of the Chieftain in 1969.[200] Israel had been assisting in the design and development of the Chieftain since 1966, when two prototypes had been sent to Israel for testing, and the Israelis had suggested 70 design changes based on their combat experience and specific needs.[201] The decision to produce the Merkava using local industry and MASHA (the maintenance and repair workshops of the IDF) was made in 1969, at the urging of General Israel Tal. The Merkava emphasizes protection, ease of repair, and minimizing the possibility of fire or ammunition explosion, reflecting IDF experience in 1967 and 1973.[202]

The result of this emphasis is an outstanding tank design, which entered production after only nine years in the development stage.[203] Seventy to 80 percent of the Merkava's displacement by weight is devoted to crew protection, as compared to 50 percent in most other MBTs.[204] Merkava uses a very sophisticated Israeli-designed fire control system and modular armor.[205] The Merkava production line involves over 200 firms, producing 30,000 different parts and employing 3,000 people.[206] By 1990, approximately 800 Merkavas had been built, and older versions were all being upgraded to more recent standards.[207] The Merkava 4 tank recently entered service with the IDF, and will replace older American, British, and Russian models in IDF inventory.[208]

KFIR FIGHTER AIRCRAFT

The Kfir fighter, Israel's first effort at local production of a top-of-the-line weapons platform, integrated French and Israeli Mirage technology with American General Electric J-79 jet engines, manufactured under license by the Bet Shemesh Engine Factory.[209] The Kfir was based on the French Mirage 5 airframe, developed with Israeli assistance before the 1967 war. Complete plans for the Mirage 5, and for its ATAR-9C jet engine, were obtained through subversion of a Swiss engineer by Israeli intelligence.[210] An early version of the Kfir, known as the Barak or Nesher, reportedly flew in the October War in 1973, and the first Kfir was produced in 1975.[211]

The Kfir is equipped with Israeli avionics systems, and can perform both interceptor and ground attack roles.[212] According to one Western assessment, the Kfir is more capable than the more well-known Mirage F-1 aircraft of the Iraqi and French airforces, and almost as capable an air-to-air fighter as early versions of the Russian Su-27 Flanker.[213] The combat radius of the original Kfir is considerably greater than the Mirage III or V, and later C2 and C7 upgraded versions extended it further. It carried a greater weapons load, more effective missiles, and delivered them with greater lethality and accuracy due to Israeli-designed weapons and avionics. The canard wing technology which vastly increased its maneuverability was also an Israeli innovation.

When the Kfir was designed, supplies of modern combat aircraft to the IAF were uncertain at best. IAI quickly developed an effective substitute for imported Mirages which was superior to existing IAF aircraft. IAI could have produced Kfirs and Neshers using the stolen ATAR-9C powerplant. The availability of the US J-79 engine improved the performance of the aircraft substantially.[214] In the event that supplies of weapons were embargoed by the US, the J-79's status as a non-munitions item allowed Israel to stockpile engines and parts freely to tide them through a crisis.[215]

When analyzing the Kfir program, this context is critical, as the Kfir proved a relative failure as an export item.[216] The program was designed, however, as an import-substitution measure in response to the French embargo and US use of weapons supplies as a method of diplomatic pressure. By the late 1970s, once continuing US supplies of more advanced F-15 and F-16 aircraft were assured, maintaining the Kfir production line could no longer be justified as a national security requirement. New Kfirs were immediately mothballed and put in reserve status. Non-security factors, such as the prestige of fighter production, maintaining employment at IAI, and the vain hope of Kfir exports, are more important in explaining continued production.

'Endurance' requirements

Israeli firms produced a complete line of ammunition for IDF requirements, but the high rate of IDF consumption still meant that approximately 35 percent of IDF requirements had to be imported at this time.[217] These requirements were relatively small: according to Moshe Dayan, the US Army used 21,000 shells in one evening in Vietnam, which was more than the IDF used in both the Sinai Campaign and the Six Day War combined.[218] Maintenance and repair capability proved critical in the 1973 October War. According to one estimate, the IAF would have been down to 10 percent of its pre-war strength by the tenth day of the war.[219]

The IDF reportedly lost 900 tanks in 1973, but many of these were restored to service during or after the conflict.[220] The Yom Kippur War demonstrated that Israel's ability to quickly repair tanks and restore them to units in the field, compensated for the IDF's numerical inferiority.[221] Between 1400 on October 6, 1973 and 0800 on October 7, 1973, the IDF had over 75 percent of its deployed tank force in the Golan Heights and Sinai knocked out. Within 24 hours, 80 percent of these damaged tanks were returned to action, and some were knocked out four or five times.[222] At one point or another, every IDF tank fighting the Syrians on the Northern Front was hit by shells. In contrast, many of the 867 Syrian tanks abandoned in the Golan Heights were still in running order and were quickly repaired by the IDF. In total, the IDF listed only 100 tanks as irreparable losses after the war.[223]

Non-platform weapons

Israeli producers supplied over 90 percent of the IDF's requirements in small and light arms as well as 70–80 percent of required electronics.[224] TAAS produced the 105 mm guns for IDF tank refit programs.[225]

RAFAEL began research on AAMs in the early 1960s, and produced the Shafrir I for IAF service later in that decade. The follow-on Shafrir 2 was much more successful, and achieved a kill rate of 60–75 percent in the Yom Kippur War, destroying over 200 Arab aircraft in that conflict.[226] The Shafrir 2 cost 20 percent less than imported AAMs.[227]

IAI began production of radars and communications systems for Mirage 3 aircraft in the 1960s at the Light Industry Department, later renamed Elta.[228] The Elta 2001 radar, which became standard equipment for IAF fighters in the 1980s, was developed in response to the inability of the Mirage 3's Cyrano radar to pick up low-flying targets in 1967.[229]

Modification programs

Israel significantly increased the capability of M-48A2 tanks acquired from Germany and the US through re-equipment by installing a locally produced 105 mm gun, a new engine, and eventually a new fire-control system.²³⁰ T-54/55 tanks captured from the Arabs in 1967 and T-62 tanks captured in 1973, were upgraded with 105 mm guns and new engines. These tanks have served in the IDF for over two decades, increasing tank inventory at minimal cost.²³¹ Self-propelled artillery was created locally by setting 155 mm and 105 mm guns on older tank chassis. The L-33 SP gun, using Soltam's M-68 155 mm howitzer, entered service in 1973.²³² Tank and half-track chassis were also fitted with locally produced 120 mm and 160 mm mortars.²³³

Mirage 3 aircraft were modified with improved radar and engines, and a local modification eventually formed the basis of the Kfir design (described above). Vautour light attack bombers acquired from France in the 1950s were filled with US electronic warfare equipment and used in the War of Attrition.²³⁴

Strategic systems

Avner Cohen cites reports that Jericho-I missiles were deployed on October 7, 1973, and again from October 17–20, 1973.²³⁵ Missiles were deployed as a signal to both the US and the Soviet Union, but may also have reflected worst-case planning (as late as October 9, the situation in the Golan Heights was not fully stabilized, and nuclear use was reportedly considered).²³⁶

The Israeli nuclear program did not slow after the 1967 War. Perfunctory US inspections of the Dimona facility ceased, and production of plutonium continued. The US acknowledged – through leaks to the press – that Israel had developed a nuclear capability in 1970.²³⁷ The timing of this report – leaked to Hedrick Smith at the height of the War of Attrition – suggests that it may have been intended to influence Egyptian or Soviet calculations.²³⁸

During the October War, Israel may have had as many as 25 nuclear weapons available.²³⁹ Nuclear-capable Jericho missiles were deployed in the Judaean mountains west of Jerusalem at Hirbat Zachariah, and a squadron of F-4 aircraft was assigned for nuclear weapons delivery at Tel Nof airbase.²⁴⁰ These weapons were deliverable by air, using F-4, A-4, and possibly Mirage/Kfir aircraft, and perhaps by early versions of the Jericho missile. Israel also began development of both chemical and biological weapons during this period.²⁴¹

Overextension and decline: 1973–95

The IDF expanded and modernized in the aftermath of the October War, reflecting the military 'lessons learned' and new political-economic realities.²⁴² The IDF's active forces increased over 100 percent and reservists increased from 225,000 to 322,000 between 1971–81.²⁴³ Equipment for this expanded force was produced or modified by local industry, and also

92 *Israel*

purchased from the US. In the late 1970s Israel set a goal of producing 40 percent of total arms procurement domestically.[244]

Israeli military industry adapted quickly to the new requirements of the IDF.[245] Desire to use the local infrastructure for the rearmament process was reflected by increases in defense R&D funding: from 1974–76, Israel spend over $400 million on defense R&D.[246] In real terms, defense outlays grew at an average annual rate of five percent from 1973–81, slower than the average rate of increase in the previous decades, but still faster than growth in the economy as a whole.[247]

This period also saw dynamic increases in Israeli military exports, averaging 20–24 percent growth per year over the 1967–84 period.[248] Exports maintained production lines at full production levels, and provided important sources of foreign exchange.[249] Exports funded continued Israeli defense R&D – the Gabriel ShShM, for example, brought Israel more than $1 billion in exports, paying for its development costs more than ten times over by the mid-1980s.[250] Export production also ensured that critical equipment was available in event of a crisis.[251] For example, in 1973 50 percent of the workforce of AEL Israel Ltd. was called up for reserve duty in the October War. The firm *still* achieved two months production in one week by using most of the factories spare parts and all of the work in progress.[252]

It is clear that by 1984 Israel's economy was dependent on weapons exports to an unhealthy extent. Arms exports as a percentage of overall

Table 3.3 Israeli military expenditures and arms imports, 1972–82

Year	Defense expenditures (millions of current $US)	Defense expenditures (millions of constant $1981)	Defense expenditures as percentage of Gross National Product	Arms imports (millions of current $US)	Arms imports (millions of constant $1981)
1972	1,476	2,872	17.6	300	583
1973	3,142	5,786	34.1	230	423
1974	3,036	5,140	28.6	950	1,608
1975	3,780	5,869	31.9	725	1,125
1976	4,083	5,999	32.7	975	1,432
1977	4,103	5,694	30.0	1,100	1,526
1978	3,707	4,789	24.3	900	1,162
1979	5,232	6,232	30.8	490	583
1980	5,424	5,930	29.3	825	901
1981	4,374E	4,374E	20.3	1,100	1,100
1982	5,838E	5,507E	25.5	1,000	943

Source: ACDA, *World Military Expenditures and Arms Transfers, 1972–82*

Note
E = Estimate

industrial exports increased from 7 percent in 1967 to 15 percent in 1974, and grew to greater than 24 percent after 1977.[253] Israeli local defense production was valued at $500 million in 1974, $1.4 billion in 1980, $2.25 billion in 1984, $2.4 billion in 1988, and $3.2 billion in 1990.[254]

In 1984, the government adopted an official policy of encouraging exports.[255] At that time, almost 70 percent of the products produced by Israeli defense firms were purchased by the IDF, and about 30 percent of production was exported. By the end of the decade, that proportion had reversed. In 1990, 78 percent of IAI's $1.4 billion turnover was exported. IAI accounted for approximately two-thirds of all Israeli defense exports that year.[256] Between 1980 and 1986, RAFAEL moved from less than 10 percent export turnover to more than 50 percent.[257]

Reliance on exports exposed Israeli firms to the fluctuations of the international arms market. Defense exports also endangered the secrecy of Israeli defense products.[258] This concern was expressed by Minister of Defense Yitzhak Rabin in December, 1986, when he told the Knesset that he had permitted RAFAEL to export sensitive technologies over the objections of all of the field security agencies.[259]

Exports also complicated US–Israeli defense cooperation, raising significant political concerns on both sides. This occurred both through the transfer of Israeli technology that the US sought to control and through re-transfer of technology with significant US content. Israeli missile cooperation with South Africa led to strong protests by the US, and Israel eventually adhered to the Missile Technology Control Regime under US pressure.[260] Israel has also been accused of major transfers of US technology to China.

During this period, Israel produced most of its requirements in munitions, small and light arms, and mortars, but continued to purchase some munitions and small arms from the US. Israel became at least theoretically 'self-reliant' in major weapons platforms during this period, and production of these platforms received increasing priority. The new Merkava tank was introduced into service in limited numbers beginning in 1979. The

Table 3.4 Israel defense exports, 1974–84

Year	Exports in current $US millions	Percent share of defense exports in non-diamond industrial exports
1974	96	10
1976	322	26
1978	554	28
1981	875	21
1984	1,400	≥30

Source: Blumenthal, "Influence of Defense Industry", p. 174; Klieman and Pedatzur, *Rearming Israel...*, p. 79; Reiser, *The Israeli Arms Industry*, p. 146.

navy continued to receive the Reshef-class missile boat and also ordered the new Aliya-class.[261] The most prestigious projects were associated with the IAF – the Kfir fighter entered service in 1975, and development of the Lavi fighter began in the late 1970s.

Despite Israel's remarkable achievements in constructing missiles, platforms, and other major weapons, the most fertile area for Israeli defense industry was the field of military electronics. Investment to the electronics industry had increased markedly in the 1968–73 period, and the returns over the next decade were substantial. Over one third of all industrial investment in Israel from 1968–74 went to the metallurgical and electronics industries, and their funding increased 2.5 times from 1967 to 1968, and 3.5 times from 1967 (pre-war) to 1972.[262]

The ability to design, develop, produce, and retrofit combat electronics onto existing major weapons platforms can extend the service life of existing equipment by decades. Radar, communications, jamming equipment, electronic warfare, and missile guidance systems are all crucial to the survival and more effective operation of modern weaponry.[263] The importance of military electronics, underestimated by the IAF before the October War, became apparent as the Israel faced increasingly sophisticated Arab air defenses.[264]

Throughout the 1970s, Israeli military electronics designed and produced increasingly sophisticated equipment first for the IDF, and later with great success for the export market. The Israeli electronics complex is unusual in that, unlike production of other critical military systems, a relatively large share of the production capacity is in the hands of private industry. This led to difficulties: as Reiser has documented, from 1965 until the mid-1980s, the government frequently favored large government-owned firms over private enterprises due to economic factors and employment concerns.[265]

The election of the Likud in 1977 ushered in a new era in Israeli strategic doctrine and planning. Israeli doctrine began to focus increasingly on non-traditional threats, particularly the Soviet Union and more distant Arab states such as Iraq and Libya.[266] The test of Israel's new force structure and defense posture came in 1982, during Operation Peace for Galilee in Lebanon. Politically, the attack was a disaster. The machinations of Defense Minister Ariel Sharon ensured that both political and military leadership were unaware of the broad objectives of the conflict. Whatever political advantage Israel may have achieved in the first dramatic days of the conflict was frittered away in the siege of Beirut and the slaughter at Sabra and Shatila.[267]

The IDF invaded Lebanon on June 5, 1982. On June 9, 1982, during the fourth day of ground fighting, the IAF attacked the Syrian air defenses and wiped out 19 SAM batteries with no IAF losses.[268] This success was made possible by a sophisticated communications network, which permitted the accumulation and dispersal of near real-time intelligence. The proximity of the battle zone to Israeli territory maximized these advantages.[269] Israel coordinated ground and air strikes on the SAM batteries, using special locally-designed rocket-assisted rounds to increase the range of its 175 mm artillery.[270]

The air-to-air victory was also overwhelming.[271] After the destruction of its ground-based air defense network, Syria sent its airforce was to contest the airspace over Lebanon and the Golan Heights. In a combat enabled by locally-designed and modified Israeli electronics the IAF routed the Syrians and achieved complete air superiority.[272]

The ground war was much less successful.[273] Critics point to the failure of the IDF to maintain high rates of advance, and an unwillingness to maneuver or to fight at night, as well as a perceived preference for firepower over maneuver at odds with traditional IDF tactics.[274] 'It took only fifteen years for an army once known for its agility, flexibility, mobility, operational efficiency, and ability to respond quickly to turn into a heavy, coarse, and incredibly clumsy bureaucratic labyrinth.'[275]

During the 1973–82 period the close relationship between the military and local industry provided significant advantages for the IDF. Electronic warfare, communications, command and control, and tactical intelligence all benefited from the development and deployment of Israeli systems.[276] The development and incorporation of Remotely Piloted Vehicles (RPVs), initially designed as a private project by Tadiran, into IDF inventory facilitated the IAF's overwhelming success in annihilating SAM defenses in the 1982 war in Lebanon.[277] These and other 'blue and white' systems proved themselves magnificently in combat in 1982.

In 1983, a large infrastructure was in place for the development of sophisticated missiles, 'smart' munitions, and new generations of electronic warfare equipment. Israel was in position to take advantage of the technologies associated in US and Soviet thought with a new military-technical revolution: reconnaissance, long-range strike, and electronic warfare capabilities, and associated improvements in guidance and munitions technology.[278]

Israel instead chose to focus much of its R&D and military-industrial expertise on the Lavi fighter aircraft (see case study). This decision demonstrated the debilitating effects of political and economic interference on what had once been an efficient and cooperative relationship between Israel's security requirements and military-industrial programs. The importance of IAI as both an employer and as a symbol of Israeli competitiveness in aerospace research weighed heavily on Israeli political leadership, and there was constant pressure to provide new projects for the firm in order to keep engineers employed.[279] The high priority given to the Lavi project limited investment and research in other areas, and increased an already high level of dependence on the US for both technology and funding.

Since 1973, US security assistance, and US technology transfer, has formed an increasingly critical portion of the Israeli defense industrial effort.[280] The US financial contribution to Israeli defense is significant: in 1986, US security assistance accounted for over 40 percent of the Israeli military budget.[281] During the 1980s, increasing amounts of this were made available for use in Israel as part of the Off-Shore Procurement (OSP) fund. According to one report, from 1976–89 the US pumped $6.5 billion into the Israeli defense industry using OSP and offsets.[282]

US funding became critical in the maintenance of both military capability and military production due to Israel's severe economic turmoil in the late 1970s. Real GNP growth shrank from an annual average of almost 6 percent in 1951–73 to less than 1 percent in the next decade. Inflation averaged 45 percent per year from 1975–79, and peaked at 450 percent in 1984.[283] Israel's deteriorating economy led to the decision by a National Unity government in 1984 to take drastic fiscal measures to limit inflation. In 1984 alone, almost $1 billion was cut from the government budget, including a $258 million cut in defense expenditures.[284] Beginning in 1984, Israeli defense spending shrank rapidly, and the allocation for local purchases and imports shifted significantly.[285] Through the early 1980s, approximately 50 percent of Israeli domestic military expenditures were spent on production or R&D.[286] In June 1989, according to then-Minister of Defense Yitzhak Rabin, that figure had fallen to 35 percent,[287] and this figure continued to shrink.[288]

Israel's involvement in Lebanon (1982–85) and efforts to suppress the first Palestinian *intifada* in the late 1980s seriously strained the IDF

Table 3.5 Israeli military expenditures and arms imports, 1981–91

Year	Defense expenditures (millions of current $US)	Defense expenditures (millions of constant $1991)	Defense expenditures as percentage of Gross National Product	Arms imports (millions of current $US)	Arms imports (millions of constant $1991)
1981	6,514	9,725	22.9	1,200	1,791
1982	6,359	8,939	20.7	925	1,300
1983	7,322	9,890	22.1	500	675
1984	8,375	10,830	24.5	775	1,002
1985	7,519	9,380	20.4	1,000	1,248
1986	6,918	8,404	17.4	500	607
1987	6,308	7,428	14.3	1,800	2,120
1988	6,110	6,928	13.0	1,200	1,361
1989	6,245	6,775	12.6	1,100	1,193
1990	6,940	7,218	12.6	460	478
1991	4,992	4,992	8.1	460	460

Source: ACDA, *World Military Expenditures and Arms Transfers, 1991–92*

budget.[289] The increase in IDF active and reserve forces, and the large stocks of equipment purchased in the late 1970s, required larger financial commitments to operations and maintenance.[290] The IDF began cutting back on stockpiles to save money as early as 1987.[291] In addition, new equipment costs more to operate – the F-15 costs approximately twice as much per flight hour as the F-4.[292]

Maintenance of the post-1973 force structure at post-1984 budget levels further decreased the amounts available for local procurement and R&D.[293] IDF procurement relied heavily on American Foreign Military Sales (FMS) funds, as salary and other expenses which must be met through the local budget continued to rise. After fixed costs were accounted for, only 25–30 percent of the 'shekel budget' (the IDF budget, not including FMS funds) was left for defense industrial infrastructure and new local procurement. Forty-seven percent of the shekel budget was spent for salaries by the early 1990s.[294] As a result, the IDF increasingly bought equipment from the US that it formerly purchased from local producers.[295]

R&D spending suffered from changes in the economy and budget cuts: defense industries cut back their investments by two-thirds during this period, and decreased 'in-house' spending on R&D by 40 percent.[296] It is estimated that the Lavi program absorbed as much as 15 percent of the defense budget in the mid-1980s, and monopolized R&D and production resources to the detriment of other industries and programs.[297] This situation was not alleviated by release of funds after the Lavi was cancelled. Although $5.5 billion for new projects was supposed to become available, 42 percent of this was spent on standard operating costs of the IDF.[298]

Israeli military-related R&D expenditures remained high – at least 50–70 percent of all R&D is military related. Some analysts estimate that as much as 6.7–8.0 percent of the military budget (approximately 2.7 percent of GNP in 1987) is devoted to R&D – still a substantial drop from the 11 percent of the 1960s.[299] The future impact of cuts in R&D may be determined more by restructuring of research priorities than by the actual loss of capital.

The role of the United States in maintaining Israeli military strength also changed. During the late 1970s, the US began to use sales of advanced technology as a political instrument to gain influence with Arab states. Israel still received advanced aircraft and other systems from the United States, in addition to large amounts of military assistance,[300] but the weapons themselves were no more technologically sophisticated – in terms of hardware and basic capabilities – than those supplied to specific Arab states. By the early 1980s, the US commitment to Israeli qualitative superiority had taken the form of technology transfer, rather than weapons supply.[301] This technology transfer was far from one-sided. US designs profited from Israeli modifications, and some of these modifications became standard issue in equipment which was later exported to Arab states.[302] In short, the changing US-Israeli relationship created new dependencies on US supplies, and new constraints on Israel's ability to create, field, and export qualitatively superior weaponry.

Selected indigenous arms programs: 1973–95

Case studies: major weapons platforms and other systems

THE LAVI CONTROVERSY[303]

The most ambitious project, and greatest failure, of Israel's defense industries was the Lavi multi-purpose fighter aircraft. Originally proposed as a two-engine follow-on to the Kfir, the Lavi was re-designed as a single-engine 'second-line' fighter and approved by the Likud government in 1980.[304] Later in that year, IAI was able to convince Prime Minister Begin to approve a more sophisticated version with significantly increased air combat capability – and consequently increased unit costs.

Lavi development sapped resources and talent from all other sectors of the defense industry.[305] By the time the first prototype flew over $1.2 billion in US FMS funds had been spent, and total development costs were estimated at a minimum of $2.2 billion, of which the US would have provided $1.8 billion.[306] The number of aircraft to be produced dropped from an original estimate of 400–450 to approximately 300, only 100 of which would actually serve with the IAF.[307] It became apparent that production of the Lavi would require an increase in the IDF budget of up to $500 million annually for a decade, even assuming continuing levels of US financial support.[308]

In fact, by 1986 the IDF was facing severe budget constraints, increases in the budget were unlikely, and force quality and stockpiles were degrading from lack of funding. Minister of Defense Rabin was adamant in his opposition to the Lavi program: 'I will not let the Lavi destroy the IDF. Even if a majority in the Cabinet decides to go ahead with the project under the present conditions, I will not be able to implement that decision.' [309]

Arguments in favor of Lavi production centered around the importance of maintaining a local capability for aircraft manufacture [310] and the economic impact of ending the program.[311] Some went so far as to argue that production of the platform itself was necessary to spur innovation in sub-systems and other technological niches. This argument, of course, completely ignored 30 previous years of Israeli innovation based on modification of existing systems with locally-designed sub-systems.

In fact, the Lavi was extraordinarily dependent on US funding, technology, and expertise. Approximately 60 percent of the aircraft's parts were designed or produced in the US, and over 50 percent of the production costs would be spent in the US.[312] The military benefits of the Lavi versus other aircraft were a relatively small concern in the political debate, although the IAF provided substantial input in the design process.[313] Ultimately, the Lavi proved too expensive an investment for IDF planners and the Israeli economy. On August 30, 1987, in a 12–11 vote, the Israeli Cabinet voted to terminate the program.[314]

ARROW ATBM

Israel is currently deploying the ARROW anti-tactical ballistic missile system (ATBM), developed jointly with the United States. The project, already in the works at the time of the Gulf War, received increased priority after Iraqi missile attacks on Israel in 1991. The Arrow was designed to kill missiles at ranges of up to 90 km, and was specifically designed to attack missiles with ranges of up to 1,000 km, according to Western reports.[315]

The US agreed to fund the development of the program, but would not pay for deployment. According to one recent report, the US had provided 65 percent of the $1.1 billion cost of the program as of September 2000.[316] Another report estimates the cost at over $2 billion, and the US share at roughly $700 million as of 2000.[317] US funding appears to have been applied solely to the missile itself – the Green Pine radar was developed by Elta, and the Citron Tree battle management center was developed by Tadiran.[318] The Arrow was successfully flight-tested September 14, 2000, declared fully operational in October 2000, and was formally accepted into service in March 2001.[319] The Arrow-2 interceptor has an interception range of up to 100 km, and can engage ballistic missiles with ranges of up to 1,500 km – including most SCUD variants currently on the market.[320]

Israeli efforts to get US permission to export the Arrow system have not been successful.[321] A recent decision to give Boeing a 50 percent production share in the Arrow however, indicates the unique new realities of Israel's military-industrial policy. The decision for joint production reflects three major Israeli concerns. First, production by a US firm increases the potential for surge production, in the event that more than three batteries (with roughly 300 interceptor missiles) are required. Second, it allows Israel to pay for Arrow production with US military assistance funds. Third, Israel hopes that production in the US will provide additional leverage on future export decisions, as US employment will be affected.[322] This arrangement will ensure that final assembly and integration takes place in Israel – perhaps assuring control over secret techniques or data.

'Endurance' requirements

The IDF maintains its commitment to minimizing casualties, and this commitment is reflected in Israeli arms developments. One example of this is the design of Blazer reactive armor for tanks. This project was undertaken in the aftermath of the 1973 war, and proved itself during the 1982 conflict in Lebanon.[323] The use of body armor, while not an Israeli innovation as such, decreased small arms casualties by 20 percent in 1982.[324]

The Yom Kippur War emphasized the importance of large reserves of ammunition and spare parts. Ariel Sharon minimizes the importance of the US resupply effort in the 1973 war, but also states that in two-and-a-half weeks of combat the IDF used 25 percent of available small arms ammunition, 55 percent of available artillery shells, and 48 percent of available tank shells. Shells for the 175 mm guns were seriously depleted (these were especially important for attacking SAM sites from long distances). It appears the IDF might have found itself short of crucial ammunition had the conflict continued in the absence of US resupply and diplomatic intervention.[325]

TAAS production soared from $72 million in 1972 to $550 million in 1983.[326] IDF stockpiles nearly quadrupled from 14 days for six divisions (1973) to 28 days for 11 divisions in 1982. The Israelis were reportedly willing to pay 25 percent more than import costs for local production of sensitive munitions, in an effort to maintain local production lines.[327] By 1987, the IDF had reportedly accumulated 40 days of war reserves stocks.[328]

The development of new 'Hetz' 105 mm tank ammunition saved the IDF billions of dollars by maintaining the effectiveness of Israeli tanks armed with the 105 mm gun, at the modest cost of $200–300 million in development and ammunition procurement.[329] This ammunition was used with enormous success in the summer of 1982 during the Lebanon campaign, when kills were achieved against T-72 tanks at ranges of up to 3,500 meters.[330]

The IDF continued its long-standing commitment to maintenance, repair, and outstanding rates of readiness, and manufactured spares for most of its equipment. Bet Shemesh Engine Works, for example, produced the GE J-79 engine under license, as well as the Marbore VI turbojet for the Fouga Magister/Tzukit, the Sorek 4 expendable turbojet for RPVs, and parts for the Atar 9C engine.[331]

Non-platform weapons

Israeli firms produce a wide assortment of communications systems, radars, and other sensors for IDF ground forces. Among the most notable are the DAVID and COMBAT artillery fire control computers,[332] the Matador and Lancelot tank fire control systems[333] and a series of surveillance radars and electronic warfare systems produced by Elta. The Israeli Navy relies heavily on local electronics for surface warfare, although it imports sonars and some other equipment from the US. The IAF relies almost entirely on locally-designed and produced avionics systems.[334]

The firms of Soltam and TAAS produced three versions of the basic 60 mm mortar, three types of 81 mm mortars, two types of 120 mm mortars and the unusually large (for Western producers) 160 mm mortar.[335] The 120 mm mortar design produced by Soltam/IMI is also manufactured by Martin-Marietta for the US Army under the designation M-285.[336] Soltam has produced and modified a series of guns and howitzers for the IDF and export. These include modifications of the US M-114 155 mm howitzer, a 155 mm howitzer on a Soviet M-46 field howitzer chassis, the M-68 and M-71 155 mm Gun/Howitzers, and the Model 839 and 845 155 mm howitzers. The M-68 and M-71 were also developed as SP versions.[337] In 1990, over half the IDF's towed artillery was locally produced, but the majority of the SP equipment was imported from the US.[338] Both TAAS and RAFAEL reportedly increased the priority of providing ground force equipment, particularly missiles, during this period.[339] Israel also produces several multiple rocket launchers (MRLs), including the MAR-290 (which fires 290 mm rockets) and the LAR-160 (160 mm rockets), with a 350 mm version reportedly in development. TAAS also produces 240 mm rockets for captured Soviet MRLs used by the IDF.[340]

The IDF deployed the Merkava III tank, which is equipped with a 120 mm smoothbore cannon that was reportedly designed and developed indigenously in less than two years – although estimated production costs proved far off the mark.[341] RAMTA, a subsidiary company of IAI, has designed and produced the RBY Mk 1, and RAM V-1 and V-2 armored vehicles, which can carry machine guns, small cannon or 106 mm recoilless guns.[342]

The Gabriel ShShM was used with great success on Israeli missile boats during the 1973 conflict, and became a popular export item. The longer-range Gabriel Mk 2 was introduced into service in the mid-1970s, while the Gabriel Mk 3 joined naval service in 1979–80, and was introduced in an air-launched version in 1982. There have also been reports of an additional model of the Gabriel called the Gabriel Long Range (GLR) or Gabriel 4LR, which is reported to have a range of 1,400 km with a large enough payload to carry a nuclear weapon. Other variants have a range of over 200 km with a 240 kg explosive or sub-munition warhead.[343]

The new Sa'ar-4.5, or Aliya-class, missile attack craft was produced at ISL. Based on the Reshef design, it weighs 488 tons, and is capable of carrying a helicopter or naval RPV (HELSTAR).[344] Other vessels produced in Israel include the Ashdod and Kishon class landing craft (produced in the mid 1960s), and the Dabur and Dvora patrol boats. The Dvora has the distinction of being the smallest known missile attack craft, although they usually are armed with cannon.[345] Both the Dabur and Dvora have been offered for export, as have the Shapirit and Alligator multi-purpose patrol landing craft. ISL has also designed the Shaldag-class fast patrol boat as a private venture.[346]

In 1978, the Python 3 AAM entered service with the IAF. The Python-3 is very similar to the US AIM-9 Sidewinder, but has a much larger warhead.[347] The experience of the October War increased the IAF's demand for sophisticated air-to-ground munitions of various kinds. These include both high-accuracy and high-lethality weapons, as well as stand-off weapons for attacking SAM sites and other dangerous targets. The IAF reportedly deployed Luz-1 air-to-surface missiles in the 1970s, with a 200 kilogram explosive warhead and a range of 80 km.[348] In the 1980s, RAFAEL developed the 'Popeye' stand-off missile, which has been sold to the US Air Force for use on the B-52 as a conventional standoff weapon.[349] The IAF also deployed the Tal-1 and Tal-2 cluster bombs – developed as a result of a US decision not to sell cluster bombs to Israel – and now uses Elbit's Opher terminal guidance systems to convert regular gravity bombs into infrared-guided glide bombs.[350]

REMOTELY PILOTED VEHICLES (RPV) AND UNMANNED AERIAL VEHICLES (UAV)

The first major Israeli RPV program was initiated by Tadiran, after the successful use of a number of US target drones to deceive Arab SAM defenses in the 1973 War. Tadiran developed an RPV called the Mastiff, using in-house funding, and the first units were purchased by the IDF in 1975. Although IAI was disinterested in RPV/UAV technology when it was first available, it was encouraged to compete with Tadiran and eventually supplant it – an example of preference for state-owned companies over private industry. IAI has become the acknowledged international leader in the field.[351]

The IDF has used RPVs with enormous success, and Israeli industry has exported large numbers to the US and other customers. In the Lebanon War, RPVs reportedly were used as laser-designators for aircraft-carried smart weapons, and also may have carried cluster bombs. RPVs provided near-real-time battle damage assessment and reconnaissance capabilities for both ground and airforces, and may have been used as decoys to imitate strike aircraft.[352]

BARAK/ADAMS CLOSE-IN WEAPONS SYSTEM (CIWS)

Although IDFN missile boats are fitted with the US Phalanx CIWS, they proved difficult to operate in high seas because of the vessels' low freeboard.[353] The solution was the Barak CIWS based on vertically launched missiles, which avoids the freeboard problem and utilizes Israel's strengths in electronics and missile technology.[354] The Barak uses eight-tube launch modules and an Elta fire control radar, which allows the system to engage multiple targets at ranges of 500 meters to 12 km.[355] The ADAMS is vehicle mounted, with similar capabilities. Both systems are fully automated and have been successfully tested.[356] The Barak has been exported to the Indian navy, which prefers it to both Russian and indigenous short-ranged SAM options, and also will be deployed on Israel's Sa'ar 5 missile corvettes.[357]

Modification programs

Most US equipment is modified by the IDF shortly after delivery. US-IDF cooperation on modernization of the M-109 SP howitzer, for example, revealed that Israel and US operational requirements differ significantly: there was only a 60–70 percent commonality of design in this 'standard issue' equipment.[358] Aran Electronics developed a major modification for the radar of the Improved HAWK SAM, and Tadiran and MABAT (IAI) upgraded the Chapparal SAM.[359] These upgrades enabled the continued effective operation of aging systems at considerably lower cost than their replacement with new 'state-of-the-art' weapons.[360] In addition, Israel reportedly made major software modifications to the Patriot ATBM in response to post-combat assessment during the Gulf War.[361] Harpoon ShShMs, purchased from the US, have been fitted with Israeli-designed guidance systems.[362]

IMI and Soltam artillery and mortars designs are routinely retrofitted onto armored vehicle chassis. An armored personnel carrier, based on the Centurion chassis, was also introduced in the early 1980s, in hopes of providing infantry with better protection from Arab anti-tank weapons.[363] Most of the parts, assemblies, and systems for the Merkava-3 are manufactured locally. This enables the export of many systems based on Merkava technology which has also been used to upgrade other tanks.[364] M-48s and Centurions were modernized with indigenous fire control systems and Blazer reactive armor to permit vastly extended service lives.[365] IDF M-60 tanks have undergone significant modernization status, including installing a more powerful engine, new armor and protection against 'top-down' missile attack, and modification of the turret ring to allow refitting of a 120 mm gun if necessary.[366]

The IAF relies increasingly upon indigenous modifications of US-supplied aircraft to maintain a technological edge over Arab airforces which often receive similar equipment.[367] IAI continues modernization programs for French (Magister, Ouragan, Mirage III/V, and Kfir), US (A-4, F-4, F-5, F-15, F-16, S-2 Tracker, and Boeing 707) and Soviet (MiG-21 and MiG-23) airframes. In addition to upgrades of combat aircraft, IAI modifies civilian airframes for use as tanker aircraft, electronic and signals intelligence (ELINT/SIGINT) duties, or maritime patrol.[368] The most recent major project is the IAI/Elta PHALCON – an AEW aircraft intended to supplement or replace E-2C Hawkeyes. PHALCON costs about half as much as an AWACS.[369] PHALCON was offered to China – but the sale was canceled at US request.[370] It now appears that India will acquire a PHALCON system, based on the Russian Il-76 airframe.[371] IAI continues to provide major modifications for the F-16 project, based on specific Israeli operational requirements.[372]

104 *Israel*

Major weapons platforms

Soltam has designed and produced very capable artillery designs for the IDF and for export, including the Rascal SP 155 mm system, designed for export,[373] and the Sholef 155 mm SP system. The Sholef is reportedly an outstanding design which has not been produced because of lack of available funds for IDF procurement.[374] In general, with the exception of the Merkava tank, Israel has ceased production and development of major weapons systems.

Strategic systems

The Jericho II was tested in the Mediterranean in May 1987.[375] While exact details of the range, accuracy, and capability of the Jericho are unclear, most analysis assumes that the missile is nuclear capable, and has a range of at least 900 miles.[376] The Jericho-II variant is considerably more sophisticated than the Jericho-I, with an estimated range of 1,500 km and a 1,000 kg payload, and entered service with the IDF in 1989. The test of a missile in South Africa, reportedly almost identical to the Jericho-II, demonstrated a range of 1,400 km. The Jericho-II, like the Jericho-I, can be launched from truck or rail-based transporter-erector launchers (TELs), and 90–100 are reportedly based in the cave complex at Zachariah south of Tel Aviv.[377]

A modified Jericho II with an added third stage may serve as the 'Shavit' booster for Israel's Ofeq series satellites.[378] Reports from Lawrence Livermore Laboratories state that this booster may have a range of up to 7,500 km if modified as a ballistic missile.[379] A Jericho-III may be in development, with three solid-fuel stages and a liquid-fueled fourth stage. This would have a range of 4,800 km, in addition to probable use as an improved satellite booster.[380] According to recent reports, the Jericho-I has been retired from IDF inventory.[381]

An additional potential strategic delivery system is a locally developed cruise missile, possibly a modification of an existing RPV or the Gabriel ShShM. Reports of cooperation with Iran in the 1970s on a weapon codenamed 'Flower' may refer to such a project.[382] Israel's request for 50 Tomahawk missiles from the US in 2000 was rejected, and recent reports on the Gabriel 4LR missile speculate on a version with a 1,400 km range, optimized for submarine launch.[383]

The 1973 War spurred new developments and increased production at Dimona. According to the testimony of Mordechai Vanunu, Israel secretly expanded the capacity of the Dimona reactor during the 1970s from the original 24 megawatts (as designed in the late 1950s) to 150 megawatts.[384] This theoretically allows the production of up to 40 kg of plutonium per year.[385] Vanunu's disclosures included photographic evidence that Israel was producing lithium-6, lithium deuteride, and tritium, all of which are useful for more advanced nuclear weapons, including boosted fission, thermonuclear, and enhanced radiation devices.[386] Analysis of Vanunu's testimony suggests that Israel's nuclear arsenal includes between 60 and 300 weapons of varying yields and sophistication.[387] Israel may have created battlefield nuclear devices, and potentially enhanced radiation warheads for tactical deployment.[388]

Israel is also believed capable of producing a wide variety of chemical warfare agents.[389] A 1990 statement by Science Minister Yuval Neeman indicated that Israel might retaliate 'with the same merchandise' if attacked by Iraqi chemical weapons.[390] In October 1992, an El Al 747 cargo jet crashed in Amsterdam, with ten tons of chemical precursors for nerve agent production on board. The resulting investigation suggested that Israel had been regularly moving chemical precursors by cargo jet.[391]

Finally, Israel vigorously pursued space-based reconnaissance capabilities, although these strained the state's financial resources.[392] Israel began pursuing this capability after the 1973 war. The Offeq satellites were a prelude to later models with expanded capabilities, and the Shavit booster reportedly could manage to put a satellite into an appropriate low-earth orbit for military surveillance missions.[393]

IAI spent considerable resources developing a commercial and military space capability. It forcefully advocated development of the AMOS satellite with some defense funding, over the strong opposition of the IDF.[394] The AMOS was designed to provide phone, telex, television, and communications for the entire country, as well as having additional transponders available for foreign customers.[395]

Managing security in an uncertain world: 1995–2005

The twin themes of technological sophistication and independence imbue Israel's military industrial policies.

> Our independence and security depend to a significant extent on our scientific and technological research. Technology is particularly important in the security sphere. If we fall behind the rest of the world in technological development, our security will be imperiled.[396]
>
> If there was a genocide in Biafra — irrespective of the political issues involved — it was because the Biafrans failed to secure the arms they needed, while the Nigerians received planes and guns from Russia and Egypt.[397]

The incremental development of Israel's arms industry has been viewed, with some justification, as a suitable model for all developing military-industrial programs.[398] Israeli military industry has also been used as a primary example of a so-called 'export-oriented' model of LDC defense industry.[399]

Israel's military industry developed and prospered, in large part, because of Israel's unique security problem. Survival under conditions of existential threat, with limited financial resources, required close cooperation and linkage between military, political, economic, and industrial policies. Israel demanded high standards and efficiency from the industrial infrastructure because of the competing demands of security and economic development. The lack of assured supplies of arms forced the Israeli arms industry to provide items unavailable to the IDF, and to upgrade and modify older weapons which were available.

Military policy also provided the motivation for the development of high-technology sectors, competitive with the most advanced products in the developed world.[400] Israel's security concept demanded the construction of a force which could achieve a rapid, decisive victory through pre-emptive action on enemy territory. This required expertise in Western-style maneuver warfare, and a force structure based around tanks and aircraft. Technology was deliberately used as a force multiplier, and the government promoted high standards of technical expertise within the population by use of the IDF as a national education and training pool.

Israeli military-industrial requirements

Israel's industry must be prepared to assist and improve the IDF's military capabilities in all strategic dimensions. The critical obligations of Israel's defense industry are:

1. To provide sustenance necessary for efficient operation of the IDF in combat, and to ensure industrial 'surge capability' in event of an extended conflict.
2. To maximize quality of existing IDF inventory at minimum practical expense to national economic development.
3. To develop and produce local systems which are unavailable elsewhere or tailored to distinct Israeli requirements.[401]

The first category of production consists of 'endurance requirements': these include small arms, light arms and crew-served infantry weapons, and ammunition. In addition, the local production of spare parts and critical logistic needs (tires, uniforms, basic military gear) is emphasized, in order to allow stockpiling in times of peace and surge production if necessary in times of war to replace lost equipment.

The second category revolves around modification and modernization capabilities. The IDF traditionally relied on older cast-off equipment. Modernization programs extend service life, and increase the capability of existing systems to match newer generations of equipment, which may or may not be available on the international market at higher cost. Israeli arms industries have become adept at the retrofitting of imported equipment with local products.

The third category refers to the provision of equipment unavailable as a result of embargo, political controversy, or international arms control agreements, such as ballistic missiles, or technology designed specifically to meet local military requirements which is unavailable elsewhere. The latter category includes the Gabriel ShShM and the use of RPVs instead of manned reconnaissance aircraft.

The link between producer and consumer is extremely strong in Israel, in stark contrast to most other national arms industries. The scientist or engineer who works for the Israeli defense industry also serves as a reservist in the IDF, and is therefore intimately acquainted with the requirements for new systems, and the conditions in which they will be used. This relationship permits the local industry to focus on developing weapons and capabilities which respond directly to IDF doctrine and requirements.[402]

The high standards of the IDF have forced Israeli industry to absorb critical technological capabilities and skills, with a positive impact on the national industrial base and economy. For Israeli manufacturers to ensure continued IDF orders, particularly during the development of the industrial base, maintenance of the highest possible standards, effectively paralleling those of the industrialized West, were required. These standards

Table 3.6 Local share of value in Israeli major weapons systems procurement

	1965–70	1971–75	1976–80	1981–85	1986–90	Total
Primarily indigenous production as percentage of overall procure-ment	6.3	27.3	36.0	48.4	44.3	34.2
Licensed Production as percentage of overall procure-ment			0.4	0.8	0.0	0.2
Indigenous production as percentage of imports	6.7	37.6	56.5	95.2	79.4	52.2
Licensed production as percentage of imports			0.6	1.5	0.0	0.4
Combined local production as percentage of imports	6.7	37.6	57.1	96.8	79.4	52.6
Combined local production as percentage of total procurement of major weapons systems	6.3	27.3	36.3	49.2	44.3	34.5

Source: SIPRI data found in Ian Anthony, "The 'third tier' countries: production of major weapons", in Wulf, *Arms Industry Limited*, 370–3, 382–3. See pp. 368–9 for methodology. I have combined some of the data and created additional columns in order to further illustrate the range of indigenous efforts.

108   *Israel*

have 'spun off' into the commercial industrial sector as well, with very positive effects on Israeli industrial exports.

As a result of high standards and expanding technological expertise, the Israeli defense industry has excelled in a number of extremely profitable, high-technology areas, the most important of which are missiles and electronics. In these niches, Israeli products compete effectively with international leaders. The combination of incentive and capability, together with the close cooperation between military and industrial sectors, ensures that sophisticated equipment which responds to specific IDF requirements can be developed very rapidly.

Military industry more than adequately fulfilled its primary missions through 1973. By the early 1980s, however, Israel had to respond to changed strategic circumstances. Egypt, formerly the greatest potential threat, had been neutralized over the short-term by the Camp David Accords. Arab armies made impressive strides in absorbing modern technologies into their armed forces: while the qualitative gap had not closed, it was certainly closing relatively faster than during the 1960s.[403] The primary potential theater of the conflict shifted to the Golan Heights, where constricting terrain and the fortified positions on the Syrian border made rapid and decisive Israeli success problematic at best.[404] Rapid and decisive victory appeared increasingly unattainable on the ground: war would instead be waged by attrition, in a manner most favorable to Arab objectives and strategy.[405]

More importantly, however, the primary military threat changed from conventional forces – where Israel could counter Arab quantitative superiority with better quality, training, and doctrine – to unconventional means less amenable to qualitative solutions. First Iraq, and later Syria, Iran, and Egypt, acquired significant numbers of ballistic missiles, primarily derived from the aging SCUD. These missiles provided distant adversaries with the means to inflict significant physical and psychological damage on the Israeli populace. Many of these states also acquired chemical weapons, and pursued other forms of WMD. The Gulf War, for the first time, involved an acceptance of foreign attack without retaliation, which some analysts fear inherently undermines Israel's carefully fostered policy of deterrence through punishment.[406]

The primary threat to Israeli sovereignty and security has gradually shifted, over two decades, from a conventional external threat to an unconventional one. The *intifada* suggested for the first time that the Palestinian population of Israel and the Occupied Territories could present a major security problem for Israel. The first *intifada* was resolved through the failure of Palestinian political leadership – Yasser Arafat's foolish support of Iraq during the Gulf War – and through the initiation of the Oslo peace process, which promised Palestinians some substantial homeland in the future. This future is now endangered by the failure of the Camp David talks and events since 2001. The more recent *Al Aqsa intifada*, marked by suicide bombings and public riots backed by armed insurgents, creates a vastly more difficult security threat for Israel than anything the Palestinians have managed since 1948.

Israel's operational and technological advantages over Arab conventional forces are not easily translated into rapid, decisive success against a determined local insurgency. Israel has demonstrated enormous efficiency in urban operations – particularly the capture of Jenin – and has also leveraged its technology and intelligence advantages through policies of selective assassination and efforts to bolster internal security, including the construction of a huge defensive wall.

In addition to fundamental changes in the regional security environment, Israel must also respond to a rapidly changing international arms market. Since the collapse of the Soviet Union, the international arms trade has become largely commercial in nature. Reduced global defense spending has forced consolidation of national arms industries, increased the emphasis on joint development and production to increase efficiency, and created a highly competitive export market for a relatively smaller number of defense contracts.

This poses significant concerns for Israel's defense industry. Exports now account for over 75 percent of Israeli defense industry sales – export sales which have risen from $2.1 billion in 1999 to an anticipated $3 billion or more in 2003. The defense industry therefore depends on export orders to maintain production lines and employment. Less than 25 percent of production is for the IDF, and this figure is unlikely to increase. Costs of the Israeli-Palestinian conflict run as high as $3 billion annually, and the defense budget is declining due to the continuing budget deficit.[407]

Reliance on exports also carries risks on the political front. The Israeli-Palestinian struggle has affected Israel's export efforts, and some potential buyers have reconsidered orders in light of the ongoing violence since 2001.[408] Continuing conflict with the Palestinians effectively excludes Israel from the lucrative Middle East arms trade. It also constrains defense relationships with European states, including even Turkey – a highly promising partner in the late 1990s.[409] Delays in joint projects with the UK, reportedly at the behest of the Foreign and Commonwealth Office, have held up deliveries of UAVs from both Elbit and IAI.[410] Israel may be engaging in some joint ventures, such as the R-Darter AAM co-produced by RAFAEL and South Africa's Kentron, in an effort to bypass political objections to Israeli-produced weapons.[411]

Israel has been able to find one consistent customer – India – that remains unaffected by political tensions in the Middle East. Israeli sales of the Barak SAM to the Indian navy have proven highly profitable.[412] India purchases UAVs from Israel, as well as the Green Pine radar system used with the Arrow-2 ATBM system.[413] India has also contracted for the PHALCON airborne radar on an Il-76 airframe, and is reportedly eyeing cooperation on a range of missile systems including, possibly, the

Arrow-2.[414] Despite strengthening ties between the two governments, India cannot be counted on for sufficient sales to maintain a $2–3 billion annual export rate. Sales to China, reportedly 20 percent of Israel's total exports and therefore a very significant partner, carry the political risk of alienating both India and, more importantly, the United States.[415]

Israeli defense industries still have considerable room for rationalization. Three different firms produce and export missiles – IAI, TAAS, and RAFAEL – and three other firms compete for UAV contracts (IAI's Malat and MBT, and Elbit's Silver Arrow).[416] The mergers that created Elbit group and Elisra group led, in the case of Elbit at least, to a consolidated firm with revenues comparable to TAAS and RAFAEL. Mergers and privatization efforts among the government-owned firms, however, were less successful, and efforts to consolidate core business functions among them has, so far, failed. As a result, Israeli firms are competing with each other for foreign orders, driving down profit margins and even losing out on contracts due to corporate infighting.

European firms remain reluctant to consider joint projects with Israel due to Israeli-Palestinian conflict. There are obvious incentives for partnership agreements with US firms. There are also, however, significant barriers. One is Israel's insistence on technology transfer and offset agreements – even though US law specifically prohibits Israel from demanding offsets.[417] Another is US export control legislation, and increasing US political pressure against Israeli exports to certain countries. US industry representatives point out that Israel effectively receives nearly $500 million a year in US OSP funding for R&D, making it difficult to determine the 'true owner' of the resulting technology.[418] Israel could be indirectly funneling US aid dollars to undesirable recipients, at least from a US perspective.[419]

US assistance, as mentioned above, is critical for the maintenance of both IDF force structure and Israel's defense industry. The use of OSP funds puts the US in the unusual position of providing economic assistance for Israel to use in developing industrial products and technologies which, in theory, could compete with US defense products. In practice, Israeli officials attempt to spend OSP on specific, high-priority items which will only be produced in limited numbers and not offered on the export market.[420] If Israel designs a local product and successfully sells it to or produces it in the US, it can then use US funding to procure similar items for the IDF. US production lines have now been established for the Arrow-2, the Python-4 AAM, and the Popeye air-to-surface missile, among other systems.[421]

This shift to joint production outside the country alarms Israel's defense industry. Because Israel receives such a large percentage of its military budget in US FMS grants, this aid has a disproportionate impact on Israel's defense spending patterns.[422] US FMS dollars constituted 19.2 percent of the expanded 2001 defense budget, and OSP represented an additional 5.9 percent.[423] OSP is used primarily to sustain Israeli high-technology research and development efforts. With declining defense budgets, Israel now spends shekels (the defense budget approved by the Knesset) on operations and maintenance and personnel costs, and uses FMS dollars to purchase weapons.[424] Since the IAF receives priority in procurement and R&D, and 52 percent of the IAF budget comes from FMS, this strongly limits the ability of domestic contractors like IAI to compete for IAF weapons contracts.[425]

The shekel crunch not only affects domestic orders, but also the attractiveness of Israeli weapons on the export market – few states are willing to order weapons that are not employed by the manufacturer, or otherwise proven in combat.[426] The shekel crunch limited the ability of IAI, for example, to upgrade Israel's older F-16 fighter aircraft – a project that might lead to billions in additional export work on European F-16s of similar vintage.[427] In the mid 1990s, Israel canceled continued procurement of the famous Galil rifle in favor of the US M-16 – because the M-16 could be bought with FMS funds.[428] The new Tavor 21 5.56 mm rifle, designed in response to the new requirements of urban warfighting, remains on hold, despite its superiority to the M-16, because of shortage of funds.[429]

In effect, Israel and the US are drawing into an unequal military-industrial partnership, which is an extension of the vague but definite US commitment to Israel's security and survival. Israeli firms continue to participate in high-technology ventures with US firms that will make important contributions to US security, including Israel's participation in the Joint Strike Fighter Project as a Level 3 partner.[430] But Israel's defense industry is increasingly becoming a junior partner to US firms, and decisions regarding Israel's force structure, R&D, and procurement are dominated by US military assistance and its limitations.[431]

The future: niche production or military-industrial and strategic dysfunction?

The decisions which determine the direction of Israel's arms industry, ultimately, will be made by politicians. Despite the growing influence of IDF leadership on military policy and procurement, industrial priorities are still determined by political leadership. A small group of individuals dominates not only Israeli security decisions, but also industrial decisions, and the tension between two competing approaches has steadily increased since the 1967 Six Day War.[432]

Israeli leaders have been forced to make choices regarding procurement which affect IDF short-term readiness and the long-term viability and expansion of the defense industry. Initially, the *konenut mul hitkonenut* (preparedness versus preparation) debate provided the primary framework for determining industrial and, indeed, procurement priorities, subject to financial restrictions. Economic limitations actually provided a powerful argument in support of industrial development, as local production could eventually substitute for imports. Industrialization would not have been possible without foreign capital, however. Almost all Israeli military-industrial capability evolved from the maintenance and repair base, which indicates the primacy of preparedness as a policy in the 1948–67 period.

There were exceptions to this generalization, however. The explanation for them lies in the realm of the individual. Israel, in 1948–60, was uniquely influenced by the decisions of David Ben Gurion. No other politician in Israeli history has had as great autonomy, or the ability to act in secrecy or indeed against the wishes of the majority of his political supporters. As Avner Cohen has noted, the Israeli nuclear program could *only* have evolved in its unique opaque fashion during the 1950s, when Ben Gurion was able to capitalize on unprecedented secrecy and centralization and on a unique window of opportunity with the French Fourth Republic.[433] Ben Gurion was ably assisted by Shimon Peres, whose bureaucratic and diplomatic skills shaped the future Israeli arms industry in the 1950s.

Since 1967, however, tangential, non-military issues play an increasing role in military-industrial and procurement policy. The shock of 1973 instigated a massive buildup of all services and an expansion of existing industries, including those developed in the 1967–73 period for production of major weapons platforms. The increasing flow of capital from the United States and the commitment of the Israeli government to increase military expenditures produced a brief but illusory period of unlimited resources. Projects which would have been scrutinized carefully in the money-tight 1960s were pursued and encouraged despite the availability of equivalent or superior weapons from abroad.[434]

Domestic political factors strongly affected this absence of oversight. Defense expenditures provided both Labor and Likud governments with the means of influencing national employment and prosperity, at least at the margins.[435] The importance of local production and defense exports on the economy and the electorate was enormous, given the historical role of the Labor Federation (*Histadrut*) in Israeli elections.[436] Both Labor and Likud needed to fund 'blue-and-white' programs in order to maintain and, in some cases, increase, employment.

Finally, defense industries provide an important sense of national self-sufficiency and prestige. Grandiose national projects which require a sense of national commitment and sacrifice have a unique appeal and prestige in both developing and developed states.[437] Military industrial independence became, in the minds of political leaders, a vital symbol of Israeli national achievement: 'Israel had to apply herself to scientific and industrial development if her effective stature was to exceed the country's territorial size. The establishment of an arms industry was her first confrontation with this need.'[438]

The notion of 'self-sufficiency,' by the late 1970s, had acquired a political meaning at odds with all previous Israeli policy. Rather than focusing on limiting dependence in crucial military technologies, Israeli policy moved towards maximizing independence in technologies which were readily available from the US. The enchantment with production of expensive, multi-purpose platforms reached heights of incredible economic frivolity in the design of the Lavi, which was in essence a very sophisticated F-16.

Israel's booming defense electronics industry provides the basis for upgrades of major platforms of all types both within Israel and abroad, and maintains a competitive edge over most other producers in critical niches such as electronic warfare, avionics, and UAVs. Israel's recent launch of the Ofek series of satellites, with military intelligence gathering capabilities, provides yet another example of Israel producing sophisticated technologies to provide capabilities unavailable elsewhere.[439] The new Tactical High Energy Laser program, which includes Tadiran, IAI,

Table 3.7 US ACDA estimates of Israeli Arms Exports, 1963–91

Arms exports, Israel: 1963–1991 Year	Exports (millions of current $US)
1963	2.0
1964	1.0
1965	1.0
1966	0
1967	1.0
1968	9.0
1969	3.0
1970	5.0
1971	0
1972	10.0
1973	20.0
1974	30.0
1975	50.0
1976	140.0
1977	60.0
1978	120.0
1979	260.0
1980	140.0
1981	370.0
1982	430.0
1983	210.0
1984	575.0
1985	725.0
1986	700.0
1987	725.0
1988	460.0
1989	925.0
1990	440.0
1991	380.0

Source: ACDA, *World Military Expenditures and Arms Transfers*, various years

RAFAEL, and the US firm TRW, is aimed at a high-technology solution to the use of Katyusha type rockets by Hezbollah and other terrorist groups - a problem virtually unique to Israel.[440] Niches of excellence, therefore, remain – but the dilemma of globalization, the distorting impact of American military assistance, and the dependence on exports to retain industrial infrastructure guarantee that Israel will face difficult choices in the future.

Israel's military industry, until recently, enjoyed virtually unprecedented authority and prioritization within the domestic economy. However, after over 50 years of service, it finds itself less relevant to IDF requirements, trapped in an unstable reliance on international exports to maintain its infrastructure and capabilities, and exerting an unhealthy and possibly dysfunctional effect on the Israeli national economy. If there is a universal message to be found in Israel's military-industrial development, it lies in the fundamental limitations of LDC capabilities vis-à-vis the primary industrial producers in the international system, and the success with which a small producer can respond to specific military capabilities required within a regional military competition. 'Though it is fair to suggest that much may be learned from Israel's experience, certain aspects would not suit other countries, for no two countries have exactly the same problems. Israel's system should be adapted, but it should not be copied.'[441]

4 Iraq

Background

The development of Iraq's arms industry provides a disturbing example of the hidden industrial potential of a determined regional power. Iraq's arms industry does not fit neatly into the models of military industrialization discussed in Chapter 1: it focused neither on exports nor on incremental development of broad industrial capabilities, but instead followed a selective, pragmatic policy geared towards specific requirements. Projects selected focused on:

1. Weapons and technologies capable of being produced with existing or projected Iraqi industrial and technical infrastructure;
2. Technologies deemed desirable for long-term Iraqi military-industrial objectives; or
3. Systems not available on the international market but required for specific military or political objectives.

Iraq's military industry, as a result, repeatedly surprised Western military analysts in the late 1980s by producing or modifying weapons of considerable sophistication, particularly weapons of mass destruction (WMD).[1] The repressive and centralized nature of the Iraqi regime undoubtedly simplified military-industrial efforts: the absence of domestic opposition allowed Saddam to devote an enormous proportion of Iraq's industrial and technical resources for military ends. From 1975–90, Iraq designed and built an enormous military-industrial infrastructure that eventually employed as many as 100,000 people. Both overt and covert means were used to acquire sophisticated industrial technologies and techniques from the industrialized states, particularly those which would permit the construction of unconventional weapons. Iraq's military industries produced a wide range of goods, from basic munitions to ballistic missiles, and eventually subordinated the country's entire industrial development policy under the authority of the Ministry of Industry and Military Industrialization (MIMI).

Iraq also represents a disturbing precedent as one of the few regional powers willing to resort to the use of unconventional weaponry against both external foes and domestic opponents of the regime. Iraq's chemical weapons industry, acquired with remarkable ease and little expense from a bevy of willing Western suppliers, provided the means to save the Ba'ath regime in the 1980s. Iraq's unexpected nuclear weapons capability demonstrated the frailty of existing non-proliferation policy and safeguards. In general, the Iraqi example demonstrates the inadequacy of existing models of LDC military industrialization.

Despite the large and impressive quantities of high-technology equipment Iraq amassed during the 1970s and 1980s, the Iraqi military remained a relatively unsophisticated fighting force.[2] The Iraqi military has traditionally relied on firepower. This reflects, in part, the relative simplicity and effectiveness of modern artillery:

> Artillery is the most lethal branch of the ground forces, and has inflicted the majority of all casualties in most wars since 1914 ... for high-intensity conflict, the relative importance of artillery, as compared to infantry and armor, has greatly increased since 1945.[3]

The Iraqi armed forces therefore emphasized endurance: maintenance of adequate supplies of small arms, mortars, artillery, and ammunition was critical for Iraqi military operations. Iraq placed special emphasis on artillery in the Iran–Iraq War, where it was the primary killer of Iranian troops.[4] Western military analysts have noted that Iraq employs artillery poorly, and the general preference appears to be for massive barrages.[5] Massed artillery provided lethality at minimal cost, requiring fewer technical skills and training than maneuver warfare, and risking fewer casualties than infantry operations. It also could be applied to both internal and external threats. It is not surprising that Iraq focused on endurance as a critical military-industrial requirement.

Embargoes, financial restrictions, and military events played critical roles in the evolution of Iraqi military industry, but Iraq's policy did not focus on major weapons platforms. As a result, analysts of LDC arms industries almost completely missed the growth of the Iraqi arms industry and its military and political significance. Because that industrial development was prematurely halted, analysis of Iraq's arms industry will focus on the 1974–84 and 1984–90 periods, followed by a brief discussion of what might have been – the trends and directions of Iraqi programs in 1990, and some conjecture about what Iraqi programs might have looked like if the first Gulf War had not occurred. The strategic weapons programs, of greatest interest to the average reader and the international community, will be broken out separately.

Iraq's security perception

Iraq's security policy focuses on many of the same types of threats as Israel and India – it must cope with hostile neighbors and regional adversaries, internal unrest and secessionist movements, and extra-regional threats. Unlike India and Israel, however, where civil-military relations reflect Western traditions of civilian rule and military professionalism, a primary concern for Iraq is regime survival in the face of competing political factions – which often included the military.

As in many other LDCs, the Iraqi military has a long history of political interference.[6] The consolidation of political power in the hands of the Ba'athist regime since 1968 limited, but did not eliminate, the role of the military in Iraqi politics. The Ba'athist regime maintained close control over military appointments and decision-making, and relied on parallel military organizations to ensure a loyal armed force in the event of a coup. Despite the Ba'athists efforts to control the military, at least two military coups were attempted in the 1970s, and many others in the 1980s and 1990s.[7] Regime survival was often the primary focus of Iraqi national security policy.[8]

The Ba'ath Party's firm control over the military severely limited the role of the armed forces in military-industrial and security policy. One indication of the lack of military input in the security process is an examination of key decision-makers in Iraqi military-industrial policy. The three most important figures in Iraqi military-industrial policy in the early 1980s were Saddam Hussein, Dr. Amer Hammoudi al-Saadi, and Dr. Amer Rashid al-Ubeidi, all of whom received honorary promotions to Lt. General. Two other key figures in Iraqi security policy were cousins of Saddam Hussein: brother-in-law Adnan Khairallah, who was Minister of Defense before dying in a helicopter crash in May 1989, and son-in-law Hussain Kamil, who became the second-most powerful man in Iraq in the late 1980s, before defecting in 1995. On his inexplicable return to Iraq in 1996, Kamil was murdered by family members.

It should surprise no one that the development of the Iraqi arms industry coincided neatly with Saddam Hussein's consolidation of power, nor that its efforts were tailored to his grandiose regional ambitions.[9] These ambitions, however, were consistent with previous Iraqi regimes. Historically, Iraq seeks influence throughout the Islamic world, competing with Iran in the Gulf and with Egypt, Syria, and especially Israel in the Middle East.

Internal security concerns

The defense requirements of Iraq, like those of many other developing countries, are driven by a melange of ethnic, geographic, economic, and ideological considerations. The formation of Iraq out of portions of the Ottoman *velayets* (administrative districts) of Mosul, Baghdad, and Basra after World War I left the state with disputed borders and internal ethnic and religious tensions.

The first, and primary, concern of the Iraqi military has been to maintain and extend the central authority of Baghdad over the peripheral areas and their ethnic and religious minorities, as well as maintaining domestic security.[10] Iraqi administration, regardless of regime, has been dominated by the largely Sunni Muslim region of Baghdad, and faced potential separatist movements in the Kurdish northern province of Mosul and the predominantly Shi'ite Muslim province of Basra.[11] Every Iraqi regime has used authoritarian measures to enforce obedience to the central government. The emerging post-Saddam Iraqi regime may face a different problem, seeking to enforce authority in the center (with US and allied assistance) *against* the traditional Sunni elite.

Central control was threatened by separatist movements in the two peripheral regions, and further complicated by economic issues: while Baghdad is the dominant political center, Mosul and Basra provinces provide 60 percent and 30 percent of oil production respectively.[12] Iraq's geography provided some support for these separatist movements: the northern highlands (bordering Turkey and Iran) provide shelter for Kurdish insurgents, while the marshes and swamps of 'riverine' Iraq provide havens for rebels in the south.[13]

In the course of the Iran–Iraq rivalry, both sides attempted to exploit each others' ethnic difficulties. The Iraqis supported Baluchi rebel movements in both Pakistan and Iran.[14] On both sides of the Iraq–Iran border, the Kurdish population provided the base for a strong separatist movement. Uprisings broke out in the Kurdish region of Iraq in the 1920s, 1930s, 1940s, almost continuously in the period 1961–70, 1974–75, throughout the Iran–Iraq War, and again in the aftermath of the Gulf War.[15]

Kurdish rebels numbered only a few hundred in 1921, but by the early 1960s between 15,000 and 20,000 *peshmergas* (loosely organized Kurdish insurgents) rose against Iraq under the leadership of Mustafa al-Barzani.[16] Military requirements in the northern region escalated throughout Iraq's history. In the 1930s and 1940s, only one or two brigades of Iraqi troops were required to maintain order (or suppress rebellion). By 1963, this had risen to eight brigades, in 1969 four divisions, and by 1974 six divisions – over half the Iraqi Army – were used in government assaults on the Kurds.[17]

Substantial Kurdish minorities live in Iraq, Turkey, and Iran, with a smaller population in Syria. Kurdish rebels find sympathy, sanctuary, and support not only from Kurdish populations, but occasionally from neighboring governments.[18] Iran's willingness to provide arms and support for Kurdish rebels threatened Iraqi authority in the north. Iranian troops fought alongside the Kurds in 1969–70, and supplied Kurdish troops with artillery and anti-tank guided missiles in 1974–75.[19]

During the Iran–Iraq War, both sides attempted to use Kurdish rebel groups against the other, and in the aftermath of that conflict chemical weapons were used by Iraq in an effort to end Kurdish resistance once and for all.[20] As the Iraqi Army was destroyed in Operation Desert Storm, Kurdish rebels rose again in the north in March 1990, claiming at one point to have liberated 95 percent of 'Kurdistan'.[21] In the mid-1990s, nearly two-thirds of the Iraqi army was stationed in the north, including five of Iraq's best divisions.[22] In Operation Iraqi Freedom, Kurdish *peshmergas* combined with Coalition special forces units and the US 173rd Airborne Brigade to liberate much of northern Iraq.[23]

The threat of the Shi'ite population in the south is comparatively more recent. Although the marshes in the Basra region have always been a haven for criminals and army deserters, the southern region did not become a threat to Iraq until after the Iranian revolution, when it became a stronghold of the Shi'ite Da'wa movement.[24] After 1980, and particularly after the first Gulf War, Iraq viewed the Shi'ite population in the south as a potentially pro-Iranian force – some analysts argue that Iranian support for Shi'ite rebel forces was a critical *casus belli* in the Iran–Iraq War.[25] An abortive rising after the Gulf War was harshly suppressed by Republican Guard and regular military units, and the government drained much of the marshland in an effort to deny shelter to rebels.[26]

Regional interests and threats

Iraq's most secure border is to the northwest. Turkey ceded the province of Mosul to Iraq with some reluctance in the 1920s.[27] It made no serious efforts to redefine the border after that point, although the issue has occasionally emerged as a concern. In addition, Turkey and Iraq have similar problems with Kurdish separatists: neither state is interested in enlarging an already troublesome ethnic problem.

Iraq has been called 'the eastern flank of the Arab world': it marks for all practical purposes the meeting place of Arab and Persian cultures.[28] Ba'athist ideology calls for pan-Arab unity: the single most crucial element of this ideology is the requirement for an 'Arab solution' to the problem of Palestine.[29] Arab unity was used by Iraq to appeal for support in the Iran–Iraq War, and to appeal to the Arab masses during the Gulf conflict. Although Iraq remained engaged in both regions, the focus of Iraqi priorities shifted from the Middle East to the Gulf after the overthrow of the monarchy, despite the growing influence of Ba'athist ideology.[30]

Iraq has the potential to dominate the Persian Gulf, or at least its Arab (southern) coastline. Iran, which dominates the northern/eastern shore of the Gulf and shares a long land border with Iraq, has vastly greater population and economic resources than Iraq (see Table 4.1). Basra and Baghdad, Iraq's most important cities, lie close to the border with Iran, so strategic depth against Iranian attack is limited. Although Iran and Iraq were members of the 'northern tier' states which signed the Baghdad Pact in 1954.[31] Iranian policy since the 1960s has focused on dominating the

Table 4.1 Middle East and Persian Gulf security systems – 1990

Country	Population (in millions, 1990)	GDP (1990, $US billions)	Area (thousands of km²)
Core System			
Egypt	54.7	38.3	1,001.5
Syria	12.4	18.5	185.1
Jordan	3.1	(a) 5.2	91.5
Israel	(b) 4.4	(a) 38.0	21.0
Lebanon	3.3	2.3	10.4
Persian Gulf Subsystem			
Iran	55.6	(a) 97.6	1,648.0
Iraq	18.7	(a) 35.0	434.9
Saudi Arabia	(c) 17.1	73.0	2,149.7
Oman	(c) 1.4	7.8	212.0
Kuwait	(c) 2.1	20.5	17.8
United Arab Emirates	(c) 2.2	(a) 23.3	83.6
Other Regional			
Turkey	56.7	44.9	780.6

Source: *CIA World Factbook, 1990* (Washington, DC: 1990)

Notes
a GNP figures used instead of GDP.
b Includes Palestinian population.
c Includes expatriate and resident worker population.

Gulf region and limiting Iraqi influence. These goals have been pursued through a number of means, including massive arms purchases and encouragement of internal instability in Iraq.

The liberation of 'Arabistan' (Khuzestan) has been a consistent part of Iraqi pan-Arabist rhetoric.[32] Iraq used pan-Arab ideology as a rationale for settling nationalist and regional issues with Iran in 1980.[33] The invasion of 'Arabistan,' intended to be a rapid and decisive campaign, was astonishingly unsuccessful, and dragged Iraq and Iran into an eight-year war of attrition which drove both states to near-bankruptcy.[34]

Although the Iran–Iraq War ended in 1988, no normalization of relations or lasting peace followed. After the absorption of Kuwait Iraq surprised the rest of the world by proposing that Iran and Iraq exchange prisoners of war, accept the 1975 Algiers Agreement as the status quo, and retreat from occupied territories.[35] During the Gulf War itself, Iraq used Iran as a sanctuary for both civilian and military aircraft, apparently anticipating either use of Iranian airfields for military operations or return of the aircraft after the conflict.[36]

Iraq's strategic interest in the Gulf region increased with the expansion of oil production in the 1960s and the dramatic rise in oil prices after 1973.[37] Growing Iranian military capabilities coupled with apparent hegemonic ambitions played a critical role in refocusing Iraqi strategic

Table 4.2 Iraqi military expenditures, 1948–67

Year	Defense expenditure (millions of current dinars) (a)	Defense expenditures (millions of constant $1960) (b)	Defense expenditures as percentage of Gross Domestic Product (c)
1948	6.0	13.5	
1949	6.6	18.8	
1950	7.0	21.8	
1951	7.7	22.5	
1952	11.8	31.9	4.4
1953	15.2	47.1	5.6
1954	16.7	53.1	4.7
1955	17.2	53.2	4.1
1956	25.8	75.1	5.7
1957	29.7	82.4	6.5
1958	31.0	88.5	6.0
1959	35.8	103.1	6.7
1960	42.4	118.7	7.1
1961	44.8	123.5	6.9
1962	48.2	132.2	6.9
1963	58.3	153.6	8.3
1964	66.1	181.2	7.9
1965	80.6	223.1	8.8
1966	83.9	232.0	8.5
1967	83.8	210.8	8.4

Sources:
a *SIPRI Yearbook 1968/69*, p. 204; *SIPRI Yearbook 1974*, p. 214.
b *SIPRI Yearbook 1968/69*, p. 206.
c *SIPRI Yearbook 1973*, p. 241.

priorities from the Middle East to its eastern and southern borders.[38] In the early 1970s, Iraq provided support for pro-Ba'ath political groups in the monarchies of the southern Gulf.[39] The policy of 'moderation' in the mid-1970s, which was so successful at propelling Iraq to a position of Arab leadership, included an acceptance of the Arab Gulf regimes and an end to support for subversion in the region.

The Iran–Iraq War forced Iraq to rely on the Gulf states for financial support. Iran was able to deny Iraq access to the Gulf as an oil shipping route, and the closure of the pipeline through Syria in April 1982 further crippled the Iraqi economy.[40] Iraqi policy for the rest of the decade concentrated on access to the Gulf itself, either by arranging more favorable terms of Iraqi passage through the Shatt al-Arab (a cause of the Iran–Iraq War),[41] or by expanding its coastline adjacent to the Gulf through lease or conquest from Kuwait.[42]

Iraq's claim to Kuwait, in particular, has been a fixture of Iraqi policy. In the late 1930s, Iraq's King Ghazi demanded that Kuwait be absorbed into Iraq, a claim which lay dormant for some 20 years.[43] After Kuwait declared its independence in June 1961, then-President Qasim immediately proclaimed that Kuwait belonged to Iraq and threatened invasion. The Kuwaitis received prompt military support from Britain, and a multinational Arab force was deployed in the autumn after Kuwait was accepted into the Arab League.[44] In October 1963, after Qasim was overthrown by the military, Kuwait's independence was formally recognized by Iraq. After the 1968 Revolution, Iraqi troops occupied a strip of territory on the border for almost a decade, with Kuwaiti requests for their withdrawal met by an Iraqi demand for a lease on the Warbah and Bubiyan Islands.[45] The Gulf War resulted, at least in part, from Iraq's continuing resentment of Kuwaiti independence and desire for Kuwaiti territory.

Iraq also desires a position of leadership and influence within the Arab community and the Middle East. Iraq consistently sought to acquire or produce weapons that allowed it to strike Israel from Iraq. Israel maintains a corresponding awareness of growing Iraqi military capabilities, in both the conventional arena (particularly after the Iran–Iraq War) and in the development of weapons of mass destruction.[46] The raid on the Osirak nuclear reactor in 1981 effectively set back Iraqi nuclear weapons development by at least a decade. Saddam's famous statement of April 1, 1990, when he threatened to 'make fire eat up half of Israel' was widely interpreted as a threat to use chemical weapons.[47]

In the ideological sphere, Iraq offered a direct alternative to Egyptian leadership, particularly on the Palestine issue, and competed with Syria for leadership of the radical Arab factions.[48] In March 1968, the Ninth National Ba'athist Conference resolved that '... the Palestinian movement was the crucible of the Arab revolution and that the party must therefore exert all its energies in support of the movement.'[49] The ideological struggle with Egypt for leadership of the Arab world appeared to have ended in Iraqi triumph in November 1978.[50] The need for Egyptian support during the Iran–Iraq War, however, resulted in Iraq leading the effort to reincorporate Egypt back into the Arab world.[51]

The Ba'ath movement, originally centered in Damascus, split in 1966 due at least in part to regional differences – Syrian Ba'athism focused on the West, while Iraqi Ba'athism looked south and east.[52] Relations with Syria soured after the Baghdad Summit Conference,[53] and were further complicated by the signing of the Friendship Pact between the USSR and Syria in 1980.[54] Syrian support for Iran during the Iran–Iraq War not only broke the facade of Arab unity behind the Iraqi war effort, but also crippled the Iraqi economy.

Extra-regional objectives

Iraq's desire to lead the Arab nation manifested itself in what appeared before 1988 to be a set of grandiose objectives: according to Saddam

Hussein, 'We want our country to achieve its proper weight based on our estimation that Iraq is as great as China, as great as the Soviet Union, and as great as the United States.'[55] The abrupt collapse of Iranian morale and military capability in 1988 suddenly left Iraq, now dominant in the region, in a position to pursue some of those objectives.

In 1990, Saddam felt sufficiently confident of Iraqi power to threaten Israel with chemical attack, argue in front of the Arab Cooperation Council that Iraq was a natural defender for the Gulf region, and declare that the US could be deterred from intervening in the region by the possibility of taking substantial casualties.[56] As events later proved, Iraq could not impose its hegemony on the Gulf by force, and was unable to expand its influence through military action.

Iraq's military-industrial base

Iraq had the most educated workforce in the Arab world in 1990.[57] The literacy rate in Iraq is unusually high for an Arab state.[58] The initial establishment of a military-related scientific and technical infrastructure was assisted by a Palestinian consulting group called Arab Projects and Development, which hired as many as 4,000 scientists and researchers to work in Iraq during the period 1974–76, and designed a higher education system for the training of the future Iraqi elite. This higher education system helped the number of Iraqi students in technical fields to increase by 300 percent over the next decade to a total of 120,000.[59]

Although few reliable numbers are available on Iraq's industrial workforce, according to official figures there were approximately 170,000 industrial workers in 1984.[60] By 1990, estimates on the number of workers in Iraqi *military* industry alone ranged as high as 100,000.[61] Even if most of these 100,000 jobs were created during the 'boom years' of 1984–89, close to 40 percent of the Iraqi industrial labor force was working in military industry. Of these, 20,000 worked in the nuclear program.[62] In the words of one regional expert, '[W]hat we've found is that Iraq now has the largest technical and scientific base in the Middle East. I'd say Israel's is qualitatively better, but in terms of numbers, Iraq is the largest.'[63]

For approximately a decade, the two most important government bodies with authority in the development of military industry were the Military Industrialization Authority (MIA) and the State Organization for Technical Industries (SOTI).[64] The former body supervised the early ordnance factories and turnkey production sites, while the latter worked on advanced technological and weapons projects under the Ministry of Industry.[65] Other military-industry related developments were supervised by the Ministry of Defense through the Armed Forces Workshops, which began modifying armored vehicles in the second half of the Iran–Iraq War.[66] All these efforts were eventually combined under the leadership of Hussein

Kamil and the Ministry of Industry and Military Industrialization (MIMI) in the late 1980s.

The range of authority of Hussein Kamil indicates the bureaucratic primacy and overall importance of the Iraqi military-industrial program. By August 1990, MIMI was the only office that could finance projects independently of the Office of the President (Saddam Hussein).[67] MIMI used all the resources at its disposal to continue procuring restricted technology until the start of the Gulf War, and its resources were formidable: 'Baghdad uses aggressive covert techniques to acquire technology. The nuclear network – controlled by MIMI – uses Iraqi public sector enterprises, front companies, foreign agents, and even civilian organizations to procure technology.'[68]

MIMI was able to draw on both civilian and military-industrial resources, and had access to both legitimate and covert means of obtaining industrial technology. Kamil's new function included integrating all military and civilian industrial projects: this allowed unique opportunities for gaining access to Western technology.[69] According to a July 1990 CIA report, MIMI supervised 25–30 establishments producing primarily military supplies, spares, and weapons.[70] MIMI also controlled about 40 civilian ventures, including the Badush Dam, Petro-Chemical Complex Two (PC-2), various fertilizer factories, and truck assembly plants.[71] Military and civilian procurement were closely linked: 'Their [MIMI] facilities work closely with civilian agencies to procure equipment and technology.'[72] This included efforts to integrate specialty metals projects and civilian vehicle assembly lines to bolster tank, missile, and armored personnel carrier (APC) production – an unusual and ambitious dual-use production effort.[73] By 1990, it had become apparent that Iraq's industrial acquisition program was explicitly tailored towards military ends: 'many entities are false end-users, passing the materials acquired from foreign suppliers directly to enterprises involved in military projects, including chemical and biological warfare'[74]

According to Western intelligence sources, Baghdad had significant advantages in making this grandiose, but still substantial expansion of its defense industries a realistic goal, including cheap hydrocarbons, a positive long-term economic outlook, a large military establishment able to absorb high levels of production, an educated workforce, and a potential supply of customers on the export market for certain goods.[75] In just a decade, while fighting a major regional conflict, Iraq had created a significant and, in some fields, technologically-sophisticated military-industrial base. This development will be discussed in two stages: the formative period of 1974–84, and the maturation stage of 1984–90.

Embargo, diversification, and war: 1974–84

Iraq began acquiring large quantities of Soviet arms after the 1958 Revolution, when the new regime withdrew from the Baghdad Pact. Over the course of the next 15 years, Baghdad became dependent on Soviet supplies of arms, spares, and munitions.[76] This growing dependence on Soviet arms disrupted Iraqi foreign and domestic policies. In 1968, the Soviets used aid to the Kurds as a bargaining chip for economic concessions from Iraq, and threatened to impose an arms embargo on Iraq if the government did not negotiate with the Kurds.[77] Although the Soviets supplied relatively modern and sophisticated weaponry to Iraq, they imposed careful restrictions on maintenance and training. Soviet technicians were the only personnel allowed to maintain and repair the most modern equipment during the 1960s and 1970s.[78]

When the Ba'athist regime renewed armed conflict with the Kurds in 1974, the Soviets imposed an arms embargo.[79] The effects of this embargo, combined with Iranian assistance to the Kurds, were extremely serious: By March 1975, '... [T]he situation became extremely dangerous when our material and essential munitions cruelly began to run out. We had almost no more heavy artillery shells. Our air force had only three bombs left.'[80]

Once Iraq showed proper deference, the Soviets immediately moved to reestablish their arms connection.[81] The experience of embargo encouraged Iraqi efforts to pursue both diversification of suppliers and indigenous production of some types of arms.[82] Iraqi arms production, particularly of munitions, began on a limited scale in 1974–75.[83] The first 'turn-key' powder and propellant factories were delivered by the Soviets in 1976–78.[84] Iraq actively sought to decrease its dependency on the Soviet Union, turning to France as a supplier of arms in a major diversification

Table 4.3 Iraqi military expenditures and arms imports, 1963–73

Year	Defense expenditures (millions of current $US)	Defense expenditures (millions of constant $1972)	Defense expenditures as percentage of Gross National Product	Arms imports (millions of current $US)	Arms imports (millions of constant $1972)
1963	171.99	217.59	10.22	107.0	145.9
1964	238.10	295.71	12.49	28.0	37.6
1965	237.75	304.16	11.36	44.0	58.0
1966	235.23	295.21	10.46	35.0	44.9
1967	235.23	279.03	10.25	90.0	111.8
1968	310.84	382.38	12.34	133.0	158.9
1969	397.65	476.97	14.76	69.0	78.6
1970	403.25	452.54	13.60	45.0	48.6
1971	491.43	489.50	13.44	35.0	36.2
1972	474.31	474.31	12.77	85.0	85.0
1973	558.14	NA	NA	306.0	289.8

Source: ACDA, *World Military Expenditures and Arms Trade, 1963–1973*

effort. By 1979, Soviet supplies of arms to Iraq had dropped from 95 percent to 63 percent of total value of arms imports.[85]

Iraq also became a major contributor to the Arab Industrialization Organization in the mid-1970s, attempting to use Gulf oil wealth and existing Egyptian military-industrial infrastructure to create a pan-Arab arms industry.[86] Iraqi delegates declared at a UN Conference on Science and Technology in Vienna in 1979 that an objective for the year 2000 was '[T]he development of the armament industry in order to achieve self-reliance and national security for both Iraq and the Arab world.'[87]

From 1979–83, SOTI established a network for technology acquisition based on the existing Iraqi intelligence apparatus.[88] The support of Iraqi intelligence for covert technology procurement efforts represented a critical enabling factor in Iraqi military-industrial policy. In 1980, Amer Rashid al-Ubeidi joined Amer Hammoudi al-Saadi at SOTI, and took charge of engineering projects and licensed production ventures with France.[89] SOTI supervised the Saad General Establishments, which built factories for military purposes.[90] The State Establishment for Pesticide Production (SEPP) was created in 1980 as a front for chemical weapons production, and acted as the contracting agency for the Samarra CW facility.[91] The NASSR State Establishment for Mechanical Industries became the primary purchasing agent for missile technology and other military-industrial equipment.[92]

Table 4.4 Iraqi military expenditures and arms imports, 1972–82

Year	Defense expenditures (millions of current $US)	Defense expenditures (millions of constant $1981)	Defense expenditures as percentage of Gross National Product	Arms imports (millions of current $US)	Arms imports (millions of constant $1981)
1972	734E	1,428E	14.9	140	272
1973	1,491E	2,746E	25.5	625	1,150
1974	2,461E	4,168E	21.6	625	1,058
1975	2,398E	3,723E	16.9	675	1,048
1976	2,892E	4,249E	17.2	1,000	1,469
1977	3,633E	5,041E	18.7	1,500	2,081
1978	4,020E	5,194E	17.0	1,600	2,067
1979	5,147E	6,130E	14.9	2,300	2,739
1980	8,658E	9,466E	21.7	1,600	1,749
1981	11,864E	11,864E	48.2	3,700	3,700
1982	11,689E	11,026E	46.4	4,300	4,056

Source: ACDA, *World Military Expenditures and Arms Transfers, 1972–1982*

Note
E = Estimate

By the mid-1980s, Iraq's declaratory intentions for the arms industry closely mirrored the classic rationale for LDC arms industrialization: use of the defense industry as a leading edge for advanced civilian industries and training; activation of associated industries such as chemicals and metals; absorption/utilization of surplus labor; lower dependence and foreign exchange expenditure; acquire research and development skills and spinoffs for the civilian sector; minimize dependency and vulnerability to external actors; and reduce defense costs through local economies of scale and exports.[93] Iraq placed special emphasis on security and secrecy of locally-developed defense items.[94]

In September 1980, Iraq invaded Iran. The immediate reaction of the Soviet Union was to declare neutrality, and to impose an arms embargo on both countries. According to then-Inspector General of Iraqi Armed Forces General Mahmoud Tarek Shoukri, this embargo did not have as severe an effect as the 1974–75 embargo on Iraqi military capabilities: 'Iraq had large stocks of spare parts and Soviet-calibre munitions, and what we didn't have on hand we were able to purchase elsewhere from Egypt and other Arab countries.'[95]

The second Soviet embargo also spurred diversification efforts, as Iraq purchased arms from Brazil, China, Czechoslovakia, East Germany, Egypt, France, West Germany, the United Kingdom, Hungary, Italy, Jordan, Libya, Poland, Romania, Spain, and Switzerland during the 1980–82 period.[96] The availability of Soviet-model equipment and spares from China, Egypt, and the Warsaw Pact states partially compensated for the military effects of the Soviet embargo. Iraq also purchased systems abroad which were designed to Iraqi specifications. The most prominent of these was the EE-T4 Ogum armored gun system, which was produced in Brazil for Iraqi requirements. Iraq also imported the EE-3 and EE-9 armored/scout vehicles and the EE-11 wheeled armored personnel carrier from Brazil.[97]

Several years of war with Iran created significant financial instability. Although Baghdad had $35 billion in foreign currency reserves when the war began, these were exhausted by 1983.[98] Oil production plummeted from approximately 3.48 million barrels per day in 1979 (the last pre-war year) to 0.92 million barrels per day in 1983, and oil exports were Iraq's primary foreign exchange earner.[99] Iraq's military budget, however, remained at extremely high levels due to the Iran-Iraq conflict.

Selected indigenous arms programs: 1974–84

'Endurance' requirements

Iraq's turn-key munitions plants and rudimentary arms production efforts in this period received relatively low priority and little positive press. According to a report on the arms exhibition at Cairo in 1984

[M]uch was made of Iraq's appearance but the Iraqi booths were dominated by giant pictures of Saddam Hussein and Hosni Mubarak, which dwarfed a few artillery shells, land mines, and ammunition on display. Another Iraqi booth contained only automobile tires. The Iraqi defense industry clearly has a long way to go.[100]

Iraq's poor showing at the Cairo Exhibition in 1984 provided considerable incentive to increase indigenous efforts.[101] It appears, judging by the expansion of production in the late 1980s, that munitions production was given increased priority after the initial stalemate in the Iran–Iraq War.

During the course of the Iran–Iraq War, Iraqi engineers took increasing responsibility for maintenance and repair of various armored systems.[102] Armored production, assembly, and maintenance sites for the Iraqi armed forces have been identified at Al Ameen/Yusufiyah, Base West World, Huteen, Taji, and Samawa.[103] It is reported that during the early years of the Iran–Iraq War, Iraqi troops would abandon Chinese tanks that broke down, because they were cheaper to replace than to repair.[104]

Maintenance of the more complex and higher-technology IQAF depended heavily on foreign advisors. When the Soviets imposed their embargo on Iraq in 1980, they withdrew the technicians who serviced IQAF MiG-23s, and took the maintenance manuals with them. This severely degraded the capabilities of the IQAFs best combat aircraft.[105] Shortly after Iraq negotiated the contract with Dassault-Mirage to purchase Mirage F-1 aircraft, it began negotiations to provide depot-level maintenance and engine overhaul in Iraq, but these services were not in place during the Iran–Iraq War.[106]

Non-platform weapons

In August 1980, Iraq established the SAAD-13 project near Mosul. This plant was built by Thomson-CSF of France to produce military electronics.[107] The entire output of the factory was intended for military purposes, and by 1984 the plant was assembling man-pack radios and other sophisticated products.[108] In 1984, 250 of the total workforce of 3,000 were French 'advisors.'[109]

Major weapons platforms

Iraq expressed interest in local manufacture of aircraft as early as 1979, when it opened bidding on a contract for local production under license of advanced trainer aircraft.[110] Iraqi interest in local manufacture of advanced trainers continued through the Iran–Iraq War, and negotiations with British Aerospace were reported in 1983.[111] Decisions on aircraft manufacture were postponed until after the Iran–Iraq War.

Strategic systems

Iraq is notorious for its use of chemical weapons, first during the course of the Iran–Iraq War and later against Kurdish insurgents and civilians during 'Operation Anfal' in 1988. Up to 5,000 Kurds were killed in the chemical attack on Halabjah on February 26, 1988.[112] It has been estimated that Iraqi chemical attacks caused 40,000–50,000 Iranian casualties in the Iran–Iraq War including about 5,000 dead.[113] This amounted to approximately 5 percent of the estimated one million Iranian military and civilian casualties.[114]

The basis of Iraq's CW industry was laid in the Second Five Year Plan (1976–80), although it is likely that Iraqi interest in chemical weapons dates back at least to the 1960s.[115] The principal CW production facility was at the Samarra complex, identified as a 'pesticide plant' under the authority of the State Establishment for the Production of Pesticides. Samarra opened a production line for mustard gas (HD) in September 1983, and its first reported use in battle was in December of that year.[116] Nerve agents were used for the first time in response to the Iranian offensive at Majnoon Island in February 1984.[117]

Saddam Hussein was reportedly a strong supporter of CW production.[118] After the destruction of the Tammuz I reactor at Osriak on June 7, 1981 by the Israeli airforce, increased resources were made available for the production of CW agents.[119] At this time, construction on the Salman Pak facility was also initiated, indicating serious interest in production of biological warfare (BW) weapons.[120]

Acquisition of nuclear weapons constituted a critical part of Iraq's effort to become both the leading Gulf power and the leading Arab power. Iraq's pursuit of nuclear capability began in the 1960s, with the purchase of an IRT-2000 research reactor from the Soviet Union, which became operational in 1968.[121] The purchase of two nuclear reactors from France in 1976 provided the basis for a substantial nuclear weapons program based on plutonium extraction.[122] Purchase of the 30 Tammuz research facility from Italy in 1978 (including special 'hot cells' for the extraction of plutonium), tons of natural uranium from Niger, Portugal, and Brazil, and of the attempted purchase of 25,000 pounds of depleted uranium from the West German firm NUKEM ensured that plutonium extraction could begin immediately when the Osiraq reactor went on-line on July 1, 1981.[123] The Israeli airforce destroyed the reactor on June 7, 1981.

Pragmatism and victory: 1984–90

The Iran–Iraq War did not go as planned. The initial blitzkrieg assault failed utterly, and the war rapidly deteriorated into a drawn-out attrition contest. Iraq was forced to withdraw from Iranian soil by 1983, and fought a bloody defensive struggle in the northern mountains and the

130 *Iraq*

outskirts of Basra for three years. Early in 1986, however, Iranian troops staged a surprise attack on the Al-Faw peninsula, seizing one of Iraq's few remaining ports and inflicting a serious defeat on Iraqi troops. Iraqi counterattacks failed at a cost of thousands of casualties.

More important for Saddam and Iraq, however, were the political ramifications. Al-Faw was not particularly vital for the Iraqi war effort, but its capture was interpreted as a sign of Iraqi weakness, and endangered lines of credit from Western banks and Gulf states.[124] France threatened to suspend transfers until Baghdad paid its outstanding debts.[125] Local arms industry, therefore, received increased priority in Iraqi spending.

Supply constraints only spurred Iraqi production efforts. For example, threats to the supply of Mirage F-1 and MiG-27 fighter-bombers provided incentive for accelerated development of Iraqi missile programs.[126] Although IQAF strikes periodically targeted Tehran and other civilian centers, these attacks could only be carried out by Mirages and MiG-27s, at a high risk of losing skilled pilots and valuable aircraft. During March and April 1988, Iraq fired 203 missiles (all SCUD-B derivatives or modifications produced indigenously) against residential areas and/or economic targets.[127] These attacks produced just ten fatalities per missile (still three times greater than German V-2 attacks in World War II), but had an enormous impact on Iranian morale, resulting in mass evacuations of Tehran.[128] Locally produced missiles, therefore, successfully replaced much more complex and sophisticated foreign weapons for this mission.

The defense industries were reorganized in the 1987–88 period. Hussein

Table 4.5 Iraqi military expenditures and arms imports, 1981–91

Year	Defense expenditures (millions of current $US)	Defense expenditures (millions of constant $1991)	Defense expenditures as percentage of Gross National Product	Arms imports (millions of current $US)	Arms imports (millions of constant $1991)
1981	6,780	10,120	25.4	4,300	6,419
1982	11,290	15,870	44.7	7,100	9,981
1983	13,870	18,740	39.1	6,900	9,320
1984	16,520	21,360	44.3	9,200	11,900
1985	12,470	15,560	37.9	4,900	6,113
1986	13,780	16,750	47.4	6,000	7,289
1987	13,930	16,400	43.1	5,900	6,947
1988	13,740	15,580	40.2	5,400	6,123
1989	11,020	11,960	32.0	2,300	2,495
1990	11,890	12,370	48.0	2,800	2,912
1991	9,459	9,459	74.9	0	0

Source: ACDA, *World Military Expenditures and Arms Transfers, 1991–1992*

Kamil, a cousin and brother-in-law to Saddam Hussein, was assigned to SOTI in 1986 to work under al-Ubeidi.[129] Kamil, a former bodyguard for Saddam Hussein, was reportedly in charge of the Special Security Apparatus, also known as the Jihaz al-Amn al-Khass.[130] In January 1987, Kamil became the new head of SOTI, and probably also of SEPP, combining two of the most important defense industrial agencies under his leadership.[131] During 1987, SOTI became a full-fledged industrial ministry, and was renamed the Military Production Authority.

Under Kamil's leadership, Iraqi military-industrial efforts became more efficient and productive. Increased authority was given to project managers and priorities were focused on military requirements for the war against Iran and high technology research.[132] Streamlined procedures allowed new developmental efforts to be started almost immediately in response to requests from field commanders.

> ... Because of the war, all of us were in a hurry, and this allowed us to cut red tape. For instance, we performed no feasibility studies in the normal sense. Because we are all fighters we know the end-use of our weapons ... Sometimes a simple telephone call between a military user and myself can get the process going ... while some of us work on building a prototype, others begin designing production tools, etc.[133]

Prioritization of effort also increased the near-term impact of Iraqi military-industrial production. Hussein Kamil inherited over 80 different military-industrial projects, many of which overlapped each other and competed for resources.[134] One of Kamil's first actions in early 1987 was to give al-Saadi $400 million to expedite ballistic missile development.[135] In August 1987, the Al-Hussein missile was successfully tested, suggesting that the additional funding may have paid quick dividends.[136]

Kamil also emphasized self-sufficiency. After the Military Production Authority absorbed some of the Armed Forces Workshops from the Ministry of Defense in 1987, Western technicians at these facilities noticed that Iraqi engineers insisted on performing maintenance and repair work themselves, including rebuilding engines of armored vehicles and modifying Soviet and Chinese tanks with Western electronics.[137] Early in 1988, defense industrial structure was shuffled yet again: the new Ministry of Industrialization and Military Industrialization (MIMI) was formed from the Ministry of Heavy Industry, and Kamil's Military Production Authority.[138]

Hussein Kamil was now in charge of Iraq's entire industrial apparatus, as well as heading powerful Iraqi security/intelligence agencies which engaged in covert technology acquisition. By 1990, Kamil had appropriated the Technical Corps for Special Projects from the Ministry of Oil, and in October 1990 he became the Acting Minister of Oil.[139] The CIA report 'Iraq's Growing Arsenal: Programs and Facilities' (July 1990) identified the

State Establishment for Oil Refining and Gas Processing as '... a dedicated front for procuring chemical weapons related components and production equipment.'[140] Kamil therefore absorbed and dominated all the diverse elements of the Iraqi military industrial apparatus, from foreign espionage to actual production – a situation which both centralized and consolidated industrial efforts and provided him personally with a powerful domestic political and economic base.

In May 1989, Kamil proclaimed that Iraq was implementing a defense industrial program intended to provide all of Iraq's basic industrial supplies from indigenous sources.[141] Other intelligence reports from the summer of 1990 highlight Iraqi ambitions: 'President Saddam Hussein apparently believes an expanded arms industry will enhance Iraqi prestige and help solve security problems identified during the war such as lack of reliable arms supplies.'[142]

Selected indigenous arms programs: 1984–90

'Endurance' requirements

Iraq reportedly grew desperately short of ammunition after the Faw campaign in early 1986, and spent hundreds of millions of dollars on emergency procurement.[143] This shortage spurred efforts to upgrade munitions production to ensure adequate reserves. As early as 1986, Western observers noticed that Iraq was using larger quantities of home-built munitions.[144]

Prior to the Persian Gulf War, Iraq possessed at least 19 state-run plants manufacturing ordnance and artillery.[145] These plants were controlled by SOTI, and their products included variants of the RPG-7 anti-tank grenade launcher, hand grenades, and anti-personnel and anti-tank mines.[146] Also, 7.65 mm pistols (Type 951), 9 mm pistols (Type 70), and a number of Yugoslav small arms were produced under license, along with the the Al-Qadisiyaa 7.62 mm × 54 sharpshooter rifle (derived from the Soviet Dragounov), illuminator pistols, and 250 kg and 500 kg aircraft bombs.[147] Iraq exhibited a variety of indigenously produced light arms and munitions at Cairo in November 1987, including aerial bombs, sniper rifles and Kalashnikovs.[148] Iraq also reportedly developed anti-aircraft artillery, including a seven barreled 30 mm gun and a 'special' 57 mm gun.[149]

Iraqi ordnance factories produced ammunition for all of the weapons listed above, as well as ammunition for 7.62 mm × 39 small arms, 12.7 mm and 14.5 mm machine guns, and 23 mm and 30 mm automatic cannons.[150] In addition, Iraqi military industries were reportedly capable of producing fuel-air explosives (FAEs)[151] and cluster bombs,[152] and were developing infrared and television guided air-to-ground bombs.[153] Iraq also manufactured several varieties of naval mines.[154] By 1987, Iraq had become 'self-sufficient in ammunition, artillery ammunition, aircraft bombs, mortar bombs, RPGs, rockets, tube-launched rockets, and mortars.'[155]

By 1989, Iraq reportedly produced all mortars and mortar ammunition used by the military.[156] At an arms exhibition in Cairo in November 1987, Iraq demonstrated indigenously produced 60 mm, 81 mm, and 120 mm mortars and ammunition.[157] High-explosive, smoke, and chemical rounds for both mortars and artillery were produced indigenously, and Iraq was reportedly self-sufficient in most types of artillery projectiles, charges, and fuses.[158] According to Christopher Cowley, an engineer who worked for Gerald Bull upgrading and improving Iraqi artillery capabilities, Iraq was self-sufficient in production of shells, propellant, fuses, explosives, and replacement barrels before the Gulf War.[159] Other ammunition types produced included 100 mm, 122 mm, 130 mm, 152 mm, and 155 mm shells.[160]

Perhaps the most interesting advance in Iraqi munitions production is the evidence that they were developing a depleted uranium anti-tank round. UNSCOM inspections discovered some evidence that the Iraqis were experimenting with uranium to produce armor-piercing projectiles.[161] According to Western reports, the US sold specialized machinery to Iraq, which permitted it to build a factory to produce tungsten-carbide tool bits. These bits are used by the military for cutting and shaping depleted uranium flechettes for anti-tank rounds.[162] Iraq could obtain depleted uranium from its illicit nuclear program.

Non-platform weapons

Iraq showed great interest in modern artillery, due in part to the doctrinal emphasis on firepower. In 1986, Iraq began producing the D-30 122 mm gun under license from Yugoslavia.[163] A steel-forging plant was under development at Taji in 1990 which would eventually be capable of producing over 1,000 gun barrels per year (105 mm to 203 mm bores).[164] Dr. Gerald Bull provided Iraq with Extended-Range Full-Bore Base-Bleed (ERFB-BB) technology, which substantially increased the range of Iraqi 155 mm guns.[165] Dr. Bull assisted the Iraqis in modifying 130 mm D-46 Soviet/Chinese field guns to 155 mm, using barrels purchased abroad and then finishing the machining in-country. This substantially increased the range and destructiveness of the D-46.[166]

Iraq also began development and production of the massive Superguns. These were designed by Gerald Bull on the basis of his experience in the US 'HARP' project and on surviving design plans for World War II German V-3 long-range gun. The Supergun project, known as 'Project Babylon,' was intended to produce an experimental 350 mm prototype and two or more 1,000 mm guns with ranges of hundreds of kilometers. The purpose of these guns is still unclear. There is some speculation that they were intended for use as satellite launchers, but they were also capable of firing enormous shells carrying large quantities of chemical and or biological agents.[167] The 350 mm gun was theoretically capable of being moved about on its railway car, but the 1,000 mm guns were immobile.[168]

Other analysts, however, report that the weapons had a theoretical rate of fire of two rounds per minute, and that the initial tests of the 350 mm prototype indicate that the guns were clearly designed as weapons.[169] Bull also reportedly began design of two more mobile, but still immense, artillery pieces for Iraq: a 350 mm gun with a 100 foot barrel, and a 600 mm weapon with a 200 foot barrel. Both of these guns would have barrels which could be trained and elevated, substantially improving accuracy and permitting engagement of a wider range of potential targets.[170]

Iraq used multiple-rocket launchers of Soviet design for both conventional and chemical attacks. The M-87 system, at least portions of which were produced in Iraq before the first Gulf War, had two different configurations.[171] The Ababil 50, in service with the Iraqi Army, was a 262 mm rocket with a range of 50 km and a 95 kg warhead. The system was reportedly capable of carrying cluster and minelet warheads as well as conventional high explosive.[172] The Ababil 100, which was under development, was a 400 mm rocket with a 100 km range, also capable of carrying cluster and minelet munitions.[173] Reports after the Gulf War indicated that Ababil 100 rocket motor production might have been resumed by the Iraqis.[174]

Iraq also purchased the sophisticated Brazilian ASTROS II system.[175] The Iraqis were impressed with the high accuracy of the ASTROS system, and provided both funding and development assistance to the project.[176] Iraq manufactured rockets for the system under license, called the Sijeel 30, 40, and 60.[177] The Laith battlefield rocket is probably an upgrade of the venerable Soviet FROG (Free Rocket Over Ground) rocket, and was in service with the Iraqi military before the Gulf War.[178] A 550 mm rocket with a range of 90 km, the Laith could carry conventional, cluster, or chemical warheads.[179]

Iraq pursued a number of other short-range missile systems, many of which were modifications of Soviet surface-to-air missiles. The Kassir (reported 150 km range), Al-Rashid (reported 25 km range) and Nissan 'April 28' (reported 110 km range) were displayed at the Baghdad Arms Exhibition in May 1989.[180] Other reports mention the Barak (an SA-3 variant), and other variants based on Soviet SAMs including the Fahd (SA-1), the Nissan (SA-2), and the Kassir (SA-6).[181]

Iraq also may have gained access to data and plans for the Brazilian Piranha air-to-air missile. The team of Brazilian rocket scientists working in Iraq from 1989–90 had extensive experience with the Piranha project, and Iraq reportedly expressed interest in acquiring blueprints for the system. It is also reported that a multinational team including Iraqi, Brazilian, French, German, Argentine, and Egyptian technicians had been working on an air-to-air missile called the 'Al-Taq-Ham'.[182]

The FAO-1 anti-ballistic missile was displayed at Baghdad in 1989, where it was reported that the missile had completed two successful test firings against incoming missiles.[183] Despite the considerable propaganda value of this launch, it is clear that the Fao-1 test was rigged. There is no evidence that the FAO-1 was used during the Gulf Wars, and the missile itself reportedly bore a striking resemblance to the Soviet-designed SA-2 surface-to-air missile.[184]

ELECTRONICS

The proportion of French technicians to Iraqi engineers at the SAAD-13 complex dropped from 250 out of 3,000 in 1984 to a mere 20 advisors in 1989, evidence that most of the skills necessary for licensed production had been transferred successfully to the Iraqi workforce.[185] By 1989, other new projects and production lines included SDE-125/552 HF portable transceivers (specifically down-graded from French requirements to make them more 'grunt-resistant'),[186] microwave and hybrid circuits, and components for various communications equipment and radars.[187] An additional plant was established at Mansur to produce other defense electronics.[188] Cooperation with Thomson-CSF continued up until the Gulf War, and included licensed production of the Tigre early warning radar used on the Baghdad and Adnan AEW aircraft discussed later in this chapter.

Modification

TANKS AND OTHER ARMORED VEHICLES

Self-propelled heavy mortars, based on Soviet tracked vehicles (with four 120 mm mortars) and East German EFA 10-ton trucks (carrying 12 160 mm mortars), were assembled in Iraq. Another local modification project was a self-propelled 160 mm mortar mounted on a modified T-54 tank chassis.[189]

Tank modification programs were reported as early as 1986, which attempted to improve obsolescent T-54/55/59 tanks which made up the bulk of the Iraqi tank force. Modified T-54/55 tanks were displayed at the Baghdad Arms Exhibition in May 1989 with a retrofitted 125 mm gun, and others were provided with applique armor.[190] This applique armor was an Iraqi product, made of sandwiched layers of steel and rubber.[191] The problems of putting a 125 mm gun in a turret ring designed for a 100 mm gun were not discussed – but it seems highly doubtful that this modification could have been anything but a catastrophe.

One report states that T-55s were assembled in Iraq, and that other modernization projects were underway there.[192] Among these other projects were the retrofitting of Delft night vision equipment, and possibly of

Western fire control systems.¹⁹³ These modifications and improvements were apparently made at Iraqi Armed Forces depots, which were transferred to the authority of MIMI in 1987–88.

Iraq bought large numbers of Chinese T-59 and T-69 tanks during the Iran–Iraq War. Chinese-built T-59 tanks, an inferior copy of the T-55, were reportedly retrofitted with a 105 mm L7 gun.¹⁹⁴ Others had applique armor fitted to provide additional protection against RPG and other infantry-carried anti-tank weapons.¹⁹⁵ Type 69 tanks were modified with Western rangefinders or applique armor.¹⁹⁶ It is reported, however, that most of the Iraqi tanks destroyed during the Gulf War were standard Soviet models, indicating that modification programs were not actually fielded in great numbers.¹⁹⁷

Iraq exhibited modified versions of the Soviet BMP-1 Armored Infantry Fighting Vehicle at the Baghdad Arms Exhibition. One report states that the vehicles were being produced under license.¹⁹⁸ Modifications included replacing the main armament, attachment of applique armor to increase protection, and removal of the turret to make an ambulance version.¹⁹⁹

AIRCRAFT

The poor showing of the IQAF in the 1980–84 period inspired technological innovation in several areas: first, to provide the IQAF with capabilities which it needed but lacked; second, to acquire significant battlefield strike and interdiction capabilities for the ground forces which did not require use of the IQAF; and third, to provide long-range strike capabilities which did not risk aircraft losses.

Iraq modified existing aircraft in IQAF inventory to improve performance or provide capabilities which did not exist in Iraq and which could not be procured from abroad. Examples of this include the development of a laser-guided bombing system which combined French and Soviet technologies for the Mirage F-1 fighter²⁰⁰ and the equipment of Soviet MiG-23/27 aircraft with refueling probes.²⁰¹ Unsatisfied with the performance of Soviet AAMs, Iraq modified its large MiG-21 fleet (reportedly with Pakistani assistance) to carry French Matra 550 and 530 AAMs.²⁰² Iraq also reportedly modified An-12 and Il-76 aircraft as air-to-air refueling tankers.²⁰³ These modifications provided the IQAF with improved long-range strike capabilities and air-to-air combat performance.

The most ambitious Iraqi aircraft programs were the Baghdad and Adnan AEW, designed to cover gaps in the Iraqi air defense system. They required the integration of Western and Soviet systems originally designed for other purposes to fill a distinct Iraqi requirement. According to some reports, the Baghdad and Adnan projects had significant Indian involvement, suggesting a case of possible collaboration between two LDC industries.²⁰⁴

The Baghdad 1 was unveiled at the Baghdad Arms Exhibition in May

1989. It comprised a locally built Thomson-CSF Tigre-2 surveillance radar (manufactured under license in Iraq in a ground-based configuration) positioned in a radome under the rear of the fuselage of a Soviet Il-76 Candid transport aircraft.[205] The radar reportedly had greater than 180 degrees of scan, and could detect, track, and identify targets within a 350 km range.[206] The Baghdad 1, according to some reports, was used operationally in the last stages of the Iran–Iraq War.[207]

During the Baghdad arms exhibition in 1989, Husayn Kamil, director of MIMI, stated that an upgraded version was in development. The apparent intention was to add a fighter control capability, thereby providing more than just an AEW platform.[208] The improved version, known as the Adnan-1, had a rotodome over the fuselage, and resembled the Soviet 'Mainstay' AEW version of the Il-76 Candid.[209] Radar detection range was reported to be 'several hundred kilometers.'[210] A second version, called the Adnan-2, was test-flown shortly before the Gulf War, and was reported to be more difficult to detect with radar.[211] According to US sources at the beginning of Operation Desert Storm, the IQAF possessed at least three Baghdad/Adnan aircraft. One of these was destroyed at Al Taqqadum airfield on January 23, 1991, and the other two flew to sanctuary in Iran later that month.[212]

The Baghdad and Adnan were designed to fill gaps in the Iraqi Integrated Air Defense System (IADS). This system was equipped with a mix of standard Soviet and French systems, including some ground-based Tiger-G surveillance radars (called the SDA-G in Iraqi service) produced under license in Iraq.[213] The IADS was designed to protect against a modest-sized regional attack by Israel or Iran, and was quickly overwhelmed by Coalition air attacks in the Gulf War.[214] The Baghdad and Adnan had no impact on the air balance in the Gulf War.[215]

Major weapons platforms

ARMORED VEHICLES

In 1989, Iraq unveiled the first prototype of the 'Assad Babil' (Lion of Babylon) tank, a derivative of the Soviet T-72.[216] The agreement to produce the T-72 was reportedly reached with the Soviets in 1986, and the tank was initially assembled in Iraq, with production of some components beginning in 1989.[217] The gun barrel and breach were eventually made in Iraq, along with parts of the turret and some electrical components.[218]

It is possible, given reports of the T-55 upgrade programs, that significant portions of the T-72's turret, rangefinder and main armament were produced or assembled in Iraq – or at least that Iraq had contracted to acquire those production capabilities. Operational experience indicates that Soviet tank guns wear out quickly in combat.[219] Domestic production of gun tubes facilitates quick replacement and restoration to full combat capability. Iraqi plants also carried out maintenance of T-72s, and manufactured some parts for their repair.[220] According to Lt. General Amer al Saadi, the percentage of indigenous content in the Assad Babil was approximately 30–40 percent value added, primarily because of the high price of the electrical components.[221] According to some reports, Iraq resumed production of the Assad Babil after the first Gulf War.[222]

Iraq also attempted to develop sophisticated self-propelled (SP) artillery. At the Baghdad Arms Exhibition of 1989, Iraq unveiled two new SP artillery pieces, designed with the assistance of Dr. Bull:[223] the Al-Majnoon, a 155 mm gun-howitzer, which strongly resembled the South African G-6 SP howitzer; and the Al-Fao, a 210 mm gun-howitzer with a potential range of over 50 km.[224]

AIRCRAFT

After prolonged negotiation (including the rescheduling of payments for Iraq's formidable debt payments to France),[225] a protocol for $6.5 billion was signed with Dassault, Thomson-CSF, and Snecma on March 21, 1989 for cooperation on the construction of maintenance and assembly facilities for French aircraft in Iraq. The FAO project, originally known as Saad-25, called for the delivery of 54 Mirage-2000 fighter-bombers, the construction of depot-level maintenance facilities (including engine overhaul) for IQAF Mirage F-1s in Iraq, and the complete tooling and kits for 134 Alphajet trainers.[226]

According to a 1989 interview with Lt. Gen. Amer Rashid al-Ubaidi, Iraq intended to build an aircraft industry, and chose the advanced trainer as the first step which was both sophisticated and realistically within Iraq's industrial capacity.[227] This was confirmed by comments from General Husayn Kamil Hassan, director of Iraq's Ministry of Industry and Military Industrialization, shortly before the Baghdad Exhibition in 1989:

> We are negotiating with the Soviet Union and France to build up our own advanced jet ... clearly Iraq is not able to produce such an aircraft, though it is determined to urgently build a plant.[228]

Iraq also sought to design or license-produce an attack helicopter.[229] As evidence of their continuing interest in indigenous helicopter programs (maintenance, development, and/or production), the Iraqis established the Al-Furnas helicopter maintenance and development center at Musayib after the end of the Gulf War, despite the UN embargo.[230]

The 1990s: what might the industry have looked like?

The Gulf War, 13 years of economic sanctions and arms embargo, and Operation Iraqi Freedom effectively destroyed the Iraqi arms industry. An intriguing question, however, is how Iraq's industry *might* have evolved if Saddam had not invaded Kuwait. The following pages suggest that structural and financial obstacles would have kept Iraq from achieving some of its more grandiose ambitions, but that in fact the Iraqi military industry was capable of considerable achievements that might have contributed significantly to Iraq's military capability – if it could have avoided provoking the US and the international community.

The Iran–Iraq War ended in stalemate in 1988, although Saddam Hussein could claim a Pyrrhic victory by forcing Iran off Iraqi soil. Iraq, which had begun the war with $35 billion in foreign exchange reserves, was approximately $70–80 billion in debt.[231] In addition, as a result of the war Iraq had suffered approximately 375,000 casualties.[232] Economists and defense analysts assumed that Iraq would enter into a period of lower defense spending and place a high priority on rebuilding damaged economic infrastructure and civilian development projects.

In fact, Iraq did not release significant numbers of men from military service in 1989, and the military budget did not decline appreciably.[233]

> Iraq's 1990 military budget was $12.9 billion, or approximately $700 per citizen in a country where the average annual income was $1,950. By mid-1990, Iraq had only enough cash reserves for three months of imports and an inflation rate of 40%. If not rescheduled, the required annual principal and interest payments on the non-Arab debt alone would have consumed more than half of Iraq's estimated $13 billion 1989 oil revenue. Debt service in subsequent years would have had an equally deleterious effect.[234]

Despite these hard economic facts, military industrialization received the highest possible priority after the war.

Iraq pursued both open arms deals and also covert purchases in an effort to acquire sophisticated defense technologies as rapidly as possible. Iraq's efforts to secure unconventional weapons, intended to deter US interference in the region and to influence the Arab-Israeli struggle, expanded perceptibly. The US Customs Service detected increased efforts to procure missile, chemical and biological, and fuse technology.[235]

Iraqi spending on military industry and covert efforts to acquire technology and industrial capabilities accelerated rapidly even as imports of finished weapons were decreasing.[236] Iraq was announced its intention to invest $20 billion in the establishment of the military-industrial base.[237] Iraq's efforts to achieve military-industrial self-sufficiency elicited grudging respect and concern in Western intelligence circles: 'Although Iraq's states goals are almost certainly over ambitious, we believe the regime recognizes its limitations and holds more pragmatic aspirations in private.'[238]

The difficulties faced by Western export licensing agencies in the face of a coordinated policy of illegal acquisition were formidable, and were exacerbated by bureaucratic infighting and policy debates.[239] In the words of Representative Annunzio of Illinois:

> Even though the United States had severe restrictions on sending carbon-fiber technology abroad, Iraq was able to obtain glass-fiber technology through the United States export licensing process. The glass-fiber debacle dramatically illustrates how President Bush's mandate to increase trade with Iraq was at odds with the policy of limiting proliferation. Iraq's military industrialization strategy of mixing military and civilian production within the same complexes repeatedly caused nightmares within the export licensing process.[240]

The Al-Arabi trading network received over $1 billion in funds from Banco Nationale Lavoro-Atlanta, most of which was spent on high priority projects including ballistic missiles, the Supergun, and nuclear weapons technology.[241] The House Banking Committee, which investigated BNL-Atlanta stated that:

> The Banking Committee's investigation of BNL show that much of the $2.155 billion in loans provided to the Ministry of Industrialization and Military Industrialization ... were utilized to purchase military [sic] useful technology from the United States and Europe. BNL funds were used to purchase equipment for the new Condor II missile, the SCUD missile modifications, the short-range Ababil rocket, the 210mm and the 155mm howitzer, Gerald Bull's supercannon ... sophisticated night vision equipment, and an artillery fuze factory.[242]

In addition to the sheer bureaucratic size and authority of the military-industrial infrastructure, and the close linkage with national intelligence and security services which permitted successful technology acquisition, a final indicator of the importance of the military-industrial effort is the amount of money and trained manpower it required. The Iraqis spent $14.2 billion in 1985–89 on industrial technology, almost all of which had military applications.[243] To put this in perspective, according to US estimates Iraq spent approximately $24.5 billion on arms imports from 1985–89. Total imports of all goods amounted to $48.324 billion, so the percentage of total imports spent on arms is 50.8 percent for this five-year period.[244] Imports of defense-related manufacturing technology therefore amounted to 29.4 percent of total imports in this period. This is an enormous expenditure on industrial infrastructure during a period of continuing high-intensity conflict, and is equivalent to 21.8 percent of the estimated military budget for these years.[245]

According to Kenneth Timmerman, Iraq spent the equivalent of nearly $3 billion each year from 1984–89 on Western technology, and evidence indicates that procurement was increased even as a primary source of funds (BNL-Atlanta) was shut down by Federal investigation. Infrastructure was being acquired at a furious rate, but trained personnel did not exist to utilize it properly. In both missile and chemical weapons facilities, sophisticated machinery remained out of operation because the people with the skills or experience to fix it were in other sectors of the defense industry.[246] The nuclear program had priority over all others, and this priority was increased after the initial discoveries of Supergun parts in Europe.[247]

Iraq created a military-industrial policy that it lacked the economic and technological resources to support. Iraq's priorities lay in the unconventional weapons field, and were very close to fruition. The primary capabilities of the Iraq's military industry, it appears, would have been most efficiently focused on unconventional weaponry or endurance requirements. Modification programs and major weapons platforms were excessively demanding in terms of both technical skills and financial resources, and unnecessary for Iraq's short-term security needs. They did, however, provide useful propaganda, and had some prestige value for the regime.

Iraq's defense industry proved surprisingly resilient after the Gulf War. Early in the Gulf Crisis, a Congressional defense expert expressed disdain for the Iraqi military-industrial capability: 'A strike against Iraq using ground-hugging cruise missiles could destroy all of that country's major defense industries within hours.'[248]

In fact, Iraqi military industry was subjected to considerably more intense bombardment than a single salvo of cruise missiles. Iraq's military-industrial capability was a target for massive Coalition airstrikes during the Gulf War, and much of their manufacturing capability was degraded, if not destroyed.[249]

> By the end of the war, military production facilities had been severely damaged. At least 30 percent of Iraq's conventional weapons production capability, which made small arms, artillery, small- and large-caliber ammunition, electronic and optical systems, and repaired armored vehicles, was damaged or destroyed.[250]

Coalition air operations, however, failed to take into account the potential impact of Iraqi military industry after the war's termination phase.[251] The initial strategic bombing plan, codenamed 'Instant Thunder,' designated 84 strategic targets which, if severely punished, would theoretically degrade Iraq's military capability to wage offensive operations.[252] Only 15 so-called 'military support' facilities were included in the target list, which focused on electrical plants, communications, and leadership targets. By January 15, 1991, 62 'military support' targets had been selected. Most of the industrial targets selected, however, were missile or unconventional weapon-related.[253] These targets had priority not only because of the harm they might do to Coalition forces, but also in order to reduce Iraq's long-term threat to the Gulf and Middle East.[254]

The air campaign differed from previous strategic air campaigns in several ways. Operations focused on degrading rather than destroying enemy capability.[255]

> In Desert Storm, the overarching objective of the strategic portion of the air campaign was somewhat different ... [from the Second World War] ... Instead of attacking the vital elements of war production ... the principal threat of the 'strategic' effort against Iraq seems to have been to inhibit and paralyze the very functioning of the Iraqi government and its military forces.[256]

Iraq's weapons of mass destruction (WMD) and missile infrastructure were high priority targets. Iraq's conventional military industries, however, received a much lower priority than in previous strategic bombing campaigns. As a result, Iraq maintained significant military capabilities in the post-Gulf War period despite a continuing UN embargo.[257] The survival of Iraq's conventional military industry reflects, in part, the short war focus of the Coalition leadership, and the lack of an overall political strategy. Saddam retained the military assets necessary to reassert and retain control of the country.

Iraq made a substantial effort to relocate and/or conceal existing manufacturing capabilities before the war broke out, and that the restoration of munitions and weapons production was a high priority in Iraqi rebuilding efforts after the end of the conflict.[258] In 1992, Director of Central Intelligence Robert Gates, told the House Armed Service Committee that Iraq claimed to have repaired ' ... nearly 200 military industrial buildings and was in the process of repairing many others.'[259] Iraqi Prime Minister Muhammad al-Zubaydi told a visiting Greek delegation in August 1992 that Iraq succeeded in reconstructing 87 percent of its factories, institutions, and weapons projects and was embarking on 'new, giant strategic projects.'[260]

After the Gulf War, a considerable portion of the defense industry was reconstituted, although it operated at low productivity due to lack of machinery, spare parts, and other resources.[261] Dozens of plants resumed operating, as equipment stored before the Gulf War was moved back into facilities.[262] The status of major conventional weapons plants is uncertain, partly because many which were known to exist (primarily small arms facilities) had not been located before the conflict. Thirty-three conventional facilities had been identified before the Gulf War. As of the mid-1990s, the status of 19 were unknown. Ten were functioning or partly functioning, one was rebuilt but possibly still not functional, two were heavily damaged, and one was non-functioning.[263] Among the functioning plants were the Hutteen explosives complex, the Al Ameen, Base West

World, and Taji armored vehicle plants, the Salah-al-Din electronics facility, and the Saad 38 munitions plant at Nahrawan, which produced FAEs, cluster munitions, and critical parts for artillery shells before the Gulf War.[264]

The importance of the surviving arms facilities, particularly those dedicated to munitions production, should not be underestimated. Iraq was subject to international embargo for over 12 years from 1990–2003. In that period, it had no access to any legitimate supplies of small or medium arms ammunition, but was still able to undertake substantial, multi-division level campaigns against both Shi'ite and Kurdish rebels. Some crucial equipment, especially for air defenses, was smuggled through the UN embargo.[265] If Iraq were depending purely on smuggling, however, this level of activity could have led to shortages of critical munitions and corresponding changes in military operations, including the risk of higher casualties in an already demoralized army.

Recent military operations in Iraq suggest that Iraqi munitions plants may have continued functioning throughout the sanctions period. Several months after Operation Iraqi Freedom, American and allied units reported the existence of massive, unsecured weapons dumps. Early reports spoke of 650,000 tons of munitions in Iraq.[266] Other reports speak of more than one million tons of munitions.[267] In comparison, the US armed forces possessed 1.8 million tons of munitions in 2003 for a much larger, more sophisticated military force.[268] The sheer quantities of munitions available, after 13 years of arms embargo, suggest that Iraqi military industries either had produced or were producing significant quantities of munitions for Iraqi use. These weapons, regrettably, remain available for insurgents and opponents of the emerging new Iraqi government – a continuing legacy of Saddam's military-industrial ambitions.

The enduring puzzle: Iraq's strategic weapons

Much of our knowledge regarding Iraq's weapons of mass destruction comes from the inspections carried out after the first Gulf War by the United Nations Special Commission (UNSCOM), established under UN Security Council Resolution 687, and tasked with uncovering Iraq's various unconventional weapons programs. UNSCOM was created under the assumption that its mission would be over quickly. Instead, it became an extraordinarily powerful organization drawing on resources from a number of national intelligence agencies, tasked with breaking down an extremely effective and well-funded Iraqi deception effort. From 1991–98, UNSCOM carried out inspections of Iraqi facilities under increasingly strenuous conditions, including escalating Iraqi belligerence and official non-compliance. UNSCOM's withdrawal left many questions about Iraq's industrial capabilities unanswered, but its investigations demonstrated the massive scope of the Iraqi effort.[269]

144 *Iraq*

The results of Operation Iraqi Freedom and the ensuing US occupation have raised difficult questions about the accuracy and politicization of US and British official statements and intelligence estimates in 2002–03, and the assumptions that drove those estimates. Enormous discrepancies exist between Iraq's official admissions and the conclusions of Western and international observers based on inspections and Iraqi documentation.[270] Iraq made over a dozen 'full and final disclosures' of its WMD programs – each of which was definitively demonstrated to be inaccurate based on Iraq's own official records. These materials and capabilities, unless accounted for, will remain available to the next Iraqi regime, or to other actors or factions. The Iraqi WMD threat has not been completely destroyed.[271]

Ballistic missiles

In 1973, Iraq received its first SCUD short-range ballistic missiles (SRBMs) from the Soviet Union. For the next 15 years, Iraq continued to receive missiles, transporter-erector-launchers (TELs), spare parts, and other associated vehicles from the Soviets. The total eventually amounted to 819 missiles, 15 practice missiles, and 11 TELs. By the early 1980s, Iraq had sufficient infrastructure to maintain and repair its SCUDS.[272]

Iraq began a crash program in development and production of surface-to-surface missiles during the Iran–Iraq War. This program involved multinational cooperative efforts, technology acquisition and theft, indigenous design and development, and increasingly sophisticated modifications of existing liquid-fueled missiles. Between 1980 and 1990, Iraq spent at least $3 billion on missile research and development.[273] Among the major Iraqi missile projects were SAAD-16 (later Al-Kindi State Establishment–a research and development center), Project 395 (an umbrella project synthesizing Iraqi expertise from cooperative projects with Brazil, Argentina, Egypt, and Western Europe), Project 96 (a solid-fuel production facility), Project 124 (a missile body plant produced with Western European assistance), and Project 1728 (SCUD upgrade program).[274] Project 144 (a liquid-fuel production facility and research center) also developed special warheads for the emerging missile force, including a concrete 'kinetic energy' warhead (apparently intended for strikes against Israel's Dimona reactor) as well as chemical and biological warheads.[275]

Al-Husayn surface to surface missile

The Al-Husayn was Iraq's first modification of the Soviet-designed SCUD surface-to-surface missile, which lacked the range to hit 'strategic' targets during the Iran–Iraq War. Introduced in combat in February 1988,[276] the new Al-Husayn had a 600 km range, sufficient to hit most major cities in Iran, but achieved this increased range by sacrificing over 75 percent of the explosive payload.[277] An additional improvement was a significant reduction in 'refire time': the Al-Husayn could be reloaded and fired again in 60 minutes, compared to the SCUD's 160 minutes.[278] The 'diary' of Iraqi missile commander Lt. Gen. Hazzim 'Abd-al-Razzaq al-Ayyubbi indicates an emphasis on fire and movement due to an awareness of the possibility of counterstrikes.[279]

Initial manufacture of one Al-Husayn required the cannibalization of three SCUD-B missiles.[280] After the Iran–Iraq War it became clear that much, if not all, of the missile was produced locally.[281] One recent report states that in 1988, Iraq could produce three Al-Husayns per day.[282] Reports from the Gulf War indicate that non-scavenged content in the missiles fired in that conflict was significant:

> The Al-Husayn missiles fired at Iran in 1988 were cannibalized from Soviet-supplied SCUD missiles. However, it appears that at least some of the missiles launched in 1991 against allied forces were assembled from components obtained from West Germany and possibly elsewhere.[283]

According to recent reports, Iraq was able to produce SCUD-type missiles indigenously, and not just from parts or components supplied by the Soviets or scavenged from existing SCUDs.[284]

Al-Husayns were used extensively in the 'War of the Cities' in early 1988, and again during the Gulf War.[285] According to W. Seth Carus and Joseph Bermudez, Jr, 189 were fired during the War of the Cities, 135 of which were aimed at Tehran.[286] By January 1991, Iraq had 220 Al-Husayns and 11 unmodified SCUDs in its arsenal, as well as ten MAZ-543 TELS and four indigenous Al-Nida TELs.[287] A total of 88 missiles were fired in the Persian Gulf War (46 at the Gulf States and 42 at Israel).[288]

Al-Abbas surface to surface missile

The Al-Abbas, a longer-range derivative of the Al-Husayn, was originally tested on April 25, 1988.[289] The new missile, designed to have a 900 km range, performed somewhat below expectations, but its 800 km range was still a significant improvement over the Al-Husayn.[290] Like the Al-Husayn, the Al-Abbas achieved part of it's increased range at the expense of payload, which is estimated at 100–300 kg,[291] and could be launched from the MAZ-543 Soviet launcher or the Iraqi Al-Walid.[292] The Al-Abbas was a much more sophisticated undertaking than the Al-Hussein: it was both more complex and had a much higher level of indigenous content.

Unlike the Al-Husayn, the Al-Abbas was not just an upgraded SCUD-B. It used some of the same design specifications as the SCUD and may have used Soviet-built parts, but it was an Iraqi missile and it had rolled off an Iraqi assembly line.[293]

146 *Iraq*

It appears that the Al-Abbas was still under development during the Gulf War. After the war was over, Iraq did not declare any Al-Abbas missiles as part of the ceasefire agreement.[294]

Al-Abid Satellite Launcher/Tammuz-I medium range ballistic missile

On December 5, 1989, to the surprise of Western intelligence analysts, Iraq tested the Al-Abid satellite launch vehicle.[295] The Al-Abid was an interesting hybrid construction, consisting of a first stage of five clustered SCUD motors, a second stage with a single motor based on other Iraqi two stage rocket designs, and a previously unseen rocket motor for the third stage.[296] Western reports speculate that Dr. Gerald Bull may have been involved in this new project, as well as working on a more advanced project which involved 'clusters of eight SCUDs powered by a three-stage rocket' which could put Southern Europe within easy striking range.[297]

It is reported that the Al-Abid could launch a 350 kg satellite into space.[298] A militarized version of the Al-Abid would be capable of a range of approximately 2,000 km (approximately 1,200 miles).[299] It is also reported that a smaller version of this system was designed with a 1,200 km range, called the Al-Walid.[300] Shortly before the invasion of Kuwait, Iraq announced its intention to launch a satellite, reportedly of Sino-French origin, using the Al-Abid/Tamouz-1 booster.[301] This project, obviously, never came to fruition.

Al-Hijarah SSM

The Al-Hijarah is a ballistic missile with a reported range of 750 km. The existence of the missile was announced during the run-up to the Gulf War, and the name refers to the stones thrown by Palestinian demonstrators against Israeli forces in the Occupied Territories.[302] The Al-Hijarah was reportedly used against Israel and the Gulf States during the Gulf War, but little else is known about this system.[303] According to an Israeli report, Iraq claimed to have used Al-Hijarah missiles in an attempted attack on the Dimona nuclear facility during the Gulf War.[304] US sources believe that the Al-Hijarah is a shortened version of the Al-Hussein.[305]

Condor II/Badr-2000

The Condor solid-fuel IRBM, a joint project between Argentina, Iraq, and Egypt, never entered production. Facilities for Condor R&D and production have been identified during UNSCOM inspections in Iraq.[306] The Condor was designed to be a solid-fuel, two-stage missile capable of delivering WMD with a range of 1,000 km.[307] The Israelis estimated the total cost of the Condor project at $2.4 billion, and the cost of missiles at about $8 million each.[308]

The Condor, known in Iraq as the Badr-2000, was a genuine multinational project, involving Egypt, Iraq, and Argentina, with technical assistance from West Germany, Italy, and France. The German firm MBB was a major participant in the project, first through the cover of the independent consulting firm Consen, and later in more direct fashion.[309] MBB was responsible for transferring US Pershing-2 missile technology to the project. According to a leading Western proliferation analyst,

> The same MBB employee who worked on the Pershing at the Pentagon also represented MBB in Iraq for the Condor, and thus was in a position to transfer American missile technology to Baghdad.[310]

One reason for the apparent decline of the Condor project was the successful application of the Missile Technology Control Regime to slow or eliminate flow of crucial technologies to the participant nations.[311] Some analyses argue that the Condor project may have been a safety project, used as a hedge against the possibility that Iraq could not successfully modify SCUDs at home.[312]

This explanation, while intriguing, may understate the significance of the Condor project. In fact, it appears that Iraq attempted to synthesize the knowledge gained in the Badr-2000 project with knowledge acquired from Brazil on the SCUD modification program, under the umbrella of Project 395. The Iraqi–Brazilian cooperation in rockets and missiles dates to the early 1980s. Brazil's Aerospace Technology Center (CTA) was the organization in charge of Brazil's sounding rocket and military missile program. CTA passed technical information to the defense firm Avibras, which constructed the ASTROS battlefield rockets based on the Sonda series of sounding rockets.[313]

Iraq was involved in the financing of the ASTROS project, and cooperated in with CTA and other firms on solid and liquid fuel development in Brazil.[314] The knowledge gained there was applied in Project 395, and a team of Brazilian rocket scientists headed by Dr. Hugo Piva (former head of CTA in Brazil) entered Iraq in the spring of 1989 to train Iraqi engineers in rocket aerodynamics, flight testing, on-board electronics, and rocket propellants.[315] Despite reports of the demise of the Badr-2000 project when the Iraqis ceased funding the project in 1988, it now appears that Iraq withdrew from the multinational effort once it had obtained the necessary knowledge, and continued the project at home.

The UNSCOM 6th Report cites documents proving parallel development between the Iraqi nuclear and surface-to-surface missile projects. In one document the Ministry of Defense ordered the Iraqi Atomic Energy Commission to postpone a particular experiment until after an SSM test.[316] Badr-2000 production facilities included the Dhu al-Fiqar factory at

Falluja, the Tah al-Ma'arik factory at Latifiya, and the al-Yawm al-'Azim factory at Musayib.[317] It appears that components for the Badr-2000 continued to be produced after the Gulf War:

> Iraq is actively producing components for the BADR-2000 program, but Ambassador Ekeus has indicated that UNSCOM has identified the components of this program which cannot be activated while UNSCOM is in Iraq.[318]

This strongly suggests that the BADR-2000 program was more than a 'hedge,' and remained a priority after 1988.

Priorities within the military-industrial apparatus changed as a result of the Gulf War and subsequent UN inspections. Iraq modified its industrial plans in order to comply, on paper at least, with UN inspections and requirements. Iraq also took advantage of loopholes in existing UN resolutions. The imposition of limitations on the range of ballistic missiles to 93 miles restricted Iraqi research, development, and production of longer-range systems, but did not apply to cruise missiles. It is therefore not surprising to find that Iraq's new Ibn-al-Haytham missile research and development complex was heavily committed to cruise missile research.[319] Cruise missiles are also better delivery systems for the FAEs – and perhaps the CW and BW agents – produced by Iraqi factories.[320]

Even before the Gulf War, Baghdad expressed considerable interest in air-breathing missiles, including the Soviet SS-N-2 Styx, the Chinese HY-2 Silkworm and the French Exocet anti-ship missiles. According to Pentagon reports, Iraq had seven Silkworm launchers and approximately 50 missiles at the beginning of the Gulf War.[321] Four drones were displayed at the arms exhibition in Baghdad during October, 1988.[322] At the larger Baghdad Arms Exhibition of 1989, Iraq demonstrated a series of drones and RPVs, several of which were reportedly indigenous designs.[323]

The Iraqis had at least three versions of a cruise missile called the Faw in development before the Gulf War. The Faw was based on the SS-N-2 Styx, which used a liquid-fuelled motor, and on the Chinese versions and derivatives available on the international arms market (the HY-1 and HY-2 Silkworm).[324] The smallest version was the Faw-70, with a 70 km range, which appears to be a locally-produced version of the SS-N-2C or D Styx. It carries a warhead of about 500 kg of high explosive. The Faw 150 and Faw 200 were lengthened versions, with ranges of 150 and 200 km respectively.[325]

Iraq also worked on other cruise missiles projects. The so-called 'Ababil' (different from the battlefield rocket) was reportedly a land-attack version of the Mirach 600 RPV. This weapon was on display at the 1989 Baghdad Arms Exhibition, but apparently never entered service.[326] There have been reports of a design for ramjet-powered cruise missile with a speed of Mach 3, although this extremely ambitious design was apparently at least ten years from the prototype stage.³²⁷ During Operation Iraqi Freedom, Iraq did use 'Seersucker' shore-ship cruise missiles for an attack on the US Marine Corps Headquarters ('Camp Commando') in Kuwait – suggesting a continuing interest in cruise missiles for attacks against ground targets.³²⁸

Iraq also demonstrated an interest in Remotely Piloted Vehicles (RPV) and Unmanned Aerial Vehicles (UAV). Iraq experimented with spray tanks on both manned aircraft and pilotless vehicles.³²⁹ UNSCOM was particularly concerned with a test of a 2200 liter belly tank for a Mirage F-1, mounted on a remotely piloted MiG-21 fighter aircraft and apparently optimized for spraying biological agents.³³⁰ The US also reportedly detected an Su-22 during the Gulf War that it suspected was fitted out for BW attack.³³¹ Iraq experimented with remotely piloted versions of the MiG-21 fighter aircraft – apparently unsuccessfully – and with the L-29 jet trainer.³³² The latter conversion reportedly had a 600km range with a 160kg payload.³³³

The L-29 conversion is a significant capability, but incapable of carrying the 2000 liter spray tank – with a weight of at least 2000 kg – that Iraq tested in 1991. In the October 2, 2002 National Intelligence Estimate on the Iraqi threat, the Director, Intelligence, Surveillance, and Reconnaissance of the US airforce included a disclaimer stating that the US airforce did not agree that the Iraqis were developing UAVs *primarily* (italics in original) for CBW delivery.³³⁴ Post-war investigations have confirmed the airforce analysts' assumptions that Iraqi UAVs were, as of 2003, inadequate for CBW delivery.³³⁵

Iraq did, however, maintain two parallel RPV programs up through Operation Iraqi Freedom. The program run from Ibn Fernas worked on both traditional reconnaissance drones and also conversion of manned aircraft. This program was not declared to the UN until 2002, and was responsible for development of the RP-20, RP-30, and Pigeon RPV projects. A second RPV line, run from al-Rashid Airforce Base, remained the subject of investigation by the Iraq Survey Group after the fall of Saddam's regime.³³⁶

Iraq developed half a dozen different short-range missiles with ranges of less than 93 miles, and was accused of modifying SCUD-capable TELs for use with short-range rockets in an effort to circumvent the ceasefire agreement.³³⁷ Since Iraq demonstrated, in the Al-Abid launch program, some expertise at 'bunching' clusters of shorter range rockets to produce longer-range, multi-stage systems, it was reasonable to suspect that they might be capable of constructing a longer-range system from clusters of battlefield rockets as well.

In 1992, Dr. Ralph Ekeus (director of UNSCOM) stated that ' ... [T]here is no possibility without a major new effort to reconstruct the missile program.'³³⁸ Within six months, he had changed his mind. 'Iraq is employing its best engineers, scientists and managers in the missile area ...

It makes us very nervous to have all of the guys of any significance at the same place.'[339]

In 1995, Iraq was caught covertly importing parts and production equipment for ballistic missiles.[340] These included guidance components and gyroscopes from operational Soviet-model sea-launched ballistic missiles. One shipment was intercepted, and Iraq later admitted receiving a similar shipment earlier that year.[341] Iraq produced complete engines and other crucial systems for its missiles that were originally thought to be beyond its industrial capacity.[342] New information and Iraqi admissions cast serious doubt on the ability of the UN to confirm that it had complete knowledge of any of Iraq's many arms production projects – a condition that only exacerbated Western intelligence dilemmas throughout the 1990s and the run-up to Operation Iraqi Freedom.[343]

This confusion applied to missiles and also the more significant WMD programs. As of 1998, UNSCOM had destroyed or accounted for 817 of the 819 SCUDs supplied by the Soviet Union, as well as 19 TELs and 30 chemical and biological warheads.[344] UNSCOM supervised the destruction of 48 SCUD-type missiles and 11 mobile launchers, as well as 30 CW warheads and 20 conventional warheads for SCUD-type missiles.[345] According to a 1999 UNSCOM report, however, UNSCOM could not account for two Soviet-supplied missiles and seven domestically produced Al-Husayns.[346]

In 2002, Western intelligence sought to gain international support for resuming inspections and, later, to justify military action against Iraq. British intelligence reported that Iraq still possessed 20 Al-Husayn missiles, and was working on missiles with a range in excess of 1,000 km – although these would not be operational until 2007.[347] This report also identified important rocket and missile research complexes, including the al-Mamoun plant, which replicated pre-Gulf War facilities linked to Condor fuel production.[348] Other important missile-related facilities included the Al-Rafah North Liquid Propellant Engine Research, Development, Testing and Evaluation Facility, and the Al-Mutasim Solid Rocket Motor and Test Facility (previously associated with the Badr-2000/Condor project).[349] US intelligence believed that Saddam maintained 'a covert force of up to a few dozen SCUD-variant missiles with ranges of 650 to 900 km.'[350] Inspections after Operation Iraqi Freedom indicated that Iraq had continued producing fuel useable only by illicit SCUD variants up through 2001.[351] No al-Husayns or SCUD derivatives have been found in Iraq since 2003, however.

In 2000, Saddam ordered development of missiles with ranges from 400 to 1,000 km. These included design of clustered engine liquid propellant missiles. These projects were several years from completion, although Saddam reportedly wanted them in production within six months.[352] Postwar analysis of Iraqi documents also confirmed Iraqi efforts to purchase the North Korean *Nodong* (also known as Rodong) MRBM – and possibly an entire production facility for the missile – and indicate that Iraq made a $10 million down-payment in late 2002.[353]

UN and Western experts also expressed concern about Iraq's development of battlefield rockets. At least 50 Al-Samoud liquid fuel missiles with a range of 150 km were produced between 1998 and 2002, and Iraq was reportedly modifying the range of these systems in excess of the 150 km permitted by UN Resolution 687.[354] Four TELs for the Al-Samoud were paraded in Baghdad on December 31, 2000.[355] This report asserts that 'with substantial foreign assistance and an accommodating political environment, Iraq could flight-test an MRBM by mid-decade.'[356]

The Al-Samoud program was 'jury rigged out of Soviet-built SA-2 surface-to-air and SCUD missile components.'[357] In both 1994 and 1997, Iraqi scientists were warned not to produce a rocket with a diameter of more than 600 mm, as it would probably exceed the 93 mile/150 km range restriction. Al-Samoud 2 had a diameter of 760 mm.[358] After careful evaluation, experts reached the conclusion that the actual range of the Al-Samoud was 180 kilometers – a 20 percent increase over the UN restrictions.[359] Inspectors also determined Iraq had imported 380 rocket engines for the Al-Samoud project in violation of UN sanctions.[360] Postwar evidence indicates that Iraqi engineering teams sought to use the SA-2 SAM engine for missiles with a range of 250 km.[361]

The Ababil-100 battlefield rocket, according to British intelligence reports, had been modified to a range of 200 km.[362] Similar concerns were expressed about another project – the Al Fatah SRBM.[363] This solid-fueled rocket reportedly reached a range of 100 miles in a test.[364] Both Al-Samoud and the Ababil variants benefited from substantial foreign assistance, both in terms of supply and also in research and development.[365]

The creeping increase in Iraqi missile range and sophistication, supported by successful efforts to procure components, technologies, and even entire missiles from abroad, suggests that the 'substantial foreign assistance and accommodating political environment' US analysts worried about was actually emerging – albeit at a very gradual rate.[366] Iraq appears to have been restoring its missile development and production capability – a process that was only forestalled by international confrontation in 2002, and eventual invasion in 2003. Iraq launched 14 Ababils and Al-Samouds during Operation Iraqi Freedom – nine were successfully intercepted by Coalition defenses. One missile, fired on March 27, 2003, was intercepted just two miles from the allied command center at Camp Doha.[367]

Chemical weapons

Iraq expended, by its own admission, over 100,000 chemical munitions against Iran.[368] Iraq produced mustard gas (HD), riot control gas (CS), and the nerve agents Tabun (GA) and Sarin (GB), as well as cyclosarin (GF).

Mustard is a persistent blister agent which remains a hazard for days, attacking exposed skin, lungs (if inhaled) eyes and mucus membranes. The G-series nerve agents (sarin, tabun, cyclosarin) are more potent nerve agents that attack through inhalation or skin contact, overstimulating muscles or glands and causing convulsions and unconsciousness.[369] Sarin and cyclosarin are non-persistent agents that attack primarily through inhalation. Tabun can remain a hazard for days.[370] Iraqi weapons suffered from significant impurities – tabun (GA) and sarin (GB) agents had a shelf life of only six weeks.[371] Iraq developed sophisticated doctrines for using these weapons on the battlefield.[372]

Iraq also produced the persistent nerve agents VX and Soman (GD).[373] Iraq denied production of VX, but in 1998 UNSCOM inspectors found evidence that it had been loaded onto ballistic missile warheads during the Gulf War.[374] In addition to the production, filling and storage lines at Samarra, Iraq had three production lines for precursor chemicals under construction at Falluja.[375] A phosphate mining operation at Akashat, combined with a chemical plant at Al Qaim, provided organic phosphates for the production of Sarin and Tabun.[376] By 1990, Iraqi chemical weapons production capability was estimated at between 1,000 and 5,000 tons of all types per year.[377] This was sufficient, by one account, to fill between 250,000 and 500,000 chemical munitions each year.[378] Iraq received help, according to UN documents, from 31 major foreign suppliers – including 14 from Germany, three each from the Netherlands and Switzerland, and two each from France, the US, and Austria.[379]

Iraq attempted to conceal its CW production, leading to continuing confusion about the extent of this and other WMD programs. Iraq reported to the UN in April 1991 that it possessed 11 CW production facilities, but by late 1991 the UN had identified at least 48![380] The original declaration claimed only 105 155 mm mustard shells, but UN inspections eventually identified 12,694. Then, 45,755 filled munitions and 78,765 empty munitions were identified by 1992.[381] Iraq initially declared 355 tons of mustard and nerve agents, and only 650 tons of 'intermediate agents.'[382] By early 1992, at least 225 tons of nerve agent and 280 tons of mustard had been identified, and Iraq had modified its original assessment to include 3,173 tons of precursors.[383] By mid-1994, the UN had destroyed 28,049 chemical munitions and over 481,000 liters of chemical agents and precursors.[384] Recent intelligence estimates believe Iraq produced at least 2,850 tons of mustard gas, 210 tons of tabun (GA), 795 tons of sarin (GB), and 3.9 tons of VX.[385]

Iraq reportedly made CW agents available for use in the 1990–91 Gulf War, but did not fire them at Coalition forces.[386] The Al-Muthanna complex, the primary Iraqi CW production site, was destroyed under UN supervision in 1994.[387] UNSCOM surveyed 1,015 sites in Iraq from 1991–98, carrying out 272 inspections, and the CW complex was a particular target. UNSCOM's accomplishments included:

- destruction of 40,000 CW munitions, 2,610 tons of CW precursors, and 411 tons of CW agents;
- dismantling the prime CW complex at al-Muthanna;
- destruction of 30 CW warheads designed for ballistic missile delivery[388]

Other reports note that UNSCOM destroyed 38,500 chemical munitions, 480,000 liters of chemical agents, and 1.8 million liters of chemical precursor.[389]

British intelligence reports before Operation Iraqi Freedom noted that UNSCOM inspections had been unable to account for up to 360 tons of bulk CW agents, including 1.5 tons of VX; up to 3,000 tons of CW precursors, including 300 tons specific to VX production; and over 30,000 munitions for CW and BW delivery.[390] Over 20,000 artillery shells remained unaccounted for by the UN as of late 1998.[391] A CIA report cites discrepancies, based on information provided to UNSCOM, of 6,000 CW munitions.[392] Another CIA report states that Iraq probably retained 15,000 artillery rockets and 550 artillery shells which could carry CW.[393]

UN inspections before Operation Iraqi Freedom failed to discover these missing items. Post-war interviews with Iraqi generals have revealed little. Each has denied having access to chemical weapons, but assumed that commanders in neighboring units had them.[394] A report by the head of the Iraq Survey Group revealed little hard evidence of these missing materials or stockpiled weapons.

> Multiple sources with varied access and reliability have told ISG that Iraq did not have a large, ongoing, centrally controlled CW program after 1991. Information found to date suggests that Iraq's large-scale capability to develop, produce, and fill new CW munitions was reduced – if not completely destroyed – during Operations Desert Storm and Desert Fox, 13 years of UN sanctions and UN inspections.[395]

Review of documents and capabilities, however, suggest that Iraq could have begun producing mustard gas within two months of an order to resume production. Restoration of sarin production has been estimated at between six months and two years away.[396] These statements confirm that, despite UN inspections, Iraq maintained the ability to restore production of chemical weapons once sanctions were lifted.

Biological weapons

Iraq's biological weapons program remains the subject of great controversy and concern. Information on the program remains unreliable – for example, the date the BW program began, relative to other Iraqi WMD programs, remains a matter of some confusion.[397] Iraq admitted after the Gulf War to military research in anthrax and botulism toxins, as well as research with brucellosis and tularemia. No evidence of weapons or of facilities for filling weapons was discovered, although entire buildings from the Salman Pak complex were physically removed or detroyed prior to UN inspection.[398] However, recent reports have listed over a dozen open air Iraqi BW tests in the 1988–91 period.[399]

UNSCOM inspections did not begin to reveal the extent of the BW program until 1995.[400] Iraqi admissions, prompted by the defection of Hussein Kamil to Jordan in the summer of 1995, detail a vast and comprehensive biological weapons effort.[401] The BW complex became an important target for UNSCOM. The destruction of the Al-Hakam BW facility and its associated production equipment was a substantial blow to Iraqi BW efforts.[402]

The documents released after Kamil's defection verified that Iraq had produced both botulinum and anthrax in significant quantities.[403] These documents, and later Iraqi revelations, confirm that 1,500 gallons of anthrax toxin and 3,000 gallons of botulinum toxin were available and loaded on Iraqi missile warheads and aircraft bombs during the Gulf War. Iraq confessed to filling 25 missile warheads and 166 aerial bombs with BW agents.[404] Iraq also produced a toxin which induced gangrene.[405] Iraq admitted to production of 19,000 liters of concentrated botulinum, 8,500 liters of concentrated anthrax, and 2,200 liters of concentrated aflatoxin.[406] Iraq produced the equivalent of over ten billion doses of BW agent before 1991.[407]

In 2002, British intelligence reported that growth media for BW weapons – including up to three times the quantity of the 8,500 liters of anthrax that Iraq reported to the UN – remains at large.[408] This report identified at least *four* weaponized BW strains of concern – botulinum, anthrax, aflatoxin, and ricin.[409] US intelligence reports confirmed that ricin had been tested in artillery shells.[410] After Operation Iraqi Freedom, more evidence of the militarization of ricin was discovered.[411]

The renovation of the al-Dawrah Foot-and-Mouth Disease facility without UN approval in 2001 raised particular concern. Al-Dawrah was one of two Biocontainment Level Three facilities in Iraq, and had been utilized for BW research and production before 1991.[412]

An additional concern, raised in both intelligence reports and Secretary of State Colin Powell's February 5, 2003 address to the United Nations, was the possibility that Iraq maintained mobile BW production facilities.[413] Secretary Powell also raised the question of Iraqi research into other BW agents, mentioning gas-gangrene, plague, typhus, cholera, camel pox, and hemorrhagic fever. Other official statements have mentioned smallpox, brucella, and Congo Crimean Hemorrhagic fever.[414] David Kay noted with concern the fact that Iraq researched techniques with nonpathogenic organisms (B. Thurengiensis and medicinal plants) that could have been applied to biological weapons, including anthrax and ricin.[415] This demonstrates the dual-use nature of scientific research, and the difficulties inherent in both detecting and controlling biological warfare-related programs.

Nuclear weapons

Iraqi nuclear efforts after the 1981 Osiraq raid were secretive and circumspect. A deliberate effort was made to publicly appear to be complying with the Non-Proliferation Treaty, while pursuing covert efforts to acquire the necessary manufacturing technology.[416] Public estimates of Iraq's nuclear program in 1990 stated that it was at least five to ten years from developing nuclear weapons.[417]

These estimates were widely off the mark – a tribute to highly successful deception and camouflage efforts by Iraq. Iraq spent $7–20 billion on its nuclear effort over a period of almost two decades.[418] The nuclear program alone employed approximately 7,000 scientists and up to 20,000 workers.[419] Iraq pursued multiple methods in an effort to enrich uranium to make bomb-grade material, including gas centrifuge and chemical enrichment and electromagnetic isotope separation (EMIS). Research was also carried out in the fields of chemical exchange isotope separation and gaseous diffusion, but little progress was made in either of these areas. The EMIS facilities – which required large components known as calutrons – were the most advanced project at the time of the Gulf War.[420]

In addition, the Osiraq control panels, instrumentation systems, and computers all survived the Israeli raid in 1981, leading some UN inspectors to suspect a secret underground facility for the production of plutonium.[421] UNSCOM officials also reported evidence that Iraq was producing plutonium – a separate weapons production line.[422] A laboratory-scale plutonium separation program was identified by UNSCOM inspectors.[423] Iraq also reportedly carried out some research in laser isotope separation technologies.[424]

More disturbingly, Saddam started a crash program in 1990 to create a nuclear weapon, and some reports state that Iraq had access to 30 kg of enriched uranium – enough to create at least one nuclear device.[425] Iraqi defectors argue that a bomb design already existed in 1990 – but that it was so enormous as to be virtually undeliverable.[426] In fact, one report states specifically that '[W]e had a device capable of producing a nuclear explosion equivalent to a few kilotons of TNT .. the engineering estimates and simulation exercises we conducted put our device in the range of from one to three kilotons.'[427]

Iraqi scientists reportedly assured Saddam Hussein that when the centrifuge program was up and running, they would create enough HEU for one nuclear weapon per year.[428] Estimates of potential Iraqi nuclear weapons production run as high as 20 weapons per year, if the Gulf War had not again postponed Iraqi nuclear ambitions.[429] Iraq would have

156 *Iraq*

begun to produce significant amounts of highly-enriched uranium by 1992, and probably would have perfected a nuclear bomb design by that time.[430] The author's best estimate of Iraqi nuclear potential is included in Table 4.6. This table is based on the following assumptions.

1. Production of a nuclear weapon requires approximately 10 lbs/ 4.54 kg of plutonium,[431] or approximately 44 lbs/20 kg of weapons grade uranium[432].
2. Some 90–100 EMIS units, running at design capacity, produce approximately 15 kg of 93% HEU annually.[433] For the purposes of this analysis, the Tarmiya facility is assumed to begin operation in January 1993,[434] and the twin Ash Sharqat facility in January 1994.
3. A 100-centrifuge cascade would have been available in 1993, with an additional 500-machine cascade available in 1996.[435] The Al Furat facility was capable of producing approximately 2,000 centrifuges per year,[436] and reports state that Iraq had materials sufficient to build 10,000–20,000 centrifuges.[437] This estimate assumes that Iraq could add an additional 400 machines in 1997, and begin bringing 5,000 centrifuges on-line at a rate of 1,000 per year beginning in 1998. A 1,000 centrifuge cascade can produce enough HEU annually to make one nuclear weapon.[438]
4. Finally, that 200 tons of natural uranium is approximately enough to provide HEU for at least 50 bombs.[439] UNSCOM inspectors discovered 580 tons of natural uranium, as well as 1.7 tons of enriched uranium supplied by Italy,[440] so sufficient raw materials existed to produce at least 150 nuclear devices.

It would appear, therefore, that if Iraq had continued funding at the rate of the late 1980s, and if technology (particularly remaining materials necessary for centrifuge production) continued to be available, by 2000 Iraq might have covertly produced as many as 20 nuclear warheads. If Iraq had pursued policies of 'boosting' the yields with lithium-6, this would have been a formidable deterrent to any state.[441] In the first decade of the

Table 4.6 Iraq: potential nuclear weapons production in the absence of desert storm

Process	Year							Total
	1994	1995	1996	1997	1998	1999	2000	
Centrifuge	–	–	–	1	1	2	3	7
EMIS	1	2	2	2	2	2	2	13
Total	1	3	5	8	11	15	20	20

twenty-first century, Iraqi production rate would have continued to increase as more centrifuges came on line.

US and Western intelligence believed that Iraq still maintained a nuclear program in 2002.[442] Defector reports and interviews indicate that Saddam ordered his Special Security Organization to take charge of critical non-nuclear components from the bomb program after the first Gulf War, and that these components were successfully hidden from UNSCOM throughout the inspections.[443] One US intelligence report states that if Iraq received foreign supplies of fissile material, it could manufacture a weapon within one year. Without foreign suppliers, it could not make a weapon until the latter half of the decade.[444] The October 2002 NIE estimates that with 25,000 centrifuges, Iraq could create enough HEU for two weapons per year.[445]

Iraq was attempting to import large numbers of very small (81mm) tubes, which could be used either for centrifuges or as components of battlefield artillery rockets. Their import was specifically prohibited by the Nuclear Suppliers Group guidelines, and should have been banned to Iraq under UN sanctions.[446]

Iraq's nuclear program was the least developed of all of Iraq's WMD programs in 2003. International Atomic Energy Agency Director Mohammed El Baradei rejected US claims before the war and after several months of post-war examination, El Baradei released a statement noting that '[N]o indication of post-1991 weaponization activities were uncovered in Iraq .. [T]he agency observed a substantial degradation in facilities, financial resources and programs throughout Iraq that might support a nuclear infrastructure.'[447]

Some anecdotal evidence suggests that information was withheld from UNSCOM inspectors, and that eventually the nuclear program would have been restored.[448] A leading Iraqi nuclear scientist handed over documents and small components from the centrifuge enrichment program that he had buried in his backyard in 1991.[449] Other interviews with former scientists and other officials suggest that the program was dismantled, but might have been restored over time.[450] Iraq's nuclear program was, apparently, effectively terminated by the combination of Desert Storm and UN inspections. 'ISG [Iraq Survey Group], however, has uncovered no indication that Iraq had resumed fissile material or nuclear weapon research and development activities since 1991.'[451]

What we don't know – continuing gaps

A barrage of criticism – some politically partisan – has been leveled at the US failure to find hidden WMD stockpiles, after using the argument that their existence justified military intervention in Iraq.[452] No 'smoking gun' has been found, and no evidence of an imminent Iraqi WMD breakout (or transfer to terrorist groups) has been identified.[453] Both political and

158 *Iraq*

military analysts provided inaccurate assessments of Iraqi capabilities and doctrine.[454]

There are several possible explanations for the failure to find Iraqi WMD. The first, that the US and various intelligence agencies lied or fabricated evidence, does not seem accurate.[455] Most of the citations used in the previous sections from intelligence reports were derived from UNSCOM data focused on unresolved issues, and supplemented by other means. The UNSCOM data is based on meticulous analysis of Iraqi archives and extensive interviews of Iraqi scientists and officials. Iraq had ample opportunity to disprove the accuracy of this data, and failed. It cannot be reasonably argued, therefore, that the bulk of this initial data is a fabrication by Western intelligence.

A second explanation is US incompetence, or at least lack of foresight and proper planning. US planning for war termination was flawed at best, and troops were not properly prepared (or available in sufficient numbers) to carry out a rapid and thorough search of the country – particularly once local resistance (especially in the central Sunni region) moved from episodic to organized. The US post-OIF WMD search was poorly organized and coordinated.[456]

A third explanation is the unexpected success of Iraqi deception and concealment operations.[457] This undoubtedly accounts for part of the explanation. Iraqi deception activities have been catalogued extensively, and their efforts against UNSCOM and UNMOVIC – measured in the lack of resolution of many issues – were effective and, apparently, highly motivated.[458] The US relied heavily on defector information – information that is now suspect either as highly politicized or perhaps active Iraqi disinformation.[459] This report also points out that the Iraq Survey Group is still sifting through over 30 million pages of Iraqi documentation.

Finally, it is also entirely possible, based on interviews and intelligence reports, that the Iraqi program had been placed in mothballs until the lifting of sanctions.[460] This was originally reported by Hussein Kamel after his defection in 1995, but could not be confirmed at least in part due to active Iraqi resistance to UNSCOM. Now, many months into the occupation of Iraq and after a series of truly intrusive inspections, the mothball option appears more plausible.[461]

Conclusion

The Iraq case represents a significant exception to many of the Cold War theories of LDC arms development. Although Iraq was subject to embargo on a number of occasions, the Iraqi military industrial complex does not represent a classic case of import substitution, nor does it closely follow the ladder of production. It clearly was not an export-oriented defense industry – although if the Gulf Wars had never happened, it might have seized a role in the international missile export business, as a competitor to

North Korea. Because of Iraq's oil wealth, the size of the Iraqi military, its grandiose regional objectives, its highly centralized and repressive regime, and its relatively technically skilled population, Iraq was able to create a large military-industrial infrastructure that made tangible contributions to Iraqi national security policy.

In a relatively short time (1978–90), with the expenditure of vast amounts of capital and labor, Iraq was able to create a surprisingly capable military industry.[462] During the 1986–90 period, when military industrialization was given steadily increasing priority in Iraqi economic planning, the results were remarkable: development of a series of sophisticated ballistic missiles (with constantly expanding indigenous content), covert nuclear development that shocked international observers in 1991, establishment one of the largest chemical and biological weapons production capabilities in the world, and an expanding conventional arms production capacity which satisfied most of the Iraqi military's requirements for light arms and ammunition and was venturing into licensed production and local modification of artillery, armor, and aircraft.

Broadly speaking, the Iraqis developed two different categories of weapons: copies or licensed production of foreign systems, and hybrid designs either developed through joint ventures or with specific Iraqi modifications.[463] Initial local input was relatively limited, but by 1988–90 the industrial complex was providing innovative solutions to specific military requirements. Some of the hybrid systems combined Western and Soviet components, and substantially increased the capability of existing systems.

> ... [T]he fact that many new Iraqi systems are little more than modifications of older weapons or hybrids using established components is in reality a positive indication. In many Third World countries, and even in such states as Israel and South Africa with their developed industries, it is often the ability to adapt weapons systems to local needs that is most rewarding operationally, technically, and financially.[464]

The Iraqi defense industry's capability to respond to their military requirements should not be undervalued. Its contributions in the Iran–Iraq War were substantial. These included:

1 Production of basic munitions in large quantities (especially evident after 1986).
2 Production of low-technology, high-lethality weaponry appropriate to a high-firepower conflict (mortars, CW munitions, mines).
3 Responsiveness to military requirements, particularly when technologies were not available from abroad (ballistic missiles, aircraft modifications projects, higher-technology munitions).
4 Resourcefulness in acquiring technologies and capabilities abroad,

through theft and/or collaboration, which fulfilled specific military requirements.
5 Provision of weapons which not only fulfilled operational military needs against Iran, but which also extended Iraqi military influence into the Middle East and the struggle with Israel and, in theory, provided the basis for deterrence of extra-regional intervention by the United States.

Iraqi industry was successful in adapting systems to military needs. The military, however, was considerably less successful at utilizing the potential which both locally-produced and imported weaponry potentially provided.

> ... Iraq tended to rely on high technology and static, heavily fortified and entrenched defenses. This emphasis often appeared to verge on an obsession with sophisticated technology as a 'wonder weapon', separate from the skills and knowledge of the men using it.[465]

The absorption of technical skills and technology to *produce* weaponry within the industrial complex, apparently, was less difficult than the absorption of the military skills required to master such weaponry in combat. Although the Iraqi army was able to utilize moderately sophisticated technology with some effectiveness against Iran, the same weapons and tactics failed utterly against the Allied Coalition in the Gulf War.

In a little over a decade, Iraq engaged in two of the most significant high-intensity military conflicts in the late twentieth century. During this period, Iraq spent as much as $100 billion on advanced conventional arms and perhaps as much as $27 billion for weapons technology and supplies.[466] The industrial and technical infrastructure created by these investments is enormous, and the knowledge base of the 20,000 scientists and technicians and as many as 100,000 industrial employees who worked in these industries was relatively unaffected by the Gulf War.

The importance and utility of Iraq's military-industrial program is best calculated by two measurements: first, the enormous resources required to detect and monitor Iraqi production facilities and the continuing uncertainty surrounding the extent to which those facilities have been successfully concealed; and second, by the survival of the Ba'athist regime until April 2003. Iraq's residual military-industrial capability was more than sufficient to maintain it as a substantial and dangerous power in the Persian Gulf region, and to maintain some level of Iraqi political and military influence in the core Middle East through the Coalition invasion in March 2003.

Despite the overthrow of the Ba'athist regime, the US and Coalition occupation of Iraq, and the presence of over 1,200 US inspectors actively searching for WMD, the saga of Iraq's military industry is not over yet. A new Iraqi regime is slowly emerging in the midst of an ugly insurgency that could escalate into ethnic and religious civil war. The Bush administration has focused on efforts to construct Iraqi military and paramilitary forces – but the performance of these local troops has been uneven at best. These troops will almost certainly rely on existing stocks of arms for their equipment. Regional analysts have already expressed concerns about the resurrection of Iraq's military industry:

> The last thing Iraq needs now is a defense industry. What they need is to rebuild the country, and not to start to rearm again, and I hope that nothing will happen regarding the defense industries or military modernization in Iraq.[467]

A potentially more important issue is the question of WMD. The US will hand over government of Iraq to a regime much less committed to aggression or focused on WMD acquisition than the Ba'athist regime it replaces. Nevertheless, the new Iraqi regime will face many of the same security problems that Saddam, and every preceding Iraqi regime, has faced – a more powerful Iranian neighbor, Iraq's continuing interest in southern ports, the traditional claim to sovereignty over Kuwait, and competition in the Persian Gulf and Middle East regions. A federalized Iraqi State might inadvertently find itself used as a sanctuary by Turkish Kurdish separatists.

Iraq's security dilemma forces the government to find ways to create military power. Iraq's new military will be constrained in size, at least for a time, and focused on the difficult task of suppressing a mounting Sunni insurgency – a task Iraq's army has never faced before. This leaves Iraq, at least in theory, vulnerable to external attack – from Syria, from Iran, or even from Turkey.

This Iraqi vulnerability leaves the US with three policy alternatives – each with significant potential risk. The first is that the US can 'cut and run,' leaving Iraqi security in its own hands and getting out of the region quickly in an effort to minimize the political costs of the Iraq intervention, and freeing up forces for use elsewhere in the global war on terrorism. Some might consider this a pragmatic option. It is, almost certainly, also a recipe for the resurrection of Iraq's WMD programs. Faced with significant external threats, but lacking the economic and military resources to defend itself, an Iraqi regime would certainly find the restoration of some WMD programs a cheap and useful force multiplier. It seems difficult to believe that a US military, increasingly focused on counter-insurgency operations, would be able to eliminate Iraq's WMD capabilities before leaving, given the difficulties experienced in even locating them to date. Despite significant efforts, the Iraq Survey Group has failed to identify or locate key materials and capabilities from Saddam's programs that remain unaccounted for as of October 2005.[468] In addition, much of the necessary knowledge required to recreate some of the simpler forms of WMD reside in the thousands of scientists, technicians, and workers who survived Desert Storm and OIF. This knowledge base cannot be eliminated without massive, and unacceptable, violations of human rights.

A second option would be to focus on eliminating Iraqi WMD capabilities, even if that means more extensive US military commitment in the region in the short term. Recreating Iraq's conventional military capability in a form that is both militarily robust and politically reliable will take years – and current policy seems focused on getting Iraqi security forces into the streets as quickly as possible, accepting the risks of inadequate training and higher Iraqi casualties. An increased US presence would free up additional personnel for the WMD search, ensuring that the remaining infrastructure is attacked systematically and uprooted in a more permanent fashion. The cost, of course, is greater strain on US military resources, and larger risk to US personnel in Iraq – as well as the political cost of appearing to continue to occupy Iraq, which will act as a lightning rod in the Muslim world.

The third option is similar to US policies elsewhere, where political liberalization coincided with industrialization. If the US were to guarantee Iraq's security, and maintain forces in Iraq to provide for external security, this would alleviate Iraq's need for WMD to defend itself. This policy has worked successfully in South Korea, where US troop presence contributed not only to South Korean security and US nonproliferation objectives, but also to South Korean democracy. To a lesser extent, it has also worked in Latin America, and even in Taiwan. A credible US security guarantee, particularly at a time when US conventional military superiority is unrivaled, counteracts the attractiveness of indigenous WMD as a military force multiplier. A US commitment carries significant risks – unpopularity for the host government, continued long-term US presence in a politically volatile region, and force protection risks for US military on the ground in Iraq.

The United States must choose its Iraq policy with the WMD issue firmly in mind. Perversely enough, now that the war for Iraqi WMD is over, the future of Iraqi WMD rests in American hands. Given the unresolved nature of the Iraqi WMD complex, only continued US commitment in some form can prevent its resurrection.

5 Regional powers, security, and arms production
Conclusions

Perceptions of regional military and other security threats play critical roles in the development and direction of LDC military-industrial policy. The case studies demonstrate important patterns in the military-industrial policies of regional powers, particularly during times of serious military threat or regional crisis. These patterns appear to complement or, in some cases, contradict existing models of LDC military industrialization. The three most important observations are:

1   High levels of regional threat promote more rational, cost-effective utilization of military-industrial resources.
2   LDCs acquire, create and apply technologies in response to specific regional requirements, either creating new hardware (niche innovation) or utilizing hardware in unexpected ways (conceptual innovation).[1]
3   The role of individuals in determining the direction of LDC military industries is absolutely vital.

Each of these observations demonstrates the inadequacy of existing models of LDC military industrialization, which focus on issues of economic efficiency and dependency. A theoretical model of a security-based LDC military-industrial policy, therefore, provides additional insight into both the historical and possible future military-industrial policies of aspiring powers in the developing world. The case studies demonstrate that regional threats and opportunities provide incentives for regional powers to acquire, assimilate, produce, and sometimes design sophisticated new weapons and technologies which strongly affect regional military balances and, potentially, international security.

The collapse of the bipolar system, declining demand for new major weapons systems, and the increasing globalization of the international arms industry indicate that the future arms trade will be more commercial than ideological in nature. Unipolarity and the global war on terrorism create an unusually globalized international security environment. The US now maintains a significant presence in regions that were once relatively isolated. This significantly affects the security policies of regional powers. The unprecedented stationing of US forces in Pakistan during Operation Enduring Freedom, for example, both supported US operations and profoundly affected the evolution of the 2002 Indo–Pakistan nuclear crisis.

Armed conflict remains a common means of resolving political, social, and economic tensions both within and across national boundaries. The demands on international institutions to intervene in these conflicts are greater than ever. US and UN policy will face potential difficulties from LDC producers, as demonstrated by North Korea's proliferation of ballistic missiles, Pakistan's recent admissions of transnational nuclear proliferation, and Iraq and Iran's non-cooperation with international monitoring regimes. Arms trade links between LDC producers complicate arms control efforts, create and share significant military capabilities, and also minimize the impact of international arms embargoes. Multinational agreements and international norms banning shipment or production of certain types of weapons or technologies are, apparently, easily undercut by determined producers and suppliers.

Case studies: patterns and trends

India

Despite its relatively large military-industrial inheritance, Indian military industrial policy in the 1947–62 period reflected India's political concerns over the reliability and status of the army – essentially a domestic issue of civil-military relations – and a preference for form over substance. India focused on symbolic, high-technology projects, particularly in the aerospace field. Expensive investments in imported weapons, industrial technology, and local research and development received priority over lower-technology items repeatedly requested by the ground forces that were well within the capacity of local industry. The long-term prospects of India's conventional arms industry were essentially determined in this period by the preferences of two individuals – Prime Minister Jawaharlal Nehru and his confidante V. K. Krishna Menon. Nehru and Homi Bhabha also created the infrastructure and driving intellectual force behind India's nuclear weapons program during this period.

The 1962–74 period demonstrated the transforming impact of increased levels of regional threat on military-industrial policy. Sophisticated indigenous R&D projects were dropped or de-emphasized in favor of licensed-produced or imported systems. Local industry shifted from long-term research and high-visibility projects that exceeded India's industrial capacity to near-term production of items required by the armed forces in the new strategic environment. Endurance and non-platform weapons were emphasized, leading to improved utilization of the Ordnance Factories, greater sensitivity to requirements for spare parts and logistics, and enhanced overall military readiness, maintenance, and repair capability. Development of nuclear weapons also became a priority during this period as a result of the increased Chinese threat.

The 1975–98 period indicates the impact of declining threat on established LDC military industries. The efficient utilization of existing military-industrial infrastructure and resources were de-emphasized in favor of competition with first tier-producers in a full range of production. Local designs for major weapons platforms received inadequate funding, remained isolated from India's expanding private sector, and were not prioritized in order of relative importance – a recipe for inefficiency and waste that defeated India's efforts to move up to the top tier of producers. When military capabilities of regional opponents were enhanced, India balanced these capabilities by importing new weapons with long-term licensing agreements. Endurance requirements were gradually de-emphasized, and by the end of this period India was again susceptible to logistics shortages.

This experience suggests that military-industrial policy in an era of relative security responds primarily to non-security factors, including economic concerns, political and bureaucratic interests, and pursuit of the symbolic manifestations of great power status. Emerging threats during the 1975–98 period, such as the Soviet invasion of Afghanistan and resulting Pakistani rearmament, prompted changes in military procurement – including significant increases in defense allocations – but no urgent restructuring of military-industrial priorities. Since 1998, India has again re-evaluated its defense policy in light of the new nuclear environment and Pakistan's continuing support for insurgency in Kashmir and elsewhere. The impact on military industry, so far, is only modest. The key exception remains the nuclear/strategic sector, which clearly continues to receive both resources and bureaucratic priority.

India is normally associated with the 'import-substitution' model of military-industrialization described in Chapter 1, but this does not accurately reflect Indian policies. India *has* achieved import-substitution in critical areas, particularly production for the ground forces at the Ordnance Factories. Import-substitution of major weapons systems remains spotty, however, with priorities shifting between licensed production and indigenous development. Exports have never been an Indian priority, and the ladder of production model – mentioned in Chapter 1 – appears an inadequate methodology due to the wide separation between military and civilian industrial sectors and the relative absence of technology absorption and transfer across projects and sectors.

Indian military-industrial policy is best described in realist terms. It is practical and cost-effective under high levels of threat, but pursues prestigious and high-profile projects when the regional environment appears relatively unthreatening. Military-industrial projects have not unduly taxed Indian society, and may even have provided some positive stimulus to national economic development despite structural barriers.[2] More generally, however, Indian military-industrial efforts remain unfocused, and have not led to significant levels of global competitiveness, broader technology absorption or economic improvement. This conclusion is particularly clear when India's military-industrial achievements are compared to Israel's.

Israel

For the first 40 years of Israeli independence, geography and hostile neighbors combined to create a constant and extraordinary threat to the state's continued existence. Israeli policy was forced to prioritize between *konenut* (preparedness; immediate force structure and requirements) and *hitkonenut* (preparation; future potential), recognizing that military-industrial autarky might become a future requirement due to political isolation. This dilemma, recognizable in the cases or India and Iraq as well, is fundamental to understanding the relationship between security and LDC military-industrial policies.

From 1948–67, Israel pursued a policy which maximized the value-added benefits of local military industry. Endurance requirements were emphasized. Scarce major weapons platforms needed to be maintained at high levels of readiness and repaired immediately if damaged, while munitions and light arms were urgently required by the large but poorly armed IDF. This value-added policy led to creation of an industrial infrastructure that could be expanded to more sophisticated and challenging projects in the future, including local modification, design, and production of major weapons platforms.

Three significant long-term projects were instituted in this period – the aircraft industry, the electronics industry and the nuclear program. The firm support of David Ben Gurion drove each of these projects despite opposition from military and economic advisors, and each was enabled by the careful guidance of Shimon Peres. The role of individuals in key aspects of Israel's military infrastructure, therefore, cannot be overemphasized. When funding was available, local high-technology projects were pursued on a case-by-case basis, under the careful scrutiny of the IDF.

The victory of 1967 significantly changed Israeli assumptions regarding both the regional military balance and military-industrial priorities. The assumption that Arab forces were unlikely to attack Israel in the near future spurred a shift in industrial policy from preparedness to preparation. An influx of foreign capital and significant growth in defense budgets facilitated a general expansion of industrial capabilities.

Major weapons platforms became an industrial priority due to embargo and cancellation of contracts by European suppliers. Existing capabilities for maintenance, modernization, and light arms production expanded and remained critical for IDF force posture. The emphasis of the Israeli military-industrial policy, however, shifted to the pursuit of self-sufficiency in major weapons platforms and overall military-industrial capacity.

The 1973–95 period presented a series of dilemmas for Israeli planners. Rapid expansion in Arab military capabilities threatened Israeli battlefield superiority. Israel's economic productivity, however, suffered due to massive defense expenditures, threatening long-term economic well-being and security. The defense sector, which constituted one of the largest sectors of the national economy, became increasingly vulnerable to changes in the international arms market and IDF procurement decisions.

The US–Israeli security relationship posed threats to Israel's political independence and long-term military-industrial self-sufficiency, at the same time that it funded a steadily increasing share of Israeli military purchases and local military projects. From 1973–83, the IDF suffered from a near-embarrassment of riches. The combination of US assistance and high local defense spending allowed simultaneous expansion of force structure and qualitative upgrading of all branches of the IDF. After 1983, the availability of top-of-the-line US systems paid for with US aid dollars challenged entrenched and politically powerful sections of the industry, particularly in the aerospace sector.

Israel ultimately proved unable to sustain a policy of self-sufficiency, particularly in major weapons platforms. The former close coordination between IDF requirements, Israeli national priorities, and military industry eroded. Declining defense budgets reduced IDF orders for locally-produced goods, and the availability of US military assistance further endangered the IDF-local industry relationship. The Lavi disaster and other financial crises within the defense industry necessitated massive layoffs and a still unfinished restructuring of Israeli military-industrial infrastructure and policy.

Israel's security environment is currently in the midst of important transitions. The overthrow of the Iraqi regime removes the most significant near-term conventional and unconventional threats to Israel. The presence of the US in the region may have reduced the likelihood of a revival of some pan-Arab or 'frontline state' alliance. At least for the near-term, therefore, the requirement for conventional modernization to forestall a future Arab coalition may be receding.

However, the global war on terrorism and the continuing struggle to resolve the Palestine dilemma also create major obstacles for Israeli security planning. Israel is now menaced by a low-technology but very determined opponent that can strike publicly and with significant psychological effect inside Israel's borders. Transnational and pan-Islamic terrorist organizations threaten both Israel and the regimes of Israel's neighbors. It is conceivable that this could destabilize or even topple regimes in Saudi Arabia, Egypt, Syria, or Jordan. Existing regimes, aware of the galvanizing power of the Palestinian issue, could re-ignite or re-create pan-Arab or pan-Islamic coalitions against Israel as a means of distracting domestic populations from considering regime change. Should Israeli military industry, therefore, focus on preparedness? Or preparation? And what threat – nuclear, chemical, conventional, terrorist – should receive priority?

Israel's military goods remain among the world's best, demonstrating the potential synergy between Israeli military requirements and high-technology, locally-produced solutions. The IDF continues to demand a value-added industrial policy, with R&D spending focused on critical sophisticated sub-systems and non-platform weapons. Scaling back the industry and reverting to a strictly value-added policy, however, will have adverse economic and political impact because of the distorting role of the defense industry on Israel's national economy.

Israel is traditionally associated with two models of military-industrialization – the 'export-oriented' model and 'the ladder of production' discussed in Chapter 1. Neither of these models accurately reflect the impact of security on Israeli military-industrial policy. In the 1950s, David Ben Gurion authorized several deliberately non-incremental investments in military industry – the establishment of aerospace, electronics, and nuclear weapons programs. These programs reflected Ben Gurion's own commitment to *hitkonenut*, and his concerns over Israel's long-term vulnerability. These decisions again demonstrate the profound impact of individuals on LDC military-industrial decision making.

Decisions in the 1970s, particularly the continued pursuit of a 'blue-and-white' fighter production capability, resemble the import substitution model rather than the export model. Decisions in the 1970s and 1980s were heavily influenced by domestic economic factors and the desire for international prestige. Ultimately, however, the driving factor in Israeli military-industrial policy has been national security requirements. These requirements still affect Israeli planning today, and undeniably had positive spin-off effects on the civilian economy, particularly in electronics and other high-technology sectors.

Iraq

Unlike India and Israel, the authoritarian rule of Saddam Hussein throughout the period of Iraq's military-industrialization minimized the necessity to consider extraneous political factors. Iraq's policies reflect the demands of Saddam and a few select advisors and their perceptions of Iraq's security condition.

Iraq's early military-industrial policies, from 1974–84, reflect a classic LDC approach to the experience of embargo. The Soviet embargo of 1974, which left Iraq virtually bereft of munitions in the face of Kurdish rebellion and Iranian covert support, forced Saddam to reevaluate the reliability of his primary supplier. Technicians were sent abroad for training, foreign experts hired, and 'turn-key' industrial facilities purchased in addition to a new policy based on gradual diversification of arms suppliers. Increased emphasis was placed on unconventional weapons.

The Iran–Iraq War forced major changes in Iraqi foreign and military policies. Iraq's armed forces proved incapable of converting superior technology into decisive military advantage. Many of its weapons were too sophisticated for Iraqi personnel to operate or maintain at Western or even Soviet standards.[3] The war turned into an extended conflict of attrition, gradually threatening Iraqi political stability and economic well-being. Efforts by Arab allies and foreign suppliers to cut off credit and supplies in the mid-1980s raised the very real possibility of Iraqi defeat.

Iraq responded by using local industry to enhance endurance capabilities and to develop weapons and technologies unavailable from outside suppliers. Iraq relied increasingly on locally produced chemical weapons for both offense and defense. Locally-produced ballistic missiles replaced the ineffective Iraqi airforce for long range strikes on Iranian cities. Local modification projects increased the range and capability of Iraqi strike aircraft, resulting in increasingly effective attacks on Iranian economic targets. Improved endurance capabilities were evident in the increasing role of local technicians in depots and routine maintenance, in expanded munitions production, and in the gradual development of production facilities for the artillery and heavy mortars that played such a critical role in Iraq's firepower-intensive military operations.

Military-industrial programs continued to receive the highest possible priority in Iraq even after the defeat of Iran. Overt efforts included design of new types of artillery and an enormous production facility at Taji, licensed production of armored vehicles and tanks, and negotiations for assembly and licensed production of jet trainers and Mirage fighters. These priorities suggest that Iraq attempted to adhere, at least at some level, to the 'ladder of production' model.

Iraq also pursued symbolic capabilities, including space boosters, satellites, anti-ballistic missiles, and the exaggerated capabilities of the Baghdad and Adnan aircraft. Iraq's enormous covert procurement network emphasized unconventional weapons production, including the Supergun, ballistic missiles, and the massive nuclear, chemical, and biological warfare programs. In the aftermath of the Iran–Iraq War, then, Iraq continued to develop specific capabilities which filled political-military requirements, but also began to seek the symbolic benefits of military industry and demonstration of unexpected technological capabilities. In this respect, Iraq demonstrated an alternative model for LDC military industrialization.

Iraq's policies deliberately mixed the ladder of production and import substitution models described in Chapter 1, choosing the best or, in some cases, most feasible, of each. Throughout the Iran–Iraq War, Iraq avoided pursuing a broad spectrum of major platform production. Iraq instead prioritized by maximizing the efficient utilization of existing capabilities and infrastructure, and selectively seeking to assimilate new and critically-required capabilities determined by the leadership. The unexpected level of technological assimilation can be deduced by the surprise which greeted each successive Iraqi industrial achievement.

Iraq's military and industrial policies were suitable for regional conflict, but insufficient to compete with the global state of the art – a fact amply demonstrated from 1990–2003. Saddam's foreign policies were inadequately synchronized with the military means at his disposal, and local industry could not make up the shortfall. Iraq did demonstrate to other states that policies based on the Iraqi model might *deter* superpower military intervention – although Operation Iraqi Freedom suggests the dangers and practical limits of such policies.

Lessons learned: security and military industry

The inadequate historical perspective of existing studies of LDC military industrialization, the unwillingness to appropriately disaggregate either the hierarchy of international arms production or distinctions within the developing world, and the failure to adequately consider political-military issues or the less-easily discerned aspects of military capability have led to unreasonably pessimistic assessments of the effectiveness of LDC military industries. As the case studies reveal, LDC military industries can contribute positively to the military requirements of producer states at reasonable cost.

On consideration of all three cases, a pattern begins to emerge. During periods of relatively high military threat or vulnerability, military-industrial policies become relatively more rational – or at least efficient, in terms of achieving tangible benefits at an affordable economic cost. Emphasis is placed on projects that are applicable to regional combat and the most likely threats. Lower priority is given to symbolic projects such as Major Weapons Systems, unless supply of particular items is threatened. Pursuit of elusive concepts such as self-sufficiency and autarky temporarily ceases, and practical, cost-effective solutions within the limitations of national technical and industrial capabilities are emphasized. The military has greater input, or at least oversight, in military-industrial plans and policy.

As security threats decline military-industrial policy moves away from this rational calculus. Non-security factors, including bureaucratic preference, domestic politics, civil-military relations, prestige, and potential domestic economic benefits become more important in determining military-industrial policy. Excess capacity, especially in munitions and other low-technology items which were mass-produced for growing force structures, creates new dilemmas for LDC producers. Accepting inefficient levels of production to maintain the infrastructure is one possible solution. Another alternative is encouraging exports of excess production.

It appears that states which begin development of military industries under low-threat conditions succumb more readily to this latter set of inefficiencies and temptations. The symbolic and political aspects of arms production dominate policy decisions. This might account, in part, for the differences between arms production in Latin America, where cross-border conflicts are rare and strongly discouraged by regional treaty and the US presence, and production in more conflicted regions such as the Middle East and South Asia. Symbolic projects, including pursuit of the elusive 'across-the-board' capability and self-sufficiency in Major Weapons Systems, reflect the desires of regimes to increase their domestic and international reputation and to compete symbolically with the great powers.

A security-based model of LDC arms production, therefore, makes an important contribution to existing literature, reflecting the responses of lesser powers to more highly militarized regional military conditions. This model re-introduces the security dilemma into debate over the effectiveness of LDC production, and addresses the ramifications of local arms production for regional insecurity and stability.

A security-based model of LDC arms production

The procurement of arms, in theory, responds to existing and potential threats to the purchasing or producing state. Security factors therefore play an important role in the determination of military-industrial policy. Given limited resources, an LDC should attempt to maximize the positive impact of military-industrial policy on the civilian economy, while simultaneously lowering dependence on foreign suppliers and providing capabilities necessary to fulfill national military requirements.

According to this security-based model, the critical obligations of a lower tier defense industry are:

1. To develop an infrastructure for manufacturing or supplementing supplies of 'sustenance requirements' for the armed forces in peacetime, and to maintain the option of sustained surge production in times of war or embargo.
2. To maximize the quality of existing military equipment at minimum expense through modification and modernization programs and production of 'value-added' sub-systems and non-platform weapons.
3. To develop and produce critical military items unavailable from foreign suppliers.
4. To develop and produce items which are 'regional-specific' (appropriate for local geographic, technological, military, or political requirements), or which maximize or create local comparative advantages (niche production).

Category one: sustenance requirements

The first category of production requirements are sustenance requirements: the building blocks of military strength. These include small arms, light arms and crew-served infantry weapons, medium arms up to and including artillery, ammunition, and other consumables. Also included are maintenance, repair, and other logistics capabilities, and various forms of non-lethal military goods. In effect, this category combines the 'Endurance' category with segments of the 'Non-platform weapons' category discussed in Chapters 2 through 4.

Production of small arms provides weapons for both defense against external foes and for maintaining internal security while requiring only minimal technical and industrial sophistication. Production of small arms and small caliber ammunition, unsurprisingly, represents the most widespread military-industrial undertaking in the developing world – by the early 1980s, over 40 states produced small arms and/or ammunition locally.[4] Production of crew-served weapons, including machine guns, mortars, light and medium artillery, and light anti-aircraft guns, provides low-technology, firepower-intensive weaponry for the military at a reasonable cost relative to imported equipment.[5]

These weapons permit an LDC military to gain substantial firepower superiority over rebel or insurrectionist movements and to carry out high-firepower attrition warfare against local or extra-regional opponents. In the latter respect, firepower serves as a partial substitute for operational skill in combat. States which cannot master advanced military techniques may still be able to achieve favorable military results by simply overwhelming their opponents with shells. Mortars, for example, are relatively primitive military instruments, but are estimated to have accounted for approximately 50 percent of the casualties in World War II.[6] Artillery has inflicted the majority of all casualties in most major wars since 1914, and has increased in importance relative to other ground combat arms due to improvements in range, accuracy, and lethality.[7]

Local production of munitions and other consumables is extremely important for states with external conflicts – running out of shells and bullets is an unacceptable reason for losing a war. Regional conflicts, particularly in the regions discussed in the case studies, have become high-firepower wars: expenditure of consumables (and especially ammunition) has reached enormous levels.[8] Iraq, for instance, expended over 400 artillery rounds per gun per day in early 1986, and is reported to have expended the equivalent of one US Army 'week' of munitions per weapon per day in intense combat.[9]

Major military powers consistently underestimate the requirements for consumables in war – an experience shared by India in 1965 and 1999, Israel in 1973, and Iraq in 1974–75 and 1980. During World War I, German gunners also fired as many as 400–500 rounds per barrel per day in intense combat – far exceeding the pre-1914 estimates for ammunition expenditure – and the British Army in the Falklands expended 450 shells per gun in one evening during heavy fighting.[10]

The potential utility of local munitions production for LDCs has not received sufficient attention. Continuing production lines allow undisturbed sources of supply in the event of protracted, attritional conflicts, such as the Arab-Israeli War of Attrition or the Iran–Iraq War. The importance of this capability has sometimes been misinterpreted, given the relatively short duration of many LDC conflicts. One leading analyst of regional conflicts notes that Israel's stockpiling of munitions indicates an inability to 'surge' production in the event of conflict:

> For Third World combatants, the ability to produce consumables during peacetime has not translated into an ability to deliver sufficient resupplies to troops during combat, particularly in high attrition battle situations. This has certainly been true for the Israelis, who are forced to mobilize a citizen army for war and, in so doing, seriously deplete their industries of the highly skilled technicians needed to sustain high production rates.[11]

In point of fact, Israel provides exemptions for critical employees in the arms industries.

This analyst argues elsewhere that: "... [H]ad the war [in Lebanon] continued at its high attrition rate, Israel would have had to turn to the United States for the resupply of many spare parts and munitions for those systems originating in American industries."[12] The lack of a timeframe here is irritating. Readers and analysts might want to know *how soon* the Israelis would have required US re-supply – a week? a month? a year? Israel produces spare parts for many US systems, and even provides maintenance for a number of US aircraft based in Europe.

Israel committed about 76,000 troops to battle in 1982 in eight divisional groups.[13] The low number of troops engaged means that relatively few conscripts were mobilized, mitigating any pernicious effect conscription might have on the arms industry. In addition, these would be small divisions, and given the sporadic nature of high-intensity combat in the 1982 campaign, IDF requirements for re-supply from the US might not have been nearly as stark as Neuman portrayed them due to the existence of significant stockpiles.

These statements reflect a misunderstanding of the nature of logistics, surge production, and of Israeli military-industrial capability. *All* nations, or at least those which take the possibility of war seriously, stockpile equipment.[14] The difference between peacetime and wartime expenditure of consumables is significant – according to a report to Congress after the Gulf War, '[D]emands for some things increased 20 to 30 times the peacetime rate.'[15] No state (the US included) expects to immediately provide for this difference by direct shipments from production sites to the battlefield. There is, in fact, a distinction between 'cold-base level,' which maintains inventories sufficient to sustain troops in preparation for war and during the early stages of combat, and 'hot-base level,' which reflects wartime inventory levels. The latter are actually *lower* than cold-base levels because mobilized production lines will be constantly turning out new equipment.[16]

Surge production capacity is intended to increase production for wartime, and to make up expenditure of consumables from stocks and equipment lost in combat as quickly as possible – not to compensate for inadequate stockpiles by rapidly mobilizing industrial capacity to meet wartime demand. In the case of high-technology weapons, surge production rates can be only modest improvements over existing rates, and may take substantial time to achieve.

> Not withstanding the remarkable production increases achieved during Operation Desert Storm, substantial time was required to reach maximum production rates, even for some common, relatively inexpensive items ... six to nine months was required to achieve maximum production capacity for a variety of items. The time required to increase production rates of major items is greater still. For example, it would take 19 months to increase the AH-64 production rate from six to eight a month.[17]

A key indicator of LDC military preparedness, therefore, is stockpiles – and LDC industries can contribute substantially to these stockpiles in peacetime. LDC militaries stockpile equipment for the maintenance of war reserve stocks:

> War reserves are those stocks of material amassed in peacetime to meet wartime increases in military requirements until industrial production can meet demand. War reserves provide interim support to sustain operations until resupply began; stockage objectives are a function of, among other things, the threat and industrial base dynamics.[18]

Israel experienced the trauma of a shortage of war reserves in the 1973 conflict, when emergency US resupply was thought necessary to sustain IDF combat operations.[19] In 1973, the IDF could supply six divisions in combat for 14 days, but by 1982 it could supply 11 divisions for at least 28 days – considerably greater capability than the eight small divisions actually fielded, again raising questions about the necessity for American re-supply.[20] This capability increased to 40 days for a force of 12 divisions and 20 independent brigades in the late 1980s.[21]

Iraq had stocks for 10–30 days of intense combat distributed down to the company level in the Kuwait Theater just before the Gulf War. Over 300,000 tons of ammunition were available in Kuwait alone.[22] In the aftermath of Operation Iraqi Freedom, US forces discovered that Iraq had stockpiled between 650,000 and one *million* tons of munitions – a supply over half the size of the entire American stockpile.[23]

These basic ammunition supplies are cheap and well within the capabilities of many LDC producers, and stockpile requirements provide substantial economies of scale. Certain high-technology munitions, in fact, cannot be 'surged,' and must be stockpiled in some numbers.[24] Stockpiling from local production, then, is both rational and affordable for many LDC producers.

Maintenance and repair capabilities, as seen in the case studies, are also critical, both to military performance and also because of the linkages with both military and military-industrial proficiency.[25] Both India and Israel obtained substantial advantages over regional adversaries by being able to rapidly repair tanks on or near the battlefield.[26] Soviet analysts estimated that in combat, 85–90 percent of the 'new' equipment arriving in the hands of troops would come from the repair shops, rather than the factories.[27]

Not all LDCs can achieve significant capabilities in this arena. Despite improvements made to Iraqi maintenance capabilities during the Iran–Iraq War, US analysts estimate that at least 20 percent of the Iraqi airforce was grounded for lack of maintenance in 1991. Iraq's army lacked the ability to carry out depot-level maintenance, and repair of incapacitated systems in Kuwait was basically impossible even before the air campaign began.[28]

Maintenance and repair facilities, as described in the 'ladder of production model' can lead to enhanced production and modification capabilities. Both Israel and Iraq utilized existing army maintenance depots as the basis for later tank modification and production projects. This expansion of maintenance facilities can also contribute to supplies of spare parts – a problem which has afflicted India on numerous occasions.[29] Many other regional powers appear to be emphasizing these types of sustenance capabilities in their military-industrial policies.

These capabilities are also the area where technology as a process can be most easily transferred between the military and military industry. Familiarization with technological products through use, maintenance and repair increases the recognition of their strengths and limitations on the battlefield as well as of the process and principles behind their design and assembly. The ladder of production reflects this concept. In effect, this area of technological absorption is the place where the hierarchy of production and the hierarchy of global military culture most closely overlap.

Category two: quality maintenance

The second category revolves around modification and modernization capabilities, and production of sub-systems which enhance capabilities of existing systems within the LDC arsenal. Most LDCs maintain substantial arsenals of older equipment which may be approaching the end of its active service life. Modernization programs extend service life and can increase the capability of existing systems to match newer generations of equipment which may or may not be available on the international market at higher cost.[30]

> The costs of retrofit are considerably less than those of buying new systems. For example, the $1.56 billion to be spent by the governments of Belgium, Denmark, the Netherlands and Norway [on air force modernization] is a great deal of money. However, it will maintain over 400 modern fighter aircraft in service whereas the same money would only buy 60 to 90 (depending on the designation) of comparable performance.[31]

Once weapons systems become mature, the rate of improvement in subsystems becomes faster than the rate of improvement in the weapons systems themselves, and the systems themselves have substantially increased service lives.

> As weapons systems grow older, they have tended to last longer as the rate of development decreases. In World War I aircraft became obsolete in two years or less, but in World War II some aircraft continued in service throughout the war. Ships exhibited the same phenomenon, modernized World War I battleships doing good service in World War II.[32]

This phenomenon applies to other major systems as well – the IDF still uses Centurion tanks designed in the late 1940s, and US B-52 bombers are invariably older than their pilots.

As repair, maintenance, and/or production techniques are mastered, local modification of foreign-supplied equipment allows the regional power to improve the service life and performance of existing equipment. SIPRI analysis suggests that retrofitting offers virtually the same combat power as a new system at 20–35 percent of the cost.[33]

Modification programs allow LDC producers to increase the capability of existing forces at substantial savings in defense expenditures. They also permit LDCs to utilize existing industrial and economic comparative advantages, or in some cases to create them. Israel's sophisticated electronics industry, for instance, allows the Israeli airforce to modify US-designed fighter aircraft with substantially enhanced performance and electronic warfare capabilities, and provides fire control equipment that prolongs the service life and combat effectiveness of over 3,000 older tanks in IDF inventory. Iraq combined Western and Soviet technologies in a number of projects for increasing the effectiveness of aircraft, missiles, tanks, artillery, and guided weapons.

Category three: ability to produce systems not available from other suppliers

The third category refers to the provision of equipment unavailable as a result of embargo, political controversy, and international arms control agreements. Political restrictions and embargoes, as mentioned above, provide strong incentive for local production of arms. It should not be surprising that many of the leading LDC arms producers are associated with the proliferation of technologies which are theoretically controlled, including ballistic missiles, chemical and biological weapons, and nuclear warheads.

The supply of major weapons platforms, including tanks and aircraft, has been interrupted in some cases, creating requirements for local production by LDCs. As mentioned above, much of the existing literature on LDC arms production focuses on major weapons systems, and questions the rationale for production on economic grounds. The Israeli experience demonstrates that it is not only possible for these systems to be produced largely, albeit not entirely, with indigenous technology, but that the systems can be militarily effective and relatively affordable. Israeli production of the Kfir combat aircraft and the Merkava tank are two examples. While both depend on imported inputs (US engines), they contributed substantially to IDF force posture and potential military capability at comparable cost to imported systems. Licensed production of the MiG-21 eventually saved India considerable foreign exchange during 20 years of manufacture.

Dependence and vulnerability to embargo, however, is often exaggerated for political reasons. It is difficult to deny determined states access to both supplies *and* technology. South Africa relied largely on Mirage airframes and foreign technological assistance despite sanctions.[34] Iraq continued to smuggle industrial technology and equipment even while under strict international embargo. Iran has evaded US efforts to restrict its military capability by using Chinese, Russian, and other suppliers.

The threat of undue dependency as a rationale for MWS production by LDCs is, in most cases, receding. Increasing commercialization of the market and efforts by producer states to maintain existing infrastructure and employment provide strong incentives for exports. Both NATO and former Warsaw Pact states have large inventories of surplus equipment which can be obtained cheaply and modernized with the assistance of a variety of states, including both India and Israel.[35] Opportunities for co-development or co-production of these systems may prove attractive to some LDCs, and industrial technology continues to proliferate through offset agreements in major arms deals.[36] These new market conditions further blunt the danger of 'partial dependency,' which is unavoidable for most states in any event in the globalizing international economic system.[37]

Although LDC major weapons system production may be declining, incentives for local development and production of other weapons has increased. The Iran-Iraq and Gulf Wars demonstrated the usefulness of ballistic missiles as both military and political tools. Given efforts to control the international trade and production of both military missiles and space-launch vehicles, this is an area where continued LDC emphasis on indigenous production capability can be expected. Production of cruise missiles is well within the capabilities of many regional powers. Iraq and North Korea are examples of LDC producers that sucessfully pursued significant, and potentially exportable, production capabilities in these fields.

Less-sophisticated weapons can also be subject to controls, as recent UN embargoes have proven, but these efforts can also be foiled by local production. Iraq and Serbia both maintained sufficient domestic production of artillery, small arms, and munitions to ensure regime preservation and to maintain a formidable military capability vis-à-vis neighbors and potential external adversaries. Recent initiatives to ban the sale of land mines, and to monitor and/or control the sale of small arms, will only serve as incentives for local production.[38]

Category four: production of regional-specific weaponry and niche production

LDC military industries must also provide for military requirements specific to regional geography, environment, or combat conditions which cannot be fulfilled elsewhere. Weapons produced by the major suppliers often operate less efficiently in LDC combat conditions, even when they appear to be specialized designs.[39]

Regional combat frequently requires simpler, more robust equipment than the sophisticated devices available from primary arms suppliers. This has been recognized for decades by the US government. 'While some US high-technology equipment is entirely appropriate for low-intensity conflicts, a great deal of our standard equipment is too complex and expensive for our Third World friends and allies.'[40]

Regional combat also reflects the interplay of available technologies and weapons available to both sides, encouraging the local development of counter-measures and innovations to deny foes existing or potential advantages. Local production, in these cases, contributes to what Ze'ev Bonen, former director of the Israeli firm RAFAEL, refers to as 'qualitative arms races,' which are marked by new development in defense technology.[41]

The proliferation of weapons and technologies forces the militaries of all states to make difficult choices regarding procurement and force posture. Each service (airforce, navy, and ground forces) requires several different types of primary combat systems, depending on its perceived roles, missions, and opposition, and must continue to respond to enemy improvements. States therefore seek to obtain systems that maximize their competitiveness in various combat mediums (air, land, sea) and deny the enemy the ability to use those same mediums effectively. This often involves the creation or exploitation of new or undeveloped technologies.[42]

Focused research in these areas will lead to comparative advantages, or military-industrial 'niches', which are not only appropriate for local use but are also marketable abroad. Israel, for example, has developed globally competitive niches in missile production, RPV/UAV technology, and combat electronics, primarily in response to regional requirements. These niches created opportunities for technological surprise of opponents and provided a means for rapid response to emerging new threats.

If there is a future for LDC arms exports, it is more likely to be in the niche or quality maintenance areas – prompted by regional combat experience and comparative advantage – than in direct competition with higher-tier producers over increasingly limited numbers of expensive sophisticated major weapons platforms.

> Other countries (Israel is a good example) will compete in selected areas [of technology], such as remotely piloted vehicles and explosives technology. Indeed, if history is a guide, such countries may be able, because of their small size and focused efforts, to introduce certain technologies earlier than the wealthier but more ponderous superpowers.[43]

Even relatively under-industrialized states, such as Iraq, can create substantial arms production capabilities based on local requirements and economies of scale that may be in great demand on the international market. If Iraq had avoided the Gulf War, for instance, Iraqi SSMs might be a highly marketable item – a niche North Korea now fills as the leading exporter of ballistic missiles. China has carved a niche in less-sophisticated major weapons systems, and sells inexpensive aircraft, tanks, and ships to a wide variety of customers. Specialization in high-demand niches, therefore, can provide its own economies of scale, in addition to providing for specific regional needs. These developments may have substantial impact on the future international arms trade.

Regional powers and military industry in the evolving international system

Analysis of LDC military industries during the Cold War reflected the static, dependence-dominated focus of studies of the international arms trade. The political and economic conditions of the 1950s and 1960s, and their resulting impact on arms transfers and production, constitute significant anomalies in the longer history of the international arms trade.[44] New works on the international arms trade take a more practical and historical approach to analysis.[45]

These new analyses indicate significant changes in the international arms market in the aftermath of the Cold War, including the shift towards a more commercial market.[46] Ideology and political allegiance will play a less important role in arms sales, and supplier diversification will be easier to achieve. Financing and economic support, however, is less likely to be forthcoming from suppliers, except possibly in the form of offset agreements.

A commercialized market does not mean that supply restrictions will not occur, or that they will be applied impartially. In the post-Cold War world, embargoes and supply restrictions have become a preferred tactic for international interference in both regional and internal conflicts.[47] The primary motives for LDC military industrialization – military threats and opportunities, and avoidance of dependence on foreign arms suppliers – remain unchanged.[48]

In the emerging arms market, however, lower tier or new producers will not be able to compete with the sophistication or prices of available major weapons platforms, particularly in the aerospace sector. Even the US, the sole remaining first-tier arms producer, cannot maintain an independent arms industry, relying at least in part on transfers of foreign-made parts and technologies.[49] The wealthiest second-tier producers find local production of new generations of major platforms extravagantly expensive and inefficient.[50] Production of new 'state-of-the-art' fighter aircraft, in particular, has become almost impossible except as part of a multinational consortium.[51]

Political and economic changes in the international system therefore call into question the whole concept of dependence as defined during the Cold War. In this new international environment, LDC arms industries, and indeed arms industries in general, must be reevaluated. Existing studies focus on what LDC industries have been *unable* to accomplish through comparison with higher-tier producers. Future studies must examine the very real accomplishments of these industries on a non-global scale, and perhaps anticipate their potential in the changing international political and arms transfer systems. Security considerations have, after all, prompted both Israel and Iraq to make unexpected leaps in industrial capability and technological assimilation.

Regional warfare now poses a considerable threat to the international system. Rather than acting as a potential spark for conflict between the superpowers, however, these conflicts now pose the possibility of independently escalating to the nuclear level.[52] As regional powers achieve *de facto* nuclear status, regional conflict and extra-regional intervention carry significantly increased risks.

The predominant forms of conflict in the developing world are also changing. Regional wars during the 1960s and 1970s were brief affairs, terminated by a combination of logistic shortfalls and superpower interference. LDC militaries, particularly those of the regional powers and major

LDC producers, are now capable of undertaking and sustaining high-intensity conflicts of considerable sophistication and duration, or of funding, arming, and supporting insurgent groups in neighboring states.[53] Local production of weapons in response to regional conflict has improved the capability of regional powers to fight wars of attrition, and has decreased reliance on foreign technicians and experts. Due in part to local production, some regional powers are improving their relative positions in the global military culture.

The new international system poses several challenges for analysts. Prevailing methodology for assessing the arms trade and arms production is obsolete, and requires reevaluation. Developments in civilian and dual-use technologies offer significant potential if adapted for military use. Strategies of technology acquisition may significantly enhance long-term military capability in a number of states.[54] Regional power producers figure prominently in international markets for some of these technologies, and therefore may play important roles in their development for military functions.

A considerable portion of the value of modern MWS consists of electronic subsystems. Electronics components comprise at least 25 percent of the cost of a warship, more than 30 percent of the cost of an aircraft, and over 40 percent of the cost of a tank.[55] Licensed production of electronics, as the Iraqi case demonstrates, can be carried out by states which possess only rudimentary industrial infrastructure and are short of technicians. The increasing importance of computerized components also offers opportunities for LDCs which have not previously been viewed as important arms producers but possess or are developing hardware or software industries.

A major criticism of LDC military production, particularly from the economic perspective, is the failure of LDC military-industries to transfer technologies and useable skills to civilian industries. As we have seen, this criticism is not universally valid. Close linkages between the Israeli civilian and defense sectors increased quality standards in certain high-technology civilian goods. India, on the other hand, deliberately separated the civilian and defense industrial sectors, inhibiting transfers of technologies and skills. Iraqi policy used military industrial projects to create and expand heavy industry and manufacturing sectors of the economy – a pattern seen in the Soviet Union and Nazi Germany in the 1930s – but it is unclear how much this would have benefited the civilian economy in the long run.

The economic benefits of LDC military industrialization in the Cold War, therefore, must be viewed as mixed, and analyzed on a case-by-case basis. This is due, in part, to the technologies and industries associated with major weapons systems in the Cold War Era. Production of these weapons required development of capital and technician-intensive heavy industry, and posed severe strains on developing economies.[56] Requirements for these resources explains, in part, why many of the primary LDC producers are also larger regional powers with significant potential economies of scale.[57]

This may not be the case in coming decades. The emergence of information technology as an important economic asset may contribute to a transformation of the international economic system – the phenomenon of globalization. This may lead, as well, to significant changes not only in the social, political, and economic organization of international actors, but also in the manner in which those actors make war. Theorists are divided over whether improvements in technology benefit or harm small, weaker states in the international system.[58]

Today, many analysts argue that the international system lies on the brink of a new Revolution in Military Affairs (RMA) based on information technologies, precision-guided weapons, and stealth technology.[59] The notion of a 'system of systems' – sophisticated real-time communications and intelligence systems linked to more mobile, lethal, and widely separated forces – continues to frame the debate about defense transformation strategies and the shape and design of future military forces.[60]

These concepts are very relevant to LDC militaries and to LDC military industries. If new technologies are the key to future combat – missiles, precision-guided weapons, and pilotless aircraft, for example – this will lessen the demand or requirement for expensive, top-of-the-line military platforms that LDCs have historically produced only at significant economic inefficiencies. In regional warfare, the possession and production of such weapons may create significant military asymmetries against regional rivals – the same way that Israeli advantages in precision weapons, or Iraqi advantages in chemical weapons, created significant advantages against Arab or Iranian opponents.

Emerging technologies in the form of sensors and information systems have already been deployed by regional powers. Both Israel and India have launched satellites with significant military capabilities. Israel's use of sensors and information systems led to outstanding battle management in the 1982 Lebanon conflict, integrating near-real time intelligence with precision-guided weaponry. In Israel's case, at least, expertise in these technologies has contributed to economically productive developments in both military and commercial industries. India, an information technology powerhouse, has the potential to convert its civilian expertise into military-related capabilities, provided it can overcome institutional and political barriers between civilian and military industries.

Conversion of information technology into a strategic weapon, however, appears a distant prospect. The evidence of successful information operations, even by the United States, is rather limited. It is reported that information operations were carried out in Kosovo, but were deliberately limited in scope.[61] More recently, the Falun Gong spiritual movement jammed the Chinese government's Sinosat-1 satellite from June 23–30, 2002, affecting as many as 70 million people.[62] Information technology has proven critical in a supporting role to more traditional dimensions of warfare – information sharing, for example, is an important force multiplier for US forces today. Nevertheless, claims of a decisive role in the near future appear premature.[63]

Developments in range, guidance, and communications, however, now offer enormous potential military advantages. Some of these technologies allow long-range targeting and destruction of enemy forces with near-real-time intelligence. Others permit greatly enhanced coordination of forces in space and time for maximum military impact. Still others allow realistic simulations of military engagements at a fraction of the cost and trouble of actual exercises. Information systems, advanced data processing, simulations, precision-guidance technology, long-range strike capabilities, and advanced simulation techniques are among the primary critical technologies identified by defense analysts in the coming era.[64]

Converting these technologies to military uses is still enhanced, however, by actual hands-on military experience. Regional conflict, therefore, may help determine the direction of the next 'military revolution' – serving as a test-bed for the technologies and techniques of future warfare. Regional powers face several types of threats – low-intensity conflict against internal opponents of the state or regime, low-intensity cross-border conflict with neighbors, mid-to-high level intensity 'hot wars' within the region, and the threat of extra-regional intervention. Potential for these types of conflicts exists in East and South Asia, the Persian Gulf, and the Middle East, which are also the regions where LDC producers are most concentrated.

Existing industrial structures in some of the primary regional power producers suggest that these states possess significant potential in critical new technologies. The new technologies rely on process skills and human capital, and can be acquired through education and training. Traditional military-industrial infrastructures based on heavy industry may not be necessary for a state to compete in these new technologies. India and Israel both have large and sophisticated electronics and computer industries, in addition to existing military-industrial research and production facilities. South Korea, Singapore, and Taiwan all possess military-industrial infrastructure in addition to advanced scientific and technical sectors. Unlike the West, however, these states emphasize engineering and applied research, rather than speculative theoretical work.[65]

In the increasingly globalized commercial economy, knowledge is power. LDCs are more capable of generating competitive human capital – through domestic education and by foreign study – than capital-intensive heavy industries. As LDCs become commercially competitive in the information sector, they may become increasingly capable – at least potentially – in emerging military capabilities and in the evolving global military culture.

Integration of new commercial technologies and military industries or requirements, prompted by regional threats, creates the potential for LDC producers to make significant contributions to the evolution of military capability, and perhaps to improve their positions in the international military industrial hierarchy *and* in global military culture. Existing connections between military and industrial sectors have, in some cases, already increased national technical capabilities and process skills. Israel, for example, used military service as a means of exposing immigrants to technology and educating them to much higher standards. At least one analyst has detected similar trends in East Asian states, stating that the impact of high military participation ratios on economic performance is modest but detectable and significant.[66]

In the post-Cold War era, then, the potential of LDC military industries lies in three fields. First, they can continue to provide sustenance requirements for existing or planned armed forces, increasing their endurance and staying power, and maintaining and repairing equipment. This production can also be exported, if quality standards and production levels are high enough and there is demand for these goods on the international market

Regional power producers will also continue to produce and modify existing categories of weapons for regional requirements, based on specific environmental needs, supply restrictions, and local military balances. Few of these efforts will be competitive on the export market, as higher-tier producers will be able to achieve superior economies of scale in most weapons categories and offer superior financing and offsets on most contracts. Both of these capabilities will, however, contribute to the regional power's military capability and position in global military culture, maintaining competitiveness in regional security concerns and providing a deterrent to extra-regional intervention.

Finally, and perhaps most importantly, regional powers will continue to modify, produce, and innovate new weapons in niches and areas of comparative advantage. Integration of these efforts with existing or developing commercial industries may result in important technological developments, as occurred with Israeli RPV production. These may provide opportunities for some regional power producers to improve their standing in the international hierarchy, or even to contribute to changing the parameters of that hierarchy entirely. Cooperation in joint and co-development programs, an increasingly common phenomenon in the globalized military industry, also allows for the creation of niches of comparative excellence.

These capabilities, however, will remain limited in the near-term when compared to the United States. Regional powers, therefore, are likely to pursue indirect or asymmetric strategies when the potential for conflict with the US is high. Indirect strategies do not rely on decisive military victory, instead attempting to prolong the conflict, enlarge the theater of confrontation, and capitalize on non-military means for accomplishing political aims.[67] LDC militaries, facing a potential US threat, will be tailored for deterrence and, when possible, denying the effectiveness of critical US military capabilities. Regional forces will be unbalanced – most LDCs prioritize ground forces, and the more technically-sophisticated airforces and navies receive secondary priority.[68] Superior technology can be countered by appropriate doctrine and willingness to accept casualties – the lessons of Korea and Vietnam are still valid. Local production may create nasty surprises, like the Iraqi ballistic missile force or Israel's RPVs.

Operation Enduring Freedom (Afghanistan) and Operation Iraqi Freedom (Iraq) have demonstrated some of the tensions of the new US national security strategy – encompassing the overthrow of hostile regimes.[69] In an era where transnational terrorists thrive in regions of political chaos, the US must provide a stable successor regime or risk creating another haven of terrorism when it withdraws. This requires large US occupation forces and garrisons – stretching US military resources to their limits. Future US military interventions may, therefore, look back to the more limited wars of the 1990s as a means of degrading hostile military capability and coercing political concessions.

If the US revisits these more limited wars, leadership may also have to re-consider the strategic bombing concept behind the air campaigns against Iraq and Serbia. The US strategic bombing campaign in 1991 targeted the functioning of the Iraqi government and military, rather than attacking vital elements of war production as in World War II.[70] This focus minimized damage to Iraq's military industry – damage which was further reduced by Iraqi deception efforts and the overall lack of intelligence regarding the scope of the military-industrial effort and the location of key facilities.[71] Future air operations should reestablish military industries as high-priority targets. Local production of munitions and light arms provides the firepower edge that many regimes rely on to keep insurgent and separatist movements in check. Limiting the ability of hostile regional powers to reconstitute their military strength locally will increase US and international leverage on these regimes.

Intelligence efforts should also reflect the lessons of Iraq, in particular – but also of the successful operational deception efforts of India in the run-up to the May 1998 nuclear tests. As Operation Iraqi Freedom and the UN inspections demonstrate, intelligence collection and assessment remains far from perfect. Iraq's use of covert networks and dual-use technologies will surely be imitated, and existing military-industrial producers already have prominent commercial industries based around many of the most important technologies. In addition, we now see a new 'pariah network' of proliferation with North Korea providing missile technology to Pakistan and Iran, and Pakistan providing nuclear technology to North Korea, Iran, and Libya. The latter two efforts, in particular, apparently escaped Western intelligence collection efforts for years. Identifying linkages between commercial and military-industrial facilities will require closer cooperation and coordination among and between US and international agencies.

186 *Regional powers, security, and arms production*

The production of arms indicates national or regime interest in increasing the state's position in global military culture. This may indicate or lead to dissatisfaction with the state's relative position in global affairs – a condition which some theorists argue may increase the likelihood of war.[72] The connection between producers of conventional weapons and states suspected of proliferating unconventional arms is an additional reason for more careful monitoring of these states. Unconventional solutions to military problems are, regrettably, cheaper than conventional arms.[73]

Regional power arms industries have achieved some success in a number of areas. They have decreased dependence on outside suppliers, stimulated an increase in the position of LDC producers in global military culture, and increased the ability of those producer states to fight prolonged wars. This increased capacity acts as a deterrent to external aggression, and provides regional powers with the means to threaten and if necessary defeat neighbors by outlasting them in regional conflict. Local military industries have contributed positively to national military strength, and at times have saved foreign exchange and stimulated local civilian industries. Last but not least, local industries have developed dangerous unconventional weapons capabilities, and regional powers have used them or threatened their use in at least seven separate crises (Iraq 1984–88, 1991; Israel 1973; India and/or Pakistan 1986–87, 1990, 1999, 2001–2).

As the international system becomes more pluralist and globalized, the importance of regional military capabilities will grow. Historically, middle powers most often assert themselves when the international system is evolving, and they can create conditions which maximize their influence.[74] The potential for regional conflicts to create the conditions for either revolutionary new military capabilities or a breakdown in international norms will increase as the relative power of regional actors increases and new threats and opportunities drive changes in policies and allegiance. Regional power military industries and their relationship to regional and global military capabilities deserve serious consideration and analysis at a time when these states prepare to assert themselves militarily, politically, and economically in a 'new world order,' and when so many regional powers are threatened by, or seek to capitalize on, the global war on terrorism.

Notes

1 Introduction

1. This study will use the term 'less-developed country' (LDC) purely for convenience, although 'developing country' is probably a more accurate term. All non-European states, with the exceptions of Japan, Canada, Australia, New Zealand, and the United States, are considered LDCs for the purpose of this study.
2. Stephanie G. Neuman, 'International Stratification and Third World Military Industries,' *International Organization* 38, No. 1 (Winter 1984), 172; Michael Brzoska and Thomas Ohlson, 'Arms Production in the Third World: An Overview,' in Michael Brzoska and Thomas Ohlson (eds), *Arms Production in the Third World* (London and Philadelphia: Taylor & Francis for SIPRI, 1986), p. 9. Neuman lists Argentina, Brazil, China, Colombia, and India; Brzoska and Ohlson list Argentina, Egypt, Colombia, India, and North Korea.
3. This total includes the People's Republic of China, which the Stockholm International Peace Research Institute (SIPRI) does not include as a developing state. Michael Brzoska and Thomas Ohlson, 'Arms Production in the Third World: An Overview,' pp. 16–17 (Table 2.3); Stephanie G. Neuman, 'The Arms Market: Who's On Top,' *Orbis* 33 (Fall 1989), 512.
4. Michael Brzoska and Thomas Ohlson, 'Arms Production in the Third World: An Overview,' pp. 11–12; Ian Anthony, 'The "Third Tier" Countries: Production of Major Weapons' in Herbert Wulf (ed.), *Arms Industry Limited* (Oxford: Oxford University Press for SIPRI, 1993), pp. 362–3.
5. See: 'Navy Report Asserts Many Nations Seek Poison Gas,' *New York Times* 10 March 1991; and *Proliferation: Threat and Response* (Washington, DC: Office of the Secretary of Defense, January 2001).
6. See: *The National Security Strategy of the United States of America* (Washington, DC: The White House, September 2002), pp. 9–16.
7. Boutros Boutros-Ghali, *An Agenda for Peace* (New York: United Nations, 1992), paragraphs 60–5; Brian L. Job (ed.), *The Insecurity Dilemma: National Security of Third World States* (Boulder, CO: Lynne Rienner, 1992); David A. Lake and Patrick M. Morgan (eds), *Regional Orders: Building Security in a New World*, (University Park: Pennsylvania State University Press, 1997), and Etel Solingen, *Regional Orders at Century's Dawn: Global and Domestic Influences on Grand Strategy* (Princeton: Princeton University Press, 1998).
8. See, for example, B. M. Russett, *International Regions and the International System*, (Chicago: Rand McNally, 1967); L. J. Cantori and S. L. Spiegel (eds), *The International Politics of Regions*, (Englewood Cliffs, NJ: Prentice-Hall, 1970); R. A. Falk and S. H. Mendlovitz, *Regional Politics and World Order*,

(San Francisco: Freeman, 1973); George Liska, *The Ways of Power* (Cambridge, MA: Basil Blackwell, 1990), pp. 365–9.
9 W. Howard Wriggins with F. Gregory Gause, III, Terence Lyons, and Evelyn Colbert, *Dynamics of Regional Politics: Four Systems on the Indian Ocean Rim* (New York: Columbia University Press, 1992); David J. Myers (ed.), *Regional Hegemons: Threat Perception and Strategic Response* (Boulder, CO: Westview, 1991).
10 See David Vital, *The Inequality of States* (Oxford: Clarendon Press, 1967); August Schou and Arne Olav Brundtland (eds), *Small States in International Relations* (Stockholm: Almqvist and Wiksell, 1971); David Vital, *The Survival of Small States: Studies in Small Power/Great Power Conflict* (London: Oxford University Press, 1971); Marshall R. Singer, *Weak States in a World of Powers* (New York: The Free Press, 1972).
11 See Immanuel Wallerstein, *The Modern World System, Vol. I and II* (New York: Academic Press, 1974, 1980); Raimo Väyrynen, 'Semiperipheral Countries in the Global Economic and Military Order' in Helena Tuomi and Raimo Väyrynen (eds), *Militarization and Arms Production* (New York: St. Martin's Press, 1983), pp. 163–92.
12 See Kenneth N. Waltz, *Man, the State, and War: a Theoretical Analysis* (New York: Columbia University Press, 1954).
13 Barry Buzan, 'Third World Security in Structural and Historical Perspective,' in Brian Job (ed.), *The Insecurity Dilemma*, pp. 167–89; Barry Buzan, 'A Framework for Regional Security Analysis,' in Barry Buzan and Gowher Rizvi (eds), *South Asian Security and the Great Powers* (New York: St. Martin's Press, 1986), pp. 3–33; Barry Buzan, *People, States & Fear* (second edition) (Boulder, CO: Lynne Rienner, 1991); Robert M. Rosh, 'Third World Militarization: Security Webs and the States They Ensnare,' *Journal of Conflict Resolution* 32, (December 1988), 671–2.
14 See Abdul-Monum M. Al-Mashat, *National Security in the Third World*, (Boulder, CO: Westview Press, 1985); Mohammed Ayoob (ed.), *Regional Security in the Third World*, (Boulder, CO: Westview Press, 1986); and Ashok Kapur, *The Indian Ocean: Regional and International Power Politics*, (New York: Praeger Press, 1982).
15 Some analysts would disagree with this assertion. See, for example, Mohammed Ayoob, *The Third World Security Predicament: State Making, Regional Conflict, and the International System* (Boulder, CO: Lynne Rienner, 1995).
16 See Davis B. Bobrow and Steve Chan, 'Simple Labels and Complex Realities: National Security in the Third World,' in Edward A. Azar and Chung-in Moon (eds), *National Security in the Third World: The Management of Internal and External Threats* (Aldershot, UK: Edward Elgar, 1988), pp. 44–76.
17 See Andrew L. Ross, 'The Arming of the Third World: Patterns and Trends', *SAIS Review* 11 (Summer–Fall 1991), 69–94; and Keith Krause, 'Arms Imports, Arms Production, and the Quest for Security in the Third World,' in Brian Job (ed.), *The Insecurity Dilemma*, pp. 121–42.
18 A recent comprehensive study of security in the developing world is Robert E. Harkavy and Stephanie G. Neuman, *Warfare and the Third World* (New York: Palgrave Press, 2001). See also Timothy D. Hoyt, 'Security and Conflict in the Developing World' in Michael Brown (ed.), *Grave New World – Threats to Global Order* (Washington, DC: Georgetown University Press, 2003), pp. 213–29.
19 See Kal J. Holsti, 'International Theory and War in the Third World', in Brian

Job (ed.), *The Insecurity Dilemma*..., pp. 37–8; Kal J. Holsti, *Peace and War: Armed Contests and International Order, 1648–1989* (Cambridge: Cambridge University Press, 1991).
20 Martin Wight, *Power Politics* edited by Hedley Bull and Carsten Holbraad (New York: Holmes & Meier, 1978), p. 63.
21 See, for example, Rodney W. Jones and Steven A. Hildreth, *Modern Weapons and Third World Powers* (Boulder, CO: Westview, for the Center for Strategic and International Studies, 1984), p. 15; *Discriminate Deterrence*, Report of the Commission on Integrated Long-Term Strategy (Washington, DC: Government Printing Office, January 1988), pp. 9–10; and *The Future Security Environment*, Report of the Future Security Environment Working Group to the Commission on Long-Term Integrated Strategy (Washington, DC: The Pentagon, October 1988), pp. 3–4.
22 See Eliot A. Cohen, 'Distant Battles,' *International Security* 10 (Spring 1986), 155.
23 *From Surprise to Reckoning: The Kargil Review Committee Report* (New Delhi: SAGE, December 15, 1999), 242.
24 Michael Handel, *Weak States in the International System* (London: Frank Cass & Co., Ltd., 1990), p. 52.
25 Stephen M. Walt, *The Origins of Alliances* (Ithaca, NY: Cornell University Press, 1987), pp. 21–6.
26 Stephen M. Walt, 'Alliance, Threats, and US Grand Strategy; A Reply to Kaufman and Labs,' in *Security Studies* 1, no. 3 (Spring 1992), 465.
27 A rare exception is Yezid Sayigh, *Arab Military Industry: Capability, Performance and Impact* (London: Brassey's, 1992);
28 See Edward A. Kolodziej and Robert E. Harkavy (eds) *Security Policies of Developing Countries* (Lexington, MA: Lexington, 1982); and Stephanie G. Neuman (ed.) *Defense Planning in Less-Industrialized Countries* (Lexington, MA: Lexington, 1984).
29 Other non-military rationales exist, of course. Many states like to have a few high-technology aircraft, tanks, or large naval vessels for parades and displays. See M. Wight, *Power Politics*, p. 239.
30 Raju G. C. Thomas, 'Strategies of Recipient Autonomy: The Case of India,' in Kwang-Il Baek, Ronald D. McLaurin, and Chung-in Moon (eds), *The Dilemma of Third World Defense Industries: Supplier Control or Recipient Autonomy?* (Boulder, CO: Westview, 1989), p. 199.
31 See, for instance, W. Seth Carus, 'Israel: Some Economic and Social Considerations,' in James Everett Katz (ed.), *The Implications of Third World Military Industrialization: Sowing the Serpents' Teeth* (Lexington, MA: D. C. Heath and Co., 1986), p. 136. This was also the explicit policy of the US vis-à-vis the Soviet threat. See William J. Perry, 'Desert Storm and Deterrence', *Foreign Affairs* 70 (Fall 1991), 68.
32 Edward Luttwak and Stuart L. Koehl, *The Dictionary of Modern War* (New York: HarperCollins, 1991), p. 226.
33 See, for example, Timothy D. Hoyt, 'Military Technology and Security,' in *Grave New World – Threats to Global Order* ed. Michael Brown (Washington, DC: Georgetown University Press, 2003), pp. 17–37.
34 *Niederwerfungsstrategie* (the strategy of annihilation) seeks decisive battle as the means of achieving political ends, hoping to destroy the enemy's military capability or will to resist. *Ermattungsstrategie*, or the strategy of exhaustion, seeks means other than decisive battle to achieve political objectives, raising the costs of continued conflict until they exceed the potential benefits of success for the adversary. See Carl von Clausewitz, *On War*, edited and

translated by Michael Howard and Peter Paret (Princeton, NJ: Princeton University Press, 1976), especially pp. 577–637; Hans Delbrück, *The History of the Art of War, Vol. I: Warfare in Antiquity* translated by Walter J. Renfroe, Jr. (Lincoln, NE and London: University of Nebraska, 1975), pp. 135–43; Gordon A. Craig, 'Delbrück: The Military Historian', in Edward Mead Earle (ed.), *Makers of Modern Strategy: Military Thought from Machiavelli to Hitler* (Princeton, NJ: Princeton University Press, 1943), p. 273.

35 See Sun Tzu, *The Art of Warfare*, translated, with an introduction and commentary, by Roger Ames (New York: Ballantine, 1993), p. 107 (Chapter Two). Sun Tzu counsels against protracted war, but sometimes political objectives can only be accomplished, or enemy victory prevented, by deliberately prolonging conflict – for example, Britain's decision to continue its struggle against Nazi Germany after the fall of France in 1940, despite no immediate prospects of success.

36 Geoffrey Blainey, *The Causes of War*, 3rd edition (New York: Free Press, 1988), pp. 35–56.

37 Studies of this phenomenon include William H. McNeill, *The Rise of the West* (Chicago: University of Chicago Press, 1963); Carlo M. Cipolla, *Guns, Sails and Empires*, (Minerva Press, 1965); William H. McNeill, *The Pursuit of Power: Technology, Armed Force and Society Since A.D. 1000* (Chicago: University of Chicago Press, 1982); Geoffrey Parker, *The Military Revolution* (Cambridge: Cambridge University Press, 1988); and Clifford J. Rogers (ed.), *The Military Revolution Debate* (Boulder, CO: Westview, 1995).

38 Amelia C. Leiss, G. Kemp, J. H. Hoagland, J. S. Refson, and H. E. Fischer, *Arms Transfers to Less-Developed Countries*, (Cambridge, MA: Massachusetts Institute of Technology, Center for International Studies, 1970), which tracks data up to 1968, and SIPRI, *The Arms Trade with the Third World* (New York: Humanities Press, 1971), which covers the period 1950–69.

39 Arms transfer patterns have been described as economic, geo-political, or ideological. See Robert E. Harkavy, 'The Changing International System and the Arms Trade,' in *Annals of the American Academy of Political and Social Science* 535 (hereafter *Annals, AAPSS*), September 1994 (Robert E. Harkavy and Stephanie G. Neuman (eds), Special Issue: *The Arms Trade: Problems and Prospects in the Post Cold-War World*), pp. 11–28; SIPRI, *The Arms Trade With the Third World*, pp. 17–41.

40 Martin van Creveld. *Lessons of the Yom Kippur War: Historical Perspectives*, Washington Paper No. 24 (Beverly Hills, CA: SAGE Publications for the Center for Strategic and International Studies, 1975); and Uri Ra'anan, Robert L. Pfaltzgraff, and Geoffrey Kemp (eds), *Arms Transfers to the Third World: The Military Buildup in Less Industrialized Countries* (Boulder, CO: Westview Press, 1978).

41 Self-reliance, an Indian term, includes not only domestically produced goods but also imports from politically reliable states. R. G. C. Thomas, 'Strategies of Recipient Autonomy: The Case of India,' pp. 186–7.

42 See, for instance, James E. Katz (ed.), *The Implications of Third World Arms Industries: Sowing the Serpents' Teeth* (Lexington, MA: Lexington, 1986); *The Future Security Environment*; Andrew L. Ross, 'The Arming of the Third World . . .'

43 From 1960–70, the superpowers accounted for 80 percent of arms sales, and the next two largest suppliers only 5 percent. Robert E. Harkavy and Stephanie G. Neuman (eds) 'The Changing International System and the Arms Trade,' pp. 20, 22. In 1984, France and Germany combined for 15.5 percent of all arms sales, and the European countries (NATO and Warsaw Pact) sup-

plied 31.4 percent of the total trade. Arms Control and Disarmament Agency (ACDA), *World Military Expenditures and Arms Transfers 1986* (hereafter *WMEAT)*, (Washington, DC: Government Printing Office), pp. 9–10.
44 *WMEAT 1986*, pp. 9–10.
45 *WMEAT 1986*, pp. 6–9.
46 *WMEAT 1993–94*, p. 9.
47 See, for example, Patrice Franko Jones, *The Brazilian Defense Industry: A Case Study of Public-private Collaboration* (Boulder, CO: Westview Press, 1992); and Ken Conca, *Manufacturing Insecurity: The Rise and Fall of Brazil's Military-Industrial Complex* (Boulder, CO: Lynne Rienner Publishers, 1996).
48 See, for example, Richard A. Bitzinger *The Globalization of Arms Production: Defense Markets in Transition* (Washington, DC: Defense Budget Project, 1993); *Defense Industry Globalization: A Compendium of Papers Presented at a Conference on 'Defense Industry Globalization' Held on 16 November 2001* (Washington, DC: The Atlantic Council of the United States, February 2002).
49 Jurgen Brauer and Paul Dunne (eds), *Arming the South: The Economics of Military Expenditure, Arms Production, and Arms Trade in Developing Countries* (New York: Palgrave MacMillan, 2002); Richard Bitzinger, *Towards a Brave New Arms Industry? The Decline of the Second-Tier Arms-Producing Countries and the Emerging International Division of Labour in the Defence Industry* Adelphi Paper #356 (Oxford: Oxford University Press 2003).
50 Randall Forsberg (ed.), *The Arms Production Dilemma: Contraction and Restraint in the World Combat Aircraft Industry*, (Cambridge, MA: MIT Press, 1994); William W. Keller, *Arm in Arm: The Political Economy of the Global Arms Trade* (New York: Basic Books, 1995); Peter J. Dombrowski, Eugene Gholz, Andrew L. Ross, *Military Transformation and the Defense Industry After Next: The Defense Industrial Implications of Network-Centric Warfare* (Newport, RI: Naval War College Press, 2002).
51 Christian Catrina, 'Main Questions of Research in The Arms Trade,' in *Annals, AAPPSS* 535, p. 191.
52 See George Seldes, *Iron, Blood and Profits: An Exposure of the World-Wide Munitions Racket* (New York: Harper and Brothers Publishers, 1934); H. C. Engelbrecht and F. C. Hanighen, *Merchants of Death: A Study of the International Armament Industry* (New York: Dodd, Mead & Co., 1934); J. Noel Baker, *Disarmament* (New York: Harcourt, Brace, & Co., 1926), among others.
53 See Cindy Cannizzo, *The Gun Merchants: Politics and Policies of the Major Arms Suppliers* (New York: Pergamon Press, 1980); Anthony Sampson, *The Arms Bazaar* (New York: Viking Press, 1977); Russell Warren Howe, *Weapons: the International Game of Arms, Money, and Diplomacy* (New York, Doubleday, 1980); and George Thayer, *The War Business: The International Trade in Armaments* (New York: Simon & Schuster, 1969).
54 See, for example, Michael T. Klare, 'The Unnoticed Arms Trade: Exports of Conventional Arms-Making Technology,' *International Security* 8 (Fall 1983), 68–90; Benjamin Beit-Hallahmi, *The Israeli Connection: Who Israel Arms and Why* (New York: Pantheon Books, 1987).
55 Björn Hettne, 'Third World Arms Control and World System Conflicts,' in Thomas Ohlson (ed.), *Arms Transfer Limitations and Third World Security*. (Oxford: Oxford University Press for SIPRI, 1988), pp. 17–32.
56 Examples include Aharon Klieman, *Israel's Global Reach* (London:

Pergamon-Brassey's, 1985); Stewart Reiser, *The Israeli Arms Industry* (New York: Holmes & Meier, 1989); Ron Matthews, *Defence Production in India* (New Delhi: ABC Publishing House, 1989); and Janne Nolan, *Military Industry in Taiwan and South Korea* (New York: St. Martin's Press, 1986).

57 Examples include Nicole Ball and Milton Leitenberg (eds), *The Structure of the Defence Industry: An International Survey* (New York: St. Martin's Press, 1983), which includes one chapter on Israel and another on the developing world; James Everett Katz (ed.), *Arms Production in Developing Countries* (Lexington, MA: Lexington Books, 1984); Michael Brzoska and Thomas Ohlson, *Arms Production in the Third World*; Kwang-Il Baek, Ronald D. McLaurin, and Chung-in Moon (eds), *The Dilemma of Third World Defense Industries* ...

58 Among these are Michael Moodie, 'Sovereignty, Security, and Arms,' *The Washington Papers 58*, (Beverly Hills, CA: SAGE Publications, 1979); Ilan Peleg, 'Military Production in Third World Countries: A Political Study' in Pat McGowan and Charles W. Kegley, Jr (eds), *Threats, Weapons and Foreign Policy* (Beverly Hills, CA: SAGE, 1980), pp. 209–30; Stephanie G. Neuman, 'International stratification'; Robert M. Rosh, 'Third World Arms Production and the Evolving Interstate System,' *The Journal of Conflict Resolution* 34 (March 1990), 57–73; Robert E. Looney, *Third-World Military Expenditure and Arms Production* (New York: St. Martin's, 1988); and, A. F. Mullins, Jr., *Born Arming: Development and Military Power in New States* (Stanford, CA: Stanford University Press, 1987), p. 15, which examines states with populations of over 500,000 that became independent between January 1, 1957 and December 31, 1981.

59 The most influential of these studies are Stephanie G. Neuman, 'International stratification,' and Michael Brzoska and Thomas Ohlson, *Arms Production in the Third World*. See also Christian Catrina, *Arms Transfers and Dependence* (New York: Taylor & Francis/United Nations Institute for Disarmament Research, 1988).

60 The most comprehensive study of LDC production defines strategic and political issues in terms of changes in the international arms transfer system and dependency. The conclusion admits that political motives are predominant, but does not explicitly mention the issue of security at all, focusing instead on dependency. Michael Brzoska and Thomas Ohlson, *Arms Production in the Third World*, pp. 2–5, 279–80.

61 This technique is used by Michael Brzoska and Thomas Ohlson, *Arms Production in the Third World*; and Stephanie G. Neuman, 'International stratification'.

62 Quantitative studies of LDC arms industries include Robert M. Rosh, 'Third World Arms Production and the Evolving Interstate System'; David Kinsella, 'The Globalization of Arms Production and the Changing Third World Security Context,' paper presented at the Annual Meeting of the International Studies Association, 21–25 February 1995; Ilan Peleg, 'Military Production in Third World Countries: A Political Study,' pp. 209–30; Herbert Wulf, 'Developing Countries,' in Nichole Ball and Milton Leitenberg (eds), *The Structure of the Defense Industry: An International Survey* (New York: St. Martin's, 1983), pp. 310–43; Stephanie G. Neuman, 'International stratification ...'; and Anne Naylor-Schwarz, 'Arms Transfers and the Development of Second-Level Arms Industries' in David J. Louscher and Michael D. Salomone (eds), *Marketing Security Assistance: New Perspectives on Arms Sales* (Lexington, MA: D. C. Heath, 1987) pp. 101–30.

63 Andy Lee Ross, *Security and Self-Reliance: Military Dependence and Conven-

tional Arms Production in Developing Countries (PhD dissertation: Cornell University, August 1984); Andrew L. Ross, 'Arms Acquisition and National Security: The Irony of Military Strength' in Edward A. Azar and Chung-in Moon (eds), *National Security in the Third World*, pp. 152–87.
64 Andrew L. Ross, The Arming of the Third World'; Gerald M. Steinberg, 'Technological Transfer and the Future of The Center-Periphery System: A Realist Perspective,' in *The Jerusalem Journal of International Relations* 11 (1989), 96–117; Lewis Snider, 'Supplier Control and Recipient Autonomy,' in Kwang-Il Baek, Ronald D. McLaurin, and Chung-in Moon (eds), *The Dilemma of Third World Defense Industries*, pp. 231–70.
65 The so-called 'ladder of production models,' which attempt to standardize a rational step-by-step format for developing military industries appear to be based on the Israeli experience as described in Shimon Peres, *David's Sling*. (New York: Random House, 1970), pp. 26–7, 109–36. The simplified version of the ladder of production used in Table 1.1 is derived from a number of sources. See, for instance, Andrew L. Ross, 'The Arming of the Third World': pp. 82–3; Keith Krause, *Arms and the State*, pp. 171–4; James E. Katz, 'Understanding Arms Production in Developing Countries,' in James E. Katz (ed.), *Arms Production in Developing Countries*, pp. 8–9; Robert E. Looney, *Third-World Military Expenditure*, p. 103; and Michael Moodie, 'Sovereignty, Security, and Arms,' pp. 46–7.
66 Martin Van Creveld, *Technology and War*, 2nd edition (New York: Free Press, 1991), p. 312.
67 Stephanie G. Neuman, 'International stratification ...'; Michael Brzoska and Thomas Ohlson, 'Conclusion.'
68 See Stephanie G. Neuman, 'International stratification ...', p. 174; Michael Brzoska and Thomas Ohlson, 'Arms production in the third world: an overview,' pp. 24–5.
69 Stephanie G. Neuman, 'International stratification ...'; Stephanie G Neuman, 'The Arms Market: Who's On Top?'; Stephanie G. Neuman, 'Arms Aid and the Superpowers,' *Foreign Affairs* (Summer 1988), 1044–66.
70 Joseph J. Johnson, *The Role of the Military in Underdeveloped Countries* (Princeton, NJ: Princeton University Press, 1962) examines the positive role that militaries can play in LDCs. Emile Benoit, *Defense and Economic Growth in Developing Countries* (Lexington, MA: Lexington Books, 1973) reached the surprising and much-debated conclusion that defense spending can have positive effects on LDC economies.
71 Yezid Sayigh, *Arab Military Industries*; James Everett Katz (ed.), *The Implications of Third World Military Industrialization: Sowing the Serpent's Teeth*. The importance of military industrial policy in Japan's rise as a great power and in France's post-war economic recovery is discussed in Gerald M. Steinberg, 'Technological Transfer ...' and Shimon Peres, *David's Sling* (New York: Random House, 1970). See also Richard J. Samuels, *Rich Nation, Strong Army: National Security and the Technological Transformation of Japan* (Ithaca, NY: Cornell University Press, 1994).
72 Steve Chan and Alex Mintz (eds), *Defense, Welfare, and Growth* (New York: Routledge, 1992); Bruce Russett, 'Defense Expenditure and National Well-Being,' *American Political Science Review* 76 (December 1982), pp. 766–77; and William K. Domke, Richard C. Eichenberg and Catherine M. Kelleher, 'The Illusion of Choice: Defense and Welfare in Advanced Industrial Democracies, 1948–1978', *American Political Science Review* 77 (March 1983), 19–35.
73 Robert E. Looney, *Third-World Military Expenditure and Arms Production*.

74 See Nicole Ball, 'Defence and Development: A Critique of the Benoit Study,' in Helena Tuomi and Raimo Värynen (eds), *Militarization and Arms Production*, (New York: St. Martin's Press, 1983), pp. 39–56; United Nations, Department for Disarmament Affairs, *Economic and Social Consequences of the Arms Race and Military Expenditures* (New York: United Nations, 1983); Nicole Ball, *Security and Economy in the Third World* (Princeton, NJ: Princeton University Press, 1988); Ruth Leger Sivard, *World Military and Social Expenditures* (Leesburg, VA: World Priorities, annual).
75 See SIPRI, *The Arms Trade With The Third World*, 738–9.
76 Herbert Wulf, 'Developing Countries,' pp. 328–39; Saadet Deger, *Military Expenditure in Third World Countries: The Economic Effects* (Boston: Routledge & Kegan Paul, 1986), pp. 155–64; Carol Evans, 'Reappraising Third-World Arms Production,' *Survival* 28 (March April 1986), 99–118. The import-substitution model found in these writings is quite similar to that of the stuctural/dependency pessimists.
77 This assumption was particularly attractive given the surge in Brazilian arms exports in the late 1970s. See Ethan B. Kapstein, 'The Brazilian Defense Industry and the International System,' *Political Science Quarterly* 104: (Winter 1990–91) 4, 579–96, especially 579–85; and Scott D. Tollefson, *Brazilian Arms Transfers, Ballistic Missiles, and Foreign Policy* (PhD dissertation, Johns Hopkins University, 1991).
78 Michael Brzoska and Thomas Ohlson, 'Conclusion,' pp. 279–80. These authors conclude, on the basis of the apparent Indian failure to achieve self-sufficiency, that only an export-oriented policy makes sense for LDC producers, pp. 282, 288.
79 LDCs did make significant inroads into the arms export business in the 1980s. Most of these exports, however, were *re-exports* of previously imported arms, with or without modification. The re-export market comprised 43 percent of the international arms trade in 1988. Lewis Snider, 'Supplier Control and Recipient Autonomy,' p. 269.
80 See, for example, The Brandt Report, *North-South: A Program for Survival* (New York: Pan Books, 1980).
81 Asbjörn Eide and Marek Thee (eds), *Problems of Contemporary Militarism* (London: Croom Helm, 1980); Mary Kaldor and Asbjörn Eide, *The World Military Order: The Impact of Military Technology on the Third World* (London: Macmillan, 1979); Helena Tuomi and Raimo Värynen, *Militarization and Arms Production* (New York: St. Martin's, 1983); Helena Tuomi and Raimo Värynen, *Transnational Corporations, Armaments, and Development* (New York: St. Martin's, 1982).
82 Alexander Wendt and Michael Barnett, 'Dependent State Formation and Third World Militarization,' in *Review of International Studies* 19 (1993), 321–47; Michael Barnett and Alexander Wendt, 'The Systemic Sources of Dependent Militarization,' in Brian L. Job (ed.), *The Insecurity Dilemma* (Boulder, CO: Lynne Rienner, 1992), pp. 97–119.
83 Mary Kaldor, *The Baroque Arsenal* (New York: Hill and Wang, 1981); James Fallows, *National Defense* (New York: Random House, 1981).
84 See, for example, Herbert Wulf, 'Dependent Militarism in the Periphery and Possible Alternative Concepts,' in Stephanie G. Neuman and Robert E. Harkavy (eds), *Arms Transfers in the Modern World* (New York: Praeger Publishers, 1980), pp. 246–63.
85 Herbert Wulf, 'Developing Countries.'
86 The increasing diffusion of manufacturing technology is discussed in David J. Louscher and Michael D. Salomone, *Technology Transfer and US Security*

Assistance: The Impact of Licensed Production (Boulder, CO: Westview, 1987); David Louscher and Anne Naylor-Schwarz, 'Patterns of Future Third-World Military Technology,' in Kwang-Il Baek, Ronald D. McLaurin, and Chung-in Moon (eds), *The Dilemma of Third World Defense Industries* .., pp. 33–56; Stephanie G. Neuman, 'Coproduction, Barter and Countertrade: Offsets in the International Arms Market,' in *Orbis* 29:2 (Spring 1985), pp. 183–213; Richard Bitzinger, *Towards a Brave New Arms Industry.*'

87 See, for example, Michael T. Klare, 'The Unnoticed Arms Trade ... '.
88 This approach can be noted in Michael Moodie, 'Vulcan's New Forge: Defense Production in Less-Developed Countries,' *Arms Control Today* 10 (March 1980), 1–2, 6–8; Michael Brzoska and Thomas Ohlson, 'Conclusion,' pp. 281–2; Nichole Ball, *Security and Economy in the Third World*. It is strongly contested by Andrew Ross in 'The Arming of the Third World ...,' p. 90; and also by Anne Naylor-Schwarz, 'Arms Transfers and the Development of Second-Level Arms Industries.'
89 These books are Robert E. Harkavy, *The Arms Trade and International Systems* (Cambridge, MA: Ballinger, 1975); Keith Krause, *Arms and the State: Patterns of Military Production and Trade* (Cambridge: Cambridge University Press, 1992); Edward J. Laurance, *The International Arms Trade* (Lexington, MA: Lexington Books, 1992).
90 Raymond Vernon, *Sovereignty at Bay* (New York: Basic Books, 1971). See also Keith Krause, *Arms and the State* ..., pp. 12–34, 48–52, 64–70, 81–98; Ethan B. Kapstein (ed.), *Global Arms Production: Policy Dilemmas for the 1990s* (Lanham, MD: University Press of America, 1992), p. 111.
91 Keith Krause, *Arms and the State* ... pp. 32–3, 81–99. See also Andrew Ross. 'Full Circle: Conventional Proliferation, the International Arms Trade, and Third World Arms Exports,' in Kwang-Il Baek, Ronald D. McLaurin, and Chung-in Moon (eds), *The Dilemma of Third World Defense Industries* ..., pp. 3–32 and Ian Anthony, 'The 'third tier' countries ...' Anthony and Ross rank states on the basis of production of a 'full spectrum' of weapons systems. Krause's estimates are based on total military expenditure, total arms exports, and R&D spending.
92 Adapted from Keith Krause, *Arms and the State* ..., pp. 31–2.
93 Krause examines three systems: 1500–1840; 1840–1945; and the Cold War system. Harkavy focuses on the 1919–39 period and the Cold War, while Laurance examines the 1919–39 system and then disaggregates the Cold War system.
94 Keith Krause, *Arms and the State: Patterns of Military Production and Trade* (Cambridge: Cambridge University Press, 1992), pp. 49–52; Geoffrey Parker, *The Military Revolution* (Cambridge: Cambridge University Press, 1988), pp. 126–8, 136–45; and Carlo M. Cipolla, *Guns, Sails and Empires* (Minerva Press, 1965), pp. 90–131.
95 See Jeremy Black, *European Warfare 1660–1815* (New Haven, CT: Yale University Press, 1994), pp. 1–3, 15–24, 78–84, 200–8.
96 R. Väyrynen and T. Ohlson, 'Egypt: arms production in the transnational context' in Michael Brzoska and Thomas Ohlson (eds), *Arms Production in the Third World*, pp. 106–7; M. E. Selim, 'Egypt,' in James Everett Katz (ed.), *Arms Production in Developing Countries*, pp. 123–5.
97 Keith Krause, *Arms and the State*, pp. 68–71. For a general study including most of these cases, see David B. Ralston, *Importing The European Army: The Introduction of European Military Techniques and Institutions into the Extra-European World, 1600–1914* (Chicago: University of Chicago, 1990).
98 Robert E. Harkavy, *The Arms Trade and International Systems*, p. 93.

99 Robert E. Harkavy, *The Arms Trade and International Systems*, pp. 46, 170–2, 197–8; John Milsom, *Russian Tanks 1900–1970* (Harrisburg, PA: Stackpole Books, 1970), pp. 96–111.
100 Ethan B. Kapstein, 'Introduction: Explaining Arms Collaboration,' in Ethan B. Kapstein (ed.), *Global Arms Production* ..., pp. 6–7.
101 Thucydides, *History of the Peleponnesian War*, Translated by Rex Warner with Introduction and Notes by M. I. Finley (London: Penguin, 1954), I.76.2, p. 80.
102 Even when these factors are identified, they receive little attention. See, for instance, Herbert Wulf, 'Developing Countries,' p. 310, who identifies security, regional hegemony, and prestige as major motivations, and then fails to discuss the relationship between motivation and end-product. See also Michael Moodie, 'Sovereignty, Security, and Arms,' pp. 24–8; and James Everett Katz, 'Understanding Arms Production in the Third World,' in James Everett Katz (ed.), *Arms Production in the Third World*, pp. 3–13 for brief discussions of the importance of ambitions and threats in determining military-industrial policy.
103 Michael Brzoska and Thomas Ohlson, 'Introduction,' pp. 2–5 and 'Conclusions,' pp. 279–90, in *Arms Production in the Third World*.
104 Embargoes were identified as a key motivator in Ilan Peleg, 'Military Production ...' Robert M. Rosh, 'Third World Arms Production ...,' p. 69 concludes that states which have experienced embargoes begin military-industrial policies producing more arms than states which have not experienced embargoes.
105 Realist works include Hans J. Morgenthau, *Politics Among Nations: The Struggle for Power and Peace* sixth edition, revised by Kenneth W. Thompson (New York: Alfred A. Knopf, 1985); Arnold Wolfers, *Discord and Collaboration* (Baltimore, MD: Johns Hopkins University Press, 1962); Martin Wight, *Power Politics* edited by Hedley Bull and Carsten Holbraad (New York, Holmes & Meier, 1978); Kenneth Waltz, *Theory of International Politics* (New York: McGraw-Hill, 1979); and George Liska, *The Ways of Power*.
106 Klaus Knorr, *Military Power and Potential* (Lexington, MA: D. C. Heath, 1970), p. 9. These factors may apply simultaneously – possession of weapons, for example, may deter potential aggressors *and* compel weaker neighbors.
107 Glenn Snyder, *Deterrence and Defense: Toward a Theory of National Security* (Princeton, NJ: Princeton University Press, 1961), pp. 3–4.
108 Keith Krause, *Arms and the State* ..., pp. 2–3, 8–9, 12–18.
109 This roughly corresponds with SIPRI's category of 'geopolitical' arms sales. SIPRI, *The Arms Trade With The Third World*, pp. 17–41.
110 SIPRI refers to this as 'economic' incentives for arms transfers. SIPRI, *The Arms Trade With The Third World*, pp. 17–41.
111 Keith Krause, *Arms and the State* ..., pp. 97–8, 153, 181. Krause identifies these motives in third-tier cases in all three historical arms trade systems he examines.
112 Michael Handel, *Weak States in the International System*, 2nd edition (London: Frank Cass, 1990), p. 3.
113 See Robert E. Harkavy, *The Arms Trade* ..., pp. 183–210; and Keith Krause, *Arms and the state* ..., pp. 34–98.
114 Sweden, for example, pursued a military-industrial policy maximizing independence from foreign supply, qualitative advantages, and sophisticated technology. Per Homström and Ulf Olsson, 'Sweden,' in Nichole Ball and Milton Leitenberg (eds), *The Structure of the Defense Industry*, pp. 140–80. Sweden and Italy imported over 30 percent of their defense requirements

Notes   197

despite their industrialized status. Andrew L. Ross, 'World Order and Arms Production in the Third World,' in James Everett Katz (ed.), *The Implications of Third World Military Industrialization: Sowing the Serpents' Teeth*, p. 280.
115 Ian Anthony, 'The 'Third Tier' Countries ...', pp. 362–8. Again, SIPRI does not consider China to be a developing country.
116 I have borrowed this term from David Kinsella, in 'The Globalization of Arms Production and the Changing Third World Security Context.'
117 See, for example, Ravinder Pal Singh, 'India' in Ravinder Pal Singh (ed.), *Arms Procurement Decision Making Volume I: China, India, Israel, Japan, South Korea and Thailand* (Oxford: Oxford University Press for SIPRI, 1998), pp. 48–90.
118 See Avner Cohen, *Israel and the Bomb* (New York: Columbia University Press, 1998).
119 Michael Handel refers to two types of middle power: those with large populations and underdeveloped economies, and those with small populations but highly developed economies. Michael Handel, *Weak States* ..., p. 23. Analysis of future military developments suggests that new technologies may create 'pockets of capability' allowing small states to hold off much larger ones. Eliot A. Cohen, 'A Revolution in Warfare,' *Foreign Affairs* 75 (March/April 1996), 53.
120 US Department of Defense Directive 2000–9 (ASD-I and L), International Coproduction Projects and Agreements between the United States and Other Counties or International Organizations, 23 January 1974.
121 It was only in the 1980s that major electronics systems, such as radar, were added to the list of Major Weapons Systems. See *SIPRI Yearbook 1992*, pp. 353–4. Small arms, mortars, artillery, ammunition, and non-armored vehicles are not considered in SIPRI data.
122 This designation is drawn from Edward Luttwak and Stuart L. Koehl, *The Dictionary of Modern War*, p. 661, and differs from SIPRI's definition of an MWS. A major platform constitutes, for this analysis, a self-contained combination of weaponry, detection or fire-control systems, transport capability, and a crew.
123 See Henry Sokolski, 'Will There Be an Arms Trade Intelligence Deficit?,' *Annals AAPSS* 535, pp. 158–62; Michael Brzoska, 'Arms Transfer Data Sources,' *Journal of Conflict Resolution* 26 no. 1 (March 1982), pp. 77–108; Edward J. Laurance and Joyce A. Mullen 'Assessing and Analyzing International Arms Trade Data,' in David J. Louscher and Michael D. Salomone (eds), *Marketing Security Assistance: New Perspectives on Arms Sales*, pp. 79–108; Edward T. Fei, 'Understanding Arms Transfers and Military Expenditures: Data Problems,' in Stephanie G. Neuman and Robert E. Harkavy (eds), *Arms Transfers in the Modern World* (New York: Praeger, 1980), pp. 37–46; Nicole Ball, *Third World Security Expenditures: A Statistical Compendium* (Stockholm: National Defence Research Institute, May 1984), pp. 5–39; Keith Krause, *Arms and the State* .., pp. 216–19.
124 Ian Anthony, 'The 'Third Tier' Countries ...,' pp. 372, 378.
125 An interesting study of this phenomenon is Christopher S. Parker, 'New Weapons for Old Problems: Conventional Proliferation and Military Effectiveness in Developing States,' in *International Security*, 23:4 (Spring 1999), 119–47.

2 India

1 Until 1983, the Indian government officially held exports of military equipment in conflict with Indian foreign policy objectives. Ron Matthews, *Defence*

Production in India (New Delhi: ABC Press, 1989), p. 78; Raju G. C. Thomas, 'Defense Planning in India,' in Stephanie G. Neuman (ed.), *Defense Planning in Less-Industrialized States* (Lexington, MA: Lexington, 1984), p. 243.

2 Jawaharlal Nehru, *India's Foreign Policy: Selected Speeches September 1946–April 1961* (New Delhi: Government of India, 1961), p. 99.

3 K. M. Panikkar, *Problems of Indian Defence* (New York: Asia House, 1960), p. 125.

4 Articulated by Kautilya in *Arthashastra (Statecraft)*, the doctrine of mandala assumes that one's neighbor is an enemy, and that an enemy's neighbor is an enemy of one's enemy, and therefore a potential ally. Kautilya, *The Arthashastra*, edited, rearranged, translated and introduced by L. N. Rangarajan (Penguin Books, India (P) Ltd., 1992). See also George K. Tanham, *Indian Strategic Thought: An Interpretive Essay* (Santa Monica, CA: RAND, 1992), pp. 23, 34–5; Raju G. C. Thomas, *Indian Security Policy* (Princeton, NJ: Princeton University Press, 1986), pp. 16–17; and also George Modelski, 'Kautilya: Foreign Policy and International System in the Third World,' *American Political Science Review* 58 (September 1964), 549–60.

5 South Asia is defined here as the region including Afghanistan, Bangladesh, Bhutan, Burma, India, the Maldives, Nepal, Pakistan, and Sri Lanka. See Lt. Gen. (Retired) A. Hasnan Habib, 'Southeast Asian Perceptions of India's Strategic Development: An Indonesian View,' in Ross Babbage and Sandy Gordon (eds), *India's Strategic Future* (New York, St. Martin's, 1992), pp. 107–21.

6 According to 2004 data published in the *CIA World Factbook* at www.cia.gov/cia/publications/factbook, India's 2003 GDP of $3.002 trillion (calculated in terms of purchasing power parity) was over four times the size of the combined total for the rest of the region, and almost ten times greater than Pakistan ($317.7 billion). On Indian regional objectives, see Mohammed Ayoob, 'India in South Asia: The Quest for Regional Predominance,' *World Policy Journal* 7 (Winter 1989–90), pp. 107–33.

7 India has the third largest pool of scientisis and engineers in the world, behind the United States and Russia. 'The Asia–Pacific Region: Growth and Mobility,' *Military Technology* (April 1990), 67–9.

8 See Kanti P. Bajpai and Amitabh Mattoo (eds), *Securing India: Strategic Thought and Practice* (Essays by George K. Tanham with commentaries) (New Delhi: Manohar, 1996).

9 Raju G. C. Thomas, *Indian Security Policy*, p. 295; Stephen P. Cohen, *The Indian army: Its Contribution to the Development of a Nation* (Berkely: University of California Press, 1971).

10 Jaswant Singh, *Defending India* (London: Macmillan Press Ltd., 1999); and Ravinder Pal Singh, 'India' in Ravinder Pal Singh (ed.), *Arms Procurement Decision Making – Volume I: China, India, Israel, Japan, South Korea and Thailand* (Oxford: Oxford University Press for SIPRI, 1998), pp. 48–90.

11 Those ten occasions are: the first Kashmir Conflict (1947–48); the absorption of Hyderabad (1948); the conquest of Goa (1961); the Himalayan War with China (1962); the Rann of Kutch incident (April 1965); the Second Kashmir Conflict (late summer 1965); the liberation of Bangladesh (1971); the intervention in the Maldives (1988); the Peacekeeping Operation in Sri Lanka (1987–90); and the Kargil War of 1999.

12 Raju G. C. Thomas, *Indian Security Policy*, p. 92; Major K. C. Praval, *Indian army After Independence* (New Delhi: Lancer's International, 1990), pp. 1–93.

13 George Perkovich, *India's Nuclear Bomb* (Berkeley: University of California

Press, 1999); Raj Chengappa, *Weapons of Peace* (New Delhi: HarperCollins Publishers India Pvt Ltd, 2000); and Ashley J. Tellis, *India's Emerging Nuclear Posture: Between Recessed Deterrent and Ready Arsenal* (Santa Monica, CA: RAND, 2001).

14 Timothy D. Hoyt, 'Pakistani Nuclear Doctrine and the Dangers of Strategic Myopia,' *Asian Survey* XLI: 6 (November/December 2001), 956–77; Zafar Iqbal Cheema, 'Pakistan's Nuclear Use Doctrine and Command and Control', in Peter R. Lavoy, Scott D. Sagan, and James J. Wirtz (eds), *Planning the Unthinkable: How New Powers Will Use Nuclear, Biological, and Chemical Weapons* (Ithaca: Cornell University Press, 2000), pp. 158–81.

15 See Tanham, *Indian Strategic Thought* ..., pp. 50–69.

16 Jaswant Singh, *Defending India* and Waheguru Pal Singh Sidhu, 'India's Nuclear Use Doctrine,' in Peter R. Lavoy, Scott D. Sagan, and James J. Wirtz (eds) *Planning the Unthinkable* ..., pp. 125–57.

17 Deepa M. Ollapolly, 'Mixed Motives in India's Search for Nuclear Status', *Asian Survey* XLI, No. 6 (November/December 2001), 925–42; Jaswant Singh, 'Against Nuclear Apartheid,' *Foreign Affairs* 77:5 (September/October 1998), 41–52; 'Paper Laid on the Table of the House on Evolution of India's Nuclear Policy,' www.meadev.gov.in/govt/evolution.htm.

18 Timothy D. Hoyt, 'Kargil – The Nuclear Dimension,' in Peter Lavoy and Surinder Rana (eds), *Asymmetric Warfare in South Asia* (forthcoming).

19 Herbert Wulf, 'Developing Countries,' in Nicole Ball and Milton Leitenberg (eds), *The Structure of the Defense Industry* (New York, St. Martin's, 1983), pp. 321–39; Carol Evans, 'Reappraising Third-World Arms Production,' *Survival* 28 (March/April 1986), 99–118; Saadet Deger, *Military Expenditure in Third World Countries*, (London, Boston, and Henley: Routledge & Kegan Paul, 1986), pp. 155–64.

20 Chris Smith, *India's Ad Hoc Arsenal: Direction or Drift in Defence Policy* (Oxford: Oxford University Press for SIPRI, 1994).

21 Lorne J. Kavic, *India's Quest for Security: Defence Policies, 1947–1965* (Berkeley and Los Angeles, CA: University of California, 1967), pp. 9–10; Ashley J. Tellis, 'Securing the Barrack: The Logic, Structure and Objectives of India's Naval Expansion,' in Robert H. Bruce (ed.), *The Modern Indian Navy and the Indian Ocean: Developments and Implications* (Perth, Australia: Curtin University of Technology, 1989), pp. 8–9.

22 Lorne J. Kavic, *India's Quest* ..., pp. 13–15.

23 Barry Buzan and Gowher Rizvi (eds), *South Asian Security and the Great Powers*, (New York, St. Martin's, 1986).

24 Timothy D. Hoyt, 'The War on Terrorism in South Asia,' in Devin T. Hagerty (ed.), *South Asia in World Politics* (Lanham, MD: Rowman & Littlefield, 2005).

25 Other separatist movements in the northeast include troubles with the Kheri and Geros tribes, as well as periodic unrest in Tripura and Manipur. The Naxalite Communist movement was supported by the PRC until the mid-1970s. Raju G. C. Thomas, *Indian Security Policy*, pp. 54–65.

26 The South Asia Terrorism Portal, www.satp.org/satporgtp/countries/india/index.html

27 Timothy D. Hoyt, 'Power, Proximity and Paranoia: The Evolution of Kashmir as a Nuclear Flashpoint', and other chapters in Sumit Ganguly (ed.), *The Kashmir Question: Retrospect and Prospect* (London: Frank Cass, 2003), pp. 117–44.

28 Raju G. C. Thomas, *Indian Security Policy*, pp. 59–60; Nancy Jetly, 'India: The Domestic Dimensions of Security,' in *South Asian Security and the Great*

Powers, ed. Barry Buzan and Gowher Rizvi (New York: St. Martin's Press, 1986), pp. 52–3.
29 Sources on Indo-Pakistani relations include William J. Barnds, *India, Pakistan and the Great Powers* (New York: Praeger 1972); G. W. Choudhury, *India, Pakistan, Bangladesh, and the Major Powers* (New York: Free Press, 1975); Gulab Mishrar Prakhar, *Indo-Pakistani Relations* (Delhi: Ashish, 1987).
30 The Pakistani army's record in the former is controversial, and in the latter is deplorable. Timothy D. Hoyt, 'Pakistan's Nuclear Doctrine and the Dangers of Strategic Myopia.'
31 Timothy D. Hoyt, 'The War on Terrorism in South Asia,' and Praveen Swami, 'Terrorism in Jammu and Kashmir in Theory and Practice' in S. Ganguly (ed.), *The Kashmir Question* .., pp. 55–88.
32 An interesting twist on this relationship occurred in the mid-1990s when India purchased uranium for the Tarapur nuclear facility from China. 'India Buying Chinese Uranium,' *Washington Post,* January 8, 1995. See also 'India's Letter to Clinton on Nuclear Testing', *New York Times,* May 13, 1998.
33 Raju G. C. Thomas, 'Strategies of Recipient Autonomy,' in Kwang-Il Baek, Ronald D. McLaurin, and Chung-in Moon (eds), *The Dilemma of Third World Defense Industries: Supplier Control of Recipient Autonomy* (Boulder, CO: Westview, 1989), pp. 186–7.
34 These concepts of the differing interests of political leadership, economists, and military leaders are derived and interpreted from the various writings of Raju G. C. Thomas.
35 Lorne J. Kavic, *India's Quest* ..., p. 126 (n. 2).
36 Raju G. C. Thomas, *Indian Security Policy,* pp. 195–233.
37 In fact, through 1984 the Cabinet had never even discussed long-term strategy K. Subrahmanyam, 'Commentary: Evolution of Defence Planning in India,' in Stephanie G. Neuman (ed.), *Defense Planning in Less-Industrialized States,* pp. 269, 273 (n. 8). See also *From Surprise to Reckoning: The Kargil Committee Review Report* (New Delhi: SAGE, 1999), pp. 252–64.
38 An interesting study is Verghese Koithara, *Society, State & Security: The Indian Experience* (New Delhi: SAGE, 1999).
39 Stephen P. Cohen, *India: Emerging Power* (Washington, DC: Brookings Institution Press, 2001); George Perkovich, 'Is India a Major Power?' in *The Washington Quarterly* 27:1 (2003), 129–44.
40 In 2003 the there were 40 Ordnance Factories (OFs) and one more still in construction in Nalanda, Bihar, *Annual Report 2002–2003* (New Delhi: Ministry of Defence, Government of India), p. 41 available at: mod.nic.in/reports/welcome.html.
41 One of these units – Praga Tools Limited, which produced primarily for the civilian market – is no longer listed as a Defence Public Sector Unit by the Ministry of Defence Annual Report. See *Annual Report 2002–2003* (Government of India), p. 41.
42 Useful studies of the structure of the Indian arms industry include Thomas Graham, 'India,' in James Everett Katz (ed.), *Arms Production in Developing Countries* (Lexington, MA: Lexington, 1984), pp. 157–91; Andy Lee Ross, *Security and Self-Reliance: Military Dependence and Conventional Arms Production in Developing Countries* (Ithaca, NY: Cornell University, PhD Dissertation August 1984), especially pp. 316–455; Ron Matthews, *Defence Production in India*; Raju G. C. Thomas, *Indian Security Policy,* especially pp. 135–275; Herbert Wulf, 'India: the unfulfilled quest for self-sufficiency,' in Michael Brzoska and Thomas Ohlson (eds), *Arms Production in the Third World* ed. (London and Philadelphia: Taylor & Francis, 1986), pp. 125–45.

43 *Annual Report 2002–2003* (Government of India), p. 41.
44 Ravinder Pal Singh, 'India' in Ravinder Pal Singh (ed.), *Arms Procurement Decision Making*.., p. 57.
45 In 1993, all of the DPSUs were entirely government owned except for Goa Shipyards, Ltd. (GSL) which was a majority (51.08 percent) government-owned firm. *India 1993* (New Delhi: Ministry of Information and Broadcasting, January 1994), p. 74.
46 In 1992, the DPSUs produced Rs21.824 billion (about $750 million in 1992 $US) in defense goods and another Rs12.604 billion ($400 million) in civilian goods. Ministry of Defence, Government of India, *Annual Report 1992–93*, pp. 49–50. Production in 2001/02 was approximately Rs61 billion (approximately $1.5 billion) from the Ordnance Factories (12 percent civilian goods) and Rs76.663 billion (approximately $1.9 billion) at the DPSUs. Praga Tools Limited is no longer listed as a Defence Public Sector Undertaking. *Annual Report 2002–2003* (Government of India), pp. 40–56.
47 *Annual Report 2002–2003* (Government of India), p. 47.
48 Mohammed Abdullah, 'Beyond Bofors: India in Search of a Rational Procurement Policy,' *Military Technology* (December 1999).
49 See Herbert Wulf, 'India: the unfulfilled quest ...,' p. 133.
50 *Defense and Foreign Affairs* (April 1990), pp. 38–41; *India's Defence Public Sector: A Profile* (New Delhi: Mehta, 1983); *India 1991*, pp. 73–6; 'Industry Builds Up Strength,' *Jane's Defence Weekly* (hereafter *JDW*) (May 26, 1990), p. 1039; *Annual Report* (various years); and text.
51 Lorne J. Kavic, *India's Quest*.., p. 127.
52 *India 1991*, pp. 89–90; James Clad. 'Power amid poverty,' *FEER* (7 June 1990), 47–9; 'DRDO: Off Course,' *India Today* (September 15, 1992), 85.
53 Defence Research and Development Organization website at www.drdo.com/labs/index.shtml.
54 Defence Research and Development Organization website at www.drdo.com/genesis.shtml.
55 Ron Matthews, *Defence Production in India*, pp. 96–7.
56 Despite this cooperation, however, Indian R&D has been criticized for a lack of 'cross-fertilization,' and an obsession with pure research. See James Clad, 'Technical Knockout,' *FEER* (June 7, 1990), 47–9.
57 *Annual Report 2002–2003* (Government of India), p. 43; Matthews, *Defence Production*.., p. 91.
58 'India's Move Towards Self-Reliance, and the New Search for Defense Exports,' *Defence & Foreign Affairs* (hereafter *D&FA*) (April 1990), 29; the 2003 Report of the Comptroller and Auditor General, Government of India at www.cagindia.org/reports/defence/2003_army/index.htm.
59 *India 1991*, p. 73. See also *Annual Report 2002–2003* (Government of India) and other years.
60 *Annual Report 2002–2003* (Government of India), pp. 40–2.
61 Non-defense sales were up over 25 percent from the previous year. *Annual Report 2002–2003* (Government of India), p. 44. In the 1980s, only 3 percent of OF production was for non-military purposes. Wulf, 'India: The Unfulfilled Quest ...,' p. 131.
62 *Annual Report 2002–2003* (Government of India), p. 45.
63 Raju G. C. Thomas, *Indian Security Policy*, pp. 255–6.
64 Nehru refused to allow the Indian military to publish a pamphlet on Chinese tactics and doctrine in the early 1950s in an effort to avoid increased tensions. Lorne J. Kavic, *India's Quest* ..., p. 95.
65 See Michael Brecher, *The Struggle for Kashmir* (Toronto: Ryerson, 1953),

Major K. C. Praval, *The Indian army After Independence*, pp. 21–80; Chaudhury, *Pakistan's Relations with India, 1947–1966*, pp. 13–140. See also Dennis Kux, *Estranged Democracies* (Washington, DC: National Defense University Press, 1992), pp. 1–98 on early US–Indian relations, particularly regarding Kashmir. Excellent studies of Kashmir include Sumit Ganguly, *The Crisis in Kashmir* (Woodrow Wilson Center and Cambridge University Press, 1997); and Robert Wirsing, *India, Pakistan, and the Kashmir dispute: on regional conflict and its resolution* (New York: St. Martin's Press, 1994).

66 Dennis Kux, *Disenchanted Allies: The United States and Pakistan 1947–2000* (Baltimore, MD: The Johns Hopkins University Press, 2001). A joint US/UK embargo on both sides during the 1947–49 Kashmir dispute caused was the region's first experience of the difficulties of military dependency. Lorne J. Kavic, *India's Quest . . .*, p. 90.

67 See Chris Smith, *India's Ad Hoc Arsenal*, pp. 41–73.

68 The attitude of many leaders was best summed up by Mohandas K. (Mahatma) Gandhi, who commented: 'Today they must plough the land, dig wells, clean latrines and do every constructive work that they can, and thus turn the people's hatred of them into love.' Cited in Herbert Wulf, 'India: An Unfulfilled Quest . . . ,' p. 125.

69 See Lorne J. Kavic, *India's Quest . . .*, pp. 141–63.

70 Lorne J. Kavic, *India's Quest . . .*, p. 126.

71 '. . . it was more practical to have the capacity to manufacture a second-rate thing in one's own country than to buy a first-rate thing from outside,' cited in Ian C. Graham, 'The Indo-Soviet MiG Deal and its International Repercussions,' *Asian Survey* 4 (May 1964), 825.

72 SIPRI, *The Arms Trade With The Third World* (New York: Humanities Press, 1971) (hereafter SIPRI, *The Arms Trade (1971)*), p. 745.

73 Pushpindar Chopra, 'Spinal Cord of the Indian Air Force,' *Air International* (January 1975), 10–11, cited in Amit Gupta, 'The Indian Arms Industry: A Lumbering Giant,' *Asian Survey* 30 (September 1990), 848.

74 Amit Gupta, The 'Indian Arms Industry . . . ,' p. 848; SIPRI *The Arms Trade With The Third World*, revised edition (New York: Holmes & Meier,1975) (hereafter SIPRI, *The Arms Trade (1975)*), 33.

75 Chris Smith, *India's Ad Hoc Arsenal*, pp. 56–9.

76 George K. Tanham and Marcy Agmon, *The Indian Air Force: Trends and Prospects* (Santa Monica, CA: RAND, 1995), p. 20.

77 Raju G. C. Thomas, 'The Armed Services and the Indian Defense Budget,' *Asian Survey* 20 (March 1980), pp. 280–1; Lorne J. Kavic, *India's Quest . . ,* pp. 154–68.

78 Menon was also using the military to form a potential power base in the 1958–62 period through the manipulation of promotions and assignment of defense contracts. See Lorne J. Kavic, *India's Quest . . .*, pp. 139–68; S. S. Khera, *India's Defence Problem* (Bombay: Orient Longman, 1968), pp. 73–4; Raju G. C. Thomas, *Indian Security Policy*, p. 123; and Francis Hoeber, Yuan-li Wu, William Rood, Maclin Summers, and Ellen Heckler, *Technical Report No. 4320-3* 'Boundary Conditions of the Sino-Indian Conflict,' (Menlo Park, CA: Stanford Research Institute June 1963), pp. 75–9.

79 Lorne J. Kavic, *India's Quest . . .*, p. 128.

80 *FEER* (May 21, 1964), 370.

81 Lorne J. Kavic, *India's Quest . . .*, pp. 57–62, 140; Thomas Graham, 'India,' pp. 157–68.

82 See Chris Smith, *India's Ad Hoc Arsenal*, pp. 48–66.

83 A good description of the MiG deal written shortly after its consumation is

Ian C. Graham, 'The Indo-Soviet MiG Deal and its International Repercussions.' See also Lorne J. Kavic, *India's Quest* ..., p. 108.
84 George K. Tanham and Marcy Agmon, *The Indian Air Force* ..., pp. 20–1; Lorne J. Kavic, *India's Quest* ..., pp. 109–15.
85 The navy's share of the Indian defence budget at independence was about 2 percent. This climbed to nearly 10 percent in 1962, and dropped back to 3 percent after the Himalayan disaster at the end of that year. Hormuz Mama, 'India's Naval Future: Fewer Ships but Better,' *International Defence Review* (February 1993), 161–4.
86 Rear Admiral J. R. Hill, *Maritime Strategies for Medium Powers* (Annapolis, MD: Naval Institute Press, 1986); Ashley J. Tellis, 'The Naval Balance in the Indian Subcontinent: Demanding Missions for the Indian Navy,' *Asian Survey* 25 (December 1985), 1186–213; Sandy Gordon, 'Indian Defense Spending: Treading Water in the Fiscal Deep,' *Asian Survey* 32 (October 1992), 950.
87 SIPRI, *The Arms Trade (1975)*, 181; Lorne J. Kavic, *The Quest* ..., pp. 158–63.
88 Lorne J. Kavic, *India's Quest* ..., pp. 111–15; Ian Graham, 'The Indo–Soviet MiG Deal,' p. 825; SIPRI, *The Arms Trade* ... (1975), p. 181; George K. Tanham and Marcy Agmon, *The Indian Air Force* ..., pp. 20–3; SIPRI, *The Arms Trade* .. (1971), p. 751; Chris Smith, *India's Ad Hoc Arsenal*, p. 77.
89 See Lorne J. Kavic, *India's Quest* .. , pp. 122–5.
90 Major K. C. Praval, *Indian army After Independence*, pp. 167–71.
91 See Steven A. Hoffman, *India and the China Crisis* (Berkeley, CA: University of California Press, 1990); Shanti Prasad Varna, *Struggle for the Himalayas* (New Delhi, Sterling, 1971); Brig. Gen. J. Dalvi, *Himalayan Blunder* (Bombay: Thacker, 1969); Neville Maxwell, *India's China War* (London: Jonathan Cape, 1970); and Major K. C. Praval, *Indian army* ..., pp. 150–243.
92 Ravi Rikhye, *The Militarization of Mother India*, pp. 35–43; Chris Smith, *India's Ad Hoc Arsenal*, pp. 56–9, 68–9.
93 See David Saw, 'Light Combat Aircraft: A Recurring Trend,' *Military Technology* (October 1987), p. 69.
94 David Saw, 'Light Combat Aircraft: a Recurring Trend,' p. 69. The first Orpheus 701 came off an Indian production line on November 21, 1960. Lorne J. Kavic, *India's Quest* ..., p. 132.
95 *FEER* (February 15, 1962), 383.
96 Chris Smith, *India's Ad Hoc Arsenal*, p. 160.
97 *FEER* (December 9, 1965), 476. Production eventually ceased in 1969. 'Heading into Orbit', *FEER* (June 5, 1969), pp. 556–8.
98 See Herbert Wulf, 'India: the Unfulfilled Quest ...,' p. 134; Amit Gupta, 'The Indian Arms Industry ...,' p. 848.
99 'India to Export Aircraft,' *FEER* (January 4, 1962), p. 33.
100 Lorne J. Kavic, *India's Quest* ..., p. 134, refers to this as a 'fit of pique.'
101 *FEER* (July 13, 1961), 71.
102 Prospective partners included the US, the Soviet Union, and Egypt. Herbert Wulf, 'India: the Unfulfilled Quest ...,' p. 135 and *FEER* (December 9, 1965), p. 476.
103 *FEER* (July 26, 1962), 184; Lorne J. Kavic, *India's Quest*, p. 134.
104 Herbert Wulf, 'India: the Unfulfilled Quest ...,' 135.
105 Thomas Graham, 'India,' p. 170; *FEER* (January 30, 1964), 275.
106 Prodyut Das, 'Aircraft Resurgery Programmes: Their Role in Development of Aeronautical Design,' *Indian Defence Review* (July 1990), 113.
107 Herbert Wulf, 'India: the unfulfilled quest ...,' p. 135; Amit Gupta, 'The

Indian Arms Industry ...' pp. 848–9; *Jane's All The World's Aircraft 1977–1978*, pp. 79–80; Raju G. C. Thomas, 'Aircraft for the Indian Air Force ...,' p. 88.
108 Raju G. C. Thomas, 'The Armed Services and the Indian Defense Budget,' p. 293.
109 Herbert Wulf, 'India: an Unfulfilled Quest ...', p. 126.
110 Lorne J. Kavic, *India's Quest* ..., p. 91; SIPRI, *The Arms Trade* .. *(1971)*, p. 481.
111 *FEER* (October 18, 1974), 32; Thomas Graham, 'India,' p. 168.
112 Three versions of the Kiran were produced: the Mk. I, Mk. IA, and Mk. II. The Kiran II suffered from program delays and teething troubles when most of its staff were transferred to work on the Marut program. Lorne J. Kavic, *India's Quest* ..., p. 197.
113 SIPRI, *The Arms Trade* ... *(1971)*, p. 750.
114 Nehru sent two letters to the US on November 19, 1962. The first asked for the US to send a dozen squadrons of fighter aircraft to protect Indian cities. The second asked for two squadrons of B-47 bombers for deep strike missions. Dennis Kux, *Estranged Democracies* (Washington, DC: National Defense University Press, 1992), p. 207.
115 The US provided transport aircraft and assistance in establishing factories for the production small arms and ammunition for the Indian army. *FEER* (May 21, 1964), 370; Andy Lee Ross *Security and Self-Reliance* .., pp. 350–1; and Lorne J. Kavic, *India's Quest* ..., pp. 198–205.
116 See R. Chari, 'Indo-Soviet Military Cooperation: A Review,' in *Asian Survey* 19 (March 1979), pp. 230–44; Jyotirmoy Banerjee, 'Moscow's Indian Alliance,' in *Problems of Communism* 36 (January–February 1987), 1–12; Dilip Mukerjee, 'Indo-Soviet Economic Ties,' in *Problems of Communism* 36 (January-February 1987), 13–24.
117 Lorne J. Kavic, *India's Quest* ..., p. 202.
118 Lorne J. Kavic, *India's Quest* ..., pp. 242–3; International Institute for Strategic Studies, *The Military Balance 1975–76* (London: Brassey's, 1976), p. 54.
119 Raju G. C. Thomas, 'The Armed Services .. ,' p. 288.
120 Raju G. C. Thomas, 'The Growth of Indian Military Power: From Sufficient Defence to Nuclear Deterrence,' in Ross Babbage and Sandy Gordon (eds), *India's Strategic Future* (New York: St. Martin's, 1992), p. 53.
121 *FEER* (July 18, 1963), 158.
122 Thomas Graham, 'India,' p. 160.
123 SIPRI, *The Arms Trade* ... (1975), pp. 182–6; Lorne J. Kavic, *India's Quest* ..., p. 203; Thomas Graham, 'India,' pp. 167–8.
124 Thomas Graham, 'India,' p. 167.
125 Sumit Ganguly, *Conflict Unending: India-Pakistan Tensions since 1947* (Oxford: Oxford University Press, 2001), pp. 31–50; T.V. Paul, *Asymmetric Conflicts: War Initiation by Weaker Powers* (Cambridge: Cambridge University Press, 1994), pp. 107–25.
126 Major K. C. Praval, *Indian Army* ..., pp. 244–307; George K. Tanham and Marcy Agmon, *The Indian Air Force* ..., pp. 23–34; SIPRI, *The Arms Trade (1971)*, pp. 490–4.
127 K. Subrahmanyam, 'Unrecorded Lessons of Our Military History,' *Indian Defence Review* (July 1990), 129–32.
128 Henry Kissinger writes that in the opinion of US analysts, Pakistan was only 72 hours from annihilation at the time of the ceasefire. Henry Kissinger, *White House Years*, (Boston: Little, Brown and Co.), p. 912. This is hyperbole, but Indian army units were being moved to the Western theater.

129 For accounts of the conflict, see Robert Jackson, *South Asian Crisis* (London: Chatto & Windus, 1975); Richard Sisson and Leo B. Rose, *War and Secession: Pakistan, India, and the Creation of Bangladesh* (Berkeley, CA: University of California, 1990); Kissinger, *White House Years*, pp. 842–918; Parval, *Indian Army After Independence*, pp. 309–408; George K. Tanham and Marcy Agmon, *The Indian Air Force . . .*, pp. 34–41; Sumit Ganguly, *Conflict Unending*, pp. 51–78.
130 Raju G. C. Thomas, *Indian Security Policy*, pp. 256–7; and Herbert Wulf, 'India: the Unfulfilled Quest for Self-sufficiency,' p. 138.
131 S.S. Khera, *India's Defence Problem*, p. 50.
132 Lorne J. Kavic, *India's Quest . . .*, p. 131.
133 *FEER* (December 9, 1965), 476; and 'Arms for Oblivion,' *FEER* (July 28, 1966), 135.
134 *FEER* (October 30, 1971), 7.
135 See *IISS The Military Balance 1971–1972*, p. 50.
136 Brig. Gen. A.C. Cariappa, 'The Choice of the Main Battle Tank,' *Hindu*, 23 April 1980, cited in Raju G.C. Thomas, *Indian Security Policy*, p. 165.
137 Ian Graham, 'The Indo-Soviet MiG Deal,' pp. 824, 829.
138 Lorne J. Kavic, *India's Quest . . .*, p. 200.
139 *FEER* (December 9, 1965), 476.
140 'MiG-21M Production Ends After 10 Years,' Delhi *National Herald* in English, November 13, 1981, p. 6, in *FBIS South Asia* (December 1, 1981), E3.
141 *Jane's All The World's Aircraft 1980–81*, p. 91.
142 'India's Westward Gaze,' *JDW* (January 9, 1993), 18–19.
143 *India's Defence Public Sector: A Profile* (New Delhi: Mehta Offset Works, 1983), p. 10.
144 Chris Smith, *India's Ad Hoc Arsenal*, p. 158.
145 Raju G. C. Thomas, 'Strategies of Recipient Autonomy: The Case of India,' p. 193.
146 A recent estimate concludes that the MiG-21 still makes up roughly one-third of the IAF force posture. See *Bharat Rakshak* at www.bharat-rakshak.com/IAF/Units/Fleet.html.
147 In the 1970s, the Soviets refused to allow the Indians to provide spare parts for Egyptian MiG-21s. See Raju G. C. Thomas, 'Strategies of Recipient Autonomy . . .,' p. 193.
148 See P. R. Chari, 'Indo-Soviet Military Cooperation . . .,' p. 239.
149 SIPRI, *The Arms Trade . . (1971)*, p. 477.
150 SIPRI, *The Arms Trade . . (1971)*, p. 743.
151 SIPRI, *The Arms Trade . . (1971)*, p. 486 (n. 10).
152 SIPRI, *The Arms Trade . . (1971)*, 475–6; Lorne J. Kavic. *India's Quest . .*, p. 144; George K. Tanham and Marcy Agmon, *The Indian Air Force*, pp. 20–3.
153 *Jane's Armour and Artillery 1992–1993*, p. 643.
154 *Jane's Armour and Artillery 1992–1993*, pp. 643–4. Raju G. C. Thomas, *Indian Security Policy*, p. 169. The army had requested that these 25 pounder guns be replaced in 1958.
155 *D&FA* (April 1990), 39.
156 'Heading into orbit,' *FEER* (June 5, 1969), 556–8; *Jane's All the World's Aircraft 1977–1978*, p. 685; *SIPRI Yearbook 1985*, p. 435. Production of the SS-11 ceased in 1982–83: indigenization had reached 73 percent. *India 1991*, pp. 75–6.
157 *FEER* (April 25, 1963), 207, 'Heading into Orbit,' *FEER* (June 5, 1969): p. 556.

158 '8 Helicopters Exported to USSR Last Year,' Delhi Domestic Service in English, 0830 GMT, August 10, 1984, *FBIS South Asia* (August 13, 1984), E1.
159 *FEER* (May 24, 1962), 445; *FEER* (August 11, 1966), 285. This represents one of the relatively few cases where diffusion of arms technology mimics the product cycle, and later producers sell back to the original manufacturers as a result of lower production costs.
160 Chris Smith, *India's Ad Hoc Arsenal*, p. 125.
161 Janne E. Nolan, *Trappings of Power: Ballistic Missiles in the Third World* (Washington, DC: The Brookings Institutions, 1991), p. 41; Raju G. C. Thomas, *Indian Security Policy*, p. 245; *Jane's All The World's Aircraft 1977–1978*, pp. 714–15.
162 Patricia A. McFate and Sidney N. Graybeal, 'A New Proliferation Threat from Space?' in W. Thomas Wander and Eric H. Arnett (eds), *The Proliferation of Advanced Weaponry: Technology, Motivations, and Responses* (Washington, DC: American Academy for the Advancement of Science, 1992), p. 99.
163 Timothy McCarthy, 'India: Emerging Missile Power,' in William C. Potter and Harlan W. Jencks (eds), *The International Missile Bazaar* (Boulder, CO: Westview, 1994), p. 202.
164 Lorne J. Kavic *India's Quest* . . , pp. 27–8, n. 19.
165 A. G. Noorani, 'India's Quest for a Nuclear Guarantee,' *Asian Survey* 7 (July 1967), pp. 490–502.
166 George Perkovich, *India's Nuclear Bomb*, pp. 60–106.
167 Rodney W. Jones, Mark G. McDonough with Toby F. Dalton and Gregory D. Koblentz, *Tracking Nuclear Proliferation: A Guide in Maps and Charts, 1998* (Washington, DC: Carnegie Endowment for International Peace, 1998), p. 119, n. 11.
168 *Tracking Nuclear Proliferation: A Guide in Maps and Charts, 1998*, p. 112.
169 Indian nuclear developments from 1947–74 are covered in extraordinary detail in George Perkovich, *India's Nuclear Bomb*, pp. 1–190.
170 K. M. Panikkar, *Problems of Indian Defence*, was the first major proponent of Indian sea power. See also Admiral S. N. Kohli, *Sea Power and the Indian Ocean* (New Delhi: Tata McGraw-Hill, 1978).
171 Raju G. C. Thomas, 'The Armed Services . . . ,' p. 289.
172 The army's share of defense expenditures declined from an average of 76 percent (1962–1967) to 70 percent (1971–80) to 63.9 percent (1985–90). Air force budget share remained at approximately 20–25 percent, while navy budget share increased from an average of 4 percent (1962–67) to 13.5 percent (1985–90). Raju G. C. Thomas, 'The Armed Services and the Indian Defence Budget,' p. 283; and Sandy Gordon, 'Indian Defense Spending,' p. 942.
173 Jerrold F. Elkin and Major W. Andrew Ritezel, 'India,' p. 523; Surjit Mansingh, *India's Search for Power: Indira Gandhi's Foreign Policy, 1966–1982* (New Delhi: SAGE Publications, 1984); S. Nihal Singh, *Indira's India* (Bombay: Nachiketa Publications, 1978).
174 Jerrold F. Elkin and Major W. Andrew Ritezel, 'New Delhi's Indian Ocean Policy,' *Naval War College Review* 40 (Autumn 1987), 50–63; Devin J. Hagerty, 'India's Regional Security Doctrine,' *Asian Survey* 31 (April 1991), 351–63; Kousar J. Azam (ed.), *India's Defence Policy for the 1990s* (New Delhi: Sterling, 1992).
175 See Leonard S. Spector, *The Undeclared Bomb* (Cambridge, MA: Ballinger, 1988), pp. 120–53; Leonard S. Spector, *Nuclear Ambitions* (Boulder, CO: Westview, 1990), pp. 89–117; 'Pakistan Reported Near Atom Arms Production,' *Washington Post*, November 4, 1986; 'We Have The A-Bomb, Says

Pakistan's "Dr. Strangelove",' *Observer* (London), March 1, 1987; 'Pakistan Able to Equip F-16s for Nuclear Bombs', *Washington Times,* May 31, 1990; 'Pakistan Tells of Its A-Bomb Capacity,' *New York Times,* February 8, 1992.

176 Timothy D. Hoyt, 'Pakistani Nuclear Doctrine and the Dangers of Strategic Myopia'; and Zafar Iqbal Cheema, 'Pakistan's Nuclear Use Doctrine and Command and Control,' in Peter R. Lavoy, Scott D. Sagan, and James J. Wirtz (eds), *Planning the Unthinkable* .. The counterintuitive concept that nuclear capabilities may increase the likelihood of war is known as the 'stability-instability paradox.' See Glenn Snyder, 'The Balance of Power and the Balance of Terror,' in Paul Seabury (ed.), *The Balance of Power* (San Francisco: Chandler, 1964), pp. 184–201; Robert Jervis, *The Meaning of the Nuclear Revolution* (Ithaca, NY: Cornell University Press, 1989), pp. 19–22; and Michael Krepon and Chris Gagne (eds), *The Stability–Instability Paradox: Nuclear Weapons and Brinkmanship in South Asia* (Washington, DC: Henry L. Stimson Center, June 2001).

177 Prasun Sengupta, 'Indian Armoured Doctrine and Modernisation: Towards a Modern Armoured Capability,' *Military Technology* (May 1992), 29–35; Sandy Gordon, 'Indian Defense Spending . . .,' p. 943.

178 This policy was known in India as 'persuasive deterrence': if Pakistan caused problems in Kashmir, India would respond with a naval blockade and a rapid armored assault to the Indus River. 'A Middle-Aged Military Machine', *India Today* (April 30, 1993), 29.

179 Col. Trigunesh Mukherjee, 'Effective Defense Planning for the 1990s,' in Kousar J. Azam (ed.), *India's Defence Policy for the 1990s*, p. 33.

180 IISS *The Military Balance 2002–2003*, p. 131.

181 'A Middle Aged Military Machine,' pp. 22–30; 'On the Kashmir Beat,' *JDW* (May 21, 1994), 19–20.

182 The US threatened to declare Pakistan a supporter of terrorism because of its refusal to close down training camps in Pakistan Occupied Kashmir, also known as Azad Kashmir. Pakistan agreed in 1990 to close down 31 camps during a peacekeeping visit by Robert Gates. See 'US, Pakistan to Renew Talks,' *Washington Post,* January 11, 1995; 'A Growing Realism,' *India Today,* June 15, 1993, pp. 62–3. For recent developments, Owen Bennett Jones, *Pakistan: Eye of the Storm* (New Haven, CT: Yale University Press, 2002), p. 27; *Patterns of Global Terrorism* 2002 (Washington, DC: US Department of State, April 2003).

183 Rahul Bedi, 'Country Briefing: India – Divided Interests,' *JDW,* May 21, 2003, at www4.janes.com. An excellent study of the terrorist groups in Kashmir is Praveen Swami, 'Terrorism in Jammu and Kashmir in Theory and Practice,' in Ganguly (ed.) *The Kashmir Question: Retrospect and Prospect,* pp. 55–88.

184 'Of Brinkmanship and Limited Deterrence,' *FEER,* April 9, 1987, pp. 36–7; 'Border Backlash,' *FEER* July 27, 1989, pp. 18–19. The most thorough account of Brasstacks is Kanti P. Bajpai, P. R. Chari, Pervaiz Iqbal Cheema, Stephen P. Cohen, and Sumit Ganguly (eds), *Brasstacks and Beyond: Perception and Management of Crisis in South Asia* (Urbana, IL: The Program in Arms Control, Disarmament, and International Security, University of Illinois at Urbana-Champaign, June 1995).

185 For details, see Devin T. Hagerty, *The Consequences of Nuclear Proliferation: Lessons from South Asia* (Cambridge, MA: MIT Press, 1998); Kanti P. Bajpai, P. R. Chari, Pervaiz Iqbal Cheema, Stephen P. Cohen, and Sumit Ganguly (eds), *Brasstacks and Beyond* . . .

186 See Ravi Rikhye, *The War That Never Was: The Story of India's Strategic*

Failures (New Delhi: Chanakya Publications, 1988), p. 195; Raj Chengappa, *Weapons of Peace*, pp. 322–3; and P. N. Hoon, *Unmasking the Secrets of Turbulence* (New Delhi: Manas Publications, 2000), p. 102.
187 Sumit Ganguly, *Conflict Unending: India–Pakistan Tensions since 1947*, pp. 92–3.
188 The nuclear deployment report comes from Seymour Hersh, 'On the Nuclear Edge,' *The New Yorker* (March 29, 1993), pp. 55–73 (now available at www.newyorker.com/archive/content/?040119fr_archive02). The claim is repeated in William E. Burrows and Robert Windrem, *Critical Mass* (New York: Simon & Schuster, 1994), pp. 60–90. A less alarmist perspective is *Conflict Prevention and Confidence-Building Measures in South Asia: The 1990 Crisis* Occasional Paper no. 17 ed. Michael Krepon and Mishi Faruqee (Washington, DC: The Henry L. Stimson Center, April 1994). Recent personal interviews with former officials have persuaded this author that a nuclear device was actually assembled on the orders of then Army Chief of Staff Mirza Aslam Beg,
189 'Kashmir Issue May Draw a Summit Plea,' *Los Angeles Times*, June 1, 1990.
190 These exercises, titled 'Chequerboard' and 'Falcon,' tested Indian operations capability in the Himalayas. 'Eyeball to eyeball on the Himalayan Border,' *FEER* (April 9, 1987), 38–9; 'Tension on the Border,' *FEER* (May 7, 1987), 33–5; 'Border Backlash,' *FEER* (July 27, 1989), pp. 18–19.
191 Stephen P. Cohen, 'Why Did India "Go Nuclear",' in Raju G. C. Thomas and Amit Gupta (eds), *India's Nuclear Security* (Boulder, CO: Lynne Rienner, 2000), p. 22.
192 Raju G. C. Thomas, 'The Growth of Indian Military Power . . ', p. 53.
193 'DRDO: Off Course,' *India Today* (September 15, 1992), 85; Shekhar Gupta, 'India Redefines its Role,' *Adelphi Paper 293* (Oxford: Oxford University Press for ((SS, 1995), p. 38.
194 Up to 50 percent of the Indian airforce was reportedly grounded by the need for engine overhauls and lack of essential spares. See 'India's Military Hit By Soviet Collapse,' *Washington Post*, October 4, 1992; 'Russia, India Reach Accord on Debt, Trade, and Defense,' *Christian Science Monitor*, June 29, 1993. By 1993, the serviceability of India's MiG-29 squadrons was only 30 percent, and the airforce was cannibalizing whole squadrons of MiG-21s and An-32s in order to provide spares for other squadrons of aircraft which remained in service. 'A Middle-Aged Military Machine,' pp. 23–5.
195 *WMEAT 1991–1992*, p. 66.
196 'A Middle-Aged . . .', p. 40.
197 Production of radars, according to one official, dropped 75 percent in the early 1990s because of reduced access to foreign exchange. 'In Reverse Gear,' *India Today*, (November 15, 1991), 131.
198 Relations still remain strained through the mid-1990s. 'Rhetoric fuels US–India Rift,' *Washington Post*, February 24, 1994; John Anderson, 'Subcontinental Drift' (Op-Ed), *Washington Post*, March 20, 1994.
199 Raju G. C. Thomas, 'US Transfers of 'Dual-Use' Technologies to India,' *Asian Survey* 30 (September 1990), 825–45.
200 At one point, India was reportedly down to only two weeks worth of foreign exchange reserves, and money was unavailable for defense imports. 'SP guns battle over India,' *JDW* (August 27, 1994), p. 30; 'Chinks in the Armour,' *India Today* (November 15, 1991), 129–31. The government had to sell 90 tons of gold in 1991 to maintain liquidity. Shekhar Gupta, 'India Redefines . . .,' p. 8.
201 Foreign exchange reserves excluding gold dipped from $4.108 billion US in

1989 to $1.521 billion in 1990, and rose again to $5.757 billion by 1992. External debt rose from $55.753 billion in 1987 to $76.983 billion in 1992. The World Bank, *World Tables 1994* (Baltimore: The Johns Hopkins University Press, 1994), pp. 344–7.
202 Bimal Jalan, *India's Economic Crisis: The Way Ahead* (Delhi: Oxford India, 1992). For a more reserved assessment of the overall impact of reform, see 'The State of Reform in India,' *The Economist* (August 6, 1994), 29–30.
203 'India Stems the Fall in its Defence Spending,' *JDW* (March 12, 1994), 3.
204 'Indian Arms Buys Defy Cash Shortfall,' *JDW* (May 8, 1993), 29–30; 'India's Westward Gaze,' *JDW* (January 9, 1993), 18–19; 'Cut price weapons challenge Western Sales,' *JDW* (April 3, 1993), 12–13; 'Russia, India sign on joint aviation venture', *JDW* (9 July 1994), p. 3; 'SP Guns Battle Over India,' *JDW* (August 27, 1994), 30.
205 If R&D budgets for space and nuclear power projects were included, R&D expenses would have equalled about 7 percent of the 1982 budget. Raju G. C. Thomas, *Indian Security Policy*, pp. 239–41. By 1986, military-related R&D comprised about 40 percent of all government R&D spending. Air Vice Marshal C.V. Gole (retired), 'National Security and the Role of Industry,' in *Indian Defence Review* (July 1991), p. 126.
206 *Annual Report 1992–93*, p. 13.
207 'DRDO: Off Course,' *India Today* (15 September 1992), 85; K. Santhanam, 'Opportunities and Prospects for Indo-US Cooperation in Defense Technologies,' in *The United States and India in the Post Soviet World*, pp. 159–66.
208 Chris Smith, *India's Ad Hoc Arsenal*, pp. 112, 124–6.
209 'Plan To Build Mirage Aircraft Domestically Scrapped,' Delhi Domestic Service in English 0830 GMT 27, July 1984, in *FBIS South Asia* (July 27, 1984), E3.
210 'Deal To Purchase MIG-29 Aircraft Finalized', Bombay *The Times of India* in English, August 6, 1984, p. 6, in *FBIS South Asia* (August 13, 1984), E1. Reports of licensed production appeared in the fall. 'Review of National Defense Preparedness Discussed,' Delhi *The Hindustan Times* in English, September 20, 1984, pp. 1, 16 by MK Dhar, in *FBIS South Asia* (October 4, 1984), E1.
211 Renato Contin, 'MiG-29: A New Step in the "Mirror Policy",' *Military Technology* (April 1987), 122–9.
212 'AFP: India To Purchase MiG-29s from Soviet Union,' Hong Kong AFP in English, 0827 GMT, July 14, 1986, in *FBIS South Asia* (July 17, 1986), E1.
213 '"First Batch" of MiG-29s Arrives From USSR,' Delhi Domestic Service in English, 0240 GMT, January 4, 1987, in *FBIS South Asia* (5 January 1987), E1.
214 'Soviet Experts Arrive to Assemble MiG-29s,' Delhi *PATRIOT* in English, 4 January 1986[sic], p. 1, *FBIS South Asia* (January 12, 1987), E1; Renato Contin, 'MiG-29: A New Step in the "Mirror Policy",' p. 128; *Military Technology* (January 1989), 254.
215 See 'India's Military Hit by Soviet Collapse,' *Washington Post*, October 4, 1992; *Indian Defence Review* (June 1991), 12 states specifically that the InAF lacks spares for the MiG-29 force.
216 *Report of the Comptroller and Auditor General of India for the Year Ended 31 March 1992, No. 9 of 1993*, Union Government, 1993, cited in George K. Tanham and Marcy Agmon, *The Indian Air Force*, pp. 54–7, 69–71.
217 *Aviation Week and Space Technology* (14/21 December 1992), 17 reported that India was setting up a special overhaul facility for MiG-29s at a cost of $200 million.

210   Notes

218 'Indian Fleet To Add Two Aircraft Carriers By 2010, Navy Chief Says,' *Defense News*, December 2, 2003.
219 HAL maintained research on supersonic fighters throughout the 1970s. Ron Matthews, *Defence Production in India*, p. 99; *Jane's All The World's Aircraft 1977–1978*, p. 80; 'The Price is High', *FEER* (December 3, 1977), p. 36.
220 This engine is the Kevari turbine. 'New Engine for Jet Fighters,' Hong Kong AFP in English, 0619 GMT, April 30, 1982, in *FBIS South Asia* (May 7, 1982), E4. The Kevari still remained in development in 2003. *Annual Report 2002–2003* (Government of India), p. 61.
221 'Defense Minister on Producing Combat Aircraft,' Delhi General Overseas Service in English, 1330 GMT, March 27, 1985, in *FBIS South Asia* (March 28, 1985), E1.
222 David Saw, 'Indigenous Fighter Production,' *Military Technology*, (June 1991), 89. The GTX program has also received assistance from the French firm SNECMA: see 'Collaboration Invited for LCA Programme,' *JDW* (January 29, 1994), 8.
223 Nicholas Nugent, 'The Defence Preparedness of India: Arming for Tomorrow,' *Military Technology* (March 1991), 36; Amit Gupta, 'The Indian Arms Industry ...,' pp. 851–2.
224 'LCA Breaks Sound Barrier During Flight,' *Rediff*, August 1, 2003 at www.rediff.com.
225 'Eurofighter 2000: EF à la carte,' *International Defense Review* (January 1993), 9; 'Taiwan to Slash IDF Production,' *JDW* (April 3, 1993), p. 5.
226 'Flying Coffins? MiG-23 Even More "Lethal",' *Times of India*, July 8, 2003; 'Poor Maintenance Cause of Indian Air Force's Chronic Crashes: Report', *Agence France Presse*, August 29, 2003. According to the latter report, the Indian airforce lost 273 MiG aircraft to crashes between 1991 and 2003.
227 *SIPRI Yearbook 1982*, p. 215, and also 'India Concludes Weapons Deal With The Soviet Union,' Hong Kong AFP in English, 1841 GMT, May 27, 1980, in *FBIS South Asia* (May 28, 1980), E1.
228 'Minister on Proposal To Build T-72 Tanks,' Delhi Domestic Service in English, 0830 GMT, 14 Dec 1983, in *FBIS South Asia* (December 14, 1983), E2.
229 'Domestic Production of T-72 Tanks Begins,' Delhi Domestic Service in English, 0830 GMT, January 19, 1988, in *FBIS-NESA* (January 20, 1988), p. 61.
230 'Arjun Delays Bring Vijayanta Upgrade Back on Track,' *JDW* (July 3, 1993), 19; 'Arjun Must Fight T-72M1 for Place on the Production Line', *JDW* (September 1, 1994), 27; 'A Middle-Aged Military Machine,' p. 23; 'SP Guns Battle Over India,' *JDW* (August 27, 1994), p. 28.
231 Prasun Sengupta, 'Indian Armoured Doctrine ...', p. 32.
232 'Arjun Must Fight T-72M1 for place on the Production Line,' *JDW* (September 1, 1994), p. 27.
233 Enrico Bonsignore, 'Gulf Experience Raises Tank Survivability Issues', *Military Technology* (February 1992), 64–70.
234 'India,' *Jane's World Armies* 15 (2003) at www4.janes.com.
235 'T-90 Tank Likely to Roll Out by Dec. End,' *The Hindu*, October 17, 2003.
236 'Briefs: Battle Tank Development,' reported in Delhi *National Herald* in English, July 8, 1982, p.1, in *FBIS South Asia* (July 20, 1982), E5.
237 'Report Criticizes Delay in Tank Development,' Delhi *The Hindustan Times* in English, July 24, 1989, in *FBIS-NESA* (August 11, 1989), pp. 45–6.
238 Amit Gupta, 'The Indian Arms Industry ..,' p. 850. See also 'Review of National Defense Preparedness Discussed,' Delhi *The Hindustan Times* in

English, September 20, 1984, pp. 1, 16 by MK Dhar, in *FBIS South Asia* (October 4, 1984), E1; *Jane's Armour and Artillery 1992–1993*, p. 70.
239 'Researchers Say Tank Project Faces More Delays,' Hong Kong AFP in English, 0753 GMT, 6 April 1990, in *FBIS-NESA* (April 6, 1990); Prasun Sengupta, 'Indian Armoured Doctrine . . .,' p. 35; and Sanjiv Prakash, 'Indian Defense: A Conscious Attempt at Pragmatism,' in *D&FA* (April 1990), 43.
240 'Arjun Must Fight T-72M1 for Place on the Production Line,' *JDW* (September 1, 1994), 27.
241 *Jane's Armour and Artilley, 1992–1993*, p. 70.
242 *Jane's Armour and Artillery 1992–1993*, p. 70. Use of a rifled main gun is explicitly criticized in Eric Arnett, 'Military Technology: the Case of India,' *SIPRI Yearbook 1994*, p. 348.
243 See Prasun Sengupta, 'Indian Armoured Doctrine . . .,' pp. 29–31.
244 *Annual Report 2002–2003* (Government of India), p. 64.
245 'Arjun MBT,' *Jane's Armour and Artillery* (2003) at www4.janes.com.
246 Indramil Banerjie, 'The Integrated Guided Missile Development Programme,' *Indian Defence Review* (July 1990), 99.
247 Indramil Banerjie, 'The Integrated Guided Missile Development Programme,' 100.
248 Indramil Banerjie, 'The Integrated Guided Missile Development Programme', 101. The Trishul reportedly suffered delays from problems with key guidance technologies. 'The Missile Man,' *India Today* (April 15, 1994), 41.
249 Admiral J. G. Nadkarni, 'Riding the Waves,' *Rediff*, May 10, 2003 at www.rediff.com.
250 'Trishul is Blunt, so Naval Forces Seek Barak,' *Times of India*, August 25, 2003.
251 'Naval Chief Leaves for Moscow,' *Press Trust of India*, June 16, 2003; 'Indian Frigate Commissions Without Full Armament,' *Sea Power* (July 2000).
252 See Janne E. Nolan, *Trappings of Power* . . , p. 45; *India 1991*, p. 77; Andrew Feickert and K. Alan Kronstadt, 'Missile Proliferation and the Strategic Balance in South Asia,' *CRS Report for Congress* (Washington, DC: Library of Congress, 17 October 2003), p. 26.
253 'India Succeeds in Missile Test Launching,' *Washington Post*, February 26, 1988, 24.
254 'Army gears up to deploy Agni,' *Times of India*, September 23, 2003; 'Army to Add Firepower to Arsenal,' *Times of India*, May 12, 2003.
255 'Armed Forces – India,' *Jane's Sentinel Security Assessment – South Asia* (2004), at www4.janes.com.
256 Sanjiv Prakash, 'Indian Defense: A Conscious Attempt at Pragmatism', *D&FA* (April 1990), 44; and also 'Nag Tests Successful,' *JDW* (July 7, 1990), 18.
257 'India Negotiates MILAN Deal,' *Military Technology* (February 1992), 97.
258 'The Missile Man,' *India Today* (April 15, 1994), 41.
259 Duncan Lennox 'ATBMs and Beyond,' *JDW* (May 22, 1993); 'Testing Reactions,' *FEER* (June 8, 1989), 38–9.
260 'Akash,' *Jane's Strategic Weapons Systems* (2004) at www4.janes.com.
261 Indramil Banerjie, 'The Integrated Guided Missile Development Programme,' p. 104. This also clearly connects India's missile (IGMDP) and space launch programs (ISRO).
262 See *D&FA*, April 1990, 41 and Janne E. Nolan, *Trappings of Power* . . , p. 45.
263 Nicholas Nugent, 'The Defence Preparedness of India . . .,' p. 30.
264 'Third Agni Test Launch Fulfills "Set Objectives",' *JDW* (March 5, 1994), 18. The missile was five tons heavier, due to an increased fuel load.

212 Notes

265 See *Proliferation: Threat and Response* (Washington, DC: Office of the Secretary of Defense, January 2001); Peter Lavoy, 'Fighting Terrorism, Avoiding War: The Indo-Pakistani Situation,' *Joint Force Quarterly* (Autumn 2002), 27–34.
266 'Agni 1/2/3,' *Jane's Strategic Weapons System 40* (2003) at www4.janes.com
267 'India Tests Missile, Stirring a Region Already On Edge,' *New York Times*, January 25, 2002.
268 'Army Gears Up to Deploy Agni', *Times of India*, September 23, 2003.
269 'The Missile Man,' p. 44.
270 Timothy McCarthy, 'India: Emerging Missile Power,' p. 203.
271 See 'Advanced Surface to Surface Missile Tests Planned,' Hong Kong AFP in English, 1550 GMT, May 26, 1989 in *FBIS-NESA* (May 30, 1989), 61; 'Defense Team to Oversee Guided Missile Program,' Hong Kong AFP in English, 0753 GMT, July 20, 1988, in *FBIS-NESA* (July 22, 1988), 43–4.
272 Timothy McCarthy, 'India: Emerging Missile Power,' p. 203.
273 *Forecast International/DMS Market Intelligence Review*, June 1990 'Market Overview – India,' p. 7.
274 'India's Long Road to New Rifle', p. 30.
275 *Annual Report 1999–2000*, p. 65.
276 *Annual Report 1992–93*, pp. 41–2.
277 See 'A Middle Aged Military Machine,' p. 24.
278 *Annual Report 1992–93*, p. 14; Shekhar Gupta, 'India Redefines ...', pp. 38–43.
279 Chris Smith, *India's Ad Hoc Arsenal*, pp. 152–3; *Review of Procurement for OP VIJAY (Army)* (Delhi: Comptroller and Auditor General's Office, 2001), www.cagindia.org/reports/defence/2001_book3/review.htm.
280 '*Review of Procurement for OP VIJAY (Army)*'; 'T-90 tank likely to roll out be Dec. end', *The Hindu*, October 17, 2003.
281 *D&FA* (April 1990), 41.
282 *Indian Defence Review* (January 1991), p. 12; and Timothy McCarthy, 'India: Emerging Missile Power', p. 218.
283 See 'George Fernandes: India's Defense Minister,' *Defense News*, February 2, 2004.
284 *Jane's Armor and Artillery 1993–1993*, p. 643.
285 Bofors has been accused of paying bribes to extremely high-ranking Indian officials to secure this contract. See 'New Detonations,' *India Today* (March 15, 1992; 'Doing Business Between the Lines', *JDW* (December 11, 1993), 28.
286 'Bofors: Counter-trade Con,' *India Today* (September 30, 1991), 81–2 discusses the offset problem. See also 'India Fills Munition Gap', JDW (October 9, 1993), 21; 'SP Guns Battle Over India', *JDW* (August 27, 1994), 28; 'Indian Army Buys Defy Cash Shortfall,' *JDW* (May 8, 1993), 30.
287 *Annual Report 2000–2001*, p. 56.
288 *Review of Procurement for OP VIJAY*.
289 *India 1991*, pp. 75–6. 'India Negotiates MILAN Deal,' *Military Technology* (February 1992), 97.
290 Timothy McCarthy, 'India: Emerging Missile Power,' p. 211.
291 'Army to Add Firepower to Arsenal,' *Times of India*, May 12, 2003.
292 Ron Matthews, *Defence Production in India*, pp. 86–7. Average growth in the value of military electronics production during this decade was 14 percent.
293 Jim Bussert, 'Sonars of the Indian Navy,' *Jane's Intelligence Review* (November 1992), 511.
294 *D&FA* (April 1990), pp. 38–9.
295 See 'Defense Forces To Receive Radar From Local Firm,' Delhi Domestic

Service in English, 0830 GMT, August 28, 1988, in *FBIS-NESA* (August 30, 1988), 45; and 'Low-Flying Aircraft Radar Dedicated to Nation,' Delhi Domestic Service in English, 0730 GMT, March 26, 1989, in *FBIS-NESA* (March 28, 1989), p. 49.
296 'Industry Builds up Strength', *JDW* (May 26, 1990), 1039; 'Bharat Electronics: High Tech From India,' *Military Technology* (March 1990), 64; and 'India Boosts Electronics Capability,' *International Defence Review* (October 1991), p. 1135.
297 Reports conflict as to whether final production totalled 1,600 or 2,200 Vijayantas. *Jane's Armour and Artillery 1992–1993*, pp. 72, 137.
298 Raju G. C. Thomas, *Indian Security Policy*, p. 257. Akhtar Majeed, 'Indian Security Perspectives in the 1990s,' p. 1089.
299 See Prasun Sengupta, 'Indian Armoured Doctrine ...,' p. 31; *Jane's Armour and Artillery 1992–1993*, pp. 71–2.
300 'Arjun Delays Bring Vijayanta Upgrade Back on Track', *JDW* (July 3, 1993), 19.
301 *Jane's All The World's Aircraft 1977–78*, p. 81; *Jane's All The World's Aircraft 1980–81*, p. 88.
302 Public Accounts Committee, Seventh Lok Sabha, *Delay in Development and Manufacture of an Aircraft* (New Delhi: Government of India, 1982), p. 4, cited in Amit Gupta, 'The Indian Arms Industry ..,' p. 854.
303 The Ajeet reportedly had less than 60 percent commonality of parts with the Gnat. Andy Lee Ross, *Security and Self-Reliance ...*, p. 405.
304 'India's Westward Gaze,' *JDW* (January 9, 1993), 18–19; George K. Tanham and Marcy Agmon, *The Indian Air Force ...*, pp. 51–5; Herbert Wulf, 'India: the Unfulfilled Quest ...,' p. 134.
305 'Combat Vehicles To Be Built in Madras,' Delhi General Overseas Service in English, 1330 GMT, August 20, 1985, in *FBIS South Asia* (August 21, 1985), E7; 'First Combat Vehicle Finished,' Delhi Domestic Service in English, 1530 GMT, August 23, 1987, in *FBIS-NESA* (August 27, 1987), E2. By 1991, India was producing key components including the 30mm gun and AT-4 Spigot ATGM. *Jane's Armour and Artillery 1992–1993*, p. 389.
306 'India in $31.5 m Deal to Buy Slovak ARVs,' *JDW* (January 15, 1994), 8.
307 Raju G. C. Thomas, 'Aircraft for the Indian Air Force ...,' pp. 93–6; Akhtar Majeed, 'Indian Security Perspectives for the 1990s,' p. 1087.
308 'India to Get Jaguar Trainers,' *Aviation Week and Space Technology* (October 23, 1978), 26. Another reason was to acquire the technology for the Adour 811 jet engine. Andy Lee Ross, *Security and Self-Reliance ...*, p. 410.
309 'Indian Paper on Arms Deal Talks With US, UK,' Calcutta, *The Statesman* in English, January 20, 1981, 1, 7 in *FBIS South Asia* (February 3, 1981), E4.
310 'Pact for Licensed Production of MiG-27's Signed,' Delhi Domestic Service in English, 0830 GMT, July 29, 1983, in *FBIS South Asia* (August 2, 1983), E1.
311 'IAF's 100th Flogger "J",' *JDW*, (May 16, 1992), 839 reports that indigenous content reached 74 percent.
312 *Annual Report 2003–2003*, p. 62.
313 See 'Comprehensive Deal Planned For French Mirage', Delhi *National Herald* in English, November 24, 1981, 1, 6, in *FBIS South Asia* (December 2, 1981), E1; 'AFP: Deal Signed With France For Mirage 2000,' Hong Kong AFP in English, 0340 GMT, April 14, 1982 in *FBIS South Asia* (April 14, 1982), E1; 'Accord Signed With France For Mirage-2000's,' Hong Kong AFP in English, 0814 GMT, October 18, 1982, in *FBIS South Asia* (October 18, 1982), E1.
314 Rahul Bedi, 'Country Briefing: India – Divided Interests,' *JDW*, May 21, 2003 at www4.janes.com.

315 See 'French Minister's Visit to Boost Defence Ties,' *Times of India*, April 24, 2003, and Rahul Bedi, 'Country Briefing: India – Divided Interests'.
316 Interview with Air Chief Marshal S. K. Kaul, Chief of Air Staff, JDW (November 6, 1993), p. 56; 'India's Westward Gaze,' *JDW* (January 9, 1993), 18–19; 'A Middle-Aged Military Machine,' p. 25. The MiG accident rate is discussed in 'Flying coffins? MiG-23 Even More "Lethal"'; C. Manmohan Reddy, 'MiG Accidents and Advanced Trainers,' *The Hindu*, August 25, 2003. A defense of the MiG aircraft program can be found in AK Goel, 'Don't Shoot Down IAF Over MiG Myths', *The Indian Express*, August 13, 2003.
317 The HAWK deal, which will include assembly of 41 aircraft at the HAL Jaguar line in Bangalore, is noted in 'First Su-30 MKI Fighter to Roll Out in Dec.,' *The Hindu,* September 29, 2003.
318 *Aviation Week and Space Technology* (September 3, 1990), 25; and *Aviation Week and Space Technology* (March 9, 1987), 215.
319 'Airborne Early Warning System To Be Developed', Delhi Domestic Service in English, 1530 GMT, Apr 30, 1983, in *FBIS South Asia* (May 6, 1983), E3; 'India Launches its Own AWACS Program,' *FEER* (October 17, 1985), 12.
320 See 'USSR Offers Airborne Early Warning System,' Hong Kong AFP in English, 0757 GMT, January 5, 1987, in *FBIS South Asia* (January 5, 1987), E1; 'Paper Reports Details on Soviet AWACS Offer,' Bombay *Times of India* in English, January 5, 1987, p. 1, in *FBIS South Asia* (January 16, 1987), E2; James Smith, 'Developments in the Indian Air Force', *Jane's Intelligence Review* (November 1991), 526.
321 'Collapse of Rotodome May Have Caused Avro Crash,' *The Hindu*, January 13, 1999.
322 'Israel To Sell Radars to India,' *Wall Street Journal*, September 5, 2003; 'Phalcon Will Fly in Indian Skies, Says Israel,' *Times of India*, September 10, 2003.
323 Ron Matthews, *Defence Production in India*, pp. 100–1.
324 Amit Gupta, 'The Indian Arms Industry . . .,' p. 850.
325 'Agreement Reached With FRG Firm On Helicopters,' Delhi Domestic Service in English, 0830 GMT, July 24, 1984, in *FBIS South Asia* (July 27, 1984), E3.
326 'ALH First Flight Looms,' *JDW* (May 26, 1990), 1036.
327 'Farnborough '90: Slow Ahead,' *Military Technology* (December 1990), 80.
328 'In Reverse Gear,' p.131.
329 'On the Wings of Hope,' *India Today* (October 31, 1992), 58–9.
330 See 'Procurement, India,' *Jane's Sentinel Security Assessment – South Asia* at www4.janes.com; *Annual Report 2002–2003* (Government of India), p. 48. According to recent reports, the helicopter will be marketed by Israeli Aircraft Industries, and the US Customs Service intends to purchase as many as ten helicopters. Neelam Matthews, "Push to Save Dhruv," *Aviation Week & Space Technology* (January 12, 2004), 41.
331 'Agreement Reached With FRG on Submarine Sale,' Hamburg DPA in German, 1437 GMT, December 12, 1981, in *FBIS South Asia* (December 15, 1981), E2.
332 See *Combat Fleets of the World, 1986–1987* (Annapolis, MD: Naval Institute Press, 1986), p. 238; and *Jane's Fighting Ships, 1991–1992*, p. 260.
333 'Gandhi Stresses Need To Strengthen Navy,' Delhi Domestic Service in English, 0830 GMT, May 6, 1984, in *FBIS South Asia* (May 7, 1984), E7.
334 *Jane's Fighting Ships 1991–1992*, p. 260.
335 *Jane's Fighting Ships, 1991–1992*, p. 260; '1st Indigenously Built Submarine Launched,' Delhi Domestic Service in English, 0830 GMT, September 30, 1989, in *FBIS-NESA* (October 2, 1989), p. 51.

336 Michael Vlahos, 'Middle East, North African, and South Asian Navies,' *Proceedings* (March 1986), p. 57; Michael Vlahos, 'Regional Naval Reviews: Middle East, North Africa, and South Asia,' *Proceedings* (March 1991), 125.
337 *Khaleej Times (UAE)*, May 27, 1994.
338 'AFP: "Source" Says Submarine Reactor To Be Built,' Hong Kong AFP in English, 0535 GMT, May 11, 1983, in *FBIS South Asia* (May 11, 1983), E1.
339 'Nuclear Ambitions,' *FEER* (December 24, 1987), 18.
340 'Indian Navy Goes Nuclear,' *Military Technology* (February 1988), 87–8.
341 *Jane's Fighting Ships, 1991–1992*, p. 260. According to 'India Returns Soviet SSGN,' *JDW* (February 23, 1991), 254, high maintenance was apparently a major factor in not extending the lease.
342 See Eric Arnett, 'Military Technology: the Case of India,' pp. 362–3.
343 'Procurement, India,' *Jane's Security Sentinel – South Asia* at www4.janes.com Rahul Bedi, 'Country Briefing: India – Divided interests.'
344 See Vice-Admiral M. K. Roy (ret), 'The Indian Navy from the Bridge,' *Proceedings* (March 1990), 66–74. Ravi Rikhye, 'Nobody Asked Me, But ...,' *Proceedings* (March 1990), pp. 77–8.
345 Michael Vlahos, 'Middle Eastern, North African, and South Asian Navies', in *Proceedings* (March 1988), 64–6. According to Vlahos, the entire Indian navy budget was only Rs 6.5 billion.
346 See *Jane's Fighting Ships, 1991–1992*, p. 262; and Michael Vlahos, 'Middle East...' in *Proceedings* (March 1991), 125.
347 'Air Defence Ship Facility Inaugurated,' *The Hindu*, January 24, 2003.
348 'Nuclear Capabilities are Must', *Times of India*, July 20, 2003; 'Air Defence Ship All Set to Take Flight Next Year,' *Times of India*, December 10, 2003.
349 See *SIPRI Yearbook 1973*, p. 374; Herbert Wulf, 'India: the Unfulfilled Quest ...,' p. 139; *Jane's Fighting Ships 1991–1992*, p. 265.
350 *Jane's Fighting Ships 1991–1992*, p. 265.
351 *Jane's Fighting Ships 1991–1992*, p. 264.
352 Rahul Bedi, 'Country Briefing: India – Divided interests' and 'India's Stealth Warship to Be Launched on Friday,' *The Hindu*, April 16, 2003.
353 'India's Delhi Launched,' *JDW* (February 23, 1991), p. 295; *Jane's Fighting Ships, 1991–1992*, p. 264; Michael Vlahos, 'Middle East ...' in *Proceedings* (March 1991), 125.
354 *Jane's Fighting Ships 1991–1992*, p. 264. 'Russia Markets Latest Missile Attack Craft,' *JDW* (January 8, 1994), p. 10.
355 'Trishul is Blunt, so Naval Forces Seek Barak.'
356 See *Jane's Fighting Ships 1991–1992*, pp. 266–7.
357 *Jane's Fighting Ships 1991–1992*, p. 267.
358 Ramesh Thakur, 'India and the Soviet Union: Conjunctions and Disjunctions of Interests,' in *Asian Survey* 31 (September 1991), 832.
359 'Satellite Successfully Launched 18 July,' Delhi Domestic Service in English, 0730 GMT, July 18, 1980, in *FBIS South Asia* (July 18, 1980), E1; 'Gandhi Makes Statement on 18 July Satellite Launch,' Delhi ISI Diplomatic Service in English, 0831 GMT, July 19, 1980, in *FBIS South Asia* (July 19, 1980), E1, 2.
360 IGMDP uses ISRO test launch facilities, and the ISRO makes use of DRDO and PSDU facilities to test and manufacture new rocket and missile technologies. Timothy McCarthy, 'India: Emerging Missile Power,' pp. 203–5.
361 Anthony H. Cordesman, *Weapons of Mass Destruction in India and Pakistan: An Overview* (Washington, DC: Center for Strategic and International Studies, September 2000), pp. 3–4; 'Armed Forces, India,' *Jane's Sentinel Security Assessment – South Asia* (2004) at www4.janes.com. According to one report, the CW stock in question was mustard gas shells for WW2 vintage

25 pounder howitzers, in storage and not under Indian army operational control. See 'Chemical Weapons,' *Federation of American Scientists* website at www.fas.org/nuke/guide/india/cw.
362 'Armed Forces, India,' *Jane's Sentinel Security Assessment – South Asia* (2004) at www4.janes.com.
363 Major General Som Dutt, *India and the Bomb*, Adelphi Paper 30 (London: International Institute for Strategic Studies, 1966).
364 George Perkovich, *India's Nuclear Bomb*, p. 296.
365 Waheguru Pal Singh Sidhu discusses possible Indian doctrine and perceptions in 'India's Nuclear Use Doctrine,' in Peter R. Lavoy, Scott D. Sagan, and James J. Wirtz (eds), *Planning the Unthinkable* .., pp. 125–57. See also V. Sudarshan, 'India Had Nukes and Delivery System in 1994,' *OutlookIndia.com*, May 19, 2003 www.outlookindia.com.
366 *Proliferation: Threat and Response* (Washington, DC: Office of the Secretary of Defense, January 2001), pp. 21–30.
367 See 'The Prime Minister's Announcement of India's Three Underground Nuclear Tests on May 11, 1998,' at www.fas.org/news/india/1998/05/vajpayee1198.htm; and 'Press Conference' (Dr. R. Chidambaram (RC), Chairman, AEC & Secretary, DAE; Dr. A. P. J. Abdul Kalam (K), Scientific Advisor to Raksha Mantri and Secretary, Department of Defence Research and Development; Dr. Anil Kakodkar, Director, BARC; Dr. K. Santhanam, Chief Advisor (Technologies), DRDO) May 17, 1998,' at www.fas.org/news/india/1998/05/980500-conf.htm; and 'Press Release on India's Nuclear Tests, May 11 and 13, 1998,' at www.fas.org/news/india/1998/05/prmay1198.htm.
368 Reactor grade plutonium is typically 65–70 percent Pu-239, and has other isotopes that lower the explosive yield of the nuclear reaction. George Perkovich, *India's Nuclear Bomb*, pp. 428–9.
369 'Pakistan completes the current series of nuclear tests .. Foreign Secretary, Mr. Shamshad Ahmed's statement at the Press Conference in Islamabad on 30 May 1998' at www.fas.org/news/pakistan/1998/05/980530-gop.htm.
370 Owen Bennett Jones, *Pakistan: Eye of the Storm* (New Haven: Yale University Press, 2002), pp. 189–90.
371 For a discussion, see Hilary Synnott, *The Causes and Consequences of South Asia's Nuclear Tests*, Adelphi Paper 332 (London: International Institute for Strategic Studies, 1999), pp. 54–6, and Ashley J. Tellis, *India's Emerging Nuclear Posture*, pp. 519–22.
372 'India Ratchets Up Rhetoric against Pakistan and China,' *Agence France Presse*, New Delhi, May 18, 1998, cited in George Perkovich, *India's Nuclear Bomb*, p. 423, n. 102. See also 'Pakistan Told to Roll Back Anti-India Policy', *Times of India*, May 19, 1998.
373 'Advani Wants Troops to Strike Across LoC to Quell Proxy War in Kashmir,' *Rediff*, May 25, 1998 at www.rediff,com/news/1998/may/25geo.htm.
374 See Ashley Tellis, *India's Emerging Nuclear Posture* (Santa Monica, CA: RAND, 2001), pp. 39–58.
375 George Perkovich, *India's Nuclear Bomb*, p. 419 and n. 82.
376 A. B. Vajpayee, interviewed in *India Today*, May 25, 1998, at www.indiatoday.com/itoday/25051998/vajint.html.
377 C. Raja Mohan, *Crossing the Rubicon: The Shaping of India's New Foreign Policy* (New York: Viking, 2003).
378 On February 10, 1999, Indian Chief of Army Staff General Ved Malik said 'Having crossed the nuclear threshold does not mean that a conventional war is out.' John Cherian, 'The political and diplomatic background,' *Frontline* 16:12 (June 5–18, 1999), www.the-hindu.com/frontline/fl1612/1612080.htm.

379 *The Kargil Review Committee Report*, pp. 197–9.
380 Statement by General Musharraf dated April 12, 1999, cited in *The Kargil Review Committee Report*, p. 242. See also his remarks to the Pakistan Military Academy in 'Pak Defence Strong, Says Army Chief', *Independent*, April 19, 1999.
381 *Conflict Under the Nuclear Umbrella: Indian and Pakistani Lessons from the Kargil Crisis* Ashley J. Tellis, C. Christina Fair, Jamison Jo Medby MR-1450-USCA (Santa Monica: RAND, 2001); *The Kargil Review Committee Report*; Praveen Swami, *The Kargil War* revised edition (New Delhi: LeftWord Press, 2000).
382 Indian military plans, in fact, *always* viewed the option of infiltration or tribal and other paramilitary forces as equivalent to an invasion by Pakistani regulars. Lorne J. Kavic, *India's Quest..*, pp. 36–7.
383 See Bruce Riedel, *American Diplomacy and the 1999 Kargil Summit at Blair House*, Policy Paper Series 2002 (Philadelphia, PA: Center for the Advanced Study of India, 2002) for reports that Pakistan prepared 'nuclear tipped missiles'; and Raj Chengappa, *Weapons of Peace*, p. 437 for reports that India placed its nuclear arsenal at 'Readiness State 3' – ready to be mated with Prithvi and Agni missiles and Mirage 2000 aircraft for delivery.
384 See the Draft Nuclear Doctrine, August 17, 1999, at www.indianembassy.org/policy/CTBT/nuclear_doctrine_aug_17_1999.html.
385 'Fernandes Unveils "Limited War" Doctrine,' *The Hindu,* January 25, 2000; 'When Words Hurt: No limits on a "limited war", *Asiaweek,* March 31, 2000, vol. 26, no. 12.
386 V. R. Raghavan discusses the internal contradictions in this policy in 'Limited War and Nuclear Escalation in South Asia,' *The Nonproliferation Review* (Fall-Winter 2001), 1–17.
387 Rahul Bedi, 'A Strike Staunched,' *Frontline* 19: 12 (June 8–21, 2002).
388 Rahul Bedi, 'The Military Dynamics,' *Frontline* 19: 12 (June 8–21, 2002).
389 'Nuclear Command Authority Comes Into Being,' *The Hindu*, January 5, 2003; 'N-option seeks to allay army's fears', *Times of India*, January 6, 2003; 'Cabinet Committee on Security Reviews Progress on Operationalizing India's Nuclear Doctrine,' *Press Information Bureau, Government of India*, January 4, 2003.
390 Josy Joseph, 'The Retaliation Will Be in Minutes,' *Rediff,* May 12, 2003 at www.rediff.com; 'Nuke Panel Reviews State of the Arsenal,' *Times of India*, September 2, 2003.
391 'Nuclear Capabilities are Must,' *Times of India*, July 20, 2003; Rear Admiral Raja Menon (retired), *A Nuclear Strategy for India* (New Delhi: SAGE, 2000).
392 See Ashley J. Tellis, *India's Emerging Nuclear Posture*; Rajesh M. Basrur, 'Kargil, Terrorism and India's Strategic Shift,' *India Review* Vol. 1, No. 4 (October 2002), 39–56; Andrew C. Winner and Toshi Yoshihara, *Nuclear Stability in South Asia* (Cambridge, MA: Institute for Foreign Policy Analysis, 2002); and Rajesh M. Basrur, 'Nuclear Weapons and Indian Strategic Culture,' *Journal of Peace Research* 38:2 (2001), 181–98.
393 'Defence Budget Up As Never Before,' *Rediff,* at: www.rediff.com/business/2000/feb/29bud16.htm.
394 'Budget Allocates Rs 65,300 cr for Defense,' *Rediff*, February 28, 2003.
395 *The Kargil Review Committee Report*, p. 172.
396 'India Has Thin Edge Over Pak Military,' *Times of India*, June 13, 2002. 'Army Seeks Swift Modernisation to Counter Pak,' *Times of India*, April 13, 2003.
397 'Pakistan Closes Gap With India on Conventional Arms,' *The Statesman*, April 20, 2003.

398 'India to Acquire T-90 Tanks, AJTs,' *Rediff*, at: www.rediff.com/news/2000/may/16def.htm.
399 *Annual Report 2002–2003* (Government of India), p. 41.
400 'T-90 Tanks Likely to Roll Out by Dec. End,' *The Hindu*, October 17, 2003.
401 'Armed Forces Plan to Induct More UAVs,' *Times of India*, May 6, 2003; 'More UAVs to Step up Border Reconnaissance,' *The Hindu*, May 23, 2003; *Annual Report 2002–2003* (Government of India), p. 60.
402 *Annual Report 2002–2003* (Government of India), pp. 62–3.
403 'Naval Chief Vishnu Bhagwat Sacked,' *Times of India*, December 31, 1998; 'Bhagwat Incurred Wrath of Key Lobbies in Defence Ministry,' *Times of India*, January 7, 1999. The latter notes that Admiral Bhagwat's insistence on local procurement may have played a role in his dismissal – the first time an acting service chief was ever fired by an Indian government.
404 'First Stealth Warship Inducted into Western Fleet,' *The Hindu*, August 13, 2003.
405 'Riding the Waves,' *Rediff*, May 10, 2003, at: www.rediff.com.
406 'India to Build, Not Buy, Scorpene submarines: George,' *Times of India*, April 10, 003; 'French Minister's Visit to Boost Defence Ties,' *Times of India*, April 24, 2003.
407 *Annual Report 2002–2003* (Government of India), pp. 58–68.
408 'First BrahMos Launch From a Mobile Complex,' *The Hindu*, November 11, 2003; Rahul Bedi, 'Country Briefing: India – Divided interests.'
409 A deal was finalized in the autumn of 2003, with India agreeing to pay $1.34 billion for 66 HAWK aircraft, 25 of which would be supplied by Britain and the rest assembled in India. 'India May Buy US Patrol Aircraft', *Financial Times*, September 10, 2003; 'First Su-30 MKI Fighter to Roll Out in Dec.,' *The Hindu*, September, 2003.
410 'India Launches Stealth Combat Aircraft Program', *Aviation Week and Space Technology*, January 20, 1997.
411 'India, Russia Developing Combat Aircraft,' *Times of India*, November 10, 2003.
412 'IAF Plans Expansion to 60 Squadrons,' *Times of India*, November 7, 2003.
413 'MiG Tests to be Completed by July,' *The Hindu*, April 24, 2000. 125 MiG-21bis will receive substantial upgrades. Rahul Bedi, 'Country Briefing: India – Divided Interests.'
414 'LCA Breaks Sound Barrier During Test Flight,' *Rediff*, August 1, 2003 predicts deployment beginning in 2008–09.
415 'Talks on With Russia for Producing Su-30s,' *Times of India*, April 24, 2000; 'Rs7,317 crore Sukhoi Deal Runs into Turbulence,' *The Hindustan Times*, March 31, 2000. See also 'HAL to roll out Sukhois in 2004'; 'First Su-30 MKI Fighters to Roll Out in December.'
416 According to one report, the IAF lost 552 aircraft and over 200 pilots in over a ten-year period in the late 1980s and 1990s. 'India Rebuilds Defences a Year After Kargil: Reuters,' *Rediff*, www.rediff.com/news/2000/may/21kargil.htm. According to 'Procurement, India', *Jane's Sentinel Security Assessment – South Asia* (2004), India lost 273 aircraft from 1991–2003, and 42 per cent of the losses were the result of human error and inadequate training.
417 For a discussion of possible force postures, see Ashley J. Tellis, *India's Emerging Nuclear Posture*.
418 Brahma Chellaney, 'Tactical Nukes', *The Hindustan Times*, January 26, 1999; Gurmeet Kanwal, 'Does India Need Tactical Weapons,' *Strategic Analysis* (May 2003), www.idsa-india.org/an-may-03.html; Timothy D. Hoyt, 'The Buddha Frowns? Tactical Nuclear Weapons in South Asia,' in Brian Alexan-

der and Alistair Millar (eds), *Tactical Nuclear Weapons: Emergent Threats in an Evolving Security Environment* (Washington, DC: Brassey's, Inc., 2003), pp. 95–109.
419 'India and Pakistan's Fissile Material and Nuclear Weapons Inventory, end of 1998', www.isis-online.org/publications/southasia/stocks/1999.html.
420 Dr. P. K. Iyengar, former chief of the Indian Atomic Energy Commission, has argued both points. See 'In Testing Times,' *Times of India*, February 17, 2000; 'India Should Test Neutron Bomb, Says AEC Ex-chief,' *Times of India*, May 1, 2000.
421 'ISRO Chief Promises the Moon in 5 Years,' *Times of India*, September 3, 2003.
422 Mark Hewish and Lee Kass, 'Observation From Orbit,' *International Defense Review*, December 1, 2003; 'India, Israel Yet to Work Out Specifics of Space Cooperation,' *The Hindu*, September 10, 2003; 'Israel Offers Satellite Pictures of Kashmir,' *The Hindu*, February 12, 2004; 'Countdown Starts for PSLV-C5's Launch,' *Times of India*, October 15, 2003.
423 Figures based on *IISS The Military Balance 1970–71*.
424 Statement of retiring Indian Chief of Army Staff Sharma, June 30, 1990, cited in 'Outgoing Army Chief Sharma Interviewed,' Delhi Domestic Service in English, 1545 GMT, June 30, 1990, in *FBIS-NESA* (July 3, 1990), pp. 59–61.
425 Based on SIPRI data from Ian Anthony, 'The 'Third Tier' Countries,' pp. 362–83, in Herbert Wulf, *Arms Industry Limited* (Oxford: Oxford University Press, 1993), pp. 370–1, Table 17.1.
426 The most sophisticated version of this ladder is found in Keith Krause, *Arms and the State: Patterns of Military Production and Trade* (Cambridge: Cambridge University Press, 1992), pp. 171–4.
427 Transfer of skills is further hampered by the lack of labor mobility between the private sector and the defense sector. James Clad, 'Technical Knockout', pp. 48–9; Andy Lee Ross, *Security and Self-Reliance* ..., pp. 452–3. Thomas Graham, 'India,' p. 169 mentions the lack of forward and backward linkages with the civilian economy.
428 'Outgoing Army Chief Sharma Interviewed,' Delhi Domestic Service in English, 1545 GMT, June 30, 1990, in *FBIS-NESA* (July 3, 1990), pp. 59–61. Air Marshal C. V. Gole also argues for integration of production with the private sector. Air Vice Marshal C. V. Gole, 'National Security and the Role of Industry,' p. 131.
429 "Peace Constituency Larger Than That of Hostility: PM,' *The Hindu*, November 3, 2003.
430 See Eric Arnett, 'Military Technology: the Case of India,' pp. 343–65.
431 Manoj K. Joshi, 'Directions in India's Defence and Security Policies,' in Ross Babbage and Sandy Gordon (eds), *India's Strategic Future*, p. 77.
432 'DRDO: Off Course,' p. 85.
433 'The Missile Man,' *India Today* (April 15, 1994), 44.
434 See Raju G. C. Thomas, *Indian Security Policy*, pp. 119–28.
435 Subrahmanyam, 'Commentary ...,' pp. 269, 273; 'A Middle-Aged Military Machine,' pp. 23, 30.
436 'India: $5.5 Billion For The Military,' *New York Times*, February 5, 2004.
437 'Government to Pay Rs5,000 cr. Advance for Defence Deals,' *The Hindu*, March 5, 2004.
438 'Armed Forces, India,' *Jane's Sentinel Security Assessment – South Asia* (2004).
439 Herbert Wulf, 'India: An Unfulfilled Quest ...,' p. 127.
440 'India's Military Hit By Soviet Collapse,' *Washington Post*, October 4, 1992;

'South Asian Nations Scramble For Arms After Soviet Crackup', *Washington Post*, January 5, 1992.
441 'India's Westward Gaze,' *JDW* (January 9, 1993): pp. 18–19. Inability to replicate minor items such as these indicates an extremely lax approach towards logistics and avoidance of dependence on foreign supplies.
442 'Indian Arms Buys Defy Cash Shortfall,' pp. 29–30.
443 A comparison here is apt: both Israel and India purchased Centurion tanks from the UK in the 1950s. India's were removed from the order of battle in the early 1970s, and were sold to South Africa for scrap. Shekhar Gupta, 'India Redefines ...,' p. 48. Israel's Centurions (see Chapter 3) have been extensively modified and upgraded, and remain in service today.
444 Prodyut Das, 'Aircraft Resurgery Programmes ..'
445 'India and US To Improve Ties,' *Wall Street Journal*, January 20, 2004.
446 'Two Join Missile Defense Program,' *Washington Times*, January 14, 2004.
447 See Juli MacDonald, *Indo-US Military Relationship: Expectations and Perceptions* (Washington, DC: Office of the Secretary of Defense, Office of Net Assessment, October 2002).
448 India Test Fires Brahmos Missile,' *Times of India*, October 29, 2003.
449 'India, Russia in Talks for a New Missile,' *Times of India*, March 5, 2004.
450 'Koptev: Satellite Deal Will Be Signed Soon With India,' *Moscow Times*, January 30, 2004.
451 'Phalcon Warning System Will be Delivered in "Near Future": Shalom,' *The Hindu*, February 12, 2004; 'Now, IAF Gets Eyes in the Sky,' *Times of India*, March 8, 2004.
452 David C. Isby, 'India Seeks Missile co-Operation with Israel', *Jane's Missiles and Rockets*, November 1, 2003 at www4.janes.com.
453 'Army Drafts New War Doctrine,' *The Hindu*, March 5, 2004. This new "Cold Start" doctrine promises significant changes in both organization and equipment.

3 Israel

1 Israel's status as a 'developing country' is now, in fact, debatable. Less than 50 years ago, however, Israel's economy was dependent on two export products (citrus and diamonds), and manufacturing and industrial goods were the primary imports. Israel's national borders were imposed by colonial powers and international organizations, and the new government initially had strong socialist, anti-capitalist leanings. In short, Israel's economic structure was quite similar to other late-industrializing developing countries, and its ability to transcend these initial economic limitations should be viewed as remarkable. See Michael Barnett, *Confronting the Costs of War: Military Power, State, and Society in Egypt and Israel* (Princeton, NJ: Princeton University Press, 1992), pp. 14–17, 67–78.
2 Stockholm International Peace Research Institute (SIPRI) data indicates that from 1965–90, roughly 1/3 of Israel's high-technology MWS were acquired from local firms. Ian Anthony, 'The "Third Tier" Countries,' in Herbert Wulf (ed.), *Arms Industry Limited* (Oxford: Oxford University Press, 1993), pp. 370–1.
3 The discussion which follows is a distillation of a number of key sources on Israeli political-military doctrine and strategy. Among these are Yoav Ben-Horin and Barry Posen, *Israel's Strategic Doctrine* RAND R-2845-NA (Santa Monica, CA: The RAND Corporation, September 1981); Ze'ev Schiff, *A History of the Israeli Army: 1874 to the Present* (New York: Macmillan,

1985), especially pp. 115–23 and 145–63; Edward Luttwak and Dan Horowitz, *The Israeli Army* (New York: Harper & Row, 1975), especially pp. 119–23; Helen Chapin Metz, *Israel: A Country Study* (Washington, DC: US Government Printing Office, 1990), especially pp. 267–72; Efraim Inbar and Shmuel Sandler, 'Israel's Deterrence Strategy Revisited,' *Security Studies* 3 (Winter 1993/94), pp. 330–58; Yigal Allon, *The Making of Israel's Army* (New York: Universe Books, 1970), especially pp. 37–54, 62–71, 96–108; Efraim Inbar, 'Israel's New Military Doctrine,' *Naval War College Review* 36 (January–February 1983), pp. 26–40; Aharon Klieman and Reuven Pedatzur, *Rearming Israel: Defense Procurement Through the 1990s* (Jerusalem: Jerusalem Post, 1991), especially pp. 23–50; Michael Handel, 'The Evolution of Israeli Strategy: The Psychology of Insecurity and the Quest for Absolute Security', in Williamson Murray, MacGregor Knox, and Alvin Bernstein (eds), *The Making of Strategy: Rulers, States, and War*, (Cambridge: Cambridge University Press) pp. 534–78; and Immanuel Wald, *The Wald Report* (Boulder, CO: Westview, 1992), pp. 125–7 and 226–38.
4 Yehoshafat Harkabi, *Arab Attitudes To Israel*, translated by Misa Louvish (New York: Hart Publishing, 1970), p. 37. At the time this was written, shortly before the Six Day War, Arab pronouncements hinted darkly at genocide.
5 Immanuel Wald, *The Wald Report*, p. 125.
6 Israel's military-industrial policies in the 1950s and 1960s, based around modification of aging equipment, saved precious foreign exchange. W. Seth Carus, 'Israel: Some Economic and Social Considerations,' in James Everett Katz (ed.), *The Implications of Third World Military Industrialization: Sowing the Serpents' Teeth* (Lexington, MA: Lexington, 1986), pp. 136–7.
7 In 1948, one-sixth of the Jewish population in Palestine was concentrated in the Jerusalem area. Yuval Ne'eman, 'Conceiving a Balanced Budget for a Budding Nation,' in Zvi Lanir (ed.), *Israeli Security Planning in the 1980s: Its Economics and Politics* (New York: Praeger, 1984), p. 3. The pre-1967 borders allowed Jordan to place artillery only nine miles from the Mediterranean, and it is only 30 miles from the west end of the Golan Heights to the Mediterranean. Aharon Yariv, 'Strategic Depth,', *Jerusalem Quarterly* 6 (Fall 1980), pp. 3–12.
8 Helen Chapin Metz, *Israel: A Country Study*, p. 267; Yoav Ben-Horin and Barry Posen, *Israel's Strategic Doctrine*, p. 4; Major General Israel Tal, 'Israel's Defense Doctrine: Background and Dynamics,' *Military Review* (March 1978), 23.
9 From 1956–80, over 75 percent of the IDF budget went to the IAF and the Armored Corps, reflecting the emphasis on quick victory. Yoav Ben-Horin and Barry Posen, *Israel's Strategic Doctrine*, p. 43.
10 Efraim Inbar and Shmuel Sandler, 'Israel's Deterrence Strategy Revisited,' p. 331; and Yigal Allon, *The Making of Israel's Army*, p. 43 argue that Israel is a status quo power, seeking only to survive. For an opposing perspective, which views Israel's intentions as ultimately hegemonic, see Zachary T. Irwin, 'Israel: An Aspiring Hegemon', in David J. Myers (ed.), *Regional Hegemons: Threat Perception and Strategic Response* (Boulder, CO: Westview, 1991), pp. 63–96.
11 Michael Barnett, *Confronting the Costs of War*, p. xi.
12 Office of Technology Assessment, *Global Arms Trade*, OTA-ISC-460, (Washington, DC: US Government Printing Office, June 1991), p. 89.
13 *SIPRI Yearbook 1994*, p. 471; *SIPRI Yearbook 1994*, p. 466; *SIPRI Yearbook 2000*, p. 302.
14 'Israeli Defense Industry Has a Perennial Proving Ground for Production,' *Defense News*, June 11–16, 2001, p. 44.

15 For example, employment in state-controlled companies fell from over 40,000 in 1991 to 24,000 in 1994. The combined loss of the three state-controlled firms in this period totaled $1.6 billion. *SIPRI Yearbook 1996*, p. 448.
16 *Global Arms Trade*, p. 95.
17 Alex Mintz, 'Arms Production in Israel,' *Jerusalem Quarterly* 3 (Spring 1987), 93.
18 Aharon Klieman and Reuven Pedatzur, *Rearming Israel* . . ., pp. 144–5.
19 *Global Arms Trade*, p. 95.
20 See Avner Cohen, *Israel and the Bomb* (New York: Columbia University Press, 1998); and Avner Cohen, 'Nuclear Arms in Crisis Under Secrecy: Israel and the Lessons of the 1967 and 1973 Wars,' in Peter R. Lavoy, Scott D. Sagan, and James J. Wirtz (eds), *Planning the Unthinkable: How New Powers Will Use Nuclear, Biological, and Chemical Weapons* (New York: Columbia University Press, 2000), pp. 104–24.
21 'RAFAEL – a name to be respected,' *Military Technology* (September 1986), 146.
22 'Israeli Industry', Special Advertising Supplement, *Jane's Defence Weekly* (hereafter *JDW*), June 12, 1993, p. 10.
23 'RAFAEL,' p. 151.
24 *Global Arms Trade*, p. 96; *SIPRI Yearbook 2000*, p. 330.
25 According to a recent interview, RAFAEL only receives 15–20 percent of its total revenue from R&D funding. See interview with Giora Shalgi, President and General Manager, RAFAEL Armament Development Authority, Israel at www.defencenews.com (Mergers, Year 2000 New File).
26 RAFAEL exported 28 percent of total production in 1996, compared to Elbit's 82 percent. *SIPRI Yearbook 1996*, p. 448.
27 'IAI: A Partner for the World,' *Military Technology* (May 1992), 74.
28 *SIPRI Yearbook 2000*, p. 328; *Global Arms Trade*, p. 96. Employment dropped from 22,500 in 1986, before the cancellation of the Lavi project, to 16,000 in 1989.
29 'IAI: A Partner for the World,' p. 74. IAI annual sales, according to this article, were approximately $1.6 billion, more than 80 percent of which were export sales.
30 'Transformation and Developments at IAI: Interview with Moshe Keret, President of Israeli Aircraft Industries,' *Military Technology* (September 1991), 29.
31 See *Jane's Weapons Systems 1987–1988*, pp. 238–40, 318–20, 653–4, 701, 850–1, 893–4.
32 'IAI: A Partner for the World' p. 77.
33 Paul Hirschhom, 'Battle Fatigue,' *The Jerusalem Post Magazine* (February 26, 1993), 13.
34 *SIPRI Yearbook 1996*, p. 448; 'Business Around World Grows for Israel Aircraft Industries,' *Defense News* (May 7, 2001) 22.
35 Prior to 1990, TAAS was part of the Ministry of Defense. TAAS was renamed Israeli Military Industries (IMI) in the 1950s, and renamed TAAS again in the 1990s: the terms will be used interchangeably. *Global Arms Trade*, p. 96; 'Israel: Soaring to Singapore and Points Beyond,' Special Advertising Supplement, *JDW*, February 19, 1994, 11.
36 'Industry: Riding on the Wave of New Demands,' *JDW*, February 15, 1992, 238; see also *Global Arms Trade*, p. 96.
37 'Industry: Riding' p. 236. Reductions in IDF orders in the late 1980s had disastrous effects on TAAS' financial condition. *Global Arms Trade*, p. 96.
38 *Global Arms Trade*, p. 97; *SIPRI Yearbook 2000*, p. 330.

39 'Israel Plans to Privatize IMI,' *Defense News*, November 19–25, 2001, p. 16.
40 *SIPRI Yearbook 1996*, 448; *SIPRI Yearbook 1997*, p. 241.
41 'Israeli Merger Success Eludes Government Firms,' at www.defensenews.com (Mergers, Year 2000 News File); 'Israeli Companies Merge Missile Marketing Efforts,' *Defense News*, June 11–17, 2001, p. 24.
42 *Global Arms Trade*, p. 97.
43 These firms are owned by the Histadrut through the Koor industrial holding company.
44 Tadiran is the second source contractor for the US Army's SINCGARS communications system. *Military Technology*, October 1988, 198.
45 Employment fell from a high of 13,000 in 1986 to 6,500 in 1991. *Global Arms Trade*, p. 96. Sales remained stable, growing from $620 million in 1986 to $700 million in 1991, indicating a substantial increase in productivity. During this period, however, Tadiran sold its 50 percent share of the Mazlat firm, which specialized in RPVs, to IAI. This effectively removed it from the RPV/UAV market, despite the fact that Tadiran's efforts had pioneered the Israeli RPV industry.
46 'Israel: Soaring to Singapore,' pp. 4–5; *Jane's Weapons Systems 1987–1988*, pp. 894–86.
47 'Industry: Riding,' p. 239; *Jane's Weapons Systems 1987–1988*, pp. 701–2.
48 'Israel Merger Success Eludes Government Firms.'
49 *Global Arms Trade*, p. 99. Sales rose from $87 million in 1987 to $130 million ($87 million in exports) in 1992. 'Israeli Industry': p. 6.
50 'Industry: Riding,' p. 239.
51 *Jane's Weapons Systems 1987–1988*, p. 375.
52 'Israeli Industry,' p. 4.
53 'Industry: Riding,' p. 239; *Global Arms Trade*, p. 99.
54 'Israel: Soaring to Singapore,' p. 3.
55 *Jane's Weapons Systems 1987–1988*, pp. 70–2; *Military Technology* (May 1987), 78.
56 'Industry: Riding, p. 240; 'Israel: Soaring,' pp. 3–4.
57 'Israeli Industry,' p. 4.
58 Interview with Yossi Ackerman, President and Chief Executive Officer, Elbit Systems Ltd. at www.defensenews.com (Mergers, Year 2000 News File).
59 See www.defensenews/com/current/top100/2001chart3.html; Timothy D. Hoyt, 'Israel's Military Industry – The Other Side of Globalization,' *Defense Industry Globalization: A Compendium of Papers Presented at a Conference on 'Defense Industry Globalization' Held on 16 November 2001* (Washington, DC: The Atlantic Council, February 2002), pp. 193–205.
60 Total turnover in 1989 was only $22 million, 82 percent of which was exports. *Global Arms Trade*, pp. 86, 99.
61 According to contemporary reports, the US navy used six trained technicians, working twelve hours to identify less than 60 percent of the potential electronics malfunctions on one of their aircraft. ATE does the job with 100 percent accuracy in half an hour. 'Rada Rides Shifts in Defense Market,' *Jerusalem Post*, August 9, 1990.
62 'Israel: Soaring to Singapore,' p. 8.
63 'Avionics on the Up,' *Jerusalem Post*, October 11, 1991; 'Local Firm Manufactures Computers for F-16s,' Jerusalem Israel Television Network in Hebrew, 1900 GMT, December 5, 1990, in *FBIS-NESA*, December 19, 1990, p. 42.
64 Yigal Allon, *The Making of Israel's Army*, p. 4;. Ze'ev Schiff, *A History of the Israeli Army*, p. 1.

65 Ze'ev Schiff, *A History of the Israeli Army*, p. 2; and David Ben Gurion, *Israel: A Personal History*, (New York: Funk & Wagnall, 1971), pp. 824–5.
66 Helen Chapin Metz, *Israel: A Country Study*, p. 253; Ze'ev Schiff *A History of the Israeli Army*, pp. 2–3.
67 Ze'ev Schiff, *A History of the Israeli Army*, pp. 6–18. While the Haganah's primary mission remained defensive, more militant groups emerged from factions within the Zionist leadership in the late 1930s. The most famous of these was *Irgun Zva'i Leumi* (also called *Irgun* or *Etzel*), led by Menachim Begin. The other was *Lohamei Herut Israel* (also known as Lehi or 'The Stern Gang' after its leader, Avraham Stern). The *Haganah* later formed elite strike units, called the *Palmach*, which formed the core of the IDF during the War of Independence. Yoram Peri, 'Civilian Control During a Protracted War,' in Zvi Lanir (ed.), *Israeli Security Planning in the 1980s*, p. 65; Yitzhak Rabin, *The Rabin Memoirs*, p. 45; and Nadav Safran, *Israel: The Embattled Ally* (Cambridge, MA: Belknap, 1981), p. 320.
68 Efraim Inbar, 'The Development of the Israeli Defense Industry,' p. 119. Other early products included American and Russian rifle grenades. See Yigal Allon, *Shield of David* (New York: Random House, 1970), p. 161.
69 The metal for the weapons was acquired from wrecked aircraft in the Negev desert. TAAS also re-machined the barrels of ancient rifles, and produced large amounts of small arms ammunition. These mortars were also copied from standard British issue. Yigal Allon, *Shield of David*, pp. 162–4.
70 Stewart Reiser, *The Israeli Arms Industry* (New York: Holmes & Meier, 1989), p. 13; Shimon Peres, *David's Sling*, (New York: Random House, 1970), p. 109; David Ben Gurion, *Israel: A Personal History*, pp. 118, 248.
71 Address by Yisrael Galili, Commander in Chief of the Haganah, to the National Council of Histadrut (General Federation of Labor) in September 1947, cited in Yigal Allon, *The Making of the Israeli Army*, p. 177.
72 David Ben Gurion, *Israel: A Personal History*, p. 55.
73 Some of the machinery was put to immediate use. Other machinery was too complicated to be used and remained in storage until the 1960s when Israeli workers finally acquired sufficient skills to employ it productively. Yigal Allon, *Shield of David*, p. 187; David Ben Gurion, *Israel: A Personal History*, p. 56; Shimon Peres, *David's Sling*, p. 110.
74 David Ben Gurion, *Israel: A Personal History*, p. 59.
75 Stewart Reiser, *The Israeli Arms Industry*, p. 3; and Aharon Klieman and Reuven Pedatzur, *Rearming Israel ...*, p. 71.
76 Anthony H. Cordesman, *The Arab–Israeli Military Balance and the Art of Operations* (Lanham, MD: University of America Press, 1987), p. 9. Helen Chapin Metz, *Israel: A Country Study*, p. 256; Major General Israel Tal, 'Israel's Defense Doctrine: Background and Dynamics,' *Military Review* (March 1978), 24–6.
77 David Ben Gurion, *Israel: A Personal History*, pp. 268–9.
78 Michael Barnett, *Confronting the Costs of War ...*, pp. 16, 169; Samuel J. Roberts, *Survival or Hegemony: The Foundations of Israeli Foreign Policy* (Baltimore, MD: The Johns Hopkins University Press, 1973), pp. 18–19.
79 Stewart Reiser, *The Israeli Arms Industry*, p. 18. The number of TAAS employees increased from 1,000 to 2,300 in the 1949–50 period. Efraim Inbar, 'The Development of the Israeli Defense Industry,' pp. 121–2.
80 Stewart Reiser, *The Israeli Arms Industry*, pp. 24–5; Aharon Klieman and Reuven Pedatzur, *Rearming Israel*, p. 71; Gerald M. Steinberg, 'Israel: Case Study for International Missile Trade and Non-Proliferation,' in William C.

Potter and Harlan W. Jencks (eds), *The International Missile Bazaar: The New Suppliers' Network* (Boulder, CO: Westview, 1994), pp. 235–6.
81 *Global Arms Trade*, pp. 93–4.
82 Stewart Reiser, *The Israeli Arms Industry*, p. 26.
83 David Ben Gurion, *Israel: A Personal History*, p. 630.
84 Shimon Peres, *David's Sling*, pp. 132–5.
85 Shimon Peres, *David's Sling*, p. 28.
86 Stewart Reiser, *The Israeli Arms Industry*, p. 34.
87 Yuval Ne'eman, 'Conceiving a Balanced Budget . . ,' p. 8.
88 Michael Barnett, *Confronting the Costs of War* . . ., p. 167.
89 The value of German reparations payments from 1953–66 has been estimated at between $700–821 million: see Stewart Reiser, *The Israeli Arms Industry*, pp. 29–30, and Michael Barnett, *Confronting the Costs of War* . . , p. 64. According to Barnett, German reparations funds accounted for 20–25 percent of the government development budget from 1953–66, and the Diaspora contributed an additional $120 million during this period. From 1950–73, the state had little reliance on private capital for investment. Michael Michaely, 'Israel's Dependence on Capital Imports,' *Jerusalem Quarterly* 3 (Spring 1977), pp. 42–9.
90 Protests by opposition leader Menachim Begin nearly brought the state to civil war. Michael Barnett, *Confronting the Costs of War*, p. 64.
91 Approximately 38 percent of all German reparations payments took the form of ships, machinery, and equipment. Stewart Reiser, *The Israeli Arms Industry*, p. 30.
92 Egypt and Israel received matching supplies of equipment from the UK under the terms of the Tripartite Agreement. Israel, Syria, and Egypt, for example, all received Meteor fighters in 1952–53. SIPRI, *The Arms Trade With the Third World* revised edition (New York: Holmes & Meier, 1975) (hereafter SIPRI, *The Arms Trade (1975)*), pp. 211–12.
93 Shimon Peres, *David's Sling*, p. 26.
94 Yigal Allon, *The Making of Israel's Army*, p. 49.
95 Aharon Klieman, *Israel's Global Reach: Arms Sales as Diplomacy* (New York: Brassey's, 1985), p. 17.
96 Shimon Peres, *David's Sling*, pp. 36–50; Benjamin Kagan, *The Secret Battle for Israel*, (Cleveland and New York: World Publishing Co., 1966), pp. 157–89.
97 Edward Luttwak and Dan Horowitz, *The Israeli Army*, pp. 132–3; Yigal Allon, *The Making of Israel's Army*, pp. 51–2.
98 For accounts of Israeli military success in 1956, see Edward Luttwak and Dan Horowitz, *The Israeli Army*, pp. 138–64; Ze'ev Schiff, *A History of the Israeli Army*, pp. 86–100; Chaim Herzog, *The Arab-Israeli Wars*, (New York: Random House, 1984), pp. 109–41; Ariel Sharon, *Warrior: An Autobiography* with David Chanoff, (London: MacDonald, 1989), pp. 133–53.
99 Peres states that the IDF received M-48 tanks from the Bundeswehr as the Germans received newer models, and notes that Israel received military equipment valued by the Arabs at 500 million Israeli pounds without ever paying a cent. Shimon Peres, *David's Sling*, pp. 77–85.
100 Shimon Peres, *David's Sling*, pp. 31–65, 114–17.
101 Stewart Reiser, *The Israeli Arms Industry*, pp. 23–5, 33–5, 41.
102 Shimon Peres, *David's Sling*, pp. 128–9. Israeli engineers made multiple modifications to the Magister, and the aircraft continued in IAF service for decades after extensive modernization. Stewart Reiser, *The Israeli Arms Industry*, p. 54; *Jane's All The World's Aircraft 1991–1992*, p. 149.

103 Leonard Spector, *Nuclear Ambitions* with Jacqueline R. Smith (Boulder, CO: Westview Press, 1990), pp. 149–74; Seymour M. Hersh, *The Samson Option* (New York: Random House, 1991), pp. 33–71; Sylvia Crosbie, *A Tacit Alliance* (Princeton, NJ: Princeton University Press, 1974); Avner Cohen, *Israel and the Bomb*.
104 Gerald M. Steinberg, 'Israel: A Case Study...', pp. 235–7.
105 Gerald M. Steinberg, 'Israel: A Case Study...', p. 235.
106 W. Seth Carus, 'Israel: Some Economic and Social Considerations,' p. 136.
107 Yigal Allon, *The Making of Israel's Army*, p. 68.
108 'IDF–Barn door of opportunity,' *Jerusalem Post*, May 17, 1991.
109 Eliezer Sheffer, 'The Economic Burden of the Arms Race Between the Confrontation States and Israel,' in Zvi Lanir (ed), *Israeli Security Planning...*, pp. 142–65.
110 Stewart Reiser, *The Israeli Arms Industry*, p. 50.
111 Aharon Klieman and Reuven Pedatzur, *Rearming Israel...*, p. 75.
112 The value of major weapons systems produced in Israel, either under license or with significant local content, as a percentage of total major weapons procurement, amounted to only about 6.8 percent in 1965, 4.8 percent in 1966, and 1.9 percent in 1967. Percentages based on SIPRI data in Ian Anthony, 'The 'Third-Tier Countries'...', Table 17.1, pp. 370–1.
113 Stewart Reiser, *The Israeli Arms Industry*, p. 72.
114 Stewart Reiser, *The Israeli Arms Industry*, pp. 55, 60.
115 IAI has attempted to maintain a foothold in the civilian aerospace market, but local designs have rarely been successful. 'Israel Arms Exports Spur Concern,' *Aviation Week and Space Technology*, (December 1976), p. 13; 'Swords to Ploughshares turns Loss to Profit,' *Jerusalem Post*, July 4, 1989; Efraim Inbar, 'The Development of the Israeli Defense Industry,' p. 123.
116 Emigration, particularly in the science and engineering sectors, is always an issue of concern in Israel. From 1948 to 1986, between 400,000 and 500,000 Israelis emigrated. Helen Chapin Metz, *Israel: A Country Study*, p. 89.
117 SIPRI, *The Arms Trade (1975)*, p. 208; SIPRI, *The Arms Trade With The Third World* (New York: Humanities Press, 1971) (hereafter SIPRI, *The Arms Trade (1971)*), pp. 768–81.
118 Abraham Rabinovich, *The Boats of Cherbourg* (New York: Seaver Books, Henry Holt and Company, 1988), p. 29. An Egyptian frigate bombarded Tel Aviv on October 31, 1956 during the Sinai Campaign. Chaim Herzog, *The Arab-Israeli Wars*, p. 138.
119 Abraham Rabinovich, *The Boats of Cherbourg*, p. 27. Among the options considered were the establishment of an 'all-commando' navy or elimination of the surface force and concentration on submarines.
120 Commander Eli Rahav, Israeli Navy (Retired), 'Missile Boat Warfare: Israeli Style,' *Proceedings* (March 1986), pp. 107–13.
121 The Jaguars were purchased with a $60 million defense grant provided by the West German government in March, 1960. Abraham Rabinovich, *The Boats of Cherbourg*, p. 41.
122 Captain Peleg Lapid, Israeli Navy (retired), 'Electronics in the Israeli Navy,' *IDF Journal*, (December 1984) pp. 13–18.
123 Abraham Rabinovich, *The Boats of Cherbourg*, pp. 57, 60, 179.
124 Abraham Rabinovich, *The Boats of Cherbourg*, pp. 67, 73.
125 *Jane's Fighting Ships 1991–1992*, pp. 297–8.
126 For more description of the naval campaign in 1973, see Commander Eli Rahav, 'Missile Boat Warfare: Israeli Style,' pp. 112–13; Abraham Rabinovich, *The Boats of Cherbourg*, pp. 177–306; Edward Luttwak and Dan

Horowitz, *The Israeli Army*, pp. 394–5; Chaim Herzog, *The Arab–Israeli Wars*, pp. 311–14; Anthony Cordesman and Abraham R. Wagner, *The Lessons of Modern Warfare* Volume I: The Arab Israeli Conflicts 1973–1989 (Boulder, CO: Westview, 1990), pp. 104–8.
127 Shimon Peres, *David's Sling*, pp. 128–9.
128 Gerald Steinberg, 'Israel,' in Nicole Ball and Milton Leitenberg (eds), *The Structure of the Defence Industry: A Comparative Study* (New York: St. Martin's, 1983), p. 300.
129 SIPRI, *The Arms Trade . . . (1971)*, pp. 768–9.
130 SIPRI, *The Arms Trade . . . (1971)*, pp. 768–9.
131 'After Years of Relying On Its Own Weapons, Israel Looks Abroad,' *Wall Street Journal*, June 27, 1995.
132 Edward Luttwak and Dan Horowitz, *The Israeli Army*, pp. 217–18.
133 Edward Luttwak and Dan Horowitz, *The Israeli Army*, pp. 126–30.
134 David Eshel, *Chariots of the Desert* (Oxford: Brassey's, 1989) pp. 29–30; 54; *Jane's Armor and Artillery 1992–1993*, pp. 86–7.
135 David Eshel, *Chariots of the Desert*, pp. 52–5; *Jane's Armour and Artillery 1992–1993*, pp. 84–7; Anthony Cordesman and Abraham R. Wagner, *The Lessons of Modern Warfare*, vol. I, pp. 58–9, Table 2.9.
136 Shimon Peres, *David's Sling*, p. 26.
137 'The Artillery Corps, 1948-Present,' *IDF Journal*, vol. 4, no. 2 (Spring 1987); Edward Luttwak and Dan Horowitz, *The Israeli Army*, pp. 180, 218, 329; Enrico Po, 'Self-Propelled Artillery for the 90s,' in *Military Technology* (December 1986), 18–39, 20–1; *Jane's Armor and Artillery 1992–1993*, pp. 575–6.
138 Lon Nordeen, *Fighters Over Israel* (New York: Orion Books, 1990), p. 201.
139 Edward Luttwak and Dan Horowitz, *The Israeli Army*, pp. 195, 199.
140 Gerald Steinberg, 'Israel,' p. 281.
141 Shimon Engel, 'The Long Road from Molotov Cocktails to Missiles, Tanks, and Lasers,' *IDF Journal* (Summer 1988), p. 26; Gerald M. Steinberg, 'Israel: A Case Study . .'
142 Shimon Peres, *David's Sling*, p. 105.
143 Stewart Reiser, *The Israeli Arms Industry . . .*, pp. 44, 60–1; Shlomo Aronson, *The Politics and Strategy of Nuclear Weapons in the Middle East: Opacity, Theory and Reality, 1960–1991*, with Oded Brosh, (Albany, NY: State University of New York Press, 1992), p. 86.
144 Avner Cohen, *Israel and the Bomb*, p. 232.
145 SIPRI, *The Arms Trade With The Third World* (1971), pp. 780–1. The MD-620 reportedly had serious technical problems. 'Israel to Receive Lance Missiles, F-15s,' *Aviation Week and Space Technology* (September 15, 1975), 16.
146 Seymour M. Hersh, *The Samson Option*; Leonard Spector, *Nuclear Ambitions*, pp. 149–74; Shlomo Aronson, *The Politics and Strategy . .*; Frank Barnaby, *The Invisible Bomb: The Nuclear Arms Race in the Middle East* (London, I. B. Taurus, 1989); Peter Pry, *Israel's Nuclear Arsenal* (Boulder, CO: Westview, 1984); Avner Cohen, *Israel and the Bomb*.
147 Avner Cohen, *Israel and the Bomb*, p. 54.
148 Avner Cohen, *Israel and the Bomb*, p. 59.
149 Avner Cohen, *Israel and the Bomb*, p. 64.
150 Shlomo Aronson, *The Politics and Strategy*, p. 62.
151 Avner Cohen, *Israel and the Bomb*, p. 71.
152 Avner Cohen, *Israel and the Bomb*, p. 67.
153 Avner Cohen, *Israel and the Bomb*, p. 236.
154 Avner Cohen, *Israel and the Bomb*, pp. 171, 203.

155 Avner Cohen, *Israel and the Bomb*, pp. 227–33.
156 According to Cohen, Israel created two nuclear devices on May 28, 1967. Avner Cohen, *Israel and the Bomb*, pp. 273–4. For CIA estimates, see Leonard Spector, *Nuclear Ambitions*, p. 153; Seymour M. Hersh, *The Samson Option*, p. 186.
157 For accounts of Israel's victory, which increased the territory of the state by almost 35 percent (not including the Sinai), see Chaim Herzog, *The Arab–Israeli Wars*, pp. 143–91; Edward Luttwak and Dan Horowitz, *The Israeli Army*, pp. 209–98; Ze'ev Schiff, *A History of the Israeli Army*, pp. 124–44; Ariel Sharon, *Warrior*, pp. 179–203; Yitzhak Rabin, *The Rabin Memoirs* pp. 100–21; Raful Eitan, *A Soldier's Story* (New York: Shapolsky Publishers, 1992), pp. 95–108; Brig. Gen. S. L. A. Marshall, 'The Army of Israel,' *Military Review* (April 1968), pp. 3–9; Michael B. Oren, *Six Days of War: June 1967 and the Making of the Modern Middle East* (Oxford: Oxford University Press, 2002).
158 Yitzhak Rabin, *The Rabin Memoirs*, p. 132; David Pollock, *The Politics of Pressure: American Arms and Israeli Policy Since the Six Day War* (Westport, CT: Greenwood Press, 1982).
159 Anwar el-Sadat, *In Search of Identity* (New York: Harper & Row, 1977), p. 188.
160 Defense expenditure rose, in real terms, approximately 20 percent per year from 1967–73, compared to GNP growth of about 10 percent per year. Eliezer Sheffer, 'The Economic Burden of the Arms Race,' pp. 143, 150.
161 Stewart Reiser, *The Israeli Arms Industry*, p. 79. The defense industry share of new employment in industry was over 36 percent – of 55,000 new industrial jobs created, 20,000 were in the defense industry. Naftali Blumenthal, 'The Influence of Defense Industry Investment on Israel's Economy,' in Zvi Lanir (ed.), *Israeli Security Planning*, p. 173.
162 Aharon Klieman and Reuven Pedatzur, *Rearming Israel*, pp. 76–7.
163 Aharon Klieman and Reuven Pedatzur, *Rearming Israel . . .*, p. 73.
164 Naftali Blumenthal, 'The Influence of Defense Industry Investment,' pp. 169–71.
165 Nadav Safran, *Israel: The Embattled Ally*, p. 117.
166 *Global Arms Trade*, p. 94. After 1967, military R&D expenditures surpassed all civilian R&D expenditures combined. Stewart Reiser, *The Israeli Arms Industry*, pp. 96–7.
167 Michael Barnett, *Confronting the Costs of War*, p. 199.
168 Yoram Peri, 'Political-Military Partnership in Israel', *International Political Science Review* 2 (1981), p. 304.
169 Helen Chapin Metz, *Israel: A Country Study*, p. 260; Chaim Herzog, *The Arab–Israeli Wars*, p. 227.
170 Edward Luttwak and Dan Horowitz, *The Israeli Army*, pp. 360–1.
171 Naftali Blumenthal, 'The Influence of Defense Industry Investment,' p. 169.
172 Stewart Reiser, *The Israeli Arms Industry*, pp. 111–12.
173 Yitzhak Rabin, *The Rabin Memoirs*, p. 64; Stewart Reiser, *The Israeli Arms Industry*, pp. 84–5; Gerald Steinberg, 'Israel: High Technology Roulette,' in Michael Brzoska and Thomas Ohlson (eds), *Arms Production in the Third World* (London and Philadelphia: Taylor and Francis, 1986), p. 167.
174 Stewart Reiser, *The Israeli Arms Industry*, pp. 99–100, 195; Gerald M. Steinberg, 'High Technology Roulette', p. 175. In the 1973 war Britain also refused to supply the Israelis with spares and ammunition for their Centurion tanks. Robert E. Harkavy and Stephanie Neuman, 'Israel,' pp. 193–223, in James E. Katz (ed.), *Arms Production in the Third World* (Lexington, MA: Lexington, 1984), p. 196.

175 Gerald M. Steinberg 'High Technology Roulette,' p. 175; Aharon Klieman and Reuven Pedatzur, *Rearming Israel* ..., p. 170; *Jane's Armour and Artillery, 1992–1993*, p. 154.
176 Yitzhak Rabin, *The Rabin Memoirs*, 141–2. An alternate account is Avner Cohen, *Israel and the Bomb*, pp. 312–15.
177 Yitzhak Rabin, *The Rabin Memoirs*, pp. 54–5; Stewart Reiser, *The Israeli Arms Industry*, pp. 44–5; Alex Mintz, 'The Military-Industrial Complex: American Concepts and Israeli Realities,' *Journal of Conflict Resolution* 29 (December 1985), 627.
178 Aharon Klieman and Reuven Pedatzur, *Rearming Israel* ..., pp. 73–4; Stewart Reiser, *The Israeli Arms Industry*, pp. 44, 55, 193–4; Yitzhak Rabin, *The Rabin Memoirs*, pp. 54–5; Efraim Inbar, 'The American Arms Transfer to Israel,' *Middle East Review* 15 (Fall 1982, Winter 1982/3), 46.
179 Edward Luttwak and Dan Horowitz, *The Israeli Army*, pp. 360–1.
180 Edward Luttwak and Dan Horowitz, *The Israeli Army*, pp. 318–19; Ze'ev Schiff, *A History of the Israeli Army*, pp. 178–82; Immanuel Wald, *The Wald Report*, p. 201.
181 Stewart Reiser, *The Israeli Arms Industry*, pp. 93–6; Chaim Herzog, *The Arab–Israeli Wars*, pp. 210–23; Ze'ev Schiff, *A History of the Israeli Army*, pp. 181–9; Edward Luttwak and Dan Horowitz, *The Israeli Army*, pp. 314–27; Avi Schlaim and Raymond Tanter, 'Decision Process, Choice, and Consequence: Israel's Deep Penetration Bombing in Egypt, 1970,' *World Politics* 30 (July 1978), 483–516.
182 Immanuel Wald, *The Wald Report*, p. 200; Martin Van Creveld, *The Sword and the Olive: A Critical History of the Israeli Defense Force* (New York: PublicAffairs, 1998), pp. 195–267.
183 Stewart Reiser, *The Israeli Arms Industry*, pp. 153–4; Edward Luttwak and Dan Horowitz, *The Israeli Army*, pp. 347–52.
184 Nadav Safran, *Israel: The Embattled Ally*, pp. 488–9; Seymour M. Hersh, *The Samson Option*, pp. 223–40; 'How Israel Got The Bomb,' *Time* (April 12, 1976), 39–40. More recent analysis suggests that these reports were exaggerated. Avner Cohen, 'Nuclear Arms in Crisis Under Secrecy ..,' pp. 117–22.
185 Edward Luttwak and Dan Horowitz, *The Army of Israel*, pp. 337–97; Chaim Herzog, *The Arab–Israeli Wars*, pp. 227–323; Anthony Cordesman and Abraham R. Wagner, *Lessons of Modern Warfare*, vol. I., pp. 14–113; Ze'ev Schiff, *A History of the Israeli Army*, pp. 207–29; Martin Van Creveld, 'Military Lessons of the Yom Kippur War,' *Jerusalem Quarterly* 3 (Fall 1977), 114–24.
186 Avi Schlaim, 'Failures in National Intelligence Estimates: The Case of the Yom Kippur War,' *World Politics* 27 (April 1976), 348–88.
187 See Yuval Ne'eman, 'Conceiving a Balanced Budget ...,' pp. 10–11; Chaim Herzog, *The Arab–Israeli Wars*, pp. 227–8; Edward Luttwak and Dan Horowitz, *The Israeli Army*, p. 337; Ze'ev Schiff, *A History of the Israeli Army*, p. 215.
188 Edward Luttwak and Dan Horowitz, *The Israeli Army*, p. 362.
189 Anthony Cordesman and Abraham R. Wagner, *Lessons of Modern Warfare*, Vol. I, p. 21; Ze'ev Schiff, *A History of the Israeli Army*, p. 215.
190 Major Richard A. Gabriel, 'Lessons of War: The IDF in Lebanon,' *Military Review* (August 1984), 62.
191 Martin Van Creveld, *The Sword and the Olive*, p. 252; Hirsh Goodman, *Israel's Strategic Reality: The Impact of the Arms Race* (Washington, DC: The Washington Institute for Near East Policy, 1985), p. 8.

192 Abraham Rabinovich, *The Boats of Cherbourg*, pp. 205–306.
193 Ze'ev Schiff, *A History of the Israeli Army*, p. 223.
194 The IAF lost a total of 104 aircraft in the conflict, but only *six* in air-to-air combat. The Arabs lost 277 aircraft in air-to-air combat: 183 to Mirages and Neshers, and 94 to F-4s. Ze'ev Schiff, *A History of the Israeli Army*, pp. 217, 220; Lon Nordeen, *Fighters over Israel*, p. 200.
195 Aharon Klieman and Reuven Pedatzur, *Rearming Israel ...*, p. 128; Eliezer Cohen, *Israel's Best Defense* (New York: Orion Books, 1993), p. 426.
196 Nadav Safran, *Israel: The Embattled Ally*, p. viii.
197 In 1950, Egypt's GNP was 4.5 times that of Israel, while by 1967 the difference had shrunk to only 1.5 times. Nadav Safran, *Israel: The Embattled Ally*, pp. 260–1.
198 Eliezer Sheffer, 'The Economic Burden of the Arms Race,' p. 152, Table 8.4.
199 Nadav Safran, *Israel: The Embattled Ally*, p. 496; Sharon R. Murphy, *The Foreign Policies of Israel and South Africa: A Comparative Study* (PhD dissertation, University of Notre Dame, April 1985), p. 109.
200 Peter Hellman, 'Israel's Chariot of Fire,' in *Atlantic Monthly* 255 (March 1985), 81–95; David Eshel, *Chariots of the Desert*, pp. 155–69.
201 Major (Reserve) Louis Williams and Lt. Col. Yehuda Weinraub, 'The Merkava: A National Enterprise,' *IDF Journal* (May 1984), 46; Zvi Volk, 'Tanks Lead the Way,' *IDF Journal* (Summer 1990), 22–3.
202 According to the IDF, Merkava crewmen suffered 50 percent fewer casualties than the crews of other tank models in the 1982 Lebanon conflict, and no Merkava crewmen suffered burns. *IDF Journal* (Fall 1985), 7; Major Richard A. Gabriel, 'Lessons of War,' pp. 50–1.
203 Zvi Volk, 'Tanks Lead the Way,' p. 25.
204 David Eshel, 'Merkava Mk.3: Israel's New Spearhead,' *Military Technology* (July 1989), 67; Richard Simpkin, 'From Array to Disarray: Tactical Aspects of Active and Reactive Armor,' in *Military Technology* (April 1986), 23. This is possible, at least in part, because of the positioning of the engine in the front of the tank, where it provides additional protection for the crew.
205 David Eshel, 'Merkava Mk. 3 ...,' p. 68, and 'IDF Takes Off the Wraps. New Merkava "Arguably Best Tank in the World",' *Jerusalem Post*, May 4, 1989.
206 Zvi Volk, 'Tanks Lead the Way,' p. 25.
207 Christopher Foss, 'MBT Update,' pp. 345–52, *JDW*, September 1, 1990, 347.
208 'Merkava Mk 4 MBT' *Jane's Armour and Artillery* (2003) at www4.janes.com
209 Bet Shemesh produced the J-79 under license, but it relied on the US for provision of 40 percent of the parts. *Global Arms Trade*, p. 97; Gerald M. Steinberg, 'Israel: High-Technology Roulette,' pp. 167, 174.
210 Dan Raviv and Yossi Melman, *Every Spy a Prince* (Boston: Houghton Mifflin Company, 1990), pp. 203–4.
211 *Jane's All The World's Aircraft 1977–1978*, p. 100.
212 *Jane's All The World's Aircraft 1991–1992*, pp. 146–7.
213 James F. Dunnigan, *How To Make War* (New York: William Morrow and Company, 1988), pp. 164–165.
214 The J-79 weighs less than the French engine, produces more thrust, and is more fuel-efficient, increasing combat radius. Edward Luttwak and Stuart Koehl, *The Dictionary of Modern War*, (New York, Harper Collins, 1991), pp. 327–8 (see 'Kfir').
215 US arms export restrictions place limits on the transfer of lethal equipment, but the J-79 could be transferred freely as a non-lethal item. Israel could,

Notes 231

therefore, order as many as it could pay for, but could not export the Kfir without US approval. Stewart Reiser, *The Israeli Arms Industry*, pp. 104–5.

216 Aharon Klieman and Reuven Pedatzur, *Rearming Israel* ..., p. 140. IAI recovered $1 billion of the $2.5 billion cost in Kfir-related exports, but most of these took the form of know-how, parts, and upgrading of French Mirages in foreign service. 'State Comptroller Criticizes Decisions on Lavi,' *Jerusalem Post*, July 1, 1987, in *FBIS-NESA*, July 2, 1987, L2–3.

217 Martin J. Miller, 'Israel's Quest for Self-Sufficiency,' *Military Review* (March 1973), p. 70.

218 Moshe Dayan, *Story of My Life: An Autobiography* (New York: William Morrow and Co., 1976), p. 283.

219 'Battle Damage Repairs,' *Aerospace* (The Royal Aeronautical Society, December 1992), 12; Ze'ev Schiff, *A History of the Israeli Army*, pp. 217, 220.

220 Robert E. Harkavy, 'Arms Resupply *During* Conflict: A Framework for Analysis,' in Christian Schmidt (ed.), *The Economics of Military Expenditures* (New York: St. Martin's, 1987), p. 249; Michael Brzoska and Frederic S. Pearson, *Arms and Warfare: Escalation, De-Escalation, and Negotiation* (Columbia, SC: University of South Carolina Press, 1994), pp. 90–111.

221 Major (Reserve) Louis Williams and Lt. Col. Yehuda Weinraub, 'The Merkava: A National Enterprise,' pp. 46–63. Anthony Cordesman and Abraham R. Wagner, *Lessons of Modern Warfare*, Vol. I, p. 102.

222 John S. Coutinho, 'Battle Damage Assessment and Repair,' *Military Review* (February 1988), 54–62.

223 Chaim Herzog, *The Arab–Israeli Wars*, p. 306; Anthony Cordesman and Abraham R. Wagner, *Lessons of Modern Warfare*, vol. I, pp. 61, 102.

224 Statement by Ministry of Defense, March, 1973 cited in Stewart Reiser, *The Israeli Arms Industry*, p. 98; Martin J. Miller, 'Israel's Quest for Self-Sufficiency,' p. 68, which states that Israeli sources provide 90 percent of IDF small, light, and medium arms and ammunition.

225 Nadav Safran, *Israel: The Embattled Ally*, p. 275.

226 *Jane's Weapons Systems 1987/8*, p. 750; *Jane's All The World's Aircraft 1977–1998*, p. 687. More recent editions of Jane's have reduced some of these claims – 'Python 3' *Jane's Air-Launched Weapons* 42 (2003) at www4.janes.com states that the Shafrir 2 was responsible for over 100 kills in 1973.

227 *Military Review* (October 1973), p. 97.

228 Gerald M. Steinberg, 'Israel,' p. 281; Efraim Inbar, 'The Development of the Israeli Defense Industry', p. 123.

229 'New Capabilities Increasing Rapidly,' *Aviation Week and Space Technology*, April 10, 1978.

230 David Eshel, *Chariots of the Desert*, p. 55; *Jane's Armour and Artillery 1992–1993*, pp. 83, 154.

231 Edward Luttwak and Dan Horowitz, *The Israeli Army*, p. 329; *Jane's Armour and Artillery 1992–1993*, p. 38.

232 *Jane's Armour and Artillery 1992–1993*, pp. 575–6.

233 Edward Luttwak and Dan Horowitz, *The Israeli Army*, p. 329; David Eshel, *Chariots of the Desert*, p. 49.

234 Lon Nordeen, *Fighters Over Israel*, pp. 109, 114.

235 Avner Cohen, 'Nuclear Arms in Crisis Under Secrecy,' pp. 118–19.

236 Avner Cohen, 'Nuclear Arms in Crisis Under Secrecy,' pp. 120–1.

237 'US Assumes the Israelis Have A-Bomb Or Its Parts,' *New York Times*, July 18, 1970.

238 Avner Cohen, *Israel and the Bomb*, pp. 324–38.

239 Seymour M. Hersh, *The Samson Option*, p. 179. One of the earliest public reports concerning Israel's arming of nuclear weapons in the 1973 conflict is 'How Israel Got The Bomb,' *Time*, April 12, 1976, which reports that Israel possessed 13 weapons at the time of publication. See also 'CIA: Israel has 10–20 A-Weapons,' *Washington Post*, March 15, 1976.
240 See Seymour M. Hersh, *The Samson Option*, pp. 173, 179, 215, 225–31.
241 The best article on this subject is Avner Cohen, 'Israel and Chemical/Biological Weapons: History, Deterrence, and Arms Control,' in *The Nonproliferation Review* (Fall–Winter 2001), 27–53, available at cns.miis.edu/pubs/npr/vol08/83/83cohen.pdf . See also 'NBC Capabilities, Israel,' *Jane's Nuclear, Biological and Chemical Defence* (2003) at www4.janes.com.
242 Yitzhak Rabin, *The Rabin Memoirs*, p. 290.
243 Aryeh Shalev, 'The Arms Race in the Middle East in the 1980s,' in Zvi Lanir, *Israeli Security Planning ...*, pp. 75–90.
244 Efraim Inbar, 'The American Arms Transfer ...,' p. 48. SIPRI data indicates that Israel produced about 40 percent of the value of all major weapons system procurement in the 1974–84 period. Ian Anthony, 'The Third-Tier ..,' pp. 370–1.
245 If all domestic production in the 1973–84 period was spent instead on importing defense equipment, Israel would have spent at least $1 billion more in foreign exchange during this period. W. Seth Carus, 'Israel: Some Economic and Social Considerations,' p. 138.
246 Efraim Inbar, 'The American Arms Transfer ...,' pp. 46–7.
247 Eliezer Sheffer, 'The Economic Burden ..,' p. 144, Table 8.1.
248 Stewart Reiser, *The Israeli Arms Industry*, p. 204. Arms exports, particularly high-technology items, have a 'value-added' benefit of more than 50 percent. This is more than twice the level of diamonds, Israel's other major export item. Efraim Inbar, 'The Development of the Israeli Defense Industry,' p. 119.
249 Arms exports reportedly accounted for 25 percent of the value of all Israeli industrial exports in 1984–85. Aharon Klieman, *Israel's Global Reach*, p. 1.
250 Gerald M. Steinberg, 'Indigenous Arms Industries and Dependence: The Case of Israel,' *Defence Analysis* 2 (December 1986), p. 304.
251 Interview with Dr. Aharon Klieman, February 1993, and Aharon Klieman, *Israel's Global Reach*, p. 58.
252 'New Capabilities Increasing Rapidly,' *Aviation Week and Space Technology*, April 10, 1978.
253 Throughout this period, Israel's ratio of exports to imports was growing: from 56.6 percent in 1976 to 75.8 percent in 1985. Much of this 'healthy growth' was due to weapons exports. Aharon Klieman, *Israel's Global Reach ...*, p. 97; Stewart Reiser, *The Israeli Arms Industry*, p. 124.
254 Aharon Klieman and Reuven Pedatzur, *Rearming Israel ...*, pp. 78, 84; *Global Arms Trade*, p. 86, Table 5.2, and p. 100. IAI exported only about 8 percent of total sales in 1971, and over 70 percent in 1986. Efraim Inbar, 'The Development of the Israeli Defense Industry,' p. 123.
255 *Global Arms Trade*, p. 89.
256 'Transformation and Developments at IAI,' *Military Technology*, September 1991, 31.
257 'RAFAEL – A Name to be Respected,' *Military Technology* (September 1986), 146–51.
258 Aharon Klieman and Reuven Pedatzur, *Rearming Israel ...*, pp. 43–50.
259 *Boston Globe*, December 18, 1986, 28, cited in Stewart Reiser, *The Israeli Arms Industry*, p. 206.
260 Israel has been accused of transferring both Arrow and Jericho technology to

South Africa. 'US Suspicions Delay Computer Transfer to Israel,' *Chicago Tribune,* November 9, 1989; 'President Waives Sanctions for Israel: S. African Firm Cited in Missile Parts Deal,' *Washington Post,* October 27, 1991. 'Israel, Pressed by US, Puts Limits on Its Export of Missile Technology,' *Washington Post,* October 4, 1991. 'South Africa Engages in Row With Israel Over Past Military Ties', *Christian Science Monitor,* July 19, 1994.
261 *Jane's Fighting Ships 1991–1992,* pp. 297–8.
262 Naftali Blumenthal, 'Influence of the Defense Industry,' p. 169. See also Stewart Reiser, *The Israeli Arms Industry,* p. 80.
263 Gowri Sundaram, 'Military Electronics in Israel: Second-World Requirements in a Third-World Country,' *International Defense Review* (January 1982), pp. 59–67.
264 Shimon Engle, 'Airborne Electronic Warfare,' *IDF Journal* (Winter 1987), 34–41.
265 Stewart Reiser, *The Israeli Arms Industry,* pp. 192–5, 231–3.
266 Efraim Inbar, 'Israel's New Military Doctrine,' *Naval War College Review* 26 (January–February 1983), 26–40.
267 Ze'ev Schiff and Ehud Ya'ari, *Israel's Lebanon War* (New York: Simon & Schuster, 1984); Ariel Sharon, *Warrior ..,* pp. 408–522; Ze'ev Schiff, *A History of the Israeli Army,* pp. 239–62; Chaim Herzog, *The Arab–Israeli Wars,* pp. 339–70; Anthony Cordesman and Abraham R. Wagner, *The Lessons of Modern Warfare,* vol. I, 117–228; Major Richard A. Gabriel, 'Lessons of War'; W. Seth Carus, 'The Bekaa Valley Campaign,' *Washington Quarterly* 5 (Autumn 1982), 34–41.
268 Chaim Herzog, *The Arab–Israeli Wars,* p. 347. Four more Syrian SAM batteries were severely damaged. In the 1973 war, by comparison, only three of 36 Syrian SAM batteries were destroyed, and only five damaged. Schiff, *A History of the Israeli Army,* pp. 160–1.
269 Stanley Sienkiewicz, 'Some Military Lessons of the War in Lebanon,' in James Brown and William Snyder (eds), *The Regionalization of Warfare* (New Brunswick, NJ: Transaction Books, 1985), pp. 85–95.
270 Martin Van Creveld, *The Sword and the Olive,* p. 295.
271 Anthony Cordesman and Abraham R. Wagner, *Lessons of Modern Warfare,* vol. I, p. 202; *The Arab–Israeli Wars,* p. 362. The Syrians lost 91 aircraft in air-to-air combat. Ze'ev Schiff, *A History of The Israeli Army,* p. 162.
272 Anthony Cordesman and Abraham R. Wagner, *Lessons of Modern Warfare,* vol. I, pp. 200–10.
273 Immanuel Wald, *The Wald Report,* is extremely critical of the IDF higher command echelons, and of the capability of the ground forces to function effectively at the operational level; Major Richard A. Gabriel, 'Lessons of War,' pp. 47–9.
274 Ze'ev Schiff and Ehud Ya'ari, *Israel's Lebanon War,* pp. 168–71; Major Richard A. Gabriel, 'Lessons of War,' pp. 62, 65.
275 Immanuel Wald, *The Wald Report,* 4, p. 2.
276 Anthony Cordesman and Abraham R. Wagner, *Lessons of Modern Warfare,* vol. I, pp. 110–11, 158–64, 184. Almost all of the IAF's electronic warfare and communications systems were either locally built or modified. Robert E. Harkavy and Stephanie Neuman, 'Israel,' p. 201.
277 Stewart Reiser, *The Israeli Arms Industry,* pp. 102, 105–6, 192–5.
278 Hirsh Goodman and W. Seth Carus, *The Future Battlefield and the Arab–Israeli Conflict* (New Brunswick, NJ: Transaction Publishers, 1990).
279 Stewart Reiser, *The Israeli Arms Industry,* pp. 192–5, Aharon Klieman and Reuven Pedatzur, *Rearming Israel ...,* pp. 229–31.

280 Dore Gold, *Israel as an American Non-NATO Ally*, JCSS Study No. 19 (Jerusalem: Jerusalem Post, 1992). From 1949–63, US aid to Israel totaled $800 million. In 1973 alone, US assistance reached $2.4 billion. Nadav Safran, *Israel: The Embattled Ally*, p. viii.
281 *JCSS Middle East Military Balance 1986*, pp. 135–6, 260. US aid amounted to between 30 percent and 42 percent of Israeli military expenditures each year in the late 1980s and early 1990s. Aharon Klieman and Reuven Pedatzur, *Rearming Israel* . . ., p. 67.
282 Martha Wenger, 'The Money Tree: US Aid to Israel,' in *Middle East Report* (May–August 1990), 12.
283 Stewart Reiser, *The Israeli Arms Industry*, p. 142; Raymond J. Ahearn, 'Restructuring the Israeli Economy,' *CRS Report for Congress 92-738F* (Washington, DC: The Library of Congress, September 25, 1992).
284 Stewart Reiser, *The Israeli Arms Industry*, p. 150.
285 From 1984–90, the IDF lost 20 percent of its budget in real terms. 'Major Cuts in Israeli Defense Budget,' *Military Technology* (February 1990), 56–7.
286 In practice, this amounted to between 20–33 percent of the total defense budget. Gerald M. Steinberg, 'Israel,' p. 286; Alex Mintz, 'The Military-Industrial Complex . . .,' p. 635.
287 *Ma'ariv* in Hebrew, June 13, 1989, cited in Dore Gold, *Israel as an American Non-NATO Ally*, p. 7. Aharon Klieman and Reuven Pedatzur, *Rearming Israel* . . ., p. 67, report that domestic military contracts accounted for 45 percent of the 'shekel budget' (non-FMS funds devoted to defense) in 1985, and only 28 percent in 1989. Yitzhak Rabin stated that domestic military procurement had fallen from $2 billion in 1982 to $1 billion in 1989. Aharon Klieman and Reuven Pedatzur, *Rearming Israel* . . ., p. 79.
288 According to Reiser, local military expenditures fell from more than 20 percent of GNP in the 1970s to less than 12 percent in 1989. Stewart Reiser, *The Israeli Arms Industry*, p. 125. Other sources state that domestic military purchases fell from 11.5 percent of GDP in 1981 to 8.2 percent in 1990. Roby Nathanson, 'Recent Israeli and Worldwide Trends in Military Industries,' *IDF Journal* 21 (Fall 1990), p. 28. In FY1992, the 'shekel' portion of the defense budget was about 9 percent of GNP, or less than $3 billion, compared to $1.8 billion in US FMS grants. 'Israeli Ministries Part Paths on Military Budget Plans,' *Defense News*, August 19, 1991.
289 *The Global Arms Trade*, p. 88. The impact of the *intifada* on the IDF is discussed in Martin Van Creveld, *The Sword and the Olive*, pp. 335–52.
290 Aharon Klieman and Reuven Pedatzur, *Rearming Israel* . . ., p. 29; Pinhas Zusman, 'The Dynamics of Growth, Technological Progress, and Force Build-ups – Some Strategic Tradeoffs,' in Zvi Lanir (ed.), *Israeli Security Planning* . . ., p. 240.
291 'Uprising May Cause Stockpile Cuts,' *Jerusalem Post*, July 6, 1988, in *FBIS-NESA* (July 8, 1988), 28–9. Statement by Deputy Chief of the General Staff Ehud Barak, 'The Army's Rearguard Budget Battle,' *Jerusalem Post*, 14 April 1989.
292 Aryeh Shalev, 'The Arms Race in the Middle East in the 1980s,' in Zvi Lanir (ed.), *Israeli Security Planning* . . ., p. 83.
293 *Global Arms Trade*, p. 88; Aharon Klieman and Reuven Pedatzur, *Rearming Israel* . . ., p. 65.
294 Only about one-third of all procurement expenditures come from the shekel budget, and only 20–25 percent of these are high-technology items. Aharon Klieman and Reuven Pedatzur, *Rearming Israel* . . ., pp. 29, 63.
295 Israel stopped buying tires or uniforms at home, as it was cheaper to purchase

them abroad with US dollars. Aharon Klieman and Reuven Pedatzur, *Rearming Israel*..., pp. 165–6; *Global Arms Trade*, p. 88.
296 *Global Arms Trade*, p. 89.
297 Tim Guest, 'C'etait Lavi,' *Military Technology* (October 1987), p. 144.
298 Aharon Klieman and Reuven Pedatzur, *Rearming Israel*..., p. 95.
299 Aharon Klieman and Reuven Pedatzur, *Rearming Israel*..., pp. 56–7. Mintz states that the IDF controls about 50 percent of all government R&D spending. Alex Mintz, 'Arms Production in Israel,' pp. 89–99.
300 US military assistance allowed access to US emergency stockpiles prepositioned in Israel. This effectively saved the IDF $100 million. 'IDF Could Use Stored US Gear During Crises,' Tel Aviv *Ha'aretz* in Hebrew, September 24, 1990, in *FBIS-NESA* (September 25, 1990), 35–6; 'US, Israel Undergo Sweeping Review of Military Relations,' *Jerusalem Post*, September 16, 1992.
301 Dore Gold, *Israel as an American Non-NATO Ally*, p. 13.
302 Steven L. Spiegel, 'US Relations With Israel: The Military Benefits,' *Orbis* 30 (Fall 1986), 483, 495. IAI anticipated larger sales to the US military than it did to the Israeli military in 1989. 'Search for New Business Abroad Pays Dividends: IAI Seeks New Vistas to Keep Brains Ticking,' *Jerusalem Post*, May 23, 1989.
303 Stewart Reiser, *The Israeli Arms Industry*, pp. 171–84; Dov S. Zakheim, *Flight of the Lavi* (Washington, DC: Brassey's, 1996).
304 A production run of 400–450 aircraft was envisioned. Stewart Reiser, *The Israeli Arms Industry*, p. 175.
305 Naftali Blumenthal, 'The Impact of Defense Industry Investment...,' p. 176.
306 Graham Clark, 'Lavi Bares its Teeth,' in *Military Technology* (October 1986), 138; Anthony Cordesman and Abraham R. Wagner, *Lessons of Modern Warfare*, Vol. I., p. 258; Dore Gold, *Israel as an American*..., p. 9.
307 Stewart Reiser, *The Israeli Arms Industry*, pp. 178–9. In 1987 Israeli cost estimates assumed that over 200 units of a 300 aircraft production run would be exported. Anthony Cordesman and Abraham R. Wagner, *Lessons of Modern Warfare*, vol. I, p. 258.
308 Gerald M. Steinberg, 'Lessons of the Lavi,' *Midstream* (November 1987), p. 4.
309 'Rabin Presents Conditions for Continuing Lavi', *Ma'ariv* (in Hebrew), June 8, 1987, *FBIS-NESA* (June 9, 1987), L6–7.
310 The technologies developed in the Lavi project would be relevant primarily in the event of a follow-on aircraft project. 'State Comptroller Criticizes Decisions on Lavi,' *Jerusalem Post*, July 1, 1987, in *FBIS-NESA* (July 2, 1987), L2–3.
311 The Lavi project reportedly involved 9000 engineers and scientists, and a total of 20,000 jobs in various industries were affected by the Lavi cancellation. Gerald M. Steinberg, 'Large-scale National Projects as Public Symbols,' *Comparative Politics* 19 (April 1987), 335, 341.
312 Gerald M. Steinberg, 'Lessons of the Lavi,' 3; Statement by Yitzhak Shamir in *Military Technology* (October 1986), 146.
313 Clark, 'Lavi Bares its Teeth, p. 140.
314 'Cabinet Votes on Lavi Proposal 30 Aug: Decides to Terminate Production,' Tel Aviv *IDF* in Hebrew, 0838 GMT, August 30, 1987, in *FBIS-NESA* (August 31, 1987), L1.
315 See 'Chetz Data Revealed', *JDW*, 25 August 1990, 255.
316 'Arrow Destroys Incoming Missile in Succesful Test,' September 14, 2000 (based on Jerusalem Post reports, September 14–15, 2000, found in the Jewish Virtual Library at: us-israel.org/jsource/US-Israel/Arrow0900.html).
317 'Israel Missile Update 2000,' www.wisconsinproject.org/.

318 'Israel Unveils Arrow-2 Anti-Ballistic Missiles System,' *Middle East Intelligence Bulletin,* November 1999 at www.meib.org/artivles/9911_me3.htm. According to this report, the US funded 78 percent of the cost of the project.
319 'June 19, 2001 Israel Aircraft Industries,' Arrow Anti-Ballistic Missile System Won the Flight Award 2001,' at: iai.co.il/dows/dows/Serve/item/English/1.1.11.1.44.html
320 'Arrow 2,' *Jane's Strategic Weapons Systems 39* (2003), www4.janes.com.
321 'IAI Readies Short-list for US Arrow Partner,' *Defense News*, October 2, 2000, pp. 3, 28; 'Export Strictures Could Hamper US Missile Transfer to Allies,' *Defense News*, January 29, 2001, 3, 19; 'Turkey Seeks Permission for Arrow Buy,' *Defense News,* July 23–29, 2001, 11.
322 'Boeing to build half of the Arrow ATBM,' *Jane's Missiles and Rockets*, March 1, 2003.
323 G. R. Vered, 'Evolution of BLAZER Reactive Armour and its Adaptation to AFVs,' *Military Technology* (December 1987), 53–5.
324 Major Richard A. Gabriel, 'Lessons of War,' p. 58.
325 Ariel Sharon, *Warrior..*, p. 344.
326 Efraim Inbar, 'The Development of the Israeli Defense Industry,' p. 122.
327 'On the Cheap,' *Military Technology* (February 1987), pp. 98–100.
328 Major Richard A. Gabriel, 'Lessons of War,' pp. 60–2; Anthony H. Cordesman, *The Arab-Israeli Military Balance . . .*, pp. 50–1; 'On the Cheap,' p. 99.
329 W. Seth Carus, 'Israel: Some Economic and Social Considerations,' pp. 140–1.
330 W. Seth Carus, 'The Bekaa Valley Campaign,' p. 35. The Hetz is also in service with the US and German armies. Wolfgang Flume, 'Israeli Defense Industry: Peacetime Link in the Economic Chain,' *Military Technology* (February 1987), 95.
331 *Jane's All The World's Aircraft 1980–1981,* p. 710; *Jane's All the World's Aircraft 1985–1986,* pp. 861–2.
332 *Jane's Weapons Systems 1987–1988,* p. 71; Major Richard A. Gabriel, 'Lessons of War,' pp. 56–7.
333 Anthony Cordesman and Abraham R. Wagner, *Lessons of Modern Warfare*, vol. I, p. 184; *Jane's Weapons Systems 1987–1988,* p. 375.
334 Shimon Engle, 'Airborne Electronic Warfare,' pp. 34–41.
335 *FI/DMS,* 'Market Overview, Israel,' (September 1990), p. 15.
336 *Military Technology* (May 1988), 144, and (August 1990), 91.
337 *Jane's Armour and Artillery 1992–1993,* pp. 647–51.
338 *IISS The Military Balance 1990–1991,* p. 107. At least 300 of 579 towed pieces were Soltam 155 mm of various models.
339 Stewart Reiser, *The Israeli Arms Industry,* p. 198.
340 *Jane's Armour and Artillery 1992–1993,* pp. 729–30.
341 A critical account of the 120mm gun development can be found in Gerald Steinberg, 'Israel' in Ravinder Pal Singh (ed.), *Arms Procurement Decision Making Volume I: China, India, Israel, Japan, South Korea and Thailand* (Oxford: Oxford University Press for SIPRI, 1998), pp. 123–4.
342 *FI/DMS* 'Market Overview, Israel' (September 1990), 15 and 'Force Structure, Israel,' p. 9; *Jane's Armour and Artillery 1992–1993,* pp. 227–31.
343 *Jane's Weapons Systems 1987/8,* p. 480; 'Gabriel,' *Jane's Strategic Weapons Systems 40* (2003) at www4.janes.com.
344 *Jane's Fighting Ships 1991–1992,* p. 297.
345 *Jane's Fighting Ships 1991–1992,* pp. 298–9.
346 The SEAL teams of the US navy reportedly favored the Shaldag because of its speed and size. *International Defence Review* (October 1992), 1017; 'US Law

May Block Navy From Buying Israeli Patrol Boat,' *Defense News,* September 2, 1991.
347 See *Jane's Weapons Systems 1987–1998,* p. 750; 'Python 3,' *Jane's Air-Launched Weapons 42,* (2003), www4.janes.com.
348 *Jane's All The World's Aircraft 1977–1978,* p. 688.
349 '$8.9 million Have Nap Deal Signed,' *JDW,* April 14, 1990, 674; 'USAF Arms B-52s With Israeli Missile,' *Flight International* (August 29, 1990), 7.
350 *Jane's Weapons Systems 1987–1988,* pp. 806–7; Clifford Beal, Mark Hewish, Bill Sweetman, 'Bolt From the Blue, Part 2' *International Defence Review* (December 1992), 1179.
351 Timothy D. Hoyt, 'Revolution and Counter-Revolution: The Role of the Periphery in Technological and Conceptual Innovation,' in Emily O. Goldman and Leslie C. Eliason (eds), *The Diffusion of Military Technology and Ideas* (Stanford, CA: Stanford University Press, 2003), pp. 179–201; and Stewart Reiser, *The Israeli Arms Industry..,* for a more extensive discussion.
352 'IMI Reveals Motorized Deception Drone,' Tel Aviv *Yedi-ot Aharonot* in Hebrew, November 14, 1988, in *FBIS-NESA* (November 18, 1988), 32; W. Seth Carus, 'The Bekaa Valley Campaign,' pp. 39–41.
353 Michael Vlahos, 'Middle Eastern, North African, and South Asian Navies,' *Proceedings* (March 1989), 148–9.
354 'IAI: A Partner for the World,' p. 78.
355 Sharone Parnes, 'BARAK: Israeli Navy's Anti-Missile System,' *IDF Journal* (Summer 1990), 41–7; Martin Lewos. 'Point Defense and the Barak 1 Missile,' *IDF Journal* (Spring 1987), 39–44.
356 'Israel's Barak Missile Tests Successfully Against Decoy At Sea,' *Defense News,* August 26, 1991.
357 'Eilat (Saar5) Class (FSGHM),' *Jane's Fighting Ships* 2003, www4.janes.com; 'India Seeks Missile Co-operation With Israel,' *Jane's Missiles and Rockets,* November 1, 2003.
358 Dore Gold, *Israel as an American Non-NATO Ally,* pp. 27–8.
359 FI/DMS 'Market Overview, Israel,' (September 1990), 11.
360 'Air Force Unveils New Antiaircraft System,' Tel Aviv *Hatzofe* in Hebrew, July 15, 1987, in *FBIS-NESA* (July 16, 1987), L5.
361 'IDF Installing "Unique Improvements" in Patriot,' *Jerusalem Voice of Israel* and *IDF Radio Network* in Hebrew, 0500 GMT, January 31, 1991, in *FBIS-NESA* (January 31, 1991), 35.
362 *Jane's Fighting Ships 1991–1992,* p. 298.
363 *Jane's Armour and Artillery 1992–1993,* pp. 85–8, 575–6.
364 Zvi Volk, 'Tanks Lead the Way,' p. 26.
365 David Eshel, *Chariots of the Desert,* p. 55; W. Seth Carus, 'The Bekaa Valley Campaign,' p. 36; *Jane's Armour and Artillery 1992–1993,* pp. 83–7, 154.
366 Tamir Eshel, 'New Life for the Israeli M-60s,' *Military Technology* (June 1989), 88- 9; 'IDF Displays New Patton Model 7'. *Jerusalem Post,* February 1, 1989.
367 Dore Gold, *Israel as an American Non-NATO Ally,* pp. 14, 73; Tony Gadot, 'Israel's Aircraft Upgrading Program,' *IDF Journal* (Fall 1985), 13–18.
368 'IAI: A Partner for the World,' *Military Technology* (May 1993), 73–9; *Jane's All The World's Aircraft 1991/2,* pp. 146–50.
369 'Phalcon Set for May Delivery,' *JDW,* April 2, 1994, 10; 'Phalcon on Course for Delivery,' *International Defence Review* (October 1992), 1015; 'Phalcon AEW Aircraft Makes Public Debut,' *JDW,* June 26, 1993, 8.
370 This led Israeli officials to note that 'we can't brush up against genuine US strategic interests, even if we don't see eye to eye on what constitutes a

238 Notes

genuine strategic interest.' Kuti Mor, Deputy Director General of Israel's Ministry of Defense, in 'Israel Plans to Return Phalcon, Absent Spy Radar,' *Defense News,* July 23–29, 2001, 3.
371 'Israeli Radars for Indian AWACS,' *The Hindu,* 4 December 2003.
372 'Israel Says 'No Thanks' To F/A-22,' *Defense News,* November 24, 2003, 1. By 2009, Israel will have over 360 F-16s in operation.
373 *Military Technology* (October 1989), 166. See also *Jane's Armour and Artillery 1992–1993,* p. 574.
374 'Germany Looks Again at Foreign Howitzers,' *International Defense Review* (March 1993), 195; Aharon Klieman and Reuven Pedatzur, *Rearming Israel* ..., p. 120; *Jane's Armour and Artillery 1992–1993,* pp. 574–5.
375 'Intermediate Ballistic Missile Reportedly Tested,' Paris AFR in English, 1803 GMT, July 21, 1987 in *FBIS-NESA* (July 22, 1987), L5. Russian intelligence believes that 100 Jericho 2 missiles with a 750 km range were deployed from 1977–81, and that the tests in the late 1980s were a modified, Jericho 2B with increased range. 'Russia Spots a Gas Leak,' *The Middle East* (June 1993), p. 19.
376 Janne E. Nolan and Albert D. Wheelon, 'Third World Ballistic Missiles,' *Scientific American* (August 1990), 36.
377 'Jericho 1/2/3 (YA-1/YA-3),' *Jane's Strategic Weapons Systems* 40 (2003), www4.janes.com
378 'OFFEQ-2 Into Orbit,' *Military Technology* (May 1990), 104; 'Israel Launches Second Offeq,' *JDW,* April 14, 1990, 678.
379 Steven E. Gray, 'Israeli Missile Capabilities: A Few numbers To Think About' (New Mexico: Lawrence Livermore Laboratory/Z Division, October 7, 1988) estimates a range of 4,500 km with a 1,100 kg warhead or 7,500 km with a 500 kg warhead. Other reports estimate a range of 4,000 km with an 800 kg warhead. Steve Fetter, 'Israeli Ballistic Missile Capabilities,' *Physics and Society* 19 (July 1990), 3–4.
380 'NBC Capabilities, Israel,' *Jane's Nuclear, Biological and Chemical Defence* (2003) at: www4.janes.com
381 'Jericho 1/2/3 (YA-1/YA-3),' *Jane's Strategic Weapons Systems* 40 (2003) at www4.janes.com
382 Dan Raviv and Yossi Melman, 'The Mideast Goes MAD,' *Washington Post* (Op-Ed), July 15, 1990.
383 'Procurement, Israel,' *Jane's Sentinel Security Assessment – Eastern Mediterranean* (2003) at www4.janes.com; 'Gabriel,' *Jane's Strategic Weapons Systems* 40 (2003) at www4.janes.com
384 Vanunu's testimony is available in 'Revealed: the Secrets of Israel's Nuclear Arsenal,' *Sunday Times* (London), October 5, 1986; and 'France Admits it gave Israel A-Bomb,' *Sunday Times* (London), October 12, 1986. See also Louis Toscano, *Triple Cross: Israel, The Atomic Bomb, & The Man Who Spilled The Secrets* (New York: Birch Lane Press, 1990). Other reports rate the reactor capacity at between 75 and 200 MW. See 'NBC Capabilities, Israel,' *Jane's Nuclear, Biological and Chemical Defence* (2003) at www4.janes.com
385 Seymour M. Hersh, *The Samson Option,* pp. 202–3. US analysts believe the reactor runs at a lower output of 40–70 megawatts, which would produce approximately 15 kg of plutonium per year. Leonard Spector, *Nuclear Ambitions,* pp. 172, 173 (note b).
386 Leonard Spector, *Nuclear Ambitions,* pp. 161–2; Frank Barnaby, *The Invisible Bomb* ..., pp. 25–45. Barnaby is a former scientist in the British nuclear program, as well as a member of SIPRI, whose analysis is based on interviews with Vanunu as part of the *Sunday Times* article cited above.

387 Leonard Spector, *Nuclear Ambitions*, p. 162, estimates 60–100 weapons, some of which are boosted to the 40–50 kiloton range and others of which are 'superboosted' to 100 kilotons yield. The upper figure is based on Seymour M. Hersh, *The Samson Option*, pp. 276, 312, 318–19; and 'Dimona et al.,' *The Economist* (March 14, 1992), 46; 'NBC Capabilities, Israel,' *Jane's Nuclear, Biological and Chemical Defence* (2003) at www4.janes.com

388 For reports that the IDF has deployed both tactical and enhanced radiation 'neutron' warheads with ground forces, see Seymour M. Hersh, *The Samson Option*, pp. 276, 312, 318–19; 'NBC Capabilities, Israel,' *Jane's Nuclear, Biological and Chemical Defence* (2003) at www4.janes.com

389 Avner Cohen, 'Israel and Chemical/Biological Weapons . . ' Russian intelligence believes Israel has produced chemical weapons since the mid-1960s. 'Russia spots a gas leak.'

390 Interview with Israel radio cited in 'Israeli Sees Chemical Option Against Iraqis,' *New York Times,* July 28, 1990.

391 Avner Cohen, 'Israel and Chemical/Biological Weapons . . ' and 'NBC Capabilities, Israel,' *Jane's Nuclear, Biological and Chemical Defence* (2003) at www4.janes.com.

392 'Commentary Analyzes Need for Military Satellite,' Tel Aviv *Ha'aretz* in Hebrew, June 27, 1990 ('A Military Satellite for Israel,' Commentary by Ze'ev Schiff), in *FBIS-NESA* (28 June 1990), pp. 27–8.

393 The Offeq-2 weighed only 325 pounds, and stayed in space for two months. The earlier Offeq-1 had remained in space for 118 days. 'Israel Launches Satellite into Surveillance Orbit,' *Washington Post,* April 4, 1990; 'Israel Shoots for a Moon,' *Christian Science Monitor,* May 15, 1990.

394 IDF analysis estimated that the price tag would be at least twice IAI's $250 million development proposal. 'Clear Opposition in IDF to AMOS Satellite,' *Jerusalem Post,* October 5, 1988; 'Shamir Orders "Freeze" on Amos Satellite Project', Tel Aviv *Ha'aretz* in Hebrew, December 23, 1988, in *FBIS-NESA* (December 28, 1988), p. 36.

395 'Israel Shoots for a Moon,' *Christian Science Monitor,* May 15, 1990.

396 David Ben Gurion, *Israel: A Personal History*, p. 368.

397 Shimon Peres, *David's Sling*, p. 31.

398 The so-called 'ladder of production models' described in Chapter One, appear to be based on the Israeli experience as detailed in Shimon Peres, *David's Sling*, pp. 26–7, 109–36.

399 Saadet Deger, *Military Expenditure in Third World Countries* (London, Boston, and Henley: Routledge & Kegan Paul, 1986), pp. 155–65; Carol Evans, 'Reappraising Third-world Arms Production,' in *Survival* 28 (March/April 1986), 99–118; and Herbert Wulf, 'Developing Countries,' in Nicole Ball and Milton Leitenberg (eds), *The Structure of the Defense Industry*, pp. 336–9.

400 The military's demand for Western standards and quality control drove corresponding standards in Israeli industry. W. Seth Carus, 'Israel: Some Economic and Social Considerations,' p. 135; Aharon Klieman, *Israel's Global Reach*, p. 55; Shimon Peres, *David's Sling*, p. 114.

401 For a slightly different perspective, see Alex Mintz and Gerald Steinberg, 'Coping With Supplier Control,' pp. 147–8.

402 This results in significant economies in the development and procurement process, compared to US and European industries. Wolfgang Flume, 'Israeli Defense Industry: Peacetime Link . . ,' p. 93; Steven L. Spiegel, 'US Relations With Israel: The Military Benefits,' pp. 481–8.

403 Francis Tusa, Esq., 'Aspects of Arms Absorption in Arab Armies,' in *Defence*

Yearbook 1990 (London: Brassey's, 1990), pp. 341–54; Hirsh Goodman and W. Seth Carus, *The Future Battlefield*.., pp. 73–150.
404 Hirsh Goodman and W. Seth Carus, *The Future Battlefield*..., p. 65.
405 Stuart A. Cohen, 'Israel's Changing Military Commitments, 1982–1993: Causes and Consequences,' in *Journal of Strategic Studies* 15 (September 1992), 330–50; Dore Gold, 'Israel and the Gulf Crisis: Changing Security Requirements on the Eastern Front,' *Washington Institute for Near East Policy Memorandum 15* (Washington, DC: Washington Institute for Near East Policy, December 1990).
406 Joseph Alpher, ed., *War in the Gulf: Implications for Israel* (Jerusalem: Jerusalem Post Press, 1992), especially Parts II and IV; Efraim Inbar and Shmuel Sandler, 'Israel's Deterrence Strategy Revisited,' pp. 330–58.
407 'Israeli Defence Industry: In the Lion's Den,' *Jane's Defence Weekly*, February 26, 2003 at www4.janes.com.
408 'Mideast Violence Imperils Israeli Arms Exports,' *Defense News*, June 18–24, 2001, 12; 'Israeli Leaders Move to Combat Negative Perceptions,' *Defense News*, July 16–22, 2001, 13.
409 'Israel Lowers Public Profile on Alliance With Turkey,' *Defense News*, December 4, 2000, 34. Cooperation with Turkey has also been affected by Israeli arms exports to Greece, including new EW systems for the F-16 fighter aircraft. 'Pentagon's Waiver Allows Israeli EW Gear on Greek F-16s,' *Defense News*, December 10–16, 2001 p. 3. ISL is also producing Sa'ar 4.5 missile boats for the Greek Navy. 'Israeli Defence Industry: In the Lion's Den'.
410 'Israeli Defence Industry: In the Lion's Den ..'
411 The R-Darter, though offered as a joint product, is virtually identical to RAFAEL's Derby medium range AAM. 'Derby,' *Jane's Air-Launched Weapons 42* (2003) at www4.janes.com; and 'Air-To-Air Missiles: Command of the Air,' *Jane's Defence Weekly*, May 28, 2003 at www4.janes.com
412 'Indian Navy to Buy More Barak SAM Systems,' *Jane's Missiles and Rockets*, August 1, 2003 at www4.janes.com
413 'Israeli Defence Industry: In the Lion's Den ...'
414 'India Seeks Missile Co-operation with Israel,' *Jane's Missile and Rockets*, November 1, 2003 at www4.janes.com
415 'Israeli Defence Industry: In the Lion's Den ..'
416 'Israel: Aerospace in Depth,' *International Defense Review*, February 1, 2002 at www4janes.com
417 'Lockheed Martin Eyes Israeli Start-Ups to Satisfy Offsets,' *Defense News*, April 2, 2001, p. 20.
418 'Barak Urged to be Firm on Sales of Aircraft to China; Industry, Government Officials Bristle at US Demands,' *Defense News*, April 3, 2000 at www.defensenews.com (Exports, Technology Transfer: Year 2000 News File).
419 The US was negotiating to lower the number of 'problem nations' that required consultation before Israel could export to them. 'US, Israel Near Accords on Exports, Strategic Ties', *Defense News*, September 11, 2000, 4, 20.
420 Dore Gold, *Israel as an American Non-NATO Ally*, pp. 9–10.
421 'Israel MoD May Cancel Lockheed-Martin-RAFAEL Deal: Ministry Official Objects to US Production Line for Python-4,' *Defense News*, April 3, 2000, at www.defensenews.com (Exports, Technology Transfer: Year 2000 News File); 'Python 4, Python 5' *Jane's Air-Launched Weapons 42* (2003) at www4.janes.com
422 'Israeli Execs Decry Shift to US Buys,' *Defense News,* September 11, 2000, pp. 4, 20

423 'Limited War Forces Israel to Boost Defense Budget,' *Defense News*, November 26 – December 2, 2001, 6.
424 'Israeli Execs Decry Shift to US Buys: Israeli Critics Rap Negative Aspects of US Aid,' *Defense News*, November 19–25, 2001, 10.
425 'Air Force Claims Bulk of Israel's Procurement Funds,' *Defense News*, December 3–9, 2001, p. 30.
426 'Funding Woes Block Israeli Use of Derby Missile,' *Defense News*, May 7, 2001, p. 10.
427 'IAI Seeks Market for Upgrade Work on Aging F-16s,' *Defense News*, January 29, 2001, p. 16.
428 'After Years Of Relying On Its Own Weapons, Israel Looks Abroad,' *Wall Street Journal*, June 27, 1995.
429 'Procurement, Israel,' *Jane's Sentinel Security Assessment – Eastern Mediterranean* (2003) at www4.janes.com; 'Israeli Defence Industry: In the Lion's Den . . .'
430 'Israeli Defence Industry: In the Lion's Den . . .'
431 Aharon Klieman and Reuven Pedatzur, *Rearming Israel* . . , pp. 139–231 discuss different Israeli options for the future, one of which is growing dependency on the US.
432 *Global Arms Trade*, p. 89; Immanuel Wald, *The Wald Report*, pp. 223–38.
433 Avner Cohen, *Israel and the Bomb*, p. 341.
434 Immanuel Wald, *The Wald Report*, pp. 240–2.
435 Alex Mintz and Michael D. Ward, 'The Political Economy of Military Spending in Israel,' *American Political Science Review* 83 (June 1989), 521–33; Yoram Peri, 'Political-Military Partnership in Israel,' pp. 303–15.
436 Defense industrial investment accounts for up to 50 percent of all industrial investment in Israel. Alex Mintz and Michael D. Ward, 'The Political Economy . . .,' p. 523; Alex Mintz, 'The Military-Industrial Complex . . .,' p. 629.
437 Gerald M. Steinberg, 'Large Scale National Projects . . .'
438 Shimon Peres, *David's Sling*, p. 113.
439 The Ofek-3 satellite was launched successfully in 1995. See 'Spy Satellite Sent Aloft By Israel,' *Washington Post*, April 6, 1995. Ofek-5 was launched in 2002 to monitor Syria, Iraq, and Iran. 'Procurement, Israel' *Jane's Sentinel Security Assessment – Eastern Mediterranean* (2003) at www4.janes.com.
440 'Procurement, Israel,' *Jane's Sentinel Security Assessment – Eastern Mediterranean* (2003) at www4.janes.com.
441 Shimon Peres, *David's Sling*, p. 166.

4 Iraq

1 *The Comprehensive Revised Report of the Special Advisor to DCI on Iraq's WMD with Addendums (3 volumes)*, (Washington, DC: Government Printing Office, 2005), www.gpoaccess.gov/duelfer/index.html (herafter *Duelfer Report*) is the exhaustive official study of Iraqi WMD.
2 Kenneth M. Pollack, *Arabs at War: Military Effectiveness, 1948–1991* (Lincoln, NE: Council on Foreign Relations and University of Nebraska Press, 2002), pp. 148–267.
3 Edward Luttwak and Stuart L. Koehl, *The Dictionary of Modern War* (New York: Harper & Collins, 1991), p. 51.
4 Yezid Sayigh, *Arab Military Industry: Capability, Performance, and Impact* (London: Brassey's, 1993), p. 190; Kenneth Timmerman, *The Death Lobby: How the West Armed Iraq* (Boston, New York, and London: Houghton and Mifflin, 1991), p. 170. Iraqi artillery was responsible for over 200,000 Iranian

deaths in the Iran–Iraq War. William Scott Malone, David Halevy, and Sam Hemingway, 'The Guns of Saddam,' *Washington Post*, February 10, 1991.
5 *The Iraqi Army: Organization and Tactics* (National Training Center Handbook 100–91, 3 January 1991, Fort Irwin, CA), pp. 117–26; *Conduct of the Persian Gulf War: Final Report to Congress* (Washington, DC: Dept. of Defense, April 1992), pp. 345, 359.
6 Majid Khadduri, 'The Role of the Military in Iraqi Society,' in Sydney Nettleton Fisher, (ed.), *The Military in the Middle East* (Ohio State University Press; Columbus, OH: 1963), pp. 41–52; Mohammed A. Tarbush, *The Role of the Military in Politics: A Case Study of Iraq to 1941*, (London; KPI Limited, 1982).
7 Helen Chapin Metz (ed.), *Iraq: A Country Study* (U.S. Government Printing Office; Washington, DC: 1990), pp. 241–3; Lawrence Freedman and Efraim Karsh, *The Gulf Conflict 1990–1991* (Princeton University Press, Princeton, NJ, 1993), pp. 29–31; and Michael Eisenstadt, 'Like A Phoenix from the Ashes? The Future of Iraqi Military Power,' *Policy Papers 36* (Washington, DC: Washington Institute for Near East Policy, 1994), 9; and Kenneth M. Pollack, *The Threatening Storm: The Case for Invading Iraq* (New York: Council on Foreign Relations and Random House, 2002).
8 Samir al-Khalil, *Republic of Fear* (New York: Pantheon Books, 1989). Samar al-Khalil was a pseudonym for Kanan Makiya. Adel Darwish and Gregory Alexander, *Unholy Babylon* (New York: St Martin's Press, 1991); Judith Miller and Laurie Mylroie, *Saddam Hussein and the Crisis in the Gulf* (New York: Times Books; 1990); Efraim Karsh and Inari Rautsi, *Saddam Hussein: A Political Biography* (New York: The Free Press; 1991); and Amatzia Baram, *Building Toward Crisis: Saddam Husayn's Strategy for Survival* (Washington, DC, Washington Institute for Near East Peace, 1998).
9 Kenneth Timmerman, *The Death Lobby*; Kenneth M. Pollack, *The Threatening Storm*.
10 John Devlin, 'Iraq,' in Edward Kolodziej and Robert E. Harkavy (eds), *Security Policies of Developing Countries* (Lexington, MA: Lexington, 1982), p. 229.
11 In the first decade following the overthrow of the Iraqi monarchy in 1958, 80 percent of top government posts were controlled by Sunnis, and only 16 percent by Shi'ites. Iraq's population is approximately 20 percent percent Kurdish, and the Shi'ite and Kurdish population together constitute approximately 80 percent of Iraq's population. Lawrence Freedman and Efraim Karsh, *The Gulf Conflict ...*, pp. 8, 43, 415.
12 Norman Friedman, *Desert Victory* (Annapolis, MD: Naval Institute Press, 1991), p. 11.
13 John M. Collins, 'Military Geography of Iraq and Adjacent Arab Territory,' *CRS Report for Congress 90–431 RCO* (Library of Congress, Washington, DC, September 7, 1990).
14 Claudia Wright, 'Neutral or Neutralized: Iraq, Iran and the Superpowers,' in Shirin Tahir-Kheli and Shaheen Ayubi (eds), *The Iran–Iraq War: New Weapons, Old Conflicts* (New York: Praeger, 1983), p. 173.
15 John Devlin, 'Iraq,' p. 230.
16 Phebe Marr, *The Modern History of Iraq* (Boulder, CO: Westview; 1985), p. 176.
17 John Devlin, "Iraq," 238; Phebe Marr, *The Modern ..*, p. 222; Mirella Galletti, 'L'ultima rivolta curda in Iraq,' *Oriente Moderno 55*, 1975, 462–72, cited in Marion Farouk-Sluglett and Peter Sluglett, *Iraq Since 1958: From Revolution to Dictatorship* (London: KPI Limited, 1987), pp. 168–9.

18 Helen Chapin Metz, *Iraq ..*, p. 61; Haim Shemesh, *Soviet-Iraqi Relations, 1968–1988: In the Shadow of the Iraq–Iran Conflict* (London: Lynne Rienner, 1992), pp. 34–5, 249, 251.
19 Phebe Marr, *The Modern ..*, pp. 179, 222, 233; Haim Shemesh, *Soviet–Iraqi ..*, p. 125.
20 Mustard gas and the nerve agent GB were used on civilians, 'Press Release from Physicians for Human Rights and the Arms Project of Human Rights Watch,' April 29, 1993.
21 Lawrence Freedman and Efraim Karsh, *The Gulf Conflict ..*, p. 411.
22 Michael Eisenstadt, 'Like a Phoenix ...,' p. 48.
23 Williamson Murray and Major General Robert H. Scales, *The Iraq War: A Military History* (Cambridge, MA: Belknap Press, 2003), pp. 186–95; Andrew F. Krepinevich, *Operation Iraqi Freedom: A First-Blush Assessment* (Washington, DC: Center for Strategic and Budgetary Assessments, 2003); *Operations in Iraq: First Reflections* (London: Ministry of Defence, 2003) available at www.mod.uk/linked_files/publications/iraq2003operations.pdf.
24 Christine Moss Helms, *Iraq: Eastern Flank of the Arab World* (The Brookings Institution: Washington, DC, 1984), p. 17.
25 Claudia Wright, 'Neutral or Neutralized. ..' p. 176; Stephen R. Grummon, 'The Iran–Iraq War: Islam Embattled.' *The Washington Papers* 92 (New York: Praeger, 1982), 9; Daniel Pipes, 'A Border Adrift: Origins of the Conflict,' in Shirin Tahir-Kheli and Shaheen Ayubi (eds), *The Iran–Iraq War: New Weapons ..*, pp. 3–25; Phebe Marr, *The Modern ..*, p. 292; Anthony H. Cordesman, *The Gulf and the Search for Strategic Stability* (Boulder, CO: Westview, 1984), p. 397.
26 Michael Eisenstadt, 'Like a Phoenix ...,' p. 68; Kenneth M. Pollack, *The Threatening Storm ...*
27 Helen Chapin Metz, *Iraq ..*, p. 38.
28 Christine Moss Helms, *Iraq: Eastern ...* The Iranian province of Khuzestan (also called Arabistan), has a large Arab population and has been a focal point for Ba'athist pan-Arab rhetoric, which provided one of the pretexts for Iraq's invasion of Iran in 1980. See Nazih N. M. Ayubi, 'Arab Relations in the Gulf: The Future and Its Prologue,' in Shirin Tahir-Kheli and Shaheen Ayubi (eds), *The Iran–Iraq War: New Weapons..*, p.150
29 Haim Shemesh, *Soviet–Iraqi ..*, p. 72.
30 Christine Moss Helms, *Iraq: Eastern ..*, p. 138; Helen Chapin Metz, *Iraq ..*, p. 208.
31 Phebe Marr, *The Modern ..*, p. 117; and Peter Mansfield, *The Arabs* (Penguin: London, 1979), pp. 293, 317.
32 Nazih N. M. Ayubi, 'Arab Relations ..,' p. 150. Less than half the population of Khuszestan are ethnic Arabs: the fact that 90 percent of Iran's oil reserves are in the province probably played a critical role in Saddam Hussein's calculations. Daniel Yergin, *The Prize* (New York: Simon & Schuster, 1991), p. 710.
33 *FBIS-MEA* (September 29, 1980), E3. It is worth noting that under Gen. Qasim Iraq pressed a claim to sovereignty over the anchorage of Abadan. Phebe Marr, *The Modern ..* p. 180.
34 Iraqi casualties during this conflict are estimated at 120,000 dead, 300,000 wounded, and 70,000 prisoners. Iraq ended the war over $80 billion in debt, with reconstruction costs estimated at $320 billion. *Gulf War Air Power Survey* (hereafter *GWAPS*) Volume I, 'Planning Report,' 56 (Washington, DC, 1993); Anthony H. Cordesman and Abraham R. Wagner, *The Lessons of Modern War* Volume II: The Iran–Iraq War (Boulder, CO: Westview, 1990).
35 Lawrence Freedman and Efraim Karsh, *The Gulf Conflict ...*, pp. 107–9. This

effectively relinquished whatever minor assets Iraq had gained from eight years of bloody war, and must be seen as a major concession on the part of Saddam.
36 Michael Eisenstadt, 'Like a Phoenix ...,' p. 74; *Conduct of the Gulf War: Final Report to Congress* (Washington, DC: Government Printing Office, April 1992), p. 29. On Arab airforces and sanctuary, see Major Ronald H. Bergquist, *The Role of Airpower in the Iran–Iraq War* (Maxwell AFB, AL: Air University Press, December 1988), pp. 1–15, 69–82.
37 Oil prices rose from $1.80 per barrel in 1970 to $11.65 a barrel in December 1973. Daniel Yergin, *The Prize*, p. 625.
38 Christine Moss Helms, *Iraq: Eastern* .., p. 138.
39 Haim Shemesh, *Soviet–Iraqi* ..., p. 73; Christine Moss Helms, *Iraq: Eastern* ..., p. 139; Helen Chapin Metz, *Iraq* ..., p. 206; Claudia Wright, 'Neutral or Neutralized ...,' p. 173.
40 The 50 percent decline in Iraqi GDP from 1980–82 was due to a 76 percent decline in oil production. See Basil al-Bustany, 'Development Strategy in Iraq and the War Effort,' in M. S. El-Azhary (ed.), *The Iran–Iraq War: An Historical, Economic and Political Analysis* (New York: St. Martin's, 1984), p. 76.
41 Stephen R. Grummon, 'The Iran–Iraq War: Islam Embattled,' p. 3; Peter Hunseler, 'The Historical Antecedents of the Shatt Al-Arab Dispute,' in M. S. El-Azhary (ed.), *The Iran–Iraq War* ..., pp. 8–19.
42 On at least two occasions during the Iran–Iraq War, Saddam approached the Kuwaitis with a request to lease Warbah and Bubiyan. Frederick Axelgaard, 'A New Iraq? The Gulf War and Implications for US Policy,' *The Washington Papers* 133 (New York: Praeger, 1988), 75.
43 Lawrence Freedman and Efraim Karsh, *The Gulf Conflict* ..., p. 42.
44 Phebe Marr, *The Modern* ... p. 181.
45 Lawrence Freedman and Efraim Karsh, *The Gulf Conflict* ..., p. 44; Phebe Marr, *The Modern* ..., p. 221.
46 Dore Gold, *Israel and the Gulf Crisis: Changing Security Requirements on the Eastern Front*, Policy Focus Research Memorandum No. 15 (Washington, DC: Washington Institute for Near East Policy, December 1990), 4, 9–10.
47 Speech by Saddam Hussein on April 1, 1990, reported in *FBIS-NEA* (April 3, 1990), 35.
48 Phebe Marr, *The Modern* ..., pp. 117, 220–5.
49 Cited in Tareq Y. Ismael, 'Ideology in Recent Iraqi Foreign Policy,' in Shirin Tahir-Kheli and Shaheen Ayubi (eds), *The Iran–Iraq War* ..., p. 111. It was not until 1983 that Iraq actually accepted the 1948 UN partition of Palestine. See Helen Chapin Metz, *Iraq* ..., p. 208.
50 Nazih N. M. Ayubi, 'Arab Relations ...,' p. 150; Tareq Y. Ismael, 'Ideology ...,' p. 117; Phebe Marr, *The Modern* ..., p. 244.
51 Lawrence Freedman and Efraim Karsh, *The Gulf Conflict 1990–1991*, pp. 15, 21; Helen Chapin Metz, *Iraq* .., p. 208.
52 Christine Moss Helms, *Iraq: Eastern* .., p. 139.
53 Phebe Marr, *The Modern* ..., p. 245; Frederick W. Axelgaard, 'A New Iraq? ...,' p. 77.
54 Haim Shemesh, *Soviet-Iraqi* ... pp. 251–3.
55 Speech by Saddam Hussein, January 2, 1980, cited in *GWAPS Volume II: 'Operations,'* p. 62.
56 *GWAPS Volume I: 'Planning Report,'* p. 64.
57 July 1990 executive branch report cited in *Congressional Record,* July 27, 1992, H6699. See also Michael Adams (ed.), *The Middle East* (New York: Facts on File, 1988), pp. 213–14. Education and literacy certainly declined during more than a decade of sanctions, 1990–2003.

58 According to one report, in 1990 Iraq's illiteracy rate of 10.7 percent was lower than any country in the Middle East except for Israel (8.8 percent). *The Economist Book of Vital World Statistics* (New York: Times Books, 1990), pp. 209–10.
59 Kenneth Timmerman, *The Death Lobby* . . ., p. 19.
60 Helen Chapin Metz, *Iraq* . . , p. 148. According to *Unified Arab Economic Report 1989* (Abu Dhabi), in 1986 Iraq had a total of 193,392 employees in the manufacturing and industrial sectors.
61 Yezid Sayigh, *Arab Military Industry*, p. 107; G. Willis, 'Open Sesame: Baghdad Show Reveals Iraqi Military-industrial Capabilities,' *International Defence Review* (June 1989), 836.
62 Michael Eisenstadt, 'Like a Phoenix . . .,' p. 19.
63 Ahmed Hashim, quoted in 'US Is Building Up A Picture of Vast Iraqi Atom Program,' *New York Times*, September 27, 1991.
64 Yezid Sayigh, *Arab Military Industry*, p. 106. Sayigh refers to the 'General' Organization for Technical Industries. The State Organization for Technical Industries was the new name (as of 1975) for the former State Organization for War Industries. Kenneth Timmerman, *The Death Lobby* . . ., p. 36.
65 Yezid Sayigh, *Arab Military Industry*, p. 106.
66 Yezid Sayigh, *Arab Military Industry*, p. 107.
67 'Very Tight Inner Circle Surrounds Iraq's President,' *New York Times*, January 27, 1991.
68 CIA report from late summer 1989, cited in *Congressional Record*, August 10, 1992, H7873.
69 This was facilitated by Iraqi industrial structure. According to Lt. Gen. al-Saadi, 'Our experience in the war taught us that you can't have separate factories for civil and military products. You have to have both types of production in a single factory.' Kenneth Timmerman, *The Death Lobby* . . ., p. 289.
70 CIA Report, 'Beating Plowshares Into Swords . . .,' cited in *Congressional Record*, July 21, 1992, H6342.
71 CIA Report, 'Iraq's Growing Arsenal: Programs and Facilities,' July 1990, cited in *Congressional Record*, August 10, 1992, H7871. The Badush Dam project was used as a front for purchasing equipment for the Condor missile program, and PC-2 was used as a front for Gerald Bull's supergun project.
72 'Beating Plowshares . . .,' cited in *Congressional Record*, July 21, 1992, H6342.
73 June 1989 intelligence report, cited in *Congressional Record*, July 27, 1992, H6699.
74 July 1990 CIA Report, 'Iraq's Growing Arsenal . . .,' cited in *Congressional Record*, July 21, 1992, H6342.
75 July 1990 executive branch report cited in *Congressional Record*, July 27, 1992, H6699.
76 The Soviet share of Iraqi arms supplies was 95 percent in 1972. Kenneth Timmerman, *The Death Lobby* . . , p. 25.
77 Kenneth Timmerman, *The Death Lobby* . . ., pp. 10–11; Haim Shemesh, *Soviet–Iraqi* . . , pp. 134–5.
78 Kenneth Timmerman, *The Death Lobby* . . ., pp. 17–18.
79 Kenneth R. Timmerman, 'Iraq: Tactical and technical implications for Tomorrow's History Book,' *Military Technology* (July 1986), 128.
80 Speech by Saddam Hussein on September 17, 1980, cited in Kenneth Timmerman, *The Death Lobby* . . ., pp. 23 and 399(n).
81 Soviet military aid to Iraq had a value of $1.6 billion from 1958–74,

$1 billion in 1975 alone, and $5 billion from 1976–80. Helen Chapin Metz, *Iraq* ..., p. 229.
82 Kenneth Timmerman, *The Death Lobby* ..., p. 18; Yezid Sayigh, *Arab Military Industry* .., pp. 103, 105.
83 Interview with Lt. Gen. Amer Hammoudi al-Saadi, *Middle East Defense News* (hereafter *MEDNews*), May 8, 1989, 5.
84 *MEDNews*, May 8, 1989, 1.
85 Kenneth Timmerman, *The Death Lobby* ..., pp. 25, 120.
86 Yezid Sayigh, *Arab Military Industry* .., pp. 3, 169.
87 Cited in Simon Henderson, *Instant Empire: Saddam Hussein's Ambition for Iraq* (San Francisco, CA: Mercury House, 1991), p. 124.
88 This was assisted by the efforts of Saddam Hussein's half-brother, Barzan al-Tikriti, who was then head of the foreign branch of Iraqi intelligence. Kenneth Timmerman, *The Death Lobby* ..., p. 157. See also Simon Henderson, *Instant Empire* ..., pp. 155–68.
89 Kenneth Timmerman, *The Death Lobby* ..., p. 80. Al-Ubeidi and Al-Suadi received the complimentary rank of Lt. General, an indication of their bureaucratic stature.
90 Yezid Sayigh, *Arab Military Industry*, p. 107.
91 Kenneth Timmerman, *The Death Lobby* ..., pp. 110–11; Yezid Sayigh, *Arab Military Industry* .., p. 107.
92 Yezid Sayigh, *Arab Military Industry* .., p. 107. According to two US intelligence reports from July 1990 ('Beating Plowshares Into Swords: Iraq's Defense Industrial Program' and 'Iraq's Growing Arsenal: Programs and Facilities'), other State Establishments involved in Iraqi military industry include Badr General Establishment, Saddam State Establishment, Al QaQaa State Establishment, and Hutteen State Establishment. Cited in *Congressional Record*, July 21, 1992, H6342.
93 Interview with Ali Qasim al-Ogabi in *Al-Thawrah* (Baghdad), October 11, 1987, cited in Yezid Sayigh, *Arab Military Industry* ..., pp. 3–4, 104.
94 Yezid Sayigh, *Arab Military Industry* .., pp. 3–4.
95 Kenneth Timmerman, 'Iraq: Tactical and technical implications ...,' p. 128.
96 'Stockholm Institute Publishes Arms Suppliers List,' Vienna *Wochenpresse* in German, February 7, 1991, p. 43, in *FBIS-NES*, February 7, 1991, pp. 14–15.
97 Nick Cook and Douglas Barrie, 'Iraq's Arsenal: the Weapons Facing the West,' *Jane's Defense Weekly* (hereafter *JDW*), August 18, 1990, p. 230.
98 Kenneth Timmerman, *The Death Lobby* ..., p. 131.
99 Anthony H. Cordesman and Abraham R. Wagner, *The Lessons of Modern War*, Vol. 2, p. 47. Oil export earnings amounted to 90–95 percent of the total value of Iraqi annual exports. Patrick Clawson, 'How Has Saddam Hussein Survived? Economic Sanctions, 1990–1993,' *McNair Paper 22* (Washington, DC: National Defense University, August 1993), 12.
100 Michael Collins Dunn, 'Cairo Exhibition Report,' *Defense and Foreign Affairs*, (December 1984), p.1.
101 The Iraqis reportedly realized that they might make considerable savings if they produced munitions at home and stopped importing $600 million of Egyptian munitions annually. Kenneth Timmerman, *The Death Lobby* ..., p. 193.
102 Yezid Sayigh, *Arab Military Industry*, p. 107; Kenneth Timmerman, *The Death Lobby* ..., p. 275.
103 Michael Eisenstadt, 'Like A Phoenix ...,' pp. 95–6; 'Iraq "able to expand military capability",' *JDW*, July 10, 1993, 9.
104 Kenneth Timmerman, *The Death Lobby* ..., p. 87.

105 Kenneth Timmerman, *The Death Lobby* ..., p. 88.
106 Kenneth Timmerman, *The Death Lobby* ..., p. 26.
107 Yezid Sayigh, *Arab Military Industry*, p. 107. SAAD-13 was later re-named the Salah-al-Din project.
108 Kenneth Timmerman, *The Death Lobby* ..., p. 80.
109 *MEDNews*, May 8, 1989, 4.
110 Kenneth Timmerman, *The Death Lobby* ..., p. 56.
111 Kenneth Timmerman, *The Death Lobby* ..., p. 149.
112 Anthony H. Cordesman and Abraham R. Wagner, *The Lessons of Modern War*, Vol. 2, p. 517.
113 Mike Eisenstadt, 'The Sword of the Arabs: Iraq's Strategic Weapons,' *Policy Papers* 21 (Washington, DC: The Washington Institute for Near East Policy, 1990), 6; Anthony H. Cordesman and Abraham R. Wagner, *The Lessons of Modern War* , Vol. 2, p. 517; 'US Experts Doubt Power of Poison Gas,' *Washington Post*, December 14, 1990.
114 Anthony H. Cordesman and Abraham R. Wagner, *The Lessons of Modern War*, Vol. 2, p. 518.
115 Kenneth Timmerman, *Death Lobby* ..., pp. 35–6; Thomas L. McNaugher, 'Ballistic Missiles and Chemical Weapons: The Legacy of the Iran–Iraq War,' *International Security* 15 (Fall 1990), p. 7; William E. Burrows and Robert Windrem, *Critical Mass: The Dangerous Race for Superweapons in a Fragmenting World* (New York: Simon & Schuster, 1994), p. 46.
116 Kenneth Timmerman, *The Death Lobby*, pp. 134–5; Thomas L. McNaugher, 'Ballistic Missiles and Chemical Weapons ...,' p. 17; and Anthony H. Cordesman and Abraham R. Wagner, *The Lessons of Modern War*, Vol. 2, pp. 508–15.
117 Kenneth Timmerman, *The Death Lobby* ..., p. 135; and Anthony H. Cordesman and Abraham R. Wagner, *The Lessons of Modern War*, Vol. 2, p. 514.
118 Kenneth Timmerman, *The Death Lobby*, p. 48.
119 Kenneth Timmerman, *The Death Lobby*, pp. 105–6.
120 Kenneth Timmerman, *The Death Lobby*, p. 106. Salman Pak was the primary Iraqi facility for reseach and development of BW agents, and was heavily damaged in the Gulf War. Mike Eisenstadt, 'The Sword of the Arabs: Iraq's Strategic Weapons,' *Policy Papers* 21 (Washington, DC: The Washington Institute for Near East Policy, 1990), pp. 7–9.
121 Kenneth Timmerman, *The Death Lobby* ..., p. 29; Michael Eisenstadt, 'Like a Phoenix ...', p. 20; Leonard S. Spector, *Nuclear Ambitions* with Jacqueline R. Smith (Boulder, CO: Westview, 1990), pp. 194–5. This reactor was ultimately upgraded to five megawatts capacity.
122 The reactors in question were a 70 MW reactor (Tammuz I or Osiraq) and a smaller 800 kW research reactor (Tammuz II). Spector, *Nuclear Ambitions*, p. 187; Mike Eisenstadt, 'Sword of the Arabs ...,' pp. 10–11; Kenneth Timmerman, *The Death Lobby* ..., pp. 30–3.
123 Robert Richter, an IAEA official present at the spring 1981 inspection of the Tuwaitha complex, calculated that Iraq could manufacture a plutonium device by 1983, and be building five weapons annually by 1985. Kenneth Timmerman, *The Death Lobby* ..., pp. 59–60, pp. 98–100; Mike Eisenstadt, 'The Sword of the Arabs ...', pp. 9–11; Jed C. Snyder, 'The Road to Osiraq: Baghdad's Quest for the Bomb,' *The Middle East Journal* (Autumn 1983), pp. 565–93; Gary Milhollin, 'The Iraqi Bomb,' *The New Yorker* (February 1, 1993), 49.
124 David Segal, 'The Iran–Iraq War: A Military Analysis,' *Foreign* Affairs 66 (Summer 1988), 961.

125 Yezid Sayigh, *Arab Military Industry*, p. 105; Kenneth Timmerman, *The Death Lobby* ..., pp. 227–30, 249.
126 Kenneth Timmerman, *The Death Lobby* ..., pp. 215, 230, 249; Adel Darwish and Gregory Alexander, *Unholy Babylon*, p. 137.
127 See chart in Anthony H. Cordesman and Abraham R. Wagner, *The Lessons of Modern War*, Vol. 2, p. 366, based on a working paper by Gary Sick.
128 Thomas G. Mahnken and Timothy D. Hoyt, 'The Spread of Missile Technology to the Third World,' *Comparative Strategy* 9, 248.
129 Kenneth Katzman, 'Iraq's Campaign to Acquire and Develop High Technology,' *CRS Report for Congress* 92–611 F (Washington, DC: Library of Congress, August 3, 1992), 15.
130 Kenneth Katzman, 'Iraq's Campaign ...,' p. 9. Kamil is also identified as being head of the 'Secret Security Organization.' *Congressional Record*, August 10, 1992, H7873, citing July 1990 CIA report 'Beating Plowshares Into Swords ...'
131 Kenneth Katzman,'Iraq's Campaign ...,' p. 15. His chief deputies remained al-Ubeidi and al-Saadi.
132 Kenneth Timmerman, *The Death Lobby* ..., pp. 259, 275, 289.
133 Interview with Lt. Gen. Amer Rashid al-Ubaidi. *MEDNews*, May 8, 1989, p. 6. Al-Ubaidi, like other leaders of Iraq's military-industrial efforts, was not a professional military officer or a warfighter. He was a Ba'ath Party ideologue, but also apparently a skilled engineer and administrator.
134 *MEDNews*, May 8, 1989, 3.
135 Kenneth Timmerman, *The Death Lobby* ..., p. 255. The funds were used to expand the Saad-16 missile R&D plant, the Project 96 solid-fuel plant, the Project 124 missile body construction plant, and the Al-Anbar Space Research Center.
136 Other analysts have noted that '... the beginnings and ultimate success of the range-extension program coincided with the rise to power of Hussein Kamel.' Timothy V. McCarthy and Jonathan B. Tucker, 'Saddam's Toxic Arsenal: Chemical and Biological Weapons in the Gulf Wars,' in Peter R. Lavoy, Scott D. Sagan, and James J. Wirtz (eds), *Planning the Unthinkable: How New Powers Will Use Nuclear, Biological, and Chemical Weapons* (Ithaca, NY: Cornell University Press, 2000), p. 55 n. 28.
137 Kenneth Timmerman, *The Death Lobby* ..., p. 275.
138 Kenneth Timmerman, *The Death Lobby* ..., p. 288.
139 Kenneth Katzman, 'Iraq's Campaign ...', p. 15.
140 Cited in *Congressional Record*, July 21, 1992, H6342.
141 July 1990 intelligence report, cited in *Congressional Record*, July 27, 1992, H6699.
142 US intelligence report from the summer of 1990, cited in *Congressional Record*, July 27, 1992, H6699.
143 Anthony H. Cordesman and Abraham R. Wagner, *The Lessons of Modern War*, Vol. 2, pp. 222, 262.
144 Kenneth Timmerman, *The Death Lobby* ..., p. 231.
145 Kenneth Timmerman, *The Death Lobby* ..., p. 335.
146 These included versions of Soviet and Italian ground mines, as well as a Soviet model moored contact mine – see Norman Friedman, *Desert Victory*, p. 211.
147 *FI/DMS Market Intelligence Report, Middle East and Africa* (November 1990), 'Iraq,' p. 8.
148 *MEDNews*, May 8, 1989, 2.
149 'Minister Denies Missile Industry Cooperation,' Baghdad INA in Arabic, 1600 GMT, April 27, 1989.

150 *Forecast International/DMS* (November 1990) 'Middle East Market Overview, Iraq,' p. 3; *MEDNews*, May 8, 1989, 2.
151 'Iraq has Bomb Similar to an Atomic Weapon,' *Los Angeles Times*, October 5, 1990; 'Fuel-Air Warhead for Iraqi SCUDs,' *Flight International*, October 10, 1990, 5.
152 'Crisis in the Gulf: The Men Who Made Saddam Dangerous,' *The Independent*, August 26, 1990; Anthony H. Cordesman and Abraham R. Wagner, *The Lessons of Modern War*, Vol. 2, p. 474.
153 Yezid Sayigh, *Arab Military Industry*, p. 116, 126; W. Seth Carus, 'Cruise Missile Proliferation in the 1990s,' *Washington Papers* 159 (Westport, CT: Praeger, 1992), 68.
154 John Boatman, 'Threat from Below the Waterline', *JDW* (September 22, 1990), 502.
155 *MEDNews*, May 8, 1989, 5. See also Nick Cook and Douglas Barrie, 'Iraq's Arsenal: the Weapons Facing the West,' *JDW* (August 18, 1990), 230.
156 *MEDNews*, May 8, 1989, 5; *FI/DMS* (November 1990), 'Market Intelligence Report–Middle East and Africa: Iraq', p. 8.
157 *MEDNews*, May 8, 1989, 2. According to Yezid Sayigh, *Arab Military Industry*..., p. 108, production of mortars and shells only began in 1987.
158 'Iraq's Formidable Array of Guns,' *JDW* (February 2, 1991), p. 136. Western intelligence reported that Iraq was extremely interested in acquiring modern fuse technology: see testimony of Customs Service cited in *Congressional Record*, August 10, 1992, H7876.
159 'The Guns of Saddam,' *Washington Post*, February 10, 1991.
160 *FI/DMS* (November 1990), 'Middle East Market Overview: Iraq,' p. 3; *MEDNews*, May 8, 1989, 2.
161 *UNSCOM Report S23283* (December 12, 1991), 41 reports that at the Hatteen project at Al-Atheer, Iraqi authorities stated that 3.5 kg of uranium metal were used to build ten armor piercing 'bullets'. Iraqi authorities claimed that three of these had been used, and exhibited three more to inspectors.
162 Kenneth Timmerman, *The Death Lobby*..., p. 314; 'British Exports to Iraq,' *MEDNews*, September 2, 1991, 2.
163 *MEDNews*, May 8, 1989, 3; *Jane's Armor and Artillery, 1992–1993*, p. 647; Frank Chadwick, *Gulf War Factbook* (Bloomington, IL: GDW Inc., 1991), p. 65.
164 Alan George, 'Forging Line or Gun Barrel Project?,' *Defence* (August 1990), 478–9; Kenneth Timmerman, *The Death Lobby*..., p. 323; Michael Eisenstadt, 'Like a Phoenix...,' p. 96.
165 'Iraq: Heir to HARP Project?', *JDW* (April 21, 1990), pp. 770–1.
166 *MEDNews*, May 8, 1989, p.2. These modifications may have been based on Yugoslav kits. *Jane's Armor and Artillery 1992–93*, pp. 647, 687.
167 Ezio Bonsignore, '"Programme Babylon" and "Operation Bertha": Fact or Fiction,' *Military Technology* (June 1990), 62–5; 'US, Britain Knew of Supergun, Designer Says,' *Washington Post*, January 16, 1992. UNSCOM inspectors believe that the gun was developed for BW delivery: See 'Text of August 14, 1991 Press Briefing by Officials of UN Inspection Team on First Visit to Iraq's Biological Weapons Facilities,' pp. 1–2, and UN Press Release IK/46 which accompanied the briefing.
168 Ian Kemp, 'Dr. Gerald Bull's Deadly Legacy', *JDW*, November 24, 1990; Ian Kemp, 'The Execution of Project Babylon', *JDW*, November 24, 1990, p. 1010.
169 Kenneth Timmerman, *The Death Lobby*..., pp. 370–1; Simon Henderson, *Instant Empire*..., pp. 142–54.

170 James Adams, *Bull's Eye* (New York: Times Books, 1991), p. 261.
171 W. Seth Carus, 'Long Range Rocket Artillery in the Third World,' *Jane's Intelligence Review* (October 1991), p. 471.
172 W. Seth Carus, 'Long-range Rocket Artillery . . .,' p. 477 (chart), *MEDNews*, May 8, 1989, p. 8; *Jane's Armor and Artillery 1992–1993*, pp. 728, 744–5.
173 W. Seth Carus, 'Long-range Rocket Artillery . . .,' p. 477 (chart); *MEDNews*, May 8, 1989, p. 8; and *Jane's Armor and Artillery 1992–1993*, p. 728.
174 Tim Ripley, 'Destroying Iraq's Ballistic Missiles,' *Jane's Intelligence Review* (October 1992), p. 460. 'U.N. Team Sets Daily Inspections at Iraqi Missile Research Center,' *Washington Post*, January 27, 1993.
175 'Stockholm Institute Publishes Arms Suppliers List', Vienna *Wochenpresse* in German, February 7, 1991, 43, in *FBIS-NESA*, 7 February, 1991, 14–15. According to SIPRI data, Brazil supplied 98 Astros systems and 960 rockets for these systems in the 1979–89 period.
176 Kenneth Timmerman, *The Death Lobby* . . ., pp. 183–4.
177 W Seth Carus and Joseph Bermudez, Jr., 'Iraq's Al-Husayn Missile Program, Part I,' *Jane's Soviet Intelligence Review* (May 1990), pp. 204–9; *Jane's Armor and Artillery 1992–1993*, p. 728.
178 The Laith and the FROG share a common launcher: the Soviet-designed ZIL-135. *The Iraqi Army*, p. 9.
179 W. Seth Carus, 'Long-range Rocket Artillery . . .,' p. 477 (chart); *Jane's Armor and Artillery 1992–1993*, p. 728.
180 *MEDNews*, May 8, 1989, pp. 7–8.
181 See Duncan Lennox, 'Iraq's Short-Range Surface-to-Surface Missiles,' p. 58; and Yezid Sayigh, *Arab Military Industry*, p. 112. In August 1993, UN observers monitored an Iraqi test of a modified SA-2 missile. 'UN witnesses Iraqi rocket test', *Boston Globe*, 3 August 1993.
182 'Brazilians Probe Links with Iraq', *JDW*, 26 May 1990, p. 989; 'Brazil Rebuffs Critics of Missile Aid to Iraq,' *Insight* (September 10, 1990), 40; Scott D. Tollefson, *Brazilian Arms Transfers, Ballistic Missiles, and Foreign Policy: The Search for Autonomy* (PhD dissertation, Baltimore: Johns Hopkins University Press, 1991), pp. 335–40.
183 See 'Minister on Successful Anti-Missile Missile Test', Baghdad Domestic Service in Arabic, 1700 GMT, November 30, 1988, in *FBIS-NESA*, December 1, 1988, 29; 'TV Airs Film on Missile,' Baghdad INA in Arabic, 1730 GMT, November 30, 1988 in *FBIS-NESA*, December 1, 1988, 29.
184 Duncan Lennox, 'Iraq's Short Range . . .,' p. 58, states that the missile appeared to be a modification of the Chinese HQ-61 surface-to-air missile, a reverse-engineered version of the Soviet SA-2.
185 *MEDNews*, May 8, 1989, 4.
186 *MEDNews*, May 8, 1989, 2.
187 *MEDNews*, May 8, 1989, 4.
188 Michael Eisenstadt, 'Like a Phoenix . . .,' p. 95; 'Iraq "able to expand military capability",' *JDW*, July 10, 1993, 9; *MEDNews*, May 8, 1989, 4.
189 *MEDNews*, May 8, 1989, 2; *Jane's Armor and Artillery 1992–1993*, pp. 77, 573.
190 *Jane's Armor and Artillery 1992–1993*, pp. 76–7.
191 Yezid Sayigh, *Arab Military Industry*, p. 115.
192 Jagdeep Singh, 'After the War, The Exhibition,' *Military Technology* (August 1989), 60–2.
193 Anthony H. Cordesman and Abraham R. Wagner, *The Lessons of Modern War*, Vol. 2, p. 440; Kenneth Timmerman, *The Death Lobby* . . ., p. 275.
194 Kenneth Timmerman, *The Death Lobby* . . ., pp. 232–3.

195 Norman Friedman, *Desert Victory*, p. 295.
196 *Jane's Armor and Artillery 1992–1993*, pp. 76–7.
197 Norman Friedman, *Desert Victory*, p. 110; *Jane's Armour and Artillery, 1992–1993*, p. 77.
198 Yezid Sayigh, *Arab Military Industry*, p. 115.
199 Yezid Sayigh, *Arab Military Industry* .., p. 115; *Jane's Armour and Artillery 1992–1993*, p. 319.
200 *MEDNews*, May 8, 1989, 2. The system combined a Thomson 'Atlis' laser designator pod with the Soviet X-29L laser-guided bomb, and used Iraqi-designed software and hardware adaptors. The Soviet missile provided greater explosive power and range than existing French systems.
201 *MEDNews*, May 8, 1989, 2. According to General Husayn Kamil Hassan, director of MIMI, the MiG-23 was capable of refuelling other aircraft in mid-air. See 'Iraq Negotiating to Buy French Mirage Fighters,' *Reuters*, April 27, 1989, AM Cycle.
202 *FI/DMS* (November 1990), 'Iraq: Force Structure,' 2, 5.
203 *Jane's All the World's Aircraft 1991–1992*, p. 145; Tamir Eshel 'Iraqi Thrust Toward Strategic Weapons: A Mini-Superpower in Formation,' *Military Technology* (June 1990) 98–100; Anthony H. Cordesman and Abraham R. Wagner, *The Lessons of Modern War*, Vol.2, p. 242 and Mike Eisenstadt, 'The Sword of the Arabs .. ', p. 26.
204 'India to Test Avro-748-based AWACS Program in Mid-1991,' *Defense and Foreign Affairs Weekly*, October 15–21, 1990; James Smith, 'Developments in the Indian Air Force,' *Jane's Intelligence Review* (November 1991), 526.
205 *Jane's All the World's Aircraft 1991–1992*, p. 145; Kenneth Timmerman, *The Death Lobby . . .*, pp. 336–7.
206 *MEDNews*, May 8, 1989, 2; 'Minister Denies Missile Industry Cooperation,' Baghdad INA in Arabic, 1600 GMT, April 27, 1989, in *FBIS-NESA* (April 28, 1989), 18.
207 *Jane's All the World's Aircraft 1991–1992*, p. 145; *MEDNews*, May 8, 1989, 2.
208 'Minister Cables Saddam on Production of AWACS,' Baghdad Domestic Service in Arabic, 1800 GMT, July 3, 1989 in *FBIS-NESA* (July 5, 1989), 25; 'Baghdad TV Shows Film of Latest Military Technology, Shows Adnan-1 Airplane,' Baghdad INA in Arabic, 1750 GMT, December 7, 1989 in *FBIS-NESA* (December 8, 1989), p. 24.
209 Simon Mitchell, 'Who Owns Iraq's New AEW,' *International Defense Review* (February 1993), 156.
210 *Jane's All the World's Aircraft 1991–1992*, p. 145.
211 'Iraqis Show Off Improved Radar Plane,' *Daily Telegraph*, January 4, 1991.
212 *Jane's All the World's Aircraft 1991–1992*, p. 145. Mitchell, 'Who Owns Iraq's new AEW'.
213 *MEDNews*, May 8, 1989, 4; Kenneth R. Timmerman, 'Iraq: Tactical and Technical Implications for Tomorrow's History Book', *Military Technology* (July 1986), p. 135.
214 Norman Friedman, *Desert Victory*, pp. 148–54.
215 Norman Friedman, *Desert Victory*, p. 154.
216 Kenneth Timmerman, *The Death Lobby . . .*, p. 289; 'Iraq "Able to Expand Military Capability"', p. 9; 'Local Version of T-74 Tank Under Production,' Cairo *MENA* in Arabic, 0625 GMT, September 13, 1989, in *FBIS-NES* (September 13, 1989), 31.
217 'Industry Minister Discusses Military Production,' Cairo *Al-Akhbar* in Arabic, 7 May 1989, p. 7, in *FBIS-NESA* (May 9, 1989), 18–21.

218 'Iraq's Arsenal: the Weapons Facing the West,' p. 230.
219 Lt. Col. David Eshel (IDF, retired), 'Saddam Hussein's Spearhead – A Combat Assessment,' *Military Technology* (January 1991), 255. 'Iraq's Army: Hit Hard By The Blockade', *Newsweek,* 29 October 1990, 26; 'Iraq Tries to Offset U.S. Weapons With Low-Technology Strategies,' *New York Times*, November 25, 1990.
220 See *UNSCOM Report S23283*, p. 25; Michael Eisenstadt, 'Like A Phoenix ...,' pp. 94–5.
221 *MEDNews*, May 8, 1989, p.4.
222 Michael Eisenstadt, 'The Iraqi Armed Forces Two Years On.' *Jane's Intelligence Review* (March 1993), 121–7; 'Iraq "Able to Expand Military Capability",' p. 9.
223 Ian Kemp, 'Dr. Gerald Bull's Deadly Legacy,' p. 1009.
224 *MEDNews*, May 8, 1989, 4; Kevin Toolis, 'The Man Behind Iraq's Supergun', *New York Times Magazine,* August 26, 1990, 50; *Jane's Armour and Artillery 1992–1993*, pp. 572–3, 583–6.
225 George Graham, 'France Reaches Rescheduling Accord With Iraq For 2.4 Bn Pds Debt,' *Financial Times*, September 16, 1989.
226 *MEDNews*, May 8, 1989, 7; *Defense Electronics* (February 1989), p. 10.
227 *MEDNews*, May 8, 1989, 6.
228 'Iraq Negotiating to Buy French Mirage Fighter', *Reuters,* 27 Apr 1989, AM Cycle.
229 *MEDNews,* May 8, 1989, 6.
230 Michael Eisenstadt, 'Like a Phoenix ...,' p. 95.
231 Lawrence Freedman and Efraim Karsh, *The Gulf Conflict*, p. 39.
232 *Conduct of the Persian Gulf War*, p. 11.
233 *WMEAT 1991–1992*, p. 67.
234 *Conduct of the Persian Gulf War*, pp. 3–4; Kenneth Timmerman, *The Death Lobby* ..., p. 389.
235 Testimony of the Customs Service to the House Ways and Means Committee, 1991, cited in *Congressional Record,* August 10, 1992, H7876.
236 Steve R. Bowman, Richard F. Grimmett, Robert D. Shuey, and Zachary S. Davis, 'Weapons Proliferation and Conventional Arms Transfers: The Outlook in Mid-1992,' *CRS Report for Congress 92–994 ENR* (Washington, DC: Library of Congress, December 31, 1992), p. 35.
237 'AL-ITTAHAD on Military Industrialization,' Abu Dhabi *AL-ITTAHAD* in Arabic, November 18, 1988, p. 1 in *FBIS-NESA* (November 22, 1988), 21.
238 Intelligence report from July 1990, cited in *Congressional Record*, July 27, 1992, H6699.
239 Kenneth Timmerman, *The Death Lobby* ... ; Alan Friedman, *Spider's Web: The Secret History of How the White House Illegally Armed Iraq* (Bantam: New York, 1993).
240 *Congressional Record*, July 27, 1992, H6700.
241 *Congressional Record,* August 10, 1992, H7875–7876.
242 *Congressional Record,* September 25, 1992, H9504.
243 Kenneth Timmerman, *The Death Lobby* ..., p. 352.
244 See *WMEAT, 1991–1992*, p. 109.
245 *WMEAT 1991–1992*, p. 67.
246 Michael Eisenstadt, 'Like A Phoenix ...,' pp. 62–3, 89.
247 Kenneth Timmerman, *The Death Lobby* ..., p. 385.
248 'Missile Strike Against Iraq Mulled on Hill,' *Washington Times*, September 10, 1990.
249 'The Gulf War: Chemical Weapons Location Unknown,' *Financial Times*,

February 27, 1991, reports that '... all Iraq's factories making artillery and artillery munitions were now "non-operational" ...' according to London defense officials.
250 *Conduct of the Persian Gulf War*, p. 213.
251 This argument is developed further in Timothy D. Hoyt, 'Iraq's Military Industry: A Critical Strategic Target,' *National Security Studies Quarterly* IV, No. 2 (Spring 1998), 33–50.
252 *GWAPS* Volume I: 'Planning Report,' p. 118.
253 *GWAPS* Volume I: 'Planning,' pp. 146–7, 161.
254 'Development of this part of the air campaign plan revealed a philosophical difference between short-range military and long-range political objectives.' *GWAPS* Volume I: 'Planning,' p. 164.
255 *GWAPS* Volume II: 'Operations', p. 34.
256 *GWAPS* Volume II: 'Effects and Effectiveness', p. 10.
257 The *GWAPS* report emphasizes that analysis of attacks on Iraqi military support and industry are subsumed into the discussion of attacks on NBCW and missile production facilities. See *GWAPS* Vol. II: 'Effects and Effectiveness,' p. 273. This suggests the lower priority given to conventional military industrial infrastructure.
258 'Iraqi Factories,' *JDW*, November 3, 1990, 867; *Conduct of the Persian Gulf War* ..., p. 208; 'How Saddam is Picking Up the Pieces a Year After "Storm"', *JDW*, February 22, 1992, p. 284; 'Iraq "able to expand military capability",' p. 9; Michael Eisenstadt, 'Like a Phoenix ...,' pp. 62–5, 88–96.
259 'Testimony of Robert Gates before the House Armed Services Committee,' March 27, 1992. Gates specified that capability for limited production of artillery, munitions, and possibly armored vehicles had been restored by early 1992.
260 *MEDNews*, September 28, 1992, 3.
261 Michael Eisenstadt, 'Like a Phoenix ...,' p. 88.
262 'Iraq "able to expand military capability," p. 9.
263 Michael Eisenstadt, 'Like A Phoenix ...,' pp. 95–6.
264 Michael Eisenstadt, 'Like A Phoenix ...,' pp. 95–6; 'Iraq "able to expand military capability",' p. 9.
265 'Global Crossing, Iraqi Defenses, and The Chinese Connection,' *Newsmax.com,* March 25, 2003, www.newsmax.com;'Iraq Strengthens Air Force With French Parts,' *Washington Times*, March 7, 2003.
266 See www.cnn.com/TRANSCRIPTS/0310/01/ltm.18.html, for an interview with Eric Schmitt of the *New York Times* on October 1, 2003; 'Iraq Awash In Military Weapons', *Christian Science Monitor*, October 20, 2003.
267 'Iraqi Arms Caches Cited in Attacks,' *New York Times*, October 14, 2003.
268 'Iraq's Conventional Arms Supply Bigger Than U.S. Thought,' *Los Angeles Times*, October 17, 2003.
269 Richard Butler, *The Greatest Threat: Iraq, Weapons of Mass Destruction, and the Crisis of Global Security* (New York: PublicAffairs, 2000); Tim Trevan, *Saddam's Secrets: The Hunt for Iraq's Hidden Weapons* (London: Harper-Collins Publishers, 1999); and the idiosyncratic Scott Ritter, *Endgame: Solving the Iraq Problem – Once and For All* (New York: Simon & Schuster, 1999); Alfred B. Prados, *Iraqi Challenges and U.S. Military Responses: March 1991 through October 2002*, Report for Congress November 20, 2002, RL31641 (Washington, DC: Congressional Research Service).
270 See *Statement by David Kay on the Interim Progress Report on the Activities of the Iraq Survey Group (ISG) Before The House Permanent Select Committee on Intelligence, The House Committee on Appropriations, Subcommittee*

254   Notes

on *Defense, and the Senate Select Committee on Intelligence*, October 2, 2003 (available at the Central Intelligence Agency website, www.cia.gov/cia/public_affairs/speeches/2003/david_kay10022003.html).

271 According to David Kay, the quantities of WMD related material that remain at large could probably fit in a two-car garage. *Statement of David Kay*, p. 2.

272 Timothy V. McCarthy and Jonathan B. Tucker, 'Saddam's Toxic Arsenal,' p. 54.

273 Anthony H. Cordesman, 'Iraq and Weapons of Mass Destruction,' S. 5062.

274 See Kenneth Timmerman, *The Death Lobby* ..., pp. 252–7; 'German Intelligence Report re: Iraqi Activities in the area of nuclear technology and missile development date April 5, 1990' cited in *Congressional Record*, August 10, 1992, H7881.

275 Timothy V. McCarthy and Jonathan B. Tucker, 'Saddam's Toxic Arsenal,' p. 55; Avigdor Haselkorn, *The Continuing Storm: Iraq, Poisonous Weapons, and Deterrence* (New Haven: Yale University Press, 1999), pp. 72–3.

276 See 'President Orders Missile Code-Named "Al-Husayn".' Baghdad INA in English, 1225 GMT, 1 March 1988, in *FBIS-NESA* (2 March 1988), p. 25

277 The warhead was reduced from 800 kg to 190 kg. Seth Carus and Joseph S. Bermudez Jr., 'Iraq's Al-Husayn Missile Program: Part One,' in *Jane's Soviet Intelligence Review* (May 1990), 204–9.

278 Anthony H. Cordesman, 'Iraq and Weapons of Mass Destruction,' S. 5062. This may have been due to streamlined procedures and better training, rather than modifications to the missile or launcher.

279 'Forty Three Missiles on the Zionist Entity,' *Al-'Arab al-Yawm* (in Arabic) FBIS-NES-98-326, November 22, 1998, especially his entries for September 16–17, 1990. See also Timothy D. Hoyt, 'Revolution and Counter-Revolution: The Role of the Periphery in Technological and Conceptual Innovation,' in Emily O. Goldman and Leslie C. Eliason (eds), *The Diffusion of Military Technology and Ideas* (Stanford, CA: Stanford University Press, 2003), pp. 179–201.

280 *Duelfer Report*, Vol. 2, 'Delivery Systems,' p. 4; W. Seth Carus and Joseph Bermudez, Jr, 'Iraq's Al-Husayn .. Part One,' p. 205.

281 *MEDNews*, May 8, 1989, 7. 'This [the Al-Husayn] is clearly a case of a weapons program with significant local content.'

282 Timothy V. McCarthy and Jonathan B. Tucker, 'Saddam's Toxic Arsenal,' p. 55.

283 W. Seth Carus, 'Missiles in the Third World: The 1991 Gulf War,' *Orbis* 35 (Spring 1991), p. 253. German parts accounted for approximately 25 percent of Iraq's missile components: a larger portion than any other country except for Iraq.'German Firms Primed Iraq's War Machine,' *Washington Post*, July 23, 1992.

284 Kenneth M. Pollack, *The Threatening Storm*, p. 169.

285 *Conduct of the Persian Gulf War* ..., p. 16.

286 W. Seth Carus and Joseph Bermudez, Jr., 'Iraq's Al-Husayn Missile Program, Part 2,' *Jane's Soviet Intelligence Review* (June 1990), p. 242. Anthony H. Cordesman and Abraham R. Wagner, *The Lessons of Modern War*, Vol. 2, p. 366, use a figure of 203 missiles fired, based on data from Gary Sick.

287 Timothy V. McCarthy and Jonathan B. Tucker, 'Saddam's Toxic Arsenal,' p. 70.

288 *Conduct of the Persian Gulf War* ..., p. 226.

289 'New Missile With 900-km Range Launched 25 Apr,' Baghdad INA in Arabic, 1543 GMT, 25 April 1988 in *FBIS-NESA* (April 26, 1988), 24.

290 W. Seth Carus and Joseph Bermudez, Jr, 'Iraq's Al-Husayn Missile Program, Part 2,' p. 245.

291 Anthony H. Cordesman, 'Iraq and Weapons of Mass Destruction,' S. 5062. 'German Intelligence Report ...,' cited in *Congressional Record,* August 10, 1992, H7881, estimates the warhead at 400 kg.
292 *The Iraqi Army,* p. 9; *MEDNews,* May 8, 1989, 7.
293 Kenneth Timmerman, *The Death Lobby* ..., p. 290.
294 See *Military Technology,* (May 1991), 78.
295 W. Seth Carus and Joseph Bermudez, Jr, 'Iraq's Al-Husayn Missile Program, Part 2', p. 246. See also 'Satellite-carrier Rocket System Tested,' Baghdad Voice of the Masses in Arabic, 1136 GMT, December 7, 1989, in *FBIS-NESA* (December 8, 1989), 23, and '2,000-km Range Missiles Produced,' Baghdad Voice of the Masses in Arabic, 1230 GMT, 7 December 1989, in *FBIS-NESA* (8 December 1989), 23.
296 Duncan Lennox, 'Chemical Warfare: Extending the Range of Destruction', *JDW,* 25 August 1990, 267; Stephen J. Hedges and Brian Duffy, 'Iraqgate,' *U.S. News & World Report,* May 18, 1992, 42.
297 Pamela Pohling-Brown,'Sales Boom Expected,' *International Defense Review* (February 1993). p. 146; Ian Kemp, 'The Execution of Project Babylon,' p. 1010; James Adams, *Bull's Eye,* pp. 226–7.
298 Tamir Eshel, 'Iraqi Thrust Toward Strategic Weapons: A Mini-Superpower in Formation?,' p. 99.
299 'Countries in the Middle East Adding New Missiles to their Arsenals,' *Los Angeles Times,* December 24, 1989. According to other reports, the military version has a 1,680 mile range: see 'Ruthless Madman with a Nuclear Dream,' *Sunday Times,* April 15, 1990; 'Husayn Confers Names on Rocket, Missile Systems,' Baghdad INA in Arabic, 1125 GMT, December 9, 1989, in *FBIS-NESA* (December 12, 1989), 20.
300 Tamir Eshel, 'Iraqi Thrust Toward Strategic Weapons ...,' p. 99.
301 'Satellite Launch Planned', *JDW,* July 21, 1990, 74; 'Iraq Readies Satellite,' *Washington Post,* February 7, 1990; 'Government "Ready" To Launch Satellite,' Paris *Radio Monte Carlo* in Arabic, 1700 GMT, February 6, 1990, in *FBIS-NESA* (February 7, 1990), 22. The satellite program may also have had Brazilian assistance. 'Iraq Set to Launch First Spy Satellite,' *Insight,* December 18, 1989, 38.
302 'Saddam Claims to Have New Missile That Can Hit Israel,' *Washington Post,* October 10, 1990.
303 *Conduct of the Persian Gulf War* ..., p. 16; 'Saddam's "new" missile puzzles experts', *Financial Times,* October 10, 1990.
304 'Iraq: We Fired New Missile at Dimona', *Jerusalem Post,* February 18, 1991.
305 *GWAPS* Volume II: 'Effects and Effectiveness,' p. 319; Timothy V. McCarthy and Jonathan B. Tucker, 'Saddam's Toxic Arsenal,' p. 55.
306 *UNSCOM Report S/23165,* October 25, 1991, p. 31; Tim Ripley, 'Destroying Iraq's Ballistic Missiles,' p. 460.
307 'German Intelligence Report ...,' cited in *Congressional Record,* August 10, 1992, H7881; Duncan Lennox, 'Iraq's Short Range Surface-to-Surface Missiles,' p. 58.
308 William E. Burrows and Robert Windrem, *Critical Mass,* p. 471.
309 Kenneth Timmerman, *The Death Lobby* ..., pp. 150–4.
310 Gary Milhollin, 'Building Saddam Hussein's Bomb,' *New York Times Magazine,* March 6, 1992, p. 34; William E. Burrows and Robert Windrem, *Critical Mass,* pp. 467, 471; and Kenneth Timmerman, *The Death Lobby* ..., p. 153.
311 Andrew Slade, 'Condor Project in Disarray,' *JDW,* February 17, 1990, 295; 'Argentine Gives Missile Parts to U.S. for Disposal,' *New York Times,* 7

March 1993; Joseph S. Bermudez, Jr., 'Ballistic Missile Development in Egypt,' *Jane's Intelligence Review* (October 1992), 452–8.
312 W. Seth Carus and Joseph Bermudez, Jr, 'Iraq's Al-Husayn Missile Project, Part I', p. 204.
313 Gary Milhollin and David Dantzic, 'Must the U.S. Give Brazil and Iraq The Bomb?,' *New York Times* (Op-Ed), July 29, 1990; Alfred Manfredi, *et al.*, 'Ballistic Missile Proliferation Potential of Non-Major Military Powers: An Update,' *Congressional Research Report for Congress 87–654 SPR* (Washington, DC: Library of Congress, August 6, 1987), pp. 17–19, 25–32; 'Crisis in the Gulf: The Men Who Make Saddam Dangerous,' *Independent*, August 26, 1990.
314 Kenneth Timmerman, *The Death Lobby* ..., p. 248.
315 Gary Milhollin and David Dantzic, 'Must the US Give Brazil and Iraq The Bomb?,' 'Brazil Rebuffs Critics of Missile Aid to Iraq,' *Insight*, September 10, 1990, 40; 'Brazilians Probe Links With Iraq,' *JDW*, May 26, 1990, 989; 'Crisis in the Gulf ..., *Independent*, August 26, 1990. Scott D. Tollefson, *Brazilian Arms Transfers*..., pp. 335–43.
316 *UNSCOM Report S/23122*, October 8, 1991, 3–4. See also *UNSCOM Report S/23165*, October 25, 1991, pp. 5, 23 for linkage of SSM and nuclear research.
317 Michael Eisenstadt, 'Like a Phoenix ...', pp. 35–6.
318 Statement by Rep. Dante Fascell of Florida, *Congressional Record*, October 2, 1992, Extension of Remarks, E2884. Note that this production, detected by UNSCOM officials, was taking place 18 months after the Gulf War.
319 W. Seth Carus, 'Cruise Missile Proliferation ...,' p. 10; 'U.N. Team Sets Daily Inspections at Iraqi Missile Research Center,' *Washington Post*, January 27, 1993.
320 W. Seth Carus, 'Cruise Missile Proliferation ...,' p. 82.
321 *Conduct of the Persian Gulf War* .., p. 259; 'Stockholm Institute Publishes Arms Supplier List,' Vienna *Wochenpresse* in German, February 7, 1991, 43 in *FBIS-NESA* (February 7, 1991), 14.
322 See 'Drone' Exhibited,' Manama *WAKH* in Arabic, 2057 GMT, October 3, 1988, in *FBIS-NESA* (October 4, 1988), p. 18; 'Military Displays Locally-Made Missiles, Drones', Manama *WAKH* in Arabic, 1730 GMT, 5 October 1988 in *FBIS-NESA* (October 6, 1988), 31.
323 Norman Friedman, *Desert Victory*, pp. 109–10; Yezid Sayigh, *Arab Military Industry*, p. 119.
324 W. Seth Carus, 'Cruise Missile Proliferation ...,' p. 37.
325 *Jane's Armor and Artillery 1992–1993*, pp. 760–1.
326 W. Seth Carus, 'Cruise Missile Proliferation ...,' pp. 40, 129–30.
327 'Iraqi Missile Plan Linked to British Firms,' *Independent*, November 4, 1990; Alan George, 'UK foils Iraqi cruise missile,' *Flight International*, October 2, 1990, p. 4.
328 'A Poor Man's Air Force,' *New York Times*, June 19, 2003. *Duelfer Report*, Vol. 2, 'Delivery Systems,' pp. 37–41 details Iraqi plans to increase the Seersucker's range to 1,000 km.
329 *Iraq's Weapons of Mass Destruction: The Assessment of the British Government* (September 2002), p. 11 (hereafter *Iraq's Weapons of Mass Destruction*).
330 Avigdor Haselkorn, *The Continuing Storm*, p. 161.
331 Avigdor Haselkorn, *The Continuing Storm*, p. 31.
332 *Iraq's Weapons of Mass Destruction Programs* (Central Intelligence Agency, October 2002), p. 22 (hereafter *Iraq's Weapons of Mass Destruction Programs*).

333 Andrew Feickert, *Iraq's Weapons of Mass Destruction (WMD) Capable Missiles and Unmanned Aerial Vehicles (UAVs)* CRS Report for Congress (Congressional Research Service, March 25, 2003), p. 4.
334 See 'Key Judgments: Iraq's Continuing Programs for Weapons of Mass Destruction', available at www.fas.org/irp/cia/product/Iraq-wmd.html.
335 'Air Force Assessment Before War Said Iraqi Drones Were Minor Threat', *Baltimore Sun*, August 25, 2003; 'Air Force Doubts Drone Threat,' *Wall Street Journal*, September 10, 2003; 'Air Force Analysts Feel Vindicated On Iraqi Drones,' *Washington Post*, September 26, 2003.
336 *Statement by David Kay*, p. 8.
337 'U.N. Team Sets Daily Inspections at Iraqi Missile Research Center,' *Washington Post*, January 27, 1993; Tim Ripley, 'Destroying Iraq's Ballistic Missiles,' *Jane's Intelligence Review* (October 1992), 459–62.
338 Cited in 'For the Record' (Op-Ed), *Washington Post*, July 28, 1992.
339 'UN Team Sets Daily Inspections at Iraqi Missile Research Center,' *Washington Post*, January 27, 1993.
340 'Iraq Buying Missile Parts Covertly,' *Washington Post*, October 14, 1995; 'Jordan Seizes Missile Parts Meant for Shipment to Iraq,' *Washington Post*, December 8, 1995; 'UN Is Said To Find Russian Markings on Iraq-Bound Military Equipment,' *Washington Post*, December 15, 1995.
341 *Iraq's Weapons of Mass Destruction Programs*, p. 22.
342 'News Brief,' *Christian Science Monitor*, September 22, 1995, 2; 'Crash Nuclear Program by Iraq Is Disclosed,' *New York Times*, August 26, 1995.
343 'Iraqis Fooled Weapons Monitors,' *Washington Times*, August 23, 1995. The IAEA declared in 1994 that Iraq had 'come clean' on its nuclear program: admissions after Hussein Kamil's defection indicated that there was much the IAEA did not know about Iraqi nuclear programs.
344 Andrew Feickert, *Iraq: Weapons of Mass Destruction* .., p. 1.
345 *Iraq's Weapons of Mass Destruction*, p. 40.
346 S/1999/99 UNSCOM Report on The Status of Disarmament and Monitoring, January 29, 1999, cited in Andrew Feickert, *Iraq: Weapons of Mass Destruction* .., p. 3.
347 *Iraq's Weapons of Mass Destruction*, pp. 27, 29–30.
348 *Iraq's Weapons of Mass Destruction*, p. 30.
349 *Unclassified Report to Congress on the Acquisition of Technology Relating to Weapons of Mass Destruction and Advanced Conventional Munitions,1 January Through 30 June 2002*, p. 5, available at www.cia.gov/cia/reports/721_reports/jan_jun2002.html.
350 *Iraq's Weapons of Mass Destruction Programs*, p. 2.
351 *Statement by David Kay*, pp. 3, 8; *Duelfer Report*, Vol. 2, 'Delivery Systems,' p. 1 states that the Iraq Survey Group found no evidence Iraq had retained SCUD-type missiles after 1991.
352 *Statement by David Kay*, p. 7.
353 'Baghdad Records Show Hussein Sought Missiles, Other Aid Abroad,' *Wall Street Journal*, November 3, 2003. See also 'For The Iraqis, A Missile Deal That Went Sour,' *New York Times*, 1 December 2003.
354 *Iraq's Weapons of Mass Destruction*, p. 27.
355 *Unclassified Report to Congress on the Acquisition of Technology Relating to Weapons of Mass Destruction and Advanced Conventional Munitions, 1 July Through 31 December 2001*, p. 4 (available at www.cia.gov/cia/reports/721_reports/july_dec2001.html).
356 *Unclassified Report to Congress on the Acquisition of Technology Relating to*

Weapons of Mass Destruction and Advanced Conventional Munitions, 1 July Through 31 December 2001, p. 4.
357 'Banned Missile Might Well Be Used In A War,' Los Angeles Times, February 25, 2003.
358 'Blix Gets Aid on Iraqi Missile Issue,' Washington Post, February 4, 2003.
359 'Experts Confirm New Iraq Missile Breaks U.N. Limit,' New York Times, February 14, 2003.
360 'U.N. Weighs Blix's Plan to Test Iraq's Compliance,' Wall Street Journal, February 20, 2003.
361 Statement by David Kay, p. 7.
362 Iraq's Weapons of Mass Destruction, p. 6.
363 'Blix Gets Aid on Iraqi Missile Issue,' Washington Post, February 4, 2003; Statement by David Kay, pp. 8–9.
364 'Panel: Iraq Broke Limit On Missiles,' Washington Post, February 13, 2003.
365 Statement by David Kay, p. 9.
366 Unclassified Report to Congress on the Acquisition of Technology Relating to Weapons of Mass Destruction and Advanced Conventional Munitions, 1 July Through 31 December 2001, p. 4; Duelfer Report, Vol. 2, 'Delivery Systems,' p. 2 reports that Iraq was receiving design assistance from Russia for the Al-Sammoud II missile, and technology from several Eastern European states.
367 'A Poor Man's Air Force,' New York Times, June 19, 2003.
368 Kenneth M. Pollack, The Threatening Storm, p. 170.
369 Tabun is roughly four times as deadly as mustard. Avigdor Haselkorn, The Continuing Storm, p. 20.
370 Iraq's Weapons of Mass Destruction Programs, p. 8. Avigdor Haselkorn, The Continuing Storm, p. 27.
371 Timothy V. McCarthy and Jonathan B. Tucker, 'Saddam's Toxic Arsenal,' p. 64.
372 Timothy V. McCarthy and Jonathan B. Tucker, 'Saddam's Toxic Arsenal;' Timothy D. Hoyt, 'Revolution and Counterrevolution,' pp. 189–92; The Iraqi Army: Organization and Tactics, pp. 161–9.
373 UN Press Release IK/27, June 24, 1991, p. 2.
374 'Iraqi Nerve Gas Tests Confirmed', Washington Post, June 25, 1998. 'Tests Show Nerve Gas in Iraqi Warheads,' Washington Post, June 23, 1998.
375 UNSCOM S/23165, pp. 5, 27; Kenneth Timmerman, The Death Lobby ..., p. 233.
376 Kenneth Timmerman, The Death Lobby ..., pp. 51–2.
377 See Mike Eisenstadt, 'Sword of the Arabs ...,' p. 5; Michael Eisenstadt, 'Like A Phoenix ...,' p. 30; William E. Burrows and Robert Windrem, Critical Mass, p. 46; Anthony H. Cordesman, 'Iraq and Weapons of Mass Destruction,' S5066; Iraq's Weapons of Mass Destruction, p. 11, which estimates capacity of at least 4,000 tons per annum.
378 Mike Eisenstadt, 'The Sword of the Arabs ...,' p. 7.
379 'Iraq Chemical Arms Condemned, But West Once Looked The Other Way,' New York Times, February 13, 2003. Both US firms are now defunct.
380 Anthony H. Cordesman, 'Iraq and Weapons of Mass Destruction,' S5062.
381 Terry Gander, 'Iraq: The Chemical Arsenal,' Jane's Intelligence Review (September 1992), p. 414.
382 'Iraq Weapons Deadline Expires Without Action,' Washington Post, July 26, 1991.
383 Terry Gander, 'Iraq: The Chemical Arsenal,' p. 414; 'Iraq's Chemical Weapons Found To Be Potent,' Christian Science Monitor, January 23, 1992; UN Press Release IK/68, October 24, 1991, p. 1.

384 'Seventh Report of the Executive Chairman of UNSCOM', UNSC Document S/1994/750, June 24, 1994.
385 *Iraq's Weapons of Mass Destruction*, p. 13.
386 Timothy V. McCarthy and Jonathan B. Tucker,'Saddam's Toxic Arsenal,' p. 70.
387 'Iraqi Complex Dismantled,' *Washington Post*, June 15, 1994,
388 *Iraq's Weapons of Mass Destruction*, p. 40.
389 Sharon A. Squassoni, *Iraq: UN Inspections for Weapons of Mass Destruction* Report for Congress (Washington, DC: Congressional Research Service, 28 March 2003), p. 4.
390 *Iraq's Weapons of Mass Destruction*, p. 16.
391 *Iraq's Weapons of Mass Destruction*, p. 22; Sharon A. Squassoni, *Iraq: UN Inspections*, p. 4.
392 *Unclassified Report to Congress on the Acquisition of Technology Relating to Weapons of Mass Destruction and Advanced Conventional Munitions, 1 January through 30 June 2002*, p. 6, available at www.cia/gov/cia/reports/721_reports/jan_jun2002.html; *Iraq's Weapons of Mass Destruction Programs*, p. 10.
393 *Iraq's Weapons of Mass Destruction Programs*, p. 10.
394 'Hussein Was Sure Of Own Survival,' *Washington Post*, November 3, 2003.
395 *Statement by David Kay*, p. 6.
396 *Statement by David Kay*, p. 5. See also 'The Media Ignored the Real WMD News,' *Boston Globe*, November 9, 2003; 'Baghdad Records Show Hussein Sought Missiles, Other Aid Abroad,' *Wall Street Journal*, 3 November 2003.
397 Sharon A. Squassoni, *Iraq: UN Inspections*, p. 8; Kenneth M. Pollack, *The Threatening Storm*, pp. 176, 259; *Duelfer Report, Vol. 3*, 'Biological,' pp. 5–6.
398 'Text of 14 August 1991: Press Briefing by Officials of UN Inspection Team on First Visit to Iraq's Biological Weapons Facilities,' 1–2; IK/46 UNSCOM press release accompanying briefing; 'UN Panel Describes Iraq's Anthrax Threat,' *Washington Post*, August 15, 1991.
399 *Iraq's Weapons of Mass Destruction Programs*, 15, lists 14 separate open air tests that Baghdad has admitted.
400 Tim Trevan, *Saddam's Secrets: The Hunt for Iraq's Hidden Weapons* (London: HarperCollins, 1999); 'Iraq Had Program For Germ Warfare,' *Washington Post*, July 6, 1995; 'Iraq Admits It Produced Germ Arsenal', *New York Times*, July 6, 1995; *Iraq's Weapons of Mass Destruction Programs*, p. 15.
401 The 40 crates of documents 'discovered' shortly after Kamel's defection contained over 600,000 pages of documents – but had clearly been vetted and sanitized before release to UNSCOM. Tim Trevan, *Saddam's Secrets*, pp. 331–2.
402 *Iraq's Weapons of Mass Destruction*, p. 40; *Duelfer Report, Vol. 3*, 'Biological,' p. 1 states that the destruction of Al-Hakam effectively ended Iraq's BW program.
403 Tim Trevan, *Saddam's Secrets*, pp. 326–7.
404 Tim Trevan, *Saddam's Secrets*, pp. 331, 342.
405 'Iraq's Dirty Secrets,' *U.S. News and World Report*, September 11, 1995, pp. 41–3; '2 Monitoring Groups Accuse Iraq Of Withholding Data on Weapons,' *Washington Post*, October 12, 1995; 'Plagues in the Making,' *Newsweek*, October 9, 1995: pp. 50–1; 'Iraq Admits Working on Biological Weapons Systems,' *Washington Post*, August 19, 1995; 'U.N. Envoy Details Iraq's Admission of Germ Arsenal,' *Washington Times*, August 24, 1995.

406 Tim Trevan, *Saddam's Secrets*, p. 342.
407 Kenneth M. Pollack, *The Threatening Storm*, p. 172.
408 *Iraq's Weapons of Mass Destruction*, p. 16.
409 *Iraq's Weapons of Mass Destruction*, p. 24.
410 *Iraq's Weapons of Mass Destruction Programs*, p. 17.
411 'Iraqi Scientists Recount Effort To Make Weapon Out Of Ricin,' *Wall Street Journal*, July 18, 2003.
412 *Iraq's Weapons of Mass Destruction Programs*, p. 16.
413 This possiblity is discussed in *Iraq's Weapons of Mass Destruction Programs*, p. 17. The text of Secretary Powell's address is available at www.un.int/usa/03print_clp0205.htm. It refers to as many as seven mobile BW labs using as many as 18 trucks.
414 See 'Key Judgments..' for the October 2002 NIE's estimate that 'chances are even' that Iraq had weaponized smallpox. No evidence of smallpox weaponization has been identified. 'No Smallpox Found in Iraq Hunt,' *Philadelphia Inquirer*, September 19, 2003. The other claims were made by government officials after Operation Iraqi Freedom. See 'White House Begins New Effort To Build Iraq Support,' *Washington Post*, October 9, 2003.
415 *Statement by David Kay*, pp. 4–5.
416 William E. Burrows and Robert Windrem, *Critical Mass*, p. 41.
417 Warren H. Donnelly, *Iraq and Nuclear Weapons*, Congressional Research Issue Brief, December 21, 1990, p. 10 cited in Lawrence Freedman and Efraim Karsh, *The Gulf Conflict*, p. 220.
418 David Kay, 'Bomb Shelter,' *The New Republic*, March 15, 1993, 11–13; 'Countering Iraqi Weapons of Mass Destruction: The Gulf Crisis and Beyond,' cited in *Congressional Record*, September 30, 1992, S15748; 'Iraq Is Said To Have Hidden Nuclear Records From UN,' *New York Times*, October 14, 1991; Michael Eisenstadt, 'Like a Phoenix ...,' p. 19. A more recent report states that the nuclear program cost $18 billion over a 19-year period. Shyam Bhatia and Daniel McGrory, *Brighter Than The Baghdad Sun: Saddam Hussein's Nuclear Threat to the United States* (Washington, DC: Regnery Publishing, 2000), pp. 38, 307.
419 Michael Eisenstadt, 'Like a Phoenix ...,' p. 19; William E. Burrows and Robert Windrem, *Critical Mass*, p. 59; remarks of Director of Central Intelligence Robert M. Gates to the Comstock Club as reported in 'Gates Warns of Iraqi Nuclear Aspirations,' *Washington Post*, December 16, 1992; 'Saddam's Nuclear Weapons Dream: A Lingering Nightmare,' *Washington Post* October 3, 1991.
420 *UNSCOM Report S/23215*, November 14, 1991, p. 19.
421 Gary Milhollin, 'The Iraqi Bomb,' p. 50.
422 'Iraq Trying to Make Plutonium, Too, UN Aide Says,' *New York Times*, February 13, 1992.
423 *UNSCOM Report S/23165*, p. 5.
424 Khidhir Hamza (with Jeff Stein), *Saddam's Bombmaker: The Terrifying Inside Story of the Iraqi Nuclear and Biological Weapons Agenda* (New York: Scribner, 2000), pp. 94–105.
425 Shyam Bhatia and Daniel McGrory, *Brighter Than The Baghdad Sun*, pp. 9–10, 37–41. Khidir Hamza, *Saddam's Bombmaker*, p. 334. The program would have relied on constructing a 50-centrifuge cascade and enriching IAEA-safeguarded fuel at Tuwaitha. *Duelfer Report, Vol. 2*, 'Nuclear,' p.4.
426 Khidir Hamza, *Saddam's Bombmaker*, pp. 239–40; Shyam Bhatia and Daniel McGrory, *Brighter Than The Baghdad Sun*, p. 317; Kenneth M. Pollack, *The Threatening Storm*, p. 173.

427 Khidir Hamza, *Saddam's Bombmaker*, p. 334.
428 Shyam Bhatia and Daniel McGrory, *Brighter Than The Baghdad Sun*, p. 152.
429 William E. Burrows and Robert Windrem, *Critical Mass*, p. 59.
430 Shyam Bhatia and Daniel McGrory, *Brighter Than The Baghdad Sun*, p. 317. This report further states that by 1999, a second design existed.
431 Leonard S. Spector, *Nuclear Ambitions*, pp. 71, 150.
432 The 20 kg figure is a compromise between the 15–25 kg (33–55 lb) cited in Leonard S. Spector, *Nuclear Ambitions*, p. 154. Other reports not that Iraq's warhead designs were far too large for available missiles. Shyam Bhatia and Daniel McGrory, *Brighter Than The Baghdad Sun*, p. 317; Khidir Hamza *Saddam's Bombmaker*, pp. 239–40. Iraq was offered a more efficient nuclear design by A. Q. Khan in 1990. See Gaurav Kampani, *Proliferation Unbound: Nuclear Tales from Pakistan* (February 23, 2004), at cns.miis.edu/pubs/week/040223.htm.
433 S/22986, August 28, 1991, p. 3. The UNSCOM team believed this was the approximate capacity of the Tarmiya complex in the short term. The Ash Sharqat complex, a twin to Tarmiya, was approximately 85 percent complete, but destroyed in 1991.
434 UNSCOM inspectors felt the Tarmiya plant would be operational with 90–120 EMIS units in 6–18 months. S/22788, July 15, 1991, pp. 11–12.
435 S/23165, October 25, 1991, p. 22.
436 S/23215, November 14, 1991, p. 49.
437 Gary Milhollin, 'Building Saddam Hussein's Bomb,' *New York Times Magazine*, March 6, 1992, 34; William E. Burrows and Robert Windrem, *Critical Mass*, 59.
438 Gary Milhollin, 'A Mideast Dilemma: What Is Saddam Hussein's Nuclear Timetable?,' Washington Post (Op-Ed), November 25, 1990, estimates that 1,000 centrifuges produce about one bomb's worth of HEU annually. Recent discoveries from the A. Q. Khan network suggest that inefficient P-1 centrifuges could create 0.5–1.0 bombs per 1,000 centrifuges per year, and more efficient P-2 versions could create 0.75–1.5 weapons per 1,000 centrifuges per year. See Gaurav Kampani, *Proliferation Unbound*...
439 Gary Milhollin, 'A Mideast Dilemma...'
440 Diana Edensword and Gary Milhollin, 'Iraq's Bomb – an Update,' *New York Times* (Op-Ed), April 26, 1993.
441 Iraq planned to produce 220 pounds of lithium-6 annually. S/23615, p. 23; S/23215, p. 10; 'U.N. Says Iraq Was Building H-Bomb and Bigger A-Bomb,' *New York Times*, October 15, 1991. As of 1989, Israel had produced approximately 375 lb of lithium-6, which according to one analyst was sufficient to build 35 boosted-fission weapons of approximately 100 kt yield. Frank Barnaby, *The Invisible Bomb* (London: I.B. Taurus, 1989), p. 25.
442 See *Iraq's Weapons of Mass Destruction*; *Iraq's Weapons of Mass Destruction Programs*; 'Key Findings...'; and Kenneth M. Pollack, *The Threatening Storm*, pp. 173–5.
443 Khidir Hamza, *Saddam's Bombmaker*, p. 334; Shyam Bhatia and Daniel McGrory, *Brighter Than The Baghdad Sun*, pp. 289, 303–20.
444 *Iraq's Weapons of Mass Destruction Programs*, p. 1.
445 'Key Judgments...'
446 These tubes were specifically mentioned by Secretary of State Powell in his February 5, 2003 address to the United Nations. 'US Claim On Iraqi Nuclear Program Is Called Into Question,' *Washington Post*, January 24, 2003; 'Depiction of Threat Outgrew Supporting Evidence,' *Washington Post*, August 10, 2003.

447 'Weapons Inspectors: Iraqi Nuke Program Was In Disarray,' *USA Today* September 9, 2003.
448 *Statement by David Kay*, pp. 6–7.
449 'Scientist: Nuke Program Wasn't Restarted,' *USA Today*, July 18, 2003.
450 'Iraqi Says Hussein Planned To Revive The Nuclear Program Dismantled in 1991,' *New York Times*, June 27, 2003.
451 *Duelfer Report*, Vol. 2, 'Nuclear,' p. 6.
452 Examples of these kinds of critique include 'Where Are Iraq's WMDs?,' *Newsweek*, June 9, 2003; 'Hunt For Iraqi Arms Erodes Assumptions,' *Washington Post*, April 22, 2003; 'US To Step Up Its Search For Banned Arms,' *Los Angeles Times*, April 20, 2003.
453 See, for example, Kenneth Katzman, *Iraq: Weapons Programs, UN Requirements, and US Policy* CRS Issue Brief For Congress (Washington, DC: Congressional Research Service, September 2, 2003).
454 'Analysis of Iraqi Weapons "Wrong",' *Los Angeles Times*, May 31, 2003.
455 This argument, or at least the argument that intelligence interpretation was severely politicized, can be found in 'Straw, Powell had Serious Doubts over their Iraqi Weapons Claims,' *Guardian*, May 31, 2003.
456 'A Chronicle of Confusion In The Hunt For Hussein's Weapons,' *New York Times*, July 20, 2003. To be fair to US forces, hunting for WMD in an area the size of France while consolidating control over a conquered country and then fighting a determined insurgency is an extraordinarily difficult task. James Fallows, 'Blind Into Baghdad,' *The Atlantic Monthly* (January/February 2004) at www.theatlantic.com/issues/2004/01/fallows.htm
457 This point is well-documented in *Statement by David Kay*.
458 Ibrahim al-Marashi, 'How Iraq Conceals And Obtains Its Weapons of Mass Destruction,' *Middle East Review of International Affairs* Vol. 7, No. 1 (March 2003), available at meria.idc.ac.il/journal/2003/issue1/jv7n1a5.html.
459 'U.S. Suspects It Received False Iraq Tips,' *Los Angeles Times*, August 28, 2003.
460 Charles Duelfer, former deputy chairman of UNSCOM, makes this argument in 'No Weapons Doesn't Mean No Threat,' *Washington Post*, October 6, 2003. See also *Duelfer Report*, Vol. 1, 'Regime Strategic Intent – Key Findings,' p. 1.
461 'Blix Downgrades Prewar Assessment of Iraqi Weapons,' *Washington Post*, June 22, 2003; Kenneth M. Pollack, 'Spies, Lies, and Weapons: What Went Wrong?' *The Atlantic Monthly* (January/February 2004) at www.theatlantic.com/issues/2004/01/pollack.htm; 'Regime's Priority Was Blueprints, Not Arsenal, Defector Told UN,' *Los Angeles Times*, April 26, 2003.
462 *Duelfer Report*, Vol. 3, 'Addendum – Iraq's Military Industrial Capability – Evolution of the Military Industrialization Commission.'
463 Yezid Sayigh, *Arab Military Industry*, p. 124.
464 Yezid Sayigh, *Arab Military Industry*, p. 127.
465 Shahram Chubin and Charles Tripp, *Iran and Iraq at War* (Boulder, CO: Westview, 1988), p. 8. See also Pollack's extensive and critical analysis of Iraqi military capabilities in *Arabs at War*.
466 Statement of Senator McCain, *Congressional Record*, January 28, 1994, S346. These figures, particularly for industry, are nearly twice those used by Kenneth Timmerman in *The Death Lobby* ...
467 Retired Major General Amos Yaron, Director General of Israel's Ministry of defense, quoted in 'Rebuilding Iraq's Military,' *Defense News*, June 2, 2003. The author was personally interviewed by reporters on this subject on at least two occasions in April and May, 2003.

468 'US "All Wrong" on Weapons: Report on Iraq Contradicts Bush Administration Claims,' *Washington Post*, October 7, 2004.

5 Regional powers, security, and arms production

1 See Timothy D. Hoyt, 'Revolution and Counter-Revolution: The Role of the Periphery in Technological and Conceptual Innovation,' in Emily O. Goldman and Leslie C. Eliason (eds), *The Diffusion of Military Technology and Ideas* (Stanford, CA: Stanford University Press, 2003), pp. 179–201.
2 See Michael D. Ward, et al., 'Economic Growth, Investment, and Military Spending in India, 1950–1988,' in Steve Chan and Alex Mintz (eds), *Defense, Welfare, and Growth* (New York: Routledge, 1992), pp. 119–36.
3 *The Iraqi Army: Organization and Tactics*, National Training Center Handbook 100–91 (Fort Irwin, CA: National Training Center, January 3, 1991), p. 14; *Gulf War Air Power Survey* Volume II: 'Operations' (Washington, DC: Pentagon, 1993), pp. 33 (n. 62), 75–7.
4 See Michael Brzoska and Thomas Ohlson, 'Arms Production in the Third World: an Overview,' in Michael Brzoska and Thomas Ohlson (eds), *Arms Production in the Third World* (New York: Taylor & Francis for SIPRI, 1986), Table 2.3, pp. 16–17.
5 Ian Anthony, 'The "Third Tier" Countries: Production of Major Weapons,' in Herbert Wulf (ed.), *Arms Industry Limited* (Oxford: Oxford University Press, 1993), p. 377, points out that among the major LDC producers, large calibre artillery (100 mm and up) has been one of the items most easily produced.
6 Guy Hartcup, *The Silent Revolution: Development of Conventional Weapons, 1945–1985* (London: Brassey's, 1993), p. 156.
7 Edward Luttwak and Stuart Koehl, *The Dictionary of Modern War* (New York: HarperCollins Publishers, 1991), p. 51.
8 Michael T. Klare, 'War in the 1990s: Growing Firepower in the Third World.' *Bulletin of the Atomic Scientists* 46 (1990), pp. 4, 9–13
9 Anthony H. Cordesman and Abraham R. Wagner, *The Lessons of Modern War, Volume II: The Iran–Iraq War*, (Boulder, CO: Westview Press, 1990), p. 452.
10 Martin Van Creveld, *Command in War* (Cambridge, MA: Harvard University Press, 1985), pp. 184–5; Major General Julian Thompson, *The Lifeblood of War: Logistics in Armed Conflict* (London: Brassey's, 1991), p. 38.
11 Stephanie G. Neuman, *Military Assistance in Recent Wars: The Dominance of the Superpowers*, (New York: Praeger Press with CSIS-Georgetown University, 1986), p. 69.
12 Stephanie G. Neuman, 'Arms and Superpower Influence: Lessons From Recent Wars,' *Orbis* 30 (Winter 1987), pp. 712–13.
13 Anthony H. Cordesman and Abraham R. Wagner, *Lessons of Modern War Volume I: The Arab-Israeli Conflicts*, p. 118; and Chaim Herzog, *The Arab-Israeli Wars*, (New York: Vintage Books, 1984), p. 344.
14 Stephanie G. Neuman, 'Third World Military Industries: Capabilities and Constraints in Recent Wars,' in Stephanie G. Neuman and Robert E. Harkavy (eds), *The Lessons of Recent Wars in the Third World*, Vol. 2 (Lexington, MA: D. C. Heath 1987), p. 164.
15 *Conduct of the Persian Gulf War: Final Report to Congress*, Pursuant to Title V of The Persian Gulf Conflict Supplemental Authorization and Personnel Benefits Act of 1991 (Public Law 102–25), (Washington, DC: Pentagon, April 1992), F-55.

16 Ethan B. Kapstein, *The Political Economy of National Security: A Global Perspective* (New York: McGraw-Hill, 1992), p. 68.
17 *Conduct of the Persian Gulf War* .., F-55. The US did attempt to surge production of other items, including air-launched smart munitions, electronics, machine guns, tank ammunition, and missiles. See 'Pentagon Speeds Development, Production of Arms for Gulf Use,' *Washington Post*, December 29, 1990; 'Missile Output Reaches War Rate,' *Defense News*, September 10, 1990.
18 *Conduct of the Persian Gulf War* ..., F-59.
19 Ariel Sharon, *Warrior: An Autobiography* with David Chanoff (London: Macdonald & Co., 1989), p. 344.
20 Richard A. Gabriel, 'Lessons of War: The IDF in Lebanon,' in *Military Review* 64, no. 8 (August 1984), 45.
21 Wolfgang Flume, 'On the Cheap', *Military Technology* (February 1987), 98; *The Middle East Military Balance 1986* (Jerusalem: Jerusalem Post for the Jaffee Center for Strategic Studies, 1987), p. 264.
22 *GWAPS* Vol. I, 'Planning Report,' pp. 73–4; *GWAPS* Vol. II, 'Effects and Effectiveness,' p. 194.
23 See www.cnn.com/TRANSCRIPTS/0310/01/ltm.18.html, for an interview with Eric Schmitt of the *New York Times* on October 1, 2003; 'Iraq Awash In Military Weapons,' *Christian Science Monitor,* October 20, 2003; 'Iraq's Conventional Arms Supply Bigger Than US Thought,' *Los Angeles Times*, October 17, 2003; 'Iraqi Arms Caches Cited in Attacks,' *New York Times,* October 14, 2003.
24 See *Conduct of the Persian Gulf War* ..., F-55.
25 Christopher S. Parker, 'New Weapons for Old Problems: Conventional Proliferation and Military Effectiveness in Developing States,' in *International Security*, 23:4 (Spring 1999), 119–47.
26 Robert E. Harkavy, 'Arms Resupply *During* Conflict: A Framework for Analysis,' in Christian Schmidt (ed.), *The Economics of Military Expenditures* (New York: St. Martin's, 1987), pp. 248–9; Michael Brzoska and Frederic S. Pearson, *Arms and Warfare: Escalation, De-escalation, and Negotiation* (Columbia, SC: University of South Carolina Press, 1994).
27 Major General Julian Thompson, *The Lifeblood of War* .., p. 306.
28 *GWAPS* Volume I, 'Planning Report,' pp. 78–9.
29 Ralph Sanders, *Arms Industries: New Suppliers and Regional Security*, (Washington, DC: National Defense University, 1990), p. 43; Amit Gupta, 'Third World Military Industries: New Suppliers, Deadlier Weapons,' *Orbis* 37 (Winter 1993), 57–68.
30 David Isby, 'The International Market for Combat Aircraft,' *Military Technology* (September 1992), p. 12.
31 *SIPRI Yearbook 1991,* p. 227.
32 Archer Jones, *The Art of War in the Western World* (Urbana and Chicago, IL: University of Illinois Press, 1987), p. 548.
33 *SIPRI Yearbook 1993*, p. 456.
34 See Sanders, *Arms Industries* ..., pp. 67–75.
35 Andrew J Pierre (ed.), *Cascade of Arms: Managing Conventional Weapons Proliferation* (Washington, DC: Brookings Institution Press and World Peace Foundation, 1997).
36 Jacques Ganzler, *Affording Defense* (Cambridge, MA: MIT Press, 1989), p. 215. See also Stephen Martin (ed.), *The Economics of Offsets: Defence Procurement and Countertrade* (Amsterdam: Harwood Academic Publishers, 1996).
37 David Mussington, *Arms Unbound: The Globalization of Defense Production*

(Washington, DC: Brassey's, 1994); Richard A. Bitzinger, *The Globalization of Arms Production: Defense Markets in Transition* (Washington, DC: Defense Budget Project, 1993); Richard Bitzinger *Towards a Brave New Arms Industry? The Decline of the Second-Tier Arms-Producing Countries and the Emerging International Division of Labour in the Defence Industry* Adelphi Paper #356 (Oxford: Oxford University Press, 2003).

38 Iraq, for example, produced several types of mines, and had stocks estimated at 10 million in 1990. *The Iraqi Army: Organization and Tactics*, p. 154.
39 One example is the Soviet PT-76 amphibious light tank, designed for combat in the European theater. Used by Indian forces in the Bangladesh campaign in 1971, it proved completely inadequate: the fast current and wide rivers in the subcontinent caused the tank's engine to overheat after 30 minutes, and the tanks eventually had to be towed across the river. Major General Julian Thompson, *The Lifeblood of War..*, p. 243.
40 *Discriminate Deterrence: Report of The Commission On Integrated Long-Term Strategy* (Washington, DC: Government Printing Office, January 1988), p. 20.
41 Ze'ev Bonen, 'The Technological Arms Race,' in Zvi Lanir (ed.), *Israeli Security Planning in the 1980s: Its Politics and Economics* (New York: Praeger, 1984), pp. 108–27.
42 Timothy D. Hoyt, 'Revolution and Counter-Revolution: The Role of the Periphery in Technological and Conceptual Innovation,' for a more extensive discussion of military innovation in the developing world.
43 *The Future Security Environment*, Report of the Future Security Environment Working Group, submitted to the Commission on Integrated Long-Term Strategy (Washington, DC: The Pentagon, October 1988), p. 27.
44 Keith Krause, *Arms and the State: Patterns of Military Production and Trade* (Cambridge: Cambridge University Press, 1992), pp. 5, 207–8. The fact that the Cold War provided a poor starting point for analysis of the arms trade is becoming widely recognized. See *SIPRI Yearbook 1988*, pp. 197–8.
45 See, among others, Keith Krause, *Arms and the State ..*; Edward J. Laurance, *The International Arms Trade* (Lexington, MA: Lexington Books, 1992); Frederic S. Pearson, *The Global Spread of Arms: Political Economy of International Security* (Boulder, CO: Westview, 1994); 'The Arms Trade: Problems and Prospects in the Post-Cold War World', *The Annals of the American Academy of Political and Social Science* 535 (September 1994), special editors Robert E. Harkavy and Stephanie G. Neuman; and Barry Buzan and Eric Herring, *The Arms Dynamic in World Politics* (Boulder, CO: Lynne Rienner, 1998).
46 Robert E. Harkavy, 'The Changing International System and the Arms Trade,' in *Annals, AAPSS* 535, pp. 25–8; Frederic S. Pearson, *The Global Spread of Arms*, pp. 103–8.
47 In the period 1990–93 alone, the international community imposed twice as many arms embargoes as it had in the entire Cold War period. Ian Anthony, 'The "third tier" countries: production of major weapons,' p. 364 (note 8).
48 Ilan Peleg, 'Military Production in Third World Countries: A Political Study,' in Pat McGowan and Charles W. Kegley, Jr. (eds), *Threats, Weapons and Foreign Policy* SAGE International Yearbook of Foreign Policy Studies No. 5 (Beverly Hills: SAGE, 1980), pp. 226–7.
49 Theodore H. Moran, 'The Globalization of America's Defense Industries: Managing the Threat of Foreign Dependence,' in *International Security* 15 (Summer 1990), 57–99.
50 'Japan's Defence Industry: Slow Seppuku,' *The Economist*, June 10, 1995, 58.

51 See the Lockheed Martin brochure for the F-35, stressing the participation of eight major partners and the importance of international partners in reducing costs. Available at www.lmaeronautics.com/products/combat_air/x-35/partners.html
52 Timothy D. Hoyt, 'Power, Proximity and Paranoia: The Evolution of Kashmir as a Nuclear Flashpoint,' in *The Kashmir Question: Retrospect and Prospect* (London: Frank Cass, 2003), pp. 117–44.
53 Eliot Cohen, 'Distant Battles,' in *International Security* 10 (Spring 1986), 160; Michael T. Klare, 'The State of the Trade: Global Arms Transfer Patterns in the 1980s,' in *Journal of International Affairs* 40 (Summer 1986), 1–21; Michael T. Klare, 'War in the 1990s: Growing Firepower in the Third World,' *Bulletin of the Atomic Scientists* 46:4 (1990), 9–13.
54 Richard A. Samuels, *'Rich Nation, Strong Army': National Security and the Technological Transformation of Japan* (Ithaca, NY: Cornell University Press, 1994).
55 Helena Tuomi and Raimo Värynen, *Transnational Corporations, Armaments, and Development* (New York: St. Martin's, 1982), p. 53; Michael A. Morris, *Expansion of Third World Navies* (New York: St. Martin's, 1987), p. 59; Stephanie G. Neuman, 'International stratification and Third World military industries', *International Organization* 38 (Winter 1984), 197 (n. 79).
56 Relevant industries include the following United Nations International Standard Industrial Classifications, p. 371 (iron and steel); p. 372 (non-ferrous metal); p. 381 (metal products); p. 382 (machinery (non-electrical)); p. 383 (electrical machinery); and p. 384 (transportation). See Herbert Wulf, 'Developing Countries,' in Nicole Ball and Milton Leitenberg (eds), *The Structure of the Defense Industry* (New York: St. Martin's Press, 1983), pp. 323–5.
57 Stephanie G. Neuman, 'International stratification..', pp. 181–7.
58 Arguments that small states suffer from technological change are found in David Vital, *Weak States in the International System* (Oxford: Clarendon Press, 1967), especially Chapter 4; and Robert L. Rothstein, *Alliances and Small Powers* (New York: Columbia University Press, 1968), p. 20. Others argue that changes in technology offer the potential for weak states to redress existing imbalances. Martin Wight, *Power Politics*, Hedley Bull and Carsten Holbraad (eds) (New York: Holmes & Meier, 1978), p. 256.
59 Eliot A. Cohen, 'A Revolution in Warfare?,' *Foreign Affairs* 75, No. 2 (March/April 1996), 37–54.
60 Admiral William Owens (with Ed Offley), *Lifting the Fog of War* (New York: Farrar, Strauss and Giroux, 2000).
61 Michael G. Vickers, 'Revolution Deferred: Kosovo and the Transformation of War,' in *War Over Kosovo*, p. 196.
62 'Banned Falun Gong Movement Jammed Chinese Satellite Signal,' *Washington Post*, July 9, 2002. The operation forced the Chinese government to cancel a live broadcast of a speech by President Jiang Zemin, and transmitted Falun Gang video feed for brief periods of time.
63 Colin S. Gray, *Explorations in Strategy* (Westport, CT: Praeger, 1996), p. 102.
64 W. Seth Carus, 'Military Technology and the Arms Trade: Changes and Their Impact,' *Annals AAPSS* 535, pp. 163–74.
65 Emphasis on applied settings probably has more relevance for military applications. James Everett Katz, 'Factors Affecting Military Scientific Research in the Third World,' in James Everett Katz (ed.), *The Implications of Third World Military Industrialization: Sowing the Serpents' Teeth* (Lexington, MA: Lexington, 1986), p. 297. See also Eugene B. Skolnikoff, *The Elusive Transformation:*

Science, Technology, and the Evolution of International Politics (Princeton: Princeton University Press, 1993).
66 Erich Weede, 'Military Participation, Economic Growth, and Income Inequality: a Cross-national Study,' in Steve Chan and Alex Mintz (eds), *Defense, Welfare, and Growth*, pp. 211–30.
67 Gérard Chaliand (ed.), *The Art of War in World History* (Berkeley and Los Angeles, CA: University of California Press, 1994), p. 45.
68 Yigal Allon, *The Making of Israel's Army* (New York: Universe Books, 1970), pp. 51–2; Eliot Cohen, 'Distant Battles,' pp. 150–4.
69 *The National Security Strategy of the United States of America* (Washington, DC: The White House, September 2002). The problems of utilizing conventional military forces in a global war on terrorism are discussed in Timothy D. Hoyt, 'Military Force and the War On Terrorism,' Audrey Kurth Cronin and James M. Ludes (eds), *Attacking Terrorism: Elements of a Grand Strategy*, (Washington, DC: Georgetown University Press, 2003), pp.162–85.
70 *GWAPS* Volume II: 'Effects and Effectiveness,' p. 10.
71 Timothy D. Hoyt, 'Iraq's Military Industry: A Critical Strategic Target,' *National Security Studies Quarterly* IV, No. 2 (Spring 1998), pp. 33–50.
72 Michael David Wallace, *War and Rank Among Nations* (Lexington, MA: D.C. Heath, 1973), pp. 24, 72; Robert Gilpin, *War and Change in International Politics* (Cambridge: Cambridge University Press, 1981), pp. 30–4.
73 According to a 1969 UN report, the costs of producing mass casualties in a square kilometer was $1 for biological weapons, $600 for nerve agents, $800 for nuclear weapons, and approximately $2,000 for conventional weaponry. Cited in Richard Danzig, 'Biological Warfare: A Nation at Risk – Time to Act,' *National Defense University Strategic Forum* 58 (January 1996), p. 1.
74 Martin Wight, *Power Politics*, pp. 54, 65.

Select bibliography

General

Anthony, Ian, 'The "Third tier" Countries: Production of Major Weapons,' in Herbert Wulf (ed.), *Arms Industry Limited* (Oxford: Oxford University Press, 1993), pp. 362–83.

Arms Control and Disarmament Association (ACDA) *World Military Expenditures and Arms Transfers, 1991–1992* (Washington, DC: Government Printing Office, annual).

Aronson, Shlomo, with Oded Brosh, *The Politics and Strategy of Nuclear Weapons in the Middle East: Opacity, Theory, and Reality 1960–1991* (Albany, NY: State University of New York Press, 1992).

Ayoob, Mohammed, (ed.), *Regional Security in the Third World* (Boulder, CO: Westview Press, 1986).

Ayoob, Mohammed, *The Third World Security Predicament: State Making, Regional Conflict, and the International System* (Boulder, CO: Lynne Rienner, 1995).

Azar, Edward A and Chung-in Moon (eds), *National Security in the Third World: The Management of Internal and External Threats* (Aldershot, UK: Edward Elgar, 1988).

Baek, Kwang-Il, Ronald D. McLaurin, and Chung-in Moon (eds), *The Dilemma of Third World Defense Industries: Supplier Control or Recipient Autonomy?* (Boulder, CO: Westview, 1989).

Ball, Nicole, 'Defence and Development: A Critique of the Benoit Study', in Helena Tuomi and Raimo Värynen (eds), *Militarization and Arms Production* (London: Croom Helm, 1983), pp. 39–56.

Ball, Nicole, *Third World Security Expenditures: A Statistical Compendium* (Stockholm: National Defence Research Institute, May 1984).

Ball, Nicole, *Security and Economy in the Third World* (Princeton, NJ: Princeton University Press, 1988).

Ball, Nicole and Milton Leitenberg (eds), *The Structure of the Defence Industry: An International Survey* (New York: St. Martin's Press, 1983).

Barnett, Michael and Alexander Wendt, 'The Systemic Sources of Dependent Militarization,' in Brian L. Job (ed.), *The Insecurity Dilemma: National Security of Third World States* (Boulder, CO: Lynne Rienner, 1992), pp. 97–119.

Benoit, Emile, *Defense and Economic Growth in Developing Countries* (Lexington, MA: Lexington Books, 1973).

Bitzinger, Richard, *Towards a Brave New Arms Industry? The Decline of the Second-Tier Arms-Producing Countries and the Emerging International Division of Labour in the Defence Industry* Adelphi Paper #356 (Oxford: Oxford University Press, 2003).
Bobrow, Davis B. and Steve Chan, 'Simple Labels and Complex Realities: National Security in the Third World,' in Edward A. Azar and Chung-in Moon (eds), *National Security in the Third World: The Management of Internal and External Threats* (Aldershot, UK: Edward Elgar, 1988), pp. 44–76.
Bonen, Ze'ev, 'The Technological Arms Race,' in Zvi Lanir (ed.), *Israeli Security Planning in the 1980s: Its Politics and Economics* (New York: Praeger, 1984), pp. 108–27.
Brauer, Jurgen and Paul Dunne (eds), *Arming the South: The Economics of Military Expenditure, Arms Production, and Arms Trade in Developing Countries* (New York: Palgrave MacMillan, 2002).
Brzoska, Michael, 'Arms Transfer Data Sources,' *Journal of Conflict Resolution* 26 (March 1982), 77–108.
Brzoska, Michael and Thomas Ohlson (eds), *Arms Production in the Third World* (London and Philadelphia: Taylor & Francis for SIPRI, 1986).
Buzan, Barry, 'A Framework for Regional Security Analysis'. *South Asian Security and the Great Powers,* ed. Barry Buzan and Gowher Rizvi (New York: St. Martin's, 1986), pp. 3–33.
Buzan, Barry, *An Introduction to Strategic Studies: Military Technology and International Relations* (New York: St. Martin's Press, 1987).
Buzan, Barry, 'Third World Security in Structural and Historical Perspective', in Brian L. Job (ed.), *The Insecurity Dilemma: National Security of Third World States* (Boulder, CO: Lynne Rienner, 1992), pp. 167–89.
Buzan, Barry and Eric Herring, *The Arms Dynamic in World Politics* (Boulder, CO: Lynne Rienner, 1998).
Cahn, Anne Hessing, Joseph J. Kruzel, Peer M. Dawkins, and Jacque Huntzinger, *Controlling the Future Arms Trade* (New York: McGraw-Hill, 1976).
Cannizzo, Cindy, *The Gun Merchants: Politics and Policies of the Major Arms Suppliers* (New York: Pergamon Press, 1980).
Catrina, Christian, *Arms Transfers and Dependence* (New York: Taylor & Francis/United Nations Institute for Disarmament Research, 1988).
Catrina, Christian, 'Main Questions of Research in The Arms Trade,' in Robert E. Harkavy and Stephanie G. Neuman (eds), *The Arms Trade: Problems and Prospects in the Post Cold-War World*; Special Issue of *Annals of the American Academy of Political and Social Science* 535 (September 1994), 190–205.
Chan, Steve and Alex Mintz (eds), *Defense, Welfare, and Growth* (New York: Routledge, 1992).
Clare, Joseph F. Jr., 'Whither the Third World Arms Producers?,' *World Military Expenditures and Arms Transfers 1986* (US Arms Control and Disarmament Agency. Washington, DC: Arms Control and Disarmament Agency, 1987), pp. 23–8.
Cohen, Eliot A., 'Distant Battles,' *International Security* 10 (Spring 1986), 143–71.
Cohen, Eliot A., 'A Revolution in Warfare,' *Foreign Affairs* 75 (March/April 1996), 37–54.
Cordesman, Anthony H. and Abraham R. Wagner, *The Lessons of Modern War* (3 volumes) (Boulder, CO: Westview Press, 1990).

Cottrell, Alvin J., Robert Hanks, and Michael Moodie, *Arms Transfers and US Foreign and Military Policy* (Washington, DC: Georgetown University, 1980).
Defense Industry Globalization: A Compendium of Papers Presented at a Conference on 'Defense Industry Globalization' Held on 16 November 2001 (Washington, DC: The Atlantic Council of the United States, February 2002).
Deger, Saadet, *Military Expenditure in Third World Countries: The Economic Effects* (Boston: Routledge & Kegan Paul, 1986).
Deger, Saadet and Somnath Sen, *Military Expenditure: The Political Economy of International Security* (London: Oxford University Press, 1990).
Dombrowski, Peter J., Eugene Gholz, and Andrew L. Ross, *Military Transformation and the Defense Industry After Next: The Defense Industrial Implications of Network-Centric Warfare* (Newport, RI: Naval War College Press, 2002).
Domke, William K., Richard C. Eichenberg, and Catherine M. Kelleher, 'The Illusion of Choice: Defense and Welfare in Advanced Industrial Democracies, 1948–1978,' *American Political Science Review* 77 (March 1983), 19–35.
Evans, Carol, 'Reappraising Third-World Arms Production,' *Survival* 28 (March April 1986), 99–118.
Falk, R. A. and S. H. Mendlovitz, *Regional Politics and World Order* (San Francisco: Freeman, 1973).
Fei, Edward T., 'Understanding Arms Transfers and Military Expenditures: Data Problems,' in Stephanie G. Neuman and Robert E. Harkavy (eds), *Arms Transfers in the Modern World*, (New York: Praeger Press, 1980), pp. 37–46.
Garrity, Patrick J., *Why the Gulf War Still Matters: Foreign Perspectives on the War and the Future of International Security,* CNSS Report No. 16 (Los Alamos: Center for National Security Studies, July 1993).
Grimmett, Richard F., *Trends in Conventional Arms Transfers to the Third World by Major Supplier* (Washington, DC: Congressional Research Service, Library of Congress, annual).
Gulf War Air Power Survey (Washington, DC: Pentagon, 1993).
Gupta, Amit, 'Third World Military Industries: New Suppliers, Deadlier Weapons,' *Orbis* 37 (Winter 1993), pp. 57–68.
Handel, Michael, *Weak States in the International System,* 2nd edition (London: Frank Cass, 1990).
Harkavy, Robert E., *The Arms Trade and International Systems* (Cambridge, MA: Ballinger, 1975).
Harkavy, Robert E., 'The Pariah State System,' *Orbis* 21 (Fall 1977), 623–49.
Harkavy, Robert E., 'Arms Resupply During Conflict: A Framework for Analysis,' in Christian Schmidt (ed.), *The Economics of Military Expenditures* (New York: St. Martin's Press, 1987), pp. 239–79.
Harkavy, Robert E., 'The Changing International System and the Arms Trade,' in Robert E. Harkavy and Stephanie G. Neuman (eds), *The Arms Trade: Problems and Prospects in the Post Cold-War World,* Special Issue of *Annals of the American Academy of Political and Social Science* 535 (September 1994), 11–28.
Harkavy, Robert E. and Stephanie G. Neuman (eds), *The Arms Trade: Problems and Prospects in the Post Cold-War World.* Special Issue of *Annals of the American Academy of Political and Social Science* 535 (September 1994).
Harkavy, Robert E. and Stephanie G. Neuman, *Warfare and the Third World* (New York: Palgrave Press, 2001).

Hartcup, Guy, *The Silent Revolution: Development of Conventional Weapons, 1945–1985* (London: Brassey's, 1993).
Hartung, William D., *And Weapons for All: How America's Multibillion-Dollar Arms Trade Warps our Foreign Policy and Subverts Democracy at Home* (New York: HarperCollins Publishers, 1994).
Hettne, Björn, 'Third World Arms Control and World System Conflicts,' in Thomas Ohlson (ed.), *Arms Transfer Limitations and Third World Security* (Oxford: Oxford University Press for SIPRI, 1988), pp. 17–32.
Holsti, Kal J., 'International Theory and War in the Third World,' in Brian L. Job (ed.), *The Insecurity Dilemma: National Security of Third World States* (Boulder, CO: Lynne Rienner, 1992), pp. 37–60.
Howe, Russell Warren, *Weapons: The International Game of Arms, Money, and Diplomacy* (New York: Doubleday & Company, Inc., 1980).
Hoyt, Timothy D., 'Military Technology and Security,' in Michael Brown (ed.), *Grave New World – Threats to Global Order* (Washington, DC: Georgetown University Press, 2003), pp. 17–37.
Hoyt, Timothy D., 'Revolution and Counter-Revolution: The Role of the Periphery in Technological and Conceptual Innovation,' in Emily O. Goldman and Leslie C. Eliason (eds), *The Diffusion of Military Technology and Ideas* (Stanford, CA: Stanford University Press, 2003), pp. 179–201.
Hoyt, Timothy D., 'Security and Conflict in the Developing World,' in Michael Brown (ed), *Grave New World – Threats to Global Order* (Washington, DC: Georgetown University Press, 2003), pp. 213–29.
Job, Brian L. (ed.), *The Insecurity Dilemma: National Security of Third World States* (Boulder, CO: Lynne Rienner, 1992).
Johnson, Joseph J., *The Role of the Military in Underdeveloped Countries* (Princeton, NJ: Princeton University Press, 1962).
Jones, Rodney, 'Small Nuclear Forces,' *The Washington Papers* 103 (New York: Praeger Press, 1984).
Jones, Rodney W. and Steven A. Hildreth, *Modern Weapons and Third World Powers* (Boulder, CO: Westview, 1984).
Jones, Rodney W. and Mark G. McDonough with Toby F. Dalton and Gregory D. Koblentz, *Tracking Nuclear Proliferation: A Guide in Maps and Charts, 1998* (Washington, DC: Carnegie Endowment for International Peace, 1998).
Kapstein, Ethan B. (ed.), *Global Arms Production: Policy Dilemmas for the 1990s* (Lanham, MD: University Press of America, 1992).
Katz, James Everett (ed.), *Arms Production in Developing Countries* (Lexington, MA: Lexington Books, 1984).
Katz, James Everett (ed.), *The Implications of Third World Military Industrialization: Sowing the Serpents' Teeth* (Lexington, MA: DC Heath and Co., 1986).
Kemp, Geoffrey, 'Arms Transfers and the "Back End" Problem,' in Stephanie G. Neuman and Robert E. Harkavy (eds), *Arms Transfers in the Modern World* (New York: Praeger Press, 1979), pp. 264–75.
Kemp, Geoffrey, Robert Pfaltzgraff, and Uri Ra'anan (eds) *The Other Arms Race* (Lexington, MA: DC Heath & Co., 1975).
Kennedy, Gavin, *Defense Economics* (New York: St. Martin's, 1983).
Kennedy, Gavin, 'War Economics,' in Stephanie G. Neuman and Robert E. Harkavy (eds), *The Lessons of Recent Wars in the Third World* Vol. 2 (Lexington, MA: DC Heath 1987), pp. 91–113.

Klare, Michael T., 'The Unnoticed Arms Trade: Exports of Conventional Arms-Making Technology,' *International Security* 8 (Fall 1983), 68–90.

Klare, Michael T., 'The State of the Trade: Global Arms Transfer Patterns in the 1980s', *Journal of International Affairs* 40 (Summer 1986), 1–21.

Klare, Michael T., 'Deadly Convergence: The Perils of the Arms Trade,' *World Policy Journal* 6 (Winter 1988–89), 141–68.

Kolodziej, Edward A., *The Making and Marketing of Arms: The French Experience and its Implications for the International System* (Princeton, NJ: Princeton University Press, 1987).

Kolodziej, Edward A. and Robert E. Harkavy (eds), *Security Policies of Developing Countries* (Lexington, MA: D. C. Heath & Co., 1982).

Krause, Keith, 'Arms Imports, Arms Production, and the Quest for Security in the Third World,' in Brian L. Job (ed.), *The Insecurity Dilemma: National Security of Third World States* (Boulder, CO: Lynne Rienner, 1992), pp. 121–42.

Krause, Keith, *Arms and the State: Patterns of Military Production and Trade* (Cambridge: Cambridge University Press, 1992).

Lake, David A. and Patrick M. Morgan (eds), *Regional Orders: Building Security in a New World* (University Park: Pennsylvania State University Press, 1997).

Laurance, Edward J., *The International Arms Trade* (Lexington, MA: Lexington Books, 1992).

Leiss, Amelia C., G. Kemp, J. H. Hoagland, J.S. Refson, and H.E. Fischer, *Arms Transfers to Less-Developed Countries* (Cambridge, MA: Massachusetts Institute of Technology, Center for International Studies, 1970).

Looney, Robert E., *Third-World Military Expenditure and Arms Production* (New York: St. Martin's Press, 1988).

Louscher, David. J. and Michael D. Salomone (eds), *Marketing Security Assistance: New Perspectives on Arms Sales* (Lexington, MA: D. C. Heath & Co., 1987).

Louscher, David and Michael Salomone, *Technology Transfer and US Security Assistance: The Impact of Licensed Production* (Boulder, CO: Westview Press, 1987).

Mahnken, Thomas. G., 'Why Third World Space Systems Matter,' *Orbis* 35 (Fall 1991), 563–79.

McGowan, Pat and Charles W. Kegley, Jr. (eds), *Threats, Weapons and Foreign Policy* (SAGE International Yearbook of Foreign Policy Studies No. 5 Beverly Hills: SAGE, 1980).

McNeill, William H., *The Pursuit of Power: Technology, Armed Force, and Society since 1000 A.D.* (Chicago: University of Chicago Press, 1982).

Mellor, J.W., *Regional Power in a Multipolar World* (Boulder, CO: Westview Press, 1979).

Moodie, Michael, 'Sovereignty, Security, and Arms', *The Washington Papers* 67 (Beverly Hills, CA: SAGE Publications, 1979).

Moodie, Michael; 'Vulcan's New Forge: Defense Production in Less-Developed Countries,' *Arms Control Today* 10 (March 1980), 1–2, 6–8.

Mullins, A.F., Jr., *Born Arming: Development and Military Power in New States* (Stanford, CA: Stanford University Press, 1987).

Myers, David J. (ed.), *Regional Hegemons: Threat Perception and Strategic Response* (Boulder, CO: Westview, 1991).

Nair, Brigadier V.K., *The War in the Gulf: Lessons for the Third World* (New Delhi: Lancer International, 1991).

Naylor-Schwarz, Anne, 'Arms Transfers and the Development of Second-Level Arms Industries,' in David J. Louscher and Michael D. Salomone (eds), *Marketing Security Assistance: New Perspectives on Arms Sales* (Lexington, MA: D. C. Heath, 1987), pp. 101–30.
Neuman, Stephanie G. (ed.), *Defense Planning in Less-Industrialized Countries* (Lexington, MA: Lexington Books, 1984).
Neuman, Stephanie G., 'International Stratification and Third World Military Industries,' *International Organization* 38 (Winter 1984), 167–97.
Neuman, Stephanie G.; 'Third World Military Industries: Capabilities and Constraints in Recent Wars,' in Stephanie G. Neuman and Robert E. Harkavy (eds), *The Lessons of Recent Wars in the Third World* Vol. 2 (Lexington, MA: D. C. Heath 1987), pp. 157–97.
Neuman, Stephanie G. and Robert E. Harkavy (eds), *Arms Transfers in the Modern World* (New York: Praeger Publishers, 1980).
Neuman, Stephanie G. and Robert E. Harkavy (eds) *The Lessons of Recent Wars in the Third World* (Lexington, MA: D. C. Heath & Co., 1987).
Nolan, Janne E., *Trappings of Power: Ballistic Missiles in the Third World* (Washington, DC: The Brookings Institution, 1991).
Ohlson, Thomas (ed.), *Arms Transfer Limitations and Third World Security* (Oxford: Oxford University Press for SIPRI, 1988).
Parker, Christopher S., 'New Weapons for Old Problems: Conventional Proliferation and Military Effectiveness in Developing States,' in *International Security*, 23: (Spring 1999) 4, 119–47.
Parker, Geoffrey, *The Military Revolution: Military Innovation and the Rise of the West, 1500–1800* (Cambridge: Cambridge University Press, 1988).
Pearson, Frederic S., *The Global Spread of Arms: Political Economy of International Security* (Boulder, CO: Westview Press, 1994).
Peleg, Ilan, 'Military Production in Third World Countries: A Political Study,' in Pat McGowan and Charles W. Kegley, Jr. (eds), *Threats, Weapons and Foreign Policy* (SAGE International Yearbook of Foreign Policy Studies No. 5, Beverly Hills: SAGE, 1980), pp. 209–30.
Pierre, Andrew, *The Global Politics of Arms Sales* (Princeton, NJ: Princeton University Press, 1982).
Proliferation: Threat and Response (Washington, DC: Office of the Secretary of Defense, January 2001).
Ra'anan, Uri, Robert L. Pfaltzgraff, and Geoffrey Kemp (eds), *Arms Transfers to the Third World: The Military Buildup in Less Industrialized Countries* (Boulder, CO: Westview Press, 1978).
Ralston, David B., *Importing the European Army: The Introduction of European Military Techniques and Institutions into the Extra-European World, 1600–1914* (Chicago: University of Chicago Press, 1990).
Rogers, Clifford J. (ed.), *The Military Revolution Debate: Readings on the Military Transformation of Early Modern Europe* (Boulder, CO: Westview Press, 1995).
Rosh, Robert M., 'Third World Militarization: Security Webs and the States They Ensnare,' *Journal of Conflict Resolution* 32 (December 1988), 671–98.
Rosh, Robert M., 'Third World Arms Production and the Evolving Interstate System,' *Journal of Conflict Resolution* 34 (March 1990), pp. 57–73.
Ross, Andrew L., 'Arms Acquisition and National Security: The Irony of Military Strength,' in Edward A. Azar and Chung-in Moon (eds), *National Security in the*

Third World: The Management of Internal and External Threats (Aldershot, UK: Edward Elgar, 1988), pp. 152–87.

Ross, Andrew L., 'World Order and Arms Production in the Third World,' in James Everett Katz (ed.), *The Implications of Third World Military Industries: Sowing the Serpents' Teeth* (Lexington, MA: Lexington Books, 1986), pp. 278–92.

Ross, Andrew, 'Full Circle: Conventional Proliferation, the International Arms Trade, and Third World Arms Exports,' in Kwang-Il Baek, Ronald D. McLaurin, and Chung-in Moon (eds), *The Dilemma of Third World Defense Industries: Supplier Control or Recipient Autonomy?* (Boulder, CO: Westview Press, 1989), pp. 3–32.

Ross, Andy Lee, *Security and Self-Reliance: Military Dependence and Conventional Arms Production in Developing Countries* (PhD dissertation: Cornell University, August 1984).

Russett, B. M., *International Regions and the International System* (Chicago: Rand McNally, 1967).

Sampson, Anthony; *The Arms Bazaar: From Lebanon to Lockheed* (New York: Viking Press, 1977).

Sanders, Ralph, *Arms Industries: New Suppliers and Regional Security* (Washington, DC: National Defense University Press, 1990).

Sayigh, Yezid, *Arab Military Industry: Capability, Performance and Impact* (London: Brassey's. 1992).

Singer, Marshall R., *Weak States in a World of Powers* (New York: The Free Press, 1972).

Sivard, Ruth Leger, *World Military and Social Expenditures* (Leesburg, VA: World Priorities, annual).

Skolnikoff, Eugene B., *The Elusive Transformation: Science, Technology, and the Evolution of International Politics* (Princeton: Princeton University Press, 1993).

Snider, Lewis P., 'Supplier Control and Recipient Autonomy,' in Kwang-Il Baek, Ronald D. McLaurin, and Chung-in Moon (eds), *The Dilemma of Third World Defense Industries: Supplier Control or Recipient Autonomy?* (Boulder, CO: Westview, 1989), pp. 231–70.

Solingen, Etel, *Regional Orders at Century's Dawn: Global and Domestic Influences on Grand Strategy* (Princeton: Princeton University Press, 1998).

Spector, Leonard S., *Nuclear Ambitions: The Spread of Nuclear Weapons, 1989–1990* (Boulder, CO: Westview Press, 1990).

Stanley, John and Maurice Pearton, *The International Trade in Arms* (New York, Praeger Press, 1972).

Steinberg, Gerald M., 'Technological Transfer and the Future of The Center-Periphery System: A Realist Perspective,' *The Jerusalem Journal of International Relations* 11 (1989), 96–117.

Stockholm International Peace Research Institute, *SIPRI Yearbook of World Armaments and Disarmament* (Stockholm: Almqvist & Wiksell, annual).

Stockholm International Peace Research Institute, *The Arms Trade with the Third World* (New York: Humanities Press, 1971).

Stockholm International Peace Research Institute, *The Arms Trade With The Third World*, revised edition (New York: Holmes & Meier, 1975).

Thayer, George, *The War Business: The International Trade in Armaments* (New York: Simon & Schuster, 1969).

Tuomi, Helena and Raimo Väyrynen (eds), *Militarization and Arms Production* (New York: St. Martin's Press, 1983).
US Congress, Office of Technology Assessment, *Global Arms Trade* OTA-ISC-460 (Washington, DC: Government Printing Office, June 1991).
United Nations, Department for Disarmament Affairs, *Economic and Social Consequences of the Arms Race and Military Expenditures* (New York: United Nations, 1983).
Van Creveld, Martin, *Technology and War,* 2nd edition (New York: Free Press, 1991).
Väyrynen, Raimo, 'Semiperipheral Countries in the Global Economic and Military Order,' in Helena Tuomi and Raimo Väyrynen (eds), *Militarization and Arms Production* (New York: St. Martin's Press, 1983), pp. 163–92.
Vernon, Raymond, *Sovereignty at Bay* (New York: Basic Books, 1971).
Vital, David, *The Inequality of States* (Oxford: Clarendon Press, 1967).
Vital, David, *The Survival of Small States: Studies in Small Power/Great Power Conflict* (London: Oxford University Press, 1971).
Weede, Erich, 'Military Participation, Economic Growth, and Income Inequality: a Cross-National Study,' in Steve Chan and Alex Mintz (eds), *Defense, Welfare and Growth* (London: Routledge, 1992), pp. 211–30.
Wight, Martin, *Power Politics* edited by Hedley Bull and Carsten Holbraad (New York: Holmes & Meier, 1978).
Wolfers, Arnold, *Discord and Collaboration* (Baltimore, MD: Johns Hopkins University Press, 1962).
Wriggins, W. Howard with F. Gregory Gause, III, Terence P. Lyons, and Evelyn Colbert, *Dynamics of Regional Politics: Four Systems on the Indian Ocean Rim* (New York: Columbia University Press, 1992).
Wulf, Herbert; 'Dependent Militarism in the Periphery and Possible Alternative Concept', in Stephanie G. Neuman and Robert E. Harkavy (eds), *Arms Transfers in the Modern World* (New York: Praeger, 1979), pp. 246–63.
Wulf, Herbert, 'Developing Countries,' in Nicole Ball and Milton Leitenberg (eds), *The Structure of the Defense Industry: An International Survey*' (London: Croom Helm, 1983), pp. 310–43.
Wulf, Herbert (ed.), *Arms Industry Limited* (Oxford: Oxford University Press for SIPRI, 1993).

India

Annual Report (New Delhi: Ministry of Defence, Government of India, annual).
Arnett, Eric, 'Military Technology: the Case of India,' *SIPRI Yearbook of World Arms and Disarmament 1994* (Stockholm: Almqvist & Wiksell, 1994), pp. 343–65.
Azam, Kousar J. (ed.), *India's Defence Policy for the 1990s* (New Delhi: Sterling, 1992).
Babbage, Ross and Sandy Gordon (eds.), *India's Strategic Future* (New York: St. Martin's Press, 1992).
Bajpai, Kanti P. and Amitabh Mattoo (eds), *Securing India: Strategic Thought and Practice* (Essays by George K. Tanham with commentaries) (New Delhi: Manohar, 1996).
Bajpai, Kanti P., P. R. Chari, Pervaiz Iqbal Cheema, Stephen P. Cohen, and

Select bibliography

Sumit Ganguly (eds), *Brasstacks and Beyond: Perception and Management of Crisis in South Asia* (Urbana, IL: The Program in Arms Control, Disarmament, and International Security, University of Illinois at Urbana-Champaign, June 1995).

Barnds, William J., *India, Pakistan and the Great Powers* (New York: Praeger Press, 1972).

Basrur, Rajesh M., 'Nuclear Weapons and Indian Strategic Culture,' *Journal of Peace Research* 38:2 (2001), pp. 181–98.

Basrur, Rajesh M., 'Kargil, Terrorism and India's Strategic Shift,' *India Review* Vol. 1, No. 4 (October 2002), 39–56.

Chaudhuri, Gen. J.N., *Arms, Aims & Aspects* (Bombay: Manaktalas, 1966).

Chengappa, Raj, *Weapons of Peace* (New Delhi: HarperCollins Publishers India Pvt Ltd, 2000).

Cohen, Stephen Philip, *The Indian Army* (Berkeley, CA: University of California, 1971).

Cohen, Stephen P., *India: Emerging Power* (Washington, DC: Brookings Institution Press, 2001).

Cohen, Stephen Philip and Richard L. Park, *India: Emergent Power* (New York: Crane, Russak & Co., 1978).

Dalvi, Brig. Gen. J. P., *Himalayan Blunder* (Bombay: Thacker, 1969).

Draft Nuclear Doctrine, 17 August 1999, at www.indianembassy.org/policy/CTBT/nuclear_doctrine_aug_17_1999.html.

From Surprise to Reckoning: The Kargil Review Committee Report (New Delhi: SAGE, 1999).

Ganguly, Sumit, *Conflict Unending: India–Pakistan Tensions since 1947* (Oxford: Oxford University Press, 2001).

Graham, Thomas W., 'India,' in James Everett Katz (ed.), *Arms Production in Developing Countries* (Lexington, MA: Lexington, 1984), pp. 157–92.

Gupta, Amit; 'The Indian Arms Industry: A Lumbering Giant,' *Asian Survey* 30 (September 1990), 846–61.

Gupta, Shekhar, 'India Redefines Its Role,' *Adelphi Paper 293* (Oxford: Oxford University Press for IISS, 1995).

Hagerty, Devin T., *The Consequences of Nuclear Proliferation: Lessons from South Asia* (Cambridge, MA: MIT Press, 1998).

Hoon, P. N., *Unmasking the Secrets of Turbulence* (New Delhi: Manas Publications, 2000).

Hoyt, Timothy D., 'Pakistan's Nuclear Doctrine and the Dangers of Strategic Myopia,' *Asian Survey* Vol. XLI, No. 6 (November/December 2001 special issue), 956–77.

Hoyt, Timothy D., 'Power, Proximity and Paranoia: The Evolution of Kashmir as a Nuclear Flashpoint,' in Sumit Ganguly (ed.), *The Kashmir Question: Retrospect and Prospect* (London: Frank Cass, 2003), pp. 117–44.

Jackson, Robert, *South Asian Crisis* (London: Chatto & Windus, 1975).

Jones, Owen Bennett, *Pakistan: Eye of the Storm* (New Haven: Yale University Press, 2002).

Kapur, Ashok, *India's Nuclear Option: Atomic Diplomacy and Decision Making*. (New York: Praeger Press, 1976).

Kavic, Lorne J., *India's Quest for Security: Defence Policies, 1947–1965* (Berkeley and Los Angeles, CA: University of California Press, 1967).

Koithara, Verghese; *Society, State & Security: The Indian Experience* (New Delhi: SAGE, 1999)
Kux, Dennis, *India and the United States: Estranged Democracies*. Washington, DC: National Defense University Press, 1991.
Kux, Dennis; *Disenchanted Allies: The United States and Pakistan 1947–2000* (Baltimore, MD: The Johns Hopkins University Press, 2001).
MacDonald, Juli, *Indo–US Military Relationship: Expectations and Perceptions* (Washington, DC: Office of the Secretary of Defense, Office of Net Assessment, October 2002).
Matthews, Ron, *Defence Production in India* (New Delhi: ABC Press, 1989).
Maxwell, Neville, *India's China War* (London: Jonathan Cape, 1970).
McCarthy, Timothy V., 'India: Emerging Missile Power,' in William C. Potter and Harlan W. Jencks (eds), *The International Missile Bazaar: The New Suppliers' Network* (Boulder, CO: Westview Press, 1994), pp. 201–33.
Mohan, C. Raja, *Crossing the Rubicon: The Shaping of India's New Foreign Policy* (New York: Viking, 2003).
Ollapolly, Deepa M., 'Mixed Motives in India's Search for Nuclear Status,' *Asian Survey* XLI, No. 6 (November/December 2001), pp. 925–42.
Panikkar, K. M., *Problems of Indian Defence* (New York: Asia House, 1960).
Perkovich, George, *India's Nuclear Bomb* (Berkeley: University of California Press, 1999).
Raghavan, V. R., 'Limited War and Nuclear Escalation in South Asia,' *The Nonproliferation Review* (Fall–Winter 2001), 1–17.
Sidhu, Waheguru Pal Singh, 'India's Nuclear Use Doctrine,' in Peter R. Lavoy, Scott D. Sagan, and James J. Wirtz (eds.), *Planning the Unthinkable: How New Powers Will Use Nuclear, Biological, and Chemical Weapons* (Ithaca: Cornell University Press, 2000), pp. 125–57.
Singh, Jaswant, *Defending India* (New York: St. Martin's, 1999).
Singh, Ravinder Pal, 'India,' in Ravinder Pal Singh (ed.), *Arms Procurement Decision Making – Volume I: China, India, Israel, Japan, South Korea and Thailand* (Oxford: Oxford University Press for SIPRI, 1998), pp. 48–90.
Sisson, Richard and Leo B. Rose, *War and Secession: Pakistan, India, and the Creation of Bangladesh* (Berkeley, CA: University of California, 1990).
Smith, Chris, *India's Ad Hoc Arsenal: Direction or Drift in Defence Policy* (Oxford: Oxford University Press for SIPRI, 1994).
Subrahmanyam, K., *Nuclear Myths and Realities: India's Dilemma* (New Delhi: ABC Publishing House, 1981).
Subrahmanyam, K., 'Evolution of Defense Planning in India,' in Stephanie G. Neuman (ed.), *Defense Planning in Less-Industrialized States* (Lexington, MA: DC Heath & Co., 1984), pp. 265–74.
Tanham, George K., *Indian Strategic Thought: An Interpretive Essay* (R-4207-USDP. Santa Monica, CA: RAND Corporation, 1992).
Tanham, George K. and Marcy Agmon, *The Indian Air Force: Trends and Prospects* (Santa Monica, CA: RAND Corporation, 1995).
Tellis, Ashley J., *India's Emerging Nuclear Posture: Between Recessed Deterrent and Ready Arsenal* (Santa Monica, CA: RAND, 2001).
Tellis, Ashley J. C., Christina Fair, and Jamison Jo Medby, *Conflict Under the Nuclear Umbrella: Indian and Pakistani Lessons from the Kargil Crisis* MR-1450-USCA (Santa Monica: RAND, 2001).

Thomas, Raju G. C., *Indian Security Policy* (Princeton, NJ: Princeton University Press, 1986).
Thomas, Raju G. C., 'The Growth of Indian Military Power: From Sufficient Defense to Nuclear Deterrence,' in Ross Babbage and Sandy Gordon (eds), *India's Strategic Future* (New York: St. Martin's Press, 1992), pp. 35–66.
Thomas, Raju G. C. and Amit Gupta (eds), *India's Nuclear Security* (Boulder, CO: Lynne Rienner, 2000).
Wulf, Herbert, 'India: the Unfulfilled Quest for Self-Sufficiency,' in Michael Brzoska and Thomas Ohlson (eds), *Arms Production in the Third World* (London and Philadelphia: Taylor & Francis, 1986), pp. 125–45.

Israel

Allon, Yigal, *The Making of Israel's Army* (New York: Universe Books, 1970).
Allon, Yigal, *Shield of David: The Story of Israel's Armed Forces* (New York: Random House, 1970).
Barnett, Michael, *Confronting the Costs of War: Military Power, State, and Society in Egypt and Israel* (Princeton, NJ: Princeton University Press, 1992).
Ben Gurion, David, *Israel: A Personal History* (New York: Funk & Wagnall, 1971).
Ben-Horin, Yoav and Barry Posen, *Israel's Strategic Doctrine*, RAND R-2845-NA (Santa Monica, CA: The RAND Corporation, September 1981).
Ben-Meir, Yehuda, *National Security Decisionmaking: The Israeli Case* (Jerusalem, The Jerusalem Post, 1986).
Blumenthal, Naftali, 'The Influence of Defense Industry Investment on Israel's Economy,' in Zvi Lanir (ed.), *Israeli Security Planning in the 1980s: Its Politics and Economics* (New York: Praeger, 1984), pp. 166–77.
Carus, W. Seth, 'Israel: Some Economic and Social Considerations,' in James Everett Katz (ed.), *The Implications of Third World Military Industrialization: Sowing the Serpents' Teeth* (Lexington, MA: D. C. Heath and Co., 1986), pp. 136–50.
Cohen, Avner, *Israel and the Bomb* (New York: Columbia University Press, 1998).
Cohen, Avner, 'Nuclear Arms in Crisis under Secrecy: Israel and the Lessons of the 1967 and 1973 Wars,' in Peter R. Lavoy, Scott D. Sagan, and James J. Wirtz (eds), *Planning the Unthinkable: How New Powers Will Use Nuclear, Biological, and Chemical Weapons* (New York: Columbia University Press, 2000), pp. 104–24.
Cohen, Avner, 'Israel and Chemical/Biological Weapons: History, Deterrence, and Arms Control,' *The Nonproliferation Review* (Fall–Winter 2001), 27–53, at cns.miis.edu/pubs/npr/vol08/83/83cohen.pdf
Gold, Dore, *Israel as an American Non-NATO Ally: Parameters of Defense-Industrial Cooperation* (Jerusalem: The Jerusalem Post Press, 1992).
Goodman, Hirsh and W. Seth Carus, *The Future Battlefield and the Arab–Israeli Conflict* (New Brunswick, NJ: Transaction Publishers, 1990).
Handel, Michael I., 'The Evolution of Israeli Strategy: The Psychology of Insecurity and the Quest for Absolute Security,' in Williamson Murray, MacGregor Knox, and Alvin Bernstein (eds), *The Making of Strategy: Rulers, States, and War* (Cambridge: Cambridge University Press, 1994), pp. 534–78.
Harkabi, Y., *Arab Attitudes To Israel* (New York: Hart, 1971).

Harkavy, Robert E. and Stephanie Neuman, 'Israel,' in James E. Katz (ed.), *Arms Production in the Third World* (Lexington, MA: Lexington Books, 1984), pp. 193–223.
Hersh, Seymour M., *The Samson Option* (New York: Random House, 1991).
Herzog, Chaim, *The Arab–Israeli Wars* (New York: Vintage Books, 1984).
Hoyt, Timothy D., 'Israel's Military Industry – The Other Side of Globalization,' *Defense Industry Globalization: A Compendium of Papers Presented at a Conference on 'Defense Industry Globalization' Held on 16 November 2001* (Washington, DC: The Atlantic Council, February 2002).
Inbar, Efraim, 'The Development of the Israeli Defense Industry,' *Encyclopedia Judaica Yearbook 1988/9*, pp. 119–25.
Inbar, Efraim and Shmuel Sandler, 'Israel's Deterrence Strategy Revisited,' *Security Studies* 3 (Winter 1993/94), 330–58.
Klieman, Aharon, *Israel's Global Reach* (New York: Brassey's, 1985).
Klieman, Aharon and Reuven Pedatzur, *Rearming Israel: Defense Procurement Through the 1990s* (Jerusalem: The Jerusalem Post for the Jaffee Center for Strategic Studies, 1991).
Lanir, Zvi (ed.), *Israeli Security Planning in the 1980s: Its Politics and Economics* (New York: Praeger, 1984).
Lanir, Zvi, 'The Qualitative Factor in the Israeli-Arab Arms Race of the Late 1980s,' *IDF Journal* (Fall 1985), 27–38.
Levite, Ariel, *Offense and Defense in Israeli Military Doctrine* (Boulder, CO: Westview Press, 1988).
Luttwak, Edward, 'Defense Planning in Israel: A Brief Retrospective,' in Stephanie G. Neuman (ed.), *Defense Planning in Less-Industrialized States* (Lexington, MA: Lexington, 1984), pp. 131–44.
Luttwak, Edward and Dan Horowitz, *The Israeli Army* (New York: Harper & Row, 1975).
Michaely, Michael, 'Israel's Dependence on Capital Imports,' *Jerusalem Quarterly* 3 (Spring 1977), 42–9.
Mintz, Alex; 'The Military-Industrial Complex: American Concepts and Israeli Realities,' *Journal of Conflict Resolution* 29 (December 1985), 623–39.
Mintz, Alex, 'Arms Production in Israel,' *Jerusalem Quarterly* 13 (Spring 1987), 89–99.
Mintz, Alex and Gerald Steinberg, 'Coping with Supplier Control: The Israeli Experience,' in Kwang-Il Baek, Ronald D. McLaurin and Chung-in Moon (eds), *The Dilemma of Third World Defense Industries: Supplier Control or Recipient Autonomy* (Boulder, CO: Westview Press 1989), pp. 137–51.
Mintz, Alex and Michael D. Ward, 'The Political Economy of Military Spending in Israel', *American Political Science Review* 83 (June 1989), 521–33.
Ne'eman, Yuval, 'Conceiving a Balanced Budget for a Budding Nation,' in Zvi Lanir (ed.), *Israeli Security Planning in the 1980s* (New York: Praeger, 1984) pp. 3–13.
Peres, Shimon, *David's Sling* (New York: Random House, 1970).
Peres, Shimon, *The New Middle East* (New York: Henry Holt and Company, 1993).
Peres, Shimon, *Battling for Peace* (New York: Random House, 1995).
Rabin, Yitzhak, *The Rabin Memoirs* (Boston: Little, Brown & Co., 1979).
Reiser, Stewart, *The Israeli Arms Industry* (New York: Holmes & Meier, 1989).

Safran, Nadav, *Israel: The Embattled Ally* (Cambridge, MA: Belknap, 1981).
Schiff, Ze'ev and Ehud Ya'ari, *Israel's Lebanon War* edited and translated by Ina Friedman (New York: Simon and Schuster, 1984).
Schiff, Ze'ev, *A History of the Israeli Army: 1874 to the Present* (New York: Macmillan, 1985).
Sheffer, Eliezer, 'The Economic Burden of the Arms Race Between the Confrontation States and Israel,' in Zvi Lanir (ed.), *Israeli Security Planning in the 1980s: Its Politics and Economics* (New York: Praeger Publishing, 1984), pp. 142–65.
Steinberg, Gerald, 'Israel,' in Nicole Ball and Milton Leitenberg (eds), *The Structure of the Defence Industry: A Comparative Study* (New York: St. Martin's Press, 1983), pp. 278–309.
Steinberg, G. M., 'Israel: High Technology Roulette,' in Michael Brzoska and Thomas Ohlson (eds), *Arms Production in the Third World* (London and Philadelphia:Taylor and Francis, 1986) pp. 163–92.
Steinberg, Gerald M., 'Israel: Case Study for International Missile Trade and Non-Proliferation,' in William C. Potter and Harlan W. Jencks (eds), *The International Missile Bazaar: The New Suppliers' Network* (Boulder, CO: Westview, 1994), pp. 235–53.
Steinberg, Gerald, 'Israel,' in Ravinder Pal Singh (ed.), *Arms Procurement Decision Making Volume I: China, India, Israel, Japan, South Korea and Thailand* (Oxford: Oxford University Press for SIPRI, 1998).
Tal, Maj. Gen. Israel, 'Israel's Doctrine of National Security: Background and Dynamics,' *Jerusalem Quarterly* 3 (Summer 1977), 44–57.
Van Creveld, Martin, 'The Making of Israel's Security,' in Stephanie G. Neuman (ed.), *Defense Planning in Less Industrialized States* (Lexington, MA: D. C. Heath & Co., 1984), pp. 115–30.
Van Creveld, Martin, *The Sword and the Olive: A Critical History of the Israeli Defense Force* (New York: PublicAffairs, 1998).
Wald, Emmanuel, *The Wald Report: The Decline of Israeli National Security Since 1967* (Boulder: Westview, 1992).
Yariv, Aharon, 'Strategic Depth,' *Jerusalem Quarterly* 6 (Fall 1980), 3–12.
Zusman, Pinhas, 'The Dynamics of Growth, Technological Progress, and Force Build-ups – Some Strategic Tradeoffs,' in Zvi Lanir (ed.), *Israeli Security Planning in the 1980s: Its Politics and Economics* (New York: Praeger, 1984), pp. 239–60.

Iraq

Al-Khalil, Samir, *Republic of Fear* (New York: Pantheon Books, 1989).
Baram, Amatzia, *Building Toward Crisis: Saddam Husayn's Strategy for Survival* (Washington, DC: Washington Institute for Near East Peace, 1998).
Bhatia Shyam and Daniel McGrory, *Brighter Than The Baghdad Sun: Saddam Hussein's Nuclear Threat to the United States* (Washington, DC: Regnery Publishing, 2000).
Butler, Richard, *The Greatest Threat: Iraq, Weapons of Mass Destruction, and the Crisis of Global Security* (New York: PublicAffairs, 2000).
Carus, W. Seth, 'Defense Planning in Iraq,' in Stephanie G. Neuman (ed.), *Defense Planning in Less Industrialized States* (Lexington, MA: D. C. Heath & Co., 1984), pp. 29–52.

Comprehensive Report of the Special Advisor to the DCI on Iraq's WMD (Washington, DC: Central Intelligence Agency, September 30, 2004) at www.cia.gov/cia/reports/iraq_wmd_2004/

Chubin, Shahram and Charles Tripp, *Iran and Iraq at War* (Boulder: Westview, 1988).

Devlin, John, 'Iraq,' in Edward Kolodziej and Robert E. Harkavy (eds), *Security Policies of Developing Countries* (Lexington, MA: Lexington, 1982), pp. 227–45.

Eisenstadt, Michael, 'Like a Phoenix From The Ashes: The Future of Iraqi Military Power,' *Policy Papers 36* (Washington, DC: The Washington Institute for Near East Policy, 1994).

El Azhary, M. S. (ed.), *The Iran–Iraq War: Historical, Economic and Political Analysis* (New York: St. Martin's Press, 1984).

Farouk-Sluglett, Marion and Peter Sluglett, *Iraq Since 1958: From Revolution to Dictatorship* (London and New York: I. B. Tauris & Co. Ltd., 1990).

Freedman, Lawrence and Efraim Karsh, *The Gulf Conflict, 1990–1991: Diplomacy and War in the New World Order* (Princeton, NJ: Princeton University Press, 1993).

Gordon, Michael R. and General Bernard E. Trainor, *The Generals' War: The Inside Story of the Conflict in the Gulf* (Boston and New York: Little, Brown & Co., 1995).

Hamza, Khidhir (with Jeff Stein), *Saddam's Bombmaker: The Terrifying Inside Story of the Iraqi Nuclear and Biological Weapons Agenda* (New York: Scribner, 2000).

Helms, Christine Moss, *Iraq: Eastern Flank of the Arab World* (Washington, DC: The Brookings Institution, 1984).

Henderson, Simon, *Instant Empire: Saddam Hussein's Ambition for Iraq* (San Francisco, CA: Mercury House, Inc., 1991).

Iraq's Weapons of Mass Destruction: The Assessment of the British Government (September 2002).

Iraq's Weapons of Mass Destruction Programs (Central Intelligence Agency, October 2002).

Karsh, Efraim and Inari Rautsi, *Saddam Hussein: A Political Biography* (New York: The Free Press.

Khadduri, Majid, 'The Role of the Military in Iraqi Society,' in Sydney Nettleton Fisher (ed.), *The Military in the Middle East* (Columbus, OH: Ohio State University Press, 1963), pp. 41–52.

Marr, Phebe, *The Modern History of Iraq* (Boulder, CO: Westview Press, 1985).

McCarthy, Timothy V. and Jonathan B. Tucker, 'Saddam's Toxic Arsenal: Chemical and Biological Weapons in the Gulf Wars,' in Peter R. Lavoy, Scott D. Sagan, and James J. Wirtz (eds), *Planning the Unthinkable: How New Powers Will Use Nuclear, Biological, and Chemical Weapons* (Ithaca, NY: Cornell University Press, 2000).

Murray, Williamson and Major General Robert H. Scales, *The Iraq War: A Military History* (Cambridge, MA: Belknap Press, 2003).

Pollack, Kenneth M., *Arabs at War: Military Effectiveness, 1948–1991* (Lincoln, NE: Council on Foreign Relations and University of Nebraska Press, 2002).

Pollack, Kenneth M., *The Threatening Storm: The Case for Invading Iraq* (New York: Council on Foreign Relations and Random House, 2002).

Ritter, Scott, *Endgame: Solving the Iraq Problem – Once and For All* (New York: Simon & Schuster, 1999).

Staudenmeier, William O., 'Defense Planning in Iraq: An Alternative Perspective,' in Stephanie G. Neuman (ed.), *Defense Planning in Less Industrialized States* (Lexington, MA: D. C. Heath & Co., 1984), pp. 53–66.

The Iraqi Army: Organization and Tactics, National Training Center Handbook 100–91 (Fort Irwin, CA: National Training Center, January 3, 1991).

Timmerman, Kenneth R., *The Death Lobby: How the West Armed Iraq* (Boston, New York, and London: Houghton & Mifflin Company, 1991).

Trevan, Tim, *Saddam's Secrets: The Hunt for Iraq's Hidden Weapons* (London: HarperCollins, 1999).

Index

Ababil rockets 134, 151
Adnan aircraft 137
Advanced Light Helicopters (ALHs) 52–3
advanced trainer aircraft 52, 60, 128, 138
Advani, L. K. 57
Aerospace Surveillance and Warning Control Aircraft (ASWAC) 52
Aerospace Technology Center (CTA, Brazil) 147
Afghanistan 39–40
Agni ballistic missiles 47–8
air-to-air missiles 134
airborne self-protection systems 72
aircraft carriers 54
aircraft modification 73, 136–7
Ajeet fighters 50–1
Akash program 47
Al-Abbas missiles 145–6
Al-Abid satellite launch vehicles 146
Al-Arabi trading network 140
Al-Fatah SRBM program 151
Al-Faw 130
Al-Hijarah missiles 146
Al-Husayn missiles 144–5
Al-Samoud missiles 151
analytical frameworks of LDC arms industries *see* frameworks of LDCs arms industries
anti-ballistic missiles 135
Arab arms industry 126
Arab Industrialization Organization 126
Arab states: isolation of Israel 67, 68, 83; role of Iraq in unifying 119, 121, 122, 123; technology transference from the USA 97; use of new technologies 87, 108; wealth 88; *see also* individual countries
Arabistan (Khuzestan) 120

Arava transport 79
Arjun tanks 45–6
Armed Forces Workshops (Iraq) 123
armored vehicles 51, 81
Arms Control and Disarmament Agency (USA) 21
arms embargoes *see* embargoes
arms transfer limits 4
Arrow Anti-Tactical Ballistic Missiles 99
Artillery Saturation Rocket Systems (ASTROS) 134
Arunachalam, Dr. V. S. 64
'Assad Babil' tanks 137
Automatic Test Equipment (ATE) 73

Ba'athist Conference (1968) 122
Ba'athist regime *see* Iraqi regime
Badr-2000 project 147–8
Baghdad 118, 119
Baghdad 1 aircraft 136–7
Baghdad arms exhibition (1989) 137, 138, 148
balance of threat theory 4–5
balancing power 4
ballistic missiles: Agni series 47–8; importance 178; in Iraq 131, 144–8; in Israel 82, 104
Bangladesh 23
Barak Close-in Weapons System (CIWS) 102
battlefield rockets 151
Bedek 78, 80
Beirut 94
Ben Gurion, D. 74, 75, 112, 166, 168
Bhabha, H. 38, 164
biological weapons: Iraq's covert acquisition 124, 153–5; in Israel 91; potential of the Superguns 133–4; range 154

284 *Index*

Blainey, G. 5
body armour 100
Bonen, Z. 178
Brasstacks exercises (1986–87) 41, 57
Brazil 147
Bull, Dr. G. 133

Cairo Exhibition (1984) 128
Cairo Exhibition (1987) 132
carbon fiber technology 140
Cariappa, A. C. 36
cause/effect approach to LDCs arms industries 15
chemical weapons: as a deterrent 139; foreign supplies 152; in the Gulf War 152; in India 56; Iraqi concealment 153; Iraqi threat to Israel 122, 123; Iraq's covert acquisition 124, 126, 139; in Israel 91, 105; potential of the Superguns 132–3; relevance to Iraq's future 161–2; use against Iran 151–2; use against Kurdish rebels 118–19
Chieftain tanks 88
China: and India 41; and Israel 110; niche production 179; nuclear tests 38; and Pakistan 34
Chubin, S. 160
commercialization of arms trade 177, 180
communication systems 72, 94, 100
Condor project 145–7
cruise missiles 104, 148–9
Czechoslovakia 77

Data Transfer Equipment (DTE) 73
Defence Production Board (India, 1955) 29
Defense Ministry (Israel) 76
Defense Public Sector Undertakings (DPSUs, India) 26–7
Defense Research and Development Organization (DRDO, India) 26, 27–8, 48, 49
defense spending 21, 42, 62, 64, 70, 83, 159; *see also* individual countries
Delhi-class (type 15) destroyers 55
dependence 8–9, 15, 18
deterrence: acquisition of chemical weapons 139; importance of possession of arms 15; persuasive 41, 184–5, 186; role of Iraq 160, 170; use by India 25; use by Israel 108; use by Pakistan 40; use of missiles 91

developing world: emergence into international arms trade 2–7, 6; place in hierarchy of global power 3; structural considerations 2–3
Dimona reactor 82, 104
diplomacy 57
dominance/world approach to LDCs arms industries 11–12
Draft Nuclear Doctrine (DND, 1999) 59
Dvora craft 101

economic/development approach to LDCs arms industries 10–11
economies of scale 18, 175
education 123, 183
EE-T4 Ogum armored gun system 127
Egypt: attack on Israel 86–7; relationship with Israel 77, 82, 107; rivalry with Iraq 122
Ekeus, Dr. R. 149
El Baradei, M. 157
El-Op (Electro-Optics) 72, 73
Elbit 72–3
electronics: importance in the international system 181; in India 50; intelligence systems 71; in Israel 68, 71–2, 73, 75–6, 83–4, 90; subsystems 181
Elisra 72
embargoes 4, 107, 125–6, 127; French 85; on India/Pakistan 34; on Iraq 124, 127, 168; significance for Iraq 143; Soviet 124–5
Emet 78
employment 10, 71, 83
endurance requirements: in India 33, 37, 48–9; in Iraq 127–8, 132–3; in Israel 80–2, 90, 99–100; overview 19–20
export licensing agencies 139–40
export-oriented model 11, 18, 105–6, 168
exports 11; commercial 108; from Israel 73, 89, 92, 93, 101, 103, *113*; influence of USA 99; of major weapons platforms 105; of missile attack craft 101; of Remotely Piloted Vehicles 102; repercussions of the Israeli–Palestinian conflict 109; role in the international arms market 93, 109; to India 102

false-end users 124

Faw cruise missile programme 148
Fernandes, G. 59
fighter aircraft: in India 29, 31–3, 36, 43–4, 50–1, 61; in Israel 68, 89, 95, 98, 113, 177
fire control systems 73, 100, 103
firepower 172
force multipliers 5, 18, 183
foreign components 36
foreign exchange 26
Foreign Military Sales (FMS, USA) 97
frameworks of LDCs arms industries 7–16; broad surveys 8; cause/effect approach 15; dominance/world approach 11–12; economic/development approach 10–11; implications for study 16; the missing variable 15–16; moralist position 7; structuralist/dependency approach 8–10; study of individual states 8; systemic/historical approach 12–14; volumes/multiple case studies 8
France: arms supply to Iraq 125–6; and India 51; and Israel 78, 81, 85; technology 89
The Future Security Environment (Washington, 1988) 179
future warfare 182–3

Gabriel system 101
Gandhi, R. 47
Gates, R. 142
Germany 53
Glide path 65
globalization 7, 163
Gnat fighter aircraft 31–2, 50
Godavari class frigates 55
Great Britain *see* United Kingdom
guidance systems 78
Gulf War (1990–91): air campaign 142; effect on Iraqi arms industry 138–9, 141–2; effect on Iraq's nuclear ambitions 155–6, *156*; origins 122; presence of chemical weapons 152; significance for Israel 108; survival of Iraqi military industry 142–3

Haganah 74, 75
Handel, M. 4
Hashim, A. 123
helicopters 37, 52–3
HF-24 Marut *see* Marut
hierarchy of power 3, 180

hierarchy of production *13*
high-technology 11–12, 18; in Indian DPSUs 27; in Iraq 126, 131; value to Israel 108
Himalayan War (1962) 31
Hindustan Aeronautics Ltd (HAL) 27, 29; development of a Light Combat Aircraft 44; development of stealth aircraft 60; indigenous trainers 33; licensed productions 31; production of the Ajeet 50–1
historical/systemic approach to LDCs arms industries 12–14
hitkonenut (preparation) 86, 111, 166, 168
human capital 183
Hussein, Kamil *see* al Majid, Hussein Kamil Hasan
Hussein, Saddam 117, 122–3

import-substitution model 9, 10, 11, 18; in India 23–4, 165; in Iraq 169–70; in Israel 76, 89, 168
India: background 22–4; Brasstacks exercises 41; and China 25, 28, 31, 41; defense problems 64, 65, 66; economic development 17, 18; foreign policy 22, 33; impact of embargoes 34; and Israel 61, 66; and Pakistan 24–5, 28–9, 34, 35, 39–40, 62; political leaders 25–6, 38; and Russia 42, 65, 66; security perception 24; significance of Kashmir 25, 34, 40, 41; and the USA 42, 56, 65
Indian Air Force: defense spending 59; expansion 61; lack of an advanced trainer 52, 60; logistical problems 31
Indian army: defense spending 59; growth 40; internal security duties 40; mountain divisions 49; recruitment/reorganization 33; role in the nuclear debate 57; status 30, 39
Indian navy: defense spending 30, 59; expansion 54–6; increased budget 39; logistical problems 31; naval construction 60; nuclear role 59; use of technology 60
Indian Parliament 57, 59
Indian Small Arms System (INSAS) 48–9
Indian Space Research Organization (ISRO) 38
Indian Unmanned Aerial Vehicles 60

India's defense spending: 1948–67 30; 1963–73 34; 1972–82 39; 1981–91 43; airforce 59; army 30, 33, 59; conclusions 62; economic reforms 42; funding issues 64; importance of short campaigns 40; modernization projects 41–2, 64; navy 30, 39, 59; research and development budget 42, 59, 64; space/nuclear activities 59

India's endurance requirements: conclusions 62; importance of supplies 40; Indian Small Arms System (INSAS) 48–9; Indigenous Guided Missiles Development Program 42, 46–8; logistics problems 31, 33; quality control 49, 60, 63; role of the Ordnance Factories 37, 49, 60; spare parts diplomacy 64–5

India's indigenous arms program 42–3; aerospace projects 29; Arjun 45–6; Gnat fighter aircraft 29, 31–2, 50–1; licensed production 35–6, 62; Light Combat Aircraft (LCA) 44–5, 64; Marut fighter aircraft 32–3; MIG fighter aircraft 29, 36, 43–4, 61; modification projects 50–1; T-72 tanks 45; Vijayanta tanks 35–6, 50

India's major weapons projects: aircraft industry 44, 51–2, 52–3, 54; armored vehicles 51; indigenous trainers 33, 60; labor costs 37; local share of value 63; research and development budget 42; shipbuilding 53, 54–6, 60; stealth aircraft 60; submarines 53–4, 60; *see also* India's nuclear weapons

India's military industrial policy: defense/private sector involvement 63–4, 65; expansion of military role 40; foreign exchange 26; as a growing power 22, 24, 61, 62; import-substitution model 23–4; importance of self-reliance 25, 61; lack of national security policy 64; and the ladder of production 63; mismanagement 30–1; modernization program 41–2, 64, 65; regional concerns 39, 56; role of politicians 25–6; role of technology 25, 29, 34, 42, 65; weapons acquisition policy 5

India's non-platform weapons: ammunition manufacture 49; electronic systems 50; guided missiles 49–50; region compatible weapons 49; role of the Ordnance Factories 37

India's nuclear weapons: Draft Nuclear Doctrine (DND) 59; justification for maintaining 58; nuclear capabilities 61; nuclear submarines 54; nuclear tests 56, 57; role of Kargil War 58–9; role of military leadership 57; significance of Kashmir 41, 56, 57; significance of terrorist attacks 59

India's strategic systems: biological weapons 56; chemical weapons 56; Indigenous Guided Missiles Development Program (IGMDP) 56; nuclear programs 38; satellites 56; space programs 38, 61; *see also* India's nuclear weapons

India's structure of defense industries 26–7, 28–9, 33–4

Indigenous Guided Missile Development Program (IGMDP) 46–8, 56, 65

Indira Doctrine 40

Indo-Pakistani War (1971) 35

industrial technology 140

inertial guidance systems 78

Instant Thunder 141–2

Integrated Air Defense System (IADS, Iraq) 137

intelligence: accuracy pre-Operation Iraqi Freedom 144, 150; British 150, 153, 154; future recommendations 185

international arms trade 6–7; decline 7; effect on Israel 109; and the impact of globalization 7; introduction of the developing world 6; role of regional powers 179–86; role of the superpowers 6

international sanctions 4

intifada 107–8

Iran: cooperation with Israel 104; invasion by Iraq 127; policy towards Iraq 119–20; role in shaping Iraqi strategic priorities 120–1

Iran–Iraq War (1980–88): conclusions 169; economic effect on Iraq 139; Iraqi dependence on Gulf states 121; relevance to development of arms trade for LDCs 7; as a source of problems for Iraq 129–30; use of Kurdish rebels 118–19; as a war of attrition 173

Iraq: background 115–16; and Brazil 147; conclusions 158–62; economy 17, 121; higher education system 123; and Israel 122; and the Soviet Union 124–5; and the USA 161–2

Iraqi Air Force (IQAF): advanced trainers 138; Baghdad/Adnan AEW 136–7; helicopter programs 138; modifications 136; technological innovation 136

Iraqi regime: authoritarian measures 118; contribution to military-industrial infrastructure 115; overthrow 160–1; prestige of weapons 141; significance 117; view of indigenous arms industry 132

Iraq's defense spending: 1948–67 *121*; 1963–73 *125*; 1981–91 *130*; industrial infrastructure 140; significance 159

Iraq's electronics 128, 135

Iraq's endurance requirements: Cairo Exhibition 1984 128; foreign advisors 128; importance of artillery 116; Ordnance Factories 132; supply constraints 130

Iraq's indigenous arms program: covert operations 150; licensed production 138; local production 132, 145, 159–60; missile systems 134, 144–6; rocket launchers 134; self-sufficiency 131, 133, 139; stockpiles 174–5

Iraq's major weapons platforms 128, 137–8

Iraq's military industry: acquisition of technology 126, 131, 144; conclusions 127, 158–62; diversification efforts 127; effect of Soviet embargoes 124–5; future issues 160–1, 161–2; importance of Kamil 131–2; organization 123–4, 130–1; overview 115–16, 123–4; procurement of technology 124; role of Iran–Iraq War 129–30; role of UN inspectors 148; supply constraints 130; survival post Gulf War 142–3; theories of arms development 158–9; workforce 123

Iraq's modification programmes 135–6, 136–7

Iraq's non-platform weapons 128, 133–4, 151

Iraq's nuclear weapons: deception 155; experiments with uranium 133; hidden stockpiles 157, 158; intelligence 157; potential production 156; as a priority 141; research reactors 129; UNSCOM inspections 143, 147–8

Iraq's security perception: Arab threat 119–20, 122; extra-regional objectives 122–3; importance of Baghdad 118; importance of Kuwait 121–2; internal security concerns 117–19; regional interests 119–22; role of Kurds 118–19

Iraq's strategic systems: Condor IRBM programme 146–7; covert acquisition 116, 126, 139, 152; hidden stockpiles 157–8; range of biological weapons 154–5; range of chemical weapons 151–2; RPVs/UAVs 149; Samarra complex 129; Superguns 133–4; UNSCOM inspection 153, 154; use of chemical weapons against Kurds 129

Israel: and the Arab states 88; background 67–8; defense industry structure 69–73; and Egypt 77, 108; impact of embargoes 85, 107; and India 61, 109–10; and Iran 104; and Iraq 108; and Operation Peace for Galilee 94–5; security perception 67, 68–9, 106; significance of the Six Day War 110–11; and South Africa 93; and the UK 85, 88; and the USA 83, 85, 93, 95–6, 97–8, 110–11

Israeli Aircraft Industries (IAI) 70–1, 78; development of the Kfir aircraft 89; effect of shekel crunch 111; modifications 81, 103; origins 75; production of radars and communication systems 90; role in the Lavi project 95

Israeli airforce 87, 89, 95

Israeli Defense Force (IDF) 76, 77, 79–80, 81, 87, 95

Israeli government: control of industries 69–71; cutting defence budgets 96; diplomatic aims 75; domination of military policy 111; effect on defence expenditure 112; failure in the Lebanon 94–5; importance of Ben Gurion 112; preference for state-owned companies 102

Israeli navy (IDFN) 77, 79–80, 80, 87

Israel's defense spending: 1948–67 77; 1963–73 84; 1972–82 92; 1981–91 96; and employment 83; exports 93, 113; funding from USA 83, 95–6, 98; increases 79, 83–4, 87–8; local share of value 107; on nuclear weapons 82–3; post October War 1973 87–8; research and development 70, 74–5, 92, 95, 97; role of Defense Ministry 76

Israel's electronics industry: export market 94; investment 94; military role 94, 95; niche production 179, 182; origins 75–6; research and development 84; significance 113–14, 176; standards 68, 71–2, 102, 108; use of technology as a force multiplier 106

Israel's endurance requirements: maintenance 87; need for reserves 100; in the October War 1973 90; reactive armor 99–100; self-sufficiency 80; spare parts 87, 100, 106; trial and error 76

Israel's major weapons platforms: Arrow ATBM program 99; Kfir fighters 89; Lavi fighters 98–9; Merkava tanks 88–9

Israel's military industrial policy: conclusions 79, 106, 114, 166–8; development 75–9; diversifying weapons suppliers 78; export-orientated model 105; import-substitution model 76; ladder of production model 67–8; military exports 92–3, 107–8, 109; need for rapid victory 78; overview 106; preparation issues 67, 86, 87; relationship between military and industry 80, 111–12; and self-sufficiency 68, 93, 105, 112–13

Israel's modification programs: aircraft 81; armored vehicles 81, 91; of equipment from USA 103; fire control systems 90–1; modernization 103, 106; upgrades 73; use of technology 103

Israel's non-platform weapons 81, 90, 100, 101, 102

Israel's nuclear weapons: Dimona reactor 82; importance of the October War 1973 104–5; nuclear capabilities 70, 87, 112

Israel's strategic systems: chemical weapons 105; missiles 82, 91, 104; space-based reconnaisance capabilities 105

Jericho missiles 82, 104
Jihaz al-Amn al-Khass (Special Security Apparatus) 131
joint production 99, 109, 110, 184

Kaluchak barracks 59
Kamil, Hussein *see* al Majid Hussein Kamil Hasan
Kargil War (1999) 4, 23, 24, 25, 56, 58–9
Kashmir: nuclear weapons threat 41; role of Indian army 40; role in the nuclear debate 57; significance for India 24, 25, 56
Kashmir (1965) 34
Kfir fighter aircraft 89
Khairallah, A. 117
Khukri class corvettes 56
Khuzestan (Arabistan) 120
konenut (short-term preparedness) 86, 111, 166
Krishna Menon, V. K. 29
Kurdish rebels 118, 119–20, 124
Kuwait 121–2

labor costs 37
ladder of production: compared to Iraqi model 158–9, 169–70; in India 63, 65, 165; overview 9; relevance to Israel 67, 168
Lavi fighter aircraft 68, 95, 98–9, 113
LDCs *see* Less-Developed Countries
Leander class frigates 54–5
Lebanon 94–5, 96–7
Less-Developed Countries (LDCs): arms procurement 5–6; definition 187; and the international arms trade 6–7; relevance of external threat 3; research 2; role of internal threat 3; role of political-military rivalries 3; *see also* frameworks of LDCs arms industries
licensed production 14; compared with indigenous development 45–6; compared with indigenous production aircraft 43–5; conclusions 62, 177–8; of the Gnat 31–2; in India 35–6, 43–5, 45–6, 49, 51, 61; in Iraq 136; in Israel 89, 177
Light Combat Aircraft (LCA) 44–5

Index 289

local production: definition 19; importance in Israel 100; in India 34, 36, 44, 46; Iraq 132, 145, 159–60, 169; in Israel 88, 89, 90, 91–2, 93; of the Kfir fighter aircraft 89; of the Merkava tank 88; of missiles in Iraq 130; in the security-based model 172–3, 178–9

M-16 rifles 111
maintenance 87, 175
al Majid, Hussein Kamil Hasan 117, 123–4, 130–1, 154
major weapons platforms: in India 33, 37, 42, 63; in Iraq 128, 137–8; in Israel 104; overview 19, 20; in the security-based model 177–8
make-work projects 79
Marut 32–3
MASHA (Renovation and Maintenance Centers) 69, 75
mergers 110
Merkava tanks 88, 101, 103
metals 83–4
Middle East arms trade 109, *120*
military capability 17
military expenditure *see* defense spending
Military Industrialization Authority (MIA, Iraq) 123
Ministry of Industry and Military Industrialization (MIMI, Iraq): acquisition of restricted technology 124; authority 115; inception 131; scope of power 123–4
missile attack craft 101
missile programs: as a deterrent 91; in India 38, 46–8, 49–50, 56, 65, 66; in Iraq 130, 131, 134; in Israel 82, 91, 99
missiles: air-to-air 134; Al-Abbas 145–6; Al-Husayn 144–5; anti-ballistic 135; cruise 104; Tammuz-1 146; use against Israel 108
models of military industrialization: conclusions 163–4; Indian case 165–6; Iraqi case 168–70; Israeli case 166–8; limitations 170–1
modernization 41, 42, 64, 103, 106, 176
modification programs: effect on expenditure 176; of the IDF 76, 78, 106; in India 50–1; in Iraq 135–7; in Israel 81, 85, 90–1, 91, 101, 103;

overview 20; in the security-based model 175

Nag Anti-Tank Guided Missiles 47
Nasser, G. A. 77
naval construction 54–5, 60, 80
Nehru, J. 28, 29, 38
nerve agents 152
Neuman, S. G. 173
niche production 178–9, 184
Ninth National Ba'athist Conference (1968) 122
non-platform weapons: in India 37, 49–50; in Iraq 128, 133–5; in Israel 81, 90, 100–2; overview 20
nuclear capabilities: Iraq's covert procurement of technology 124, 133; of Israel 78, 104; as a priority for Iraq 141; UNESCOM reports 147–8
Nuclear Nonproliferation Treaty (NNT) 38, 155
nuclear reactors 82
nuclear submarines 54
nuclear tests 38, 56, 57, 58
nuclear weapons: as an insurance policy 83; dismantlement in Iraq 157; funding 83; future considerations 185; in India 23, 38, 48, 59, 61; in Iraq 123, 155–7, *156*, 161–2; in Israel 70, 78, 82–3, 87, 91; in Pakistan 23, 40; significance in the Kargil conflict 58–9

October 1973 War *see* Yom Kippur War
Offeq satellites 105
Office of Sponsored Projects (OSP) funding 110–11
oil 7, 88, 120–1, 127
Operation Enduring Freedom 185
Operation Iraqi Freedom: concealment of chemical weapons 153; effect on Iraqi arms industry 138–9; role of intelligence estimates 144; role of the Kurds 120; significance 185
Operation Peace for Galilee (1982) 94
Operation Rhino 45
Operation Trident 41
Ordnance Factories (OF): development 33–4; in India 37, 49; in Iraq 132–3; overview 28
Orpheus engines 32
Osirak nuclear reactor 122

290 Index

Pakistan: destabilizing regional power 4; and India 35, 36, 41, 51, 59; nuclear capabilities 23, 40, 41, 56; reliance on US equipment 34; role of the army 24; and USA 36, 40, 56; *see also* Kargil War
Panikkar, K. M. 22
partial dependence 16
peace studies 7–8
Peres, S. 86, 105, 112, 114
persuasive deterrence 41
PHALCON project 66
pilot training 37
politicide 68
politics 15
Powell, C. 154
preparedness 86, 87, 111
Prithvi missiles 47
private firms 72–3
process skills 20
procurement 133, 140–1
product cycle (Vernon) 12–13
Project Babylon 133–4
protectionist policies 76
public sector corporations 71–2

qualitative advantage 5
quality control 49, 53, 60, 63
quantitative advantage 5

Rabin, Y. 85, 86
Rada 73
radars 90, 100
RAFAEL (Israel Armament Development Authority) 70, 75, 83, 90
Rajiv Doctrine 40
reactive armour 99
real-time intelligence 94
reconnaissance capabilities 105
regimes 17–18, 117, 186; *see also* Iraqi regime
regional powers 4–5; asymmetrical relationships with USA 184–5; definition 4; destabilizing power balances 4; role in the international arena 4, 179–86
regional security 2, 3
regional state-systems 2–3
regional-specific weaponry 178–9
Remotely Piloted Vehicles (RPVs) 95, 102, 107, 149
Renovation and Maintenance Centres *see* MASHA
research: into regional state systems 2–3; into relevance of regional powers 4; limitations of study 5; *see also* Stockholm International Research Institute (SIPRI)
research and development: in India 27–8, 42, 46, 48, 63–4; in Israel 70, 74–5, 84, 92, 95, 97; as a means of constraining LDCs 10
resource gaps 68
retrofitting 103, 107, 135
Revolution of 1968 122
Revolution in Military Affairs (RMA) 182

Saad General Establishments 126
al Saadi, Dr. A. H. 117, 126
Sa'ar project 80, 85, 101
Samarra Chemical Weapons facility 126
sanctions 4, 151, 157
satellites 56, 61, 105, 113
Scorpene-class conventional attack submarines 60
security systems 120
security threats: assessment 3; balance of threat theory 4–5; importance in LDC military industrialization 163; in the study of LDCs arms production 15
security-based model: changing nature of technologies 1, 16, 175; deterrent effect 15; impact on military organization 21; importance of local production 172–3, 178–9; key factors 171; maintenance issues 175; niche production 178–9; production of regional-specific weaponry 178–9; production of small arms 172; quality maintenance 175–6; research overview 18–21; role of stockpiles 173–4; sustenance requirements 172–5; use of force 15
self-reliance 16, 25, 93
self-sufficiency 9; and India 61; in Iraq 131, 133, 139; Israel 68, 80, 112–13
semi-peripheral states 3
Shafrirs 90
Sharon, A. 94
shekel budget 97, 111
shipbuilding *see* naval construction
Shishumar attack submarines 53–4
Sh'ite population 120
short-range missile systems 134, 144
simulations 183

Sinai Campaign (1956) 78
Six Day War (1967) 67–8, 83
solid fuel rocket motors 78
Soltam 100, 101
sonar systems 50
South Africa 93, 177
Soviet Union *see* Union of Soviet Socialist Republics
space reconnaissance capabilities 105
spare parts: conclusions 173–5; importance to the Israel Defense Forces 76, 87, 100, 106; self-sufficiency in Israel 80; as a source of problems for India 36, 42, 49, 60, 64–5
State Establishment for Pesticide Production (SEPP, Iraq) 126
State Organization for Technical Industries (SOTI, Iraq) 123, 126, 131
stealth technology 60, 182
Stockholm International Research Institute (SIPRI) 6
stockpiles 157, 158, 173–4, 174–5
strategic systems: in India 38, 56, 61; in Israel 82–3, 91, 104–5; overview 20; *see also* Iraq's strategic systems; nuclear weapons
structuralist/dependency approach to LDCs arms industries 8–10, 15
submarines 53–4, 60
subordinate alliances 22
Suez Canal 39
Supergun project *see* Project Babylon
superpowers 6–7
supplier controls 4
surge production 99, 106, 174
Syria 86–7, 122
system of systems 182
systemic/historical approach to LDCs arms industries 12–14

T-72 tanks 45
TAAS (Ta'asiya Zvai'it) 71, 74, 90, 100
Ta'asiya Zvai'it *see* TAAS
Tadiran 71–2, 75–6, 102
Tammuz-1 missiles 146
tank armaments 35–6
tank transporters 87
tanks: armor 99; Chieftain 88; in the IDF 90–1; in Iraq 135–6; Merkava 88, 101, 103; repair 90; T-72 45
technologism 11
technology: acquisition 126, 131, 144; as an economic asset 182; complicating international relations 93; definition 19; as a force multiplier 5, 18; importance to India 26, 42, 47, 48, 53, 65; importance to Israel 95, 105; LDCs dependence on developed world 9–10, 12; negative impact 11; as a process 20; in the security-based model 175; stealth 182
Technology Experiment Satellite 61
terrorism: importance of regional actors 186; in India 56–7, 59; role in international arms trade 161–2; role of Israel 167
threats 4–5
tiers of production 12–14, *13*, 16
training 5, 40, 183
Trishul 46–7
Turkey 119

al Ubeidi, Dr. A. R. 126, 131
UK *see* United Kingdom
UN Conference on Science and Technology (1979) 126
Union of Soviet Socialist Republics (USSR): effect of invasion of Afghanistan 39–40; embargoes on Iraq 124, 127, 168; involvement in production of MIG-21 36; relationship with Israel 91; role in Indian Ocean 39; role in the international arms trade 6, 35; role in Iraq's acquisition of arms 124–5; significance of collapse 42
United Kingdom (UK) 85, 88, 150, 153, 154
United Nations sanctions 148, 151, 157
United Nations Special Commission (UNSCOM) 143, 149, 150, 152
United States of America (USA): asymmetrical relations with regional powers 184–5; funding for Israel 83, 95–6, 98–9, 110; importance of security 111; imports from Israel 72, 73; intelligence issues 150, 157, 158, 185; intervention in Indo-Pakistani conflict 35, 36; planning for war termination in Iraq 158, 162; problems with technology sharing 93; relationship with India 33, 56, 65; relationship with Israel 68, 71, 85, 89, 91, 93, 110, 167; relationship with Pakistan 39–40, 56; role in Indian Ocean 39; role in the international arms trade 6; technology transference to Arab states 97

Unmanned Aerial Vehicles (UAVs) 102, 149
UNSCOM *see* United Nations Special Commission
upgrades 73, 78, 81, 103
US export control legislation 110
USA *see* United States of America
USSR *see* Union of Soviet Socialist Republics

Vajpayee, A. B. 58, 63
Vanunu, M. 104–5
Vernon, R. 12–13

Vibhuti class corvettes 55
Vijayanta tanks 35–6, 50

Wald, I. 68
War of Attrition (1968–70) 86
War of Independence (1948) 75
World War I (1914–18) 172–3
World War II (1939–45) 14, 176
world/dominance approach to LDCs arms industries 11–12

Yom Kippur War (1973) 86–8, 91, 100, 101–2, 112

For Product Safety Concerns and Information please contact our EU representative GPSR@taylorandfrancis.com
Taylor & Francis Verlag GmbH, Kaufingerstraße 24, 80331 München, Germany

www.ingramcontent.com/pod-product-compliance
Lightning Source LLC
Chambersburg PA
CBHW071345290426
44108CB00014B/1448